EDUCATION

PAPAL TEACHINGS

EDUCATION

Selected and Arranged
by

THE BENEDICTINE MONKS OF SOLESMES

FOREWORD BY MOST REV. E. M. BORNET

Translated by

REV. ALDO REBESCHINI
Coll. Propaganda Fide

ST. PAUL EDITIONS

IMPRIMATUR:

✠ **His Eminence, Richard Cardinal Cushing**

Archbishop of Boston

August 15, 1960

Library of Congress Catalog Card Number: 60-16450

Acknowledgment

The Daughters of St. Paul gratefully acknowledge the kind permission granted by the *National Catholic Welfare Conference News Service, The Pope Speaks* Quarterly, *Catholic Truth Societies* of London and India; and *Catholic Documents* to use their translations of a number of addresses and documents, as indicated in the Index on pp. 649-662.

FOREWORD

This new volume on Education commemorates the anniversary of the Encyclical, "Divini illius Magistri," and appears in the series published by the Monks of the Abbey of Solesmes under the title, "Papal Teachings."

All the pertinent texts, from the time of Pius VII to Pius XII, have as far as possible been collated here and set forth in chronological order. The documents are followed by an analytical index with references to the authentic sources.

This book contains an outstanding collection of Papal documents, a testimony to the Church's doctrine—showing how clear and secure is her position and how unchanging and sure are her directives as she leads mankind on the way to salvation. It puts an end to the controversy among Catholics who discuss the importance of the Encyclical of Pius XI, "Divini illius Magistri" (December 31, 1929), that is to say, whether it is a doctrinal or merely disciplinary document of present-day value or not.

The book illustrates clearly that the teachings of the Supreme Pontiffs on the spiritual formation of Christians and in particular on the education of youth form a solid and harmonious body of truth. There is no shadow of doubt, no shortcoming, no lacuna in this teaching.

No aspect of the problem has been forgotten or neglected. To each of the different institutions, for example—the family, the Church and the State—in its work for the common good, its own proper place has been clearly assigned, without prejudice and with complete impartiality. It is a work whose rich content, lofty thought, balance and logic, inspire confidence and assurance in those who study it.

No one will be surprised to note that the basis of this magnificent synthesis is the Faith of which Christ's Vicar, no matter what his name may be or when he lived, remains the guardian.

Such a solid and coherent doctrine is not subject to the ups and downs of every-day life, so full of dangers for the future of civilization. It is not at the mercy of man's ignorance and passion, but is the clear reflection of an original conception of life, of this "new order" introduced by Christ which, for His disciples, put an end to the spiritual chaos of a pagan world.

"I am the Way, the Truth and the Life," He told them.

The Gospel—His "good news"—which brings with it the "True Light," enlightens every man coming into this world from his birth and baptism right up to the time of his final destiny: it raises him above the darkness of an aimless life which leads to certain death; it helps him to view the future in a new light, that is to say, in a manner in keeping with his supernatural destiny.

The Catholic School plays an essential role in the education of youth. It is not something added nor imposed by whim. The famous Encyclical of Pope Pius XI has clearly shown how it fits into the scheme of things. It is impossible to brush it aside. Its necessity in our times is akin to the necessity of Christianity itself: you cannot renounce one without renouncing the other.

The Catholic school which this volume of Papal Teachings proposes to us is the perfect school, capable of bringing Catholics to their full development—physical, intellectual, moral and religious—and of raising them to a plane that is free from disturbances and mutilations in the depths of their souls, a plane armed with solid values and principles.

It can be seen, therefore, that the atmosphere of the Catholic school system, despite its imperfections and deficiencies, is not what many of its opponents call a "ghetto," the narrow and exclusive upbringing of people who are trying their best to flee from the modern world in which they live.

Summing up, we may say that the Catholic school system achieves a positive training and formation for students, preparing each one of them, both as man and as Christian, to be a "soldier of God," vested with the weapons of God's armory, and ready to take up the battle for Truth, Justice, and Love—those eternal values of the Kingdom of God.

✝ ETIENNE-MARIS BORNET
Auxiliary Bishop of Lyons

INTRODUCTION

HOW THE DOCUMENTS ARE PRESENTED

At the head of each document is found
    a title, to facilitate understanding,
    the type of document,
    the "incipit" if the text is taken from a written document
    the address and the date of origin;
in the body of the text:
    subtitles for the longer citations.
    in italics in parentheses, a brief summary of those
        portions of the original document not cited in the
        text, because not referring directly to the subject
        being treated.

HOW TO USE THIS VOLUME

To find the texts relating to a given question:
    look first in the alphabetical index or else directly in
    the analytical index, where the numbers in heavy print
    refer the reader to the papal texts.
To clarify a text by placing it in its context in the develop-
    ment of the thought of the Popes, or by comparing it
    to parallel texts: the numbers in italics, given in paren-
    theses in the margin of the text, refer to the analytical
    index, which in turn summarizes briefly the lines of
    papal thought and indicates the relative texts.

THE NUMBERING OF THE TEXT

The numbers in heavy print, refer to the paragraphs of the
    papal pronouncements, given in chronological order
    in the text.
The numbers in italics, given in parentheses, refer to the
    divisions of the analytical index.

CONTENTS

INDEXES

PAPAL DOCUMENTS

PIUS VII
1820-1823

THE CHOSEN ONES OF THE FLOCK

Encycl. *Diu satis,* May 15, 1800.

(In praise of Pius VI.—Task of Pope and Bishops.—Doctrine.—Clergy.)

... And you must "take heed to the whole flock wherein the Holy Ghost hath placed you Bishops." (a)But it is the children and growing youth who have first claim to the care and indefatigable zeal which proceeds from your love and fatherly kindness. These are the children and the youth whom Christ, by word and example, so earnestly recommended to Us. Those who try to destroy public and private institutions and to trample on all human and divine rights have done everything possible to poison and corrupt their tender souls, hoping in this way to put them on the path of evil. Indeed, we know how soft and pliable these young people are and how easily they can be moulded into any shape. Once they have been formed they grow up hardened and clinging to it with a tenacity that defies all attempts to change them. Hence the common proverb: Raise a child in the way he should go and when he is old he will not depart from it. (b)

Take heed, then, Venerable Brethren, that the "children of this world are" not "wiser in their generation than the children of light." (a) Pay great attention to the type of person to whom you entrust children and growing youth in seminaries and colleges, to the matter in which they are instructed, to the teachers selected and to the lectures they

1
(5,
19,
80,
93)

2
(19,
111)

1a Acts 20:28.
1b Prov. 22:6.
2a Lk. 16:8.

give. Be very careful in watching over and probing every little detail. Drive off and keep far "the ravenous wolves who will not spare" the flock of innocent lambs, and if, by chance, they have already penetrated into some place, then cast them out and destroy them immediately according to the power which God has given you unto edification! (b)

(Bad books.—Press.—Duties of the King.—Evils of the Church in France.)

LEO XII
1823-1829

THE PRINCIPLE AND AIM OF TEACHING

Apost. Constitution *Quod divina sapientia,* August 28, 1824.

Having before Our eyes the teaching of divine Wisdom which is addressed to all who tread the path of salvation, namely, "My mouth shall speak truth and wickedness is an abomination to my lips" (a), We realize that Our Apostolic duty obliges Us to spare no effort to recall this maxim to the minds of those who teach sacred doctrine, human science and the liberal arts, and of all who are engaged in the instruction of youth. We feel obliged to see that they put it into practice and instill it into the minds of their pupils. The progress of religion and the salvation of the State depend upon that.

3
(5, 12, 13, 62, 92)

And since the proper organization of studies is a great help to this end, We believe that it is Our duty to devote Ourselves to a continual betterment of teaching methods in Our States.

(Reorganization prepared by Pius VII.)

To show the care and great love We have for Our sons and subjects—as it were, to point out and recall to professors and students alike the true fount of science and the liberal arts—We quote the remarks (well worthy of meditation) of Saint Augustine, Doctor of the Church, in his letter to Volusian: (a)

4
(70)

"What debates, what philosophical doctrine, what laws of any nation, can be compared with the two commandments which, Christ has told us, summarize the whole

3a Prov. 8:7.
4a Letter 137.

law and the prophets: Love the Lord thy God with all thy heart, with all thy soul, and with all thy mind, and love thy neighbor as thyself. (b)

"Therein is summarized the science of physics, because all the causes of natural things are in God their Creator. There you will find morality, since a good and honest life consists in loving Him Who gives being and him who receives it, namely God and man. Logic is there too, since the truth and the light of the rational soul is God alone. And there also is the salvation and glory of the State, since society is not well established nor adequately protected, if it is not founded on and bound together by faith and strong unity. This is guaranteed when the common good, that is, God, the true and highest good, is loved, and when men love one another sincerely in God, for Whose sake they love and from Whom they cannot hide the reason for their love."

5
(70,
101,
109)   Certainly, St. Augustine, that bright beacon of the Church, has no intention of excluding the natural sciences from the schools of humanity, nor of eliminating the practice of the liberal arts which he himself so extensively practised. But he has quite rightly warned teachers and students that all this, in truth, receives its origin from God, is in accord with reason and religion, and further, must necessarily return to God, the beginning and end of the liberal arts.

Thus he teaches us, too, to despise the obstinate opposition of false philosophers and of the friends of the prudence of the flesh (whose number, in our sad times, has grown beyond all belief) "who think and want others to think that Christian doctrine is not conducive to the good of the State, because they want the State to be founded not on sound virtue but on the impunity of vice."

(Regulations concerning studies.)

4b Matt. 22:37-39.

INFLUENCE OF CERTAIN MARRIAGES

Encycl. *Caritate Christi,* December 25, 1825.

(Extension of the Jubilee to the whole world.—Various exhortations: Sacrament of Penance.—Blasphemy.—Feast days.)

Every class of people has a claim upon your interest, but especially youth, on whom depends the future of both the Church and human society, and whom, to the peril of these two societies, impiety strives to attract with every means in its power.

6
(19, 96, 111, 113)

You are well aware that the education and instruction of youth has been neglected and warped in great part because men seem to have forgotten the sanctity and the duties of marriage. The so-called civil marriage—now the fashion in many countries—quite frequently violates the sacred laws of "this sacrament" which, according to St. Paul, "is great, in Christ and the Church." (a) In the case of marriages between Catholics and heretics there has grown up a custom whereby all the children follow the religion of the father, or the sons follow the religion of the father and the daughters that of the mother. You can well appreciate how zealous you will have to be in ensuring that the faithful adhere to Catholic teaching regarding this sacrament and obey the laws of the Church. (b) Thus with all the force of your word and authority you will remove from

---

6a Eph. 5:32.
6b Cf. C.I.C., canon 1061, § 1: Ecclesia super impedimento mixtae religionis non dispensat, nisi:
    1. Urgeant iustae ac graves causae;
    2. Cautionem praestiterit coniux acatholicus de amovendo a coniuge catholico perversionis periculo, et uterque coniux de universa prole catholice tantum baptizanda et educanda;
    3. Moralis habeatur certitudo de cautionum implemento.

the Christian people this scourge which ruins Christian education.

7
(19,
69,
111)
    And in general, do all that is possible so that growing youth may be firmly grounded in Catholic morals and teaching, and this, by insisting with both the young people themselves, and their parents and teachers. Put them on their guard against seducers and instill in them a horror of those perverse opinions and principles which the evil of our day is helping to spread. Take care that they avoid books that are hostile to religion, morals and public order, works which have done so much to swell the detestable harvest of evil.

(Priestly Vocations.—The Poor.)

2b 2 Cor. 13:10.

GREGORY XVI
1831-1846

PRINCIPAL AIM OF MODERN IRRELIGION

Letter *Cum christianae,* June 21, 1836—on the occasion of the foundation of the Congregation of the secular Clergy of the Schools of Charity.

Nothing can be of greater benefit to both Christian and civil society than a timely formation of youth in piety and virtue. Thus, the Bishops of Rome, Our predecessors, have always shown a very special partiality for those priests who have striven to their utmost, and with love, to instill the salutary truths of the Catholic faith into the tender souls and hearts of children, to guide these pliable hearts towards the exercise of virtue. If this has always been necessary, it is especially so in these bitter days, when perverse and impious men, hostile to religion and civil society alike, have formed an evil alliance that seeks to corrupt especially the souls of young people. These inexperienced souls, by the flood of irreligious and hateful ideas, by the press and certain behavior, are drawn away from the path of honesty and the right observance of justice and good, to the great detriment of society itself.

(In praise of the work of the De Cavanis brothers.— Approbation of the secular Congregation of the Schools of Charity.)

8
(5,
92,
93)

PIUS IX
1846-1878

TO ENSURE CATHOLIC COLLEGES
FOR CATHOLICS

Letter of the Congregation of Propaganda, October 9, 1847—to the Archbishop of Tuam.

(The good faith of those who have accepted the co-educational system.)

The Sacred Congregation of Propaganda, after having carefully examined the situation under all its aspects, is sceptical that these colleges will procure the desired results, and is even afraid that this sort of institution may be an imminent danger to the Catholic faith: in short the Congregation of Propaganda is convinced that these colleges will soon prove detrimental to religion. **9** *(106)*

For these reasons the Congregation has felt it its duty to warn the Archbishops and bishops of Ireland not to participate in the foundation of these colleges. The Sacred Congregation of Propaganda would have preferred that the Holy See had first been consulted by those bishops who have entered into talks with the government in order to modify the law regarding these colleges and to obtain other more favorable concessions. However, it has no doubt that now, considering the obedience to which the bishops of Ireland have always given testimony, they will withdraw whatever has been said or done contrary to this decision. But in spite of all this, if any of you have important comments to make on the question, he may freely communicate them to the Congregation of Propaganda in order to have a suitable decision on the particular points.

The Sacred Congregation is not blind to the importance of giving scientific instruction to youth, especially **10** *(65,*

67) youth of the higher classes. It therefore expects Your Excellency and your helpers to take all possible steps to make these directives known. You will have to see that the Catholic colleges already established flourish still more and that new and useful Chairs of learning are created, especially—if they lack it still—of philosophy. Steps should be taken to make the colleges accessible to a greater number of students, according to the needs of the various districts. Above all, the Sacred Congregation thinks it would be an immense advantage if the bishops were to unite to set up in Ireland a Catholic University on the lines of the one that the Bishops of Belgium have founded at Louvain.

11
(19,
111)
The Sacred Congregation urges the Bishops to preserve unity and concord, so that these measures may have the happy results desired. They must beware of party interests which drag them into situations quite alien to the sacred ministry entrusted to them. Let it be evident to all that they have no interest except the cult of God, the welfare of religion and the salvation of souls.

We are sure that you will conform to these directives with the greatest diligence, considering that they reflect the mind of Our Holy Father Pope Pius IX, who, after having obtained detailed information on the matter, has given his approval to the decisions of the Sacred Congregation and thus lent to them the weight of his authority.

VIGILANCE OF BISHOPS AND PARISH PRIESTS

Encycl. *Nostis et Nobiscum,* December 8, 1849—to the Bishops of Italy.

(The Revolution.—Merits of the Church.—Aim of the revolutionaries: to spread socialism and communism.— Remedies: religious instruction, obedience to authority, sound formation of the clergy.)

Since in any case, not all young clerics are able to do
their course of studies in seminaries, while, on the other
hand, even the young students of the secular clergy most
certainly have a claim on your pastoral solicitude, it is,
therefore your duty, Venerable Brethren, to supervise all
public and private schools and to study and labor to ensure
that the program of studies agrees with Catholic teaching on all points. The students who attend these schools
should be properly educated in real virtue and in good arts
courses, by suitable professors of unquestioned religious
probity. They must be armed with the weapons needed
in order to avoid the snares set for them by the irreligious
and thus will they be a credit and advantage to themselves
and to the Christian and the civil State.

In this respect, you must, with complete freedom, pay
special attention to the professors of the Sacred Disciplines
and all those things which belong to the domain of religion or which are closely related to it. Be very watchful
that in the schools, and above all, in matters of religion,
only those books that are free from even the slightest taint
of error be used. Enlist the assistance of the pastors of
souls in everything that concerns schools for children from
their earliest years. See that the teachers assigned to these
schools are men and women of proven honesty, and take
care that, in teaching the rudiments of the Christian faith,
they use books approved by the Holy See.

In this matter We have no doubt that parish priests
will set an example. Moreover, We are certain that these
same parish priests in response to your appeal, will devote
themselves with ever greater zeal to the teaching of the
basic points of Christian doctrine to children, since they
are fully aware that this is one of their principal duties.
They must be warned to keep before their eyes, in their
instruction both of children and of the laity, the Roman
Catechism, published by order of the Council of Trent and
of Our immortal Predecessor, St. Pius V, and which other

12
(4,
5,
12,
19,
92)

13
(45,
93,
102)

Popes, and especially Clement XIII, have again recommended to all directors of souls as "a valuable aid in warding off the deceitfulness of perverse doctrines and in spreading and establishing the true and safe doctrine." (a)

Do not be surprised, Venerable Brethren, that We dwell somewhat at length on this question. You are certainly not unaware that, in these dangerous times, both you and We must exert ourselves to the full, to study and watch carefully over all that touches education, the instruction and the training of the children and youth of both sexes. You know that today, the enemies of religion and of human society, in a spirit truly diabolic, are concentrating on the perversion of the minds and hearts of youth from their earliest years. To that end, they leave no stone unturned so that schools and institutes for the education of youth may be completely detached from the authority of the Church and the watchfulness of the Sacred Pastors.

(The Italian Princes.—Intercession of Mary.)

UNITY NEEDED IN ORDER
TO BENEFIT BY THE LAW

Instruction of the Nunciature of Paris, May 15, 1850— to the Bishops of France.

(New laws about teaching.—Progress, but not completely satisfactory.)

14
(19)   The Holy Father has also noted that, among the bishops, there is a certain difference of opinion, all the more because some of the measures of this said law do not agree with those of the Church, as, for example, the supervision of the minor seminaries; while others seem to be detrimental to episcopal dignity, such as the participation

13a Clement XIII, Encycl. *In Dominico Agro.*

of bishops in the supreme Council in which, under the terms of the law, the presence of two Protestant ministers and a Rabbi is required. So, too, is the institution, even temporary, of co-educational schools which trouble the consciences of Catholic families.

(A request for directives addressed to the Holy See.)

His Holiness, after a careful examination of this im- **15** portant question, after having heard the opinion of a spe- *(110)* cial congregation consisting of various members of the Sacred College, and after serious deliberation, has communicated these instructions which, by his orders, I hasten to transmit to Your Excellency.

Without wishing to examine the merits of the new law on education, His Holiness cannot overlook the fact that the Church, even though she does not approve of what is opposed to her principles and rights, is prepared, very often, in the interest of Christian society, to make some sacrifice, compatible with her existence and her duties, in order not to endanger further the interests of religion and place it in a more difficult situation. You are quite aware, Your Excellency, that, from the beginning of this century, France has set the world an example of hard sacrifices in the hope of preserving and restoring the Catholic religion.

Today, society is in a condition that is serious enough **16** to warrant the intervention of every possible effort to save *(111)* it. In order to achieve this aim, the surest and most efficacious means is, first of all, unity of action on the part of the clergy, as St. John Chrysostom already mentioned in speaking of the first Christians: "If there had been dissension among these disciples, all would have been lost." (a) On this point the Holy Father has incessantly besought all those of goodwill, not only to show their patience, but

16a Homily 82 on St. John, chap. 17.

also to remain united, so that bishops "may be one" with their clergy. Thus, united by the sweet bond of evangelical charity, they may "think alike" and with the ardor of their zeal, "seek the things that are Christ's." (b) Only by this union can you hope to benefit by the advantages that the new law promises, and avoid, at least partially, the obstacles to an improvement of conditions. His Holiness hopes that the goodwill and active cooperation of the government will be directed to that same end.

17
(111,
112)
He is confident, too, that those bishops who are elected by their colleagues to sit on the Supreme Council of Public Education, will know how to apply their zeal and authority, their learning and wisdom, to the courageous defence, under all circumstances, of the law of God and the Church, to the protection of the doctrines of our holy religion and to the support of sane education.

The advantages which their efforts will procure for the Church and society will compensate for their temporary absence from their Sees. If, in spite of all their efforts, their opinion on some point of Catholic doctrine or morals is not accepted, these bishops will easily be able to inform the faithful committed to their charge. And that will give them the opportunity to explain to their flock the matters on which instruction may be necessary.

18
(92,
111,
117)
The Holy Father cannot overlook the great importance of the initial religious education of children, these new plants which are the hope of the future. While he recognizes the zeal of the various bishops of France, he feels that his Apostolic ministry obliges him to recommend particularly, Your Excellency, that if in your diocese there are mixed schools, you should not hesitate to employ every possible means to ensure the benefits of separate schools for Catholic children, who, fortunately, are in the great majority almost everywhere.

16b cf. John 17:22; Philippians, 2:2, 21.

The Holy Father bitterly deplores the progress which "religious indifferentism" has made in France, as in other nations, producing innumerable evils and corrupting the faith of the people. He therefore earnestly desires that in so important a matter, pastors should never weary of raising their voice when occasion arises and of instructing the faithful entrusted to their care, on the necessity of one faith and one religion, because there is only one truth. They should recall and explain the fundamental dogma that outside the Catholic Church, there is no salvation.

These then, Your Excellency, are the considerations and instructions which I had to communicate to Your Excellency by order of Our Holy Father.

EPISCOPAL AUTHORITY IGNORED

Consistorial Allocution, November 1, 1850.

(Legislation contrary to the rights of the Church in the Kingdom of Sardinia.—Abolition of all ecclesiastical immunities.—Interference in the administration of the Sacraments.)

There are still other important things that the Sardinian government has done or established against the rights of the Church and to the detriment of religion. Among these, We must strongly deplore the baneful law which We know went into effect on October 4, 1848, regarding public education and schools of higher and secondary education, both public and private. The management of these schools, with the exception of the episcopal seminaries, is almost entirely entrusted by this law to the Royal Minister and the authorities dependent on him. This is so because article 58 of the law establishes and declares that no other authority may intervene in the management of schools or studies, in the conferring of degrees and in the choice and **19** *(109)* approval of teachers. Thus, in this Catholic State, schools of every grade and consequently, even the Chairs of sacred science (explicitly mentioned in the law) and the teaching of the elements of Christian faith to children (which is listed among the obligations of the teachers) are not under the authority of the bishops. And, to remove any doubt on the matter in the article just quoted, even spiritual directors are listed among the functionaries who must be selected and approved by the Royal Minister or the authorities under him, without the intervention of any other authority. In this way, pastors are unjustly deprived of the principal supervision they enjoyed for many centuries over many educational institutes, in virtue of Pontifical and Royal Constitutions, and in virtue of the original foundation statutes. Still worse, they are not permitted to regulate whatever concerns the teaching of the faith, Christian morals and divine cult, in the management of schools.

(The tolerance of the Church must not be strained to the extent of making her sacrifice essential rights.)

THE FREEDOM OF BISHOPS
TO WATCH OVER EDUCATION

Consistorial Allocution, September 5, 1851.

(Religious restoration in Spain after the Revolution.— Only Catholicism authorized.)

20
(19,
62)
It was consequently decided that the manner of educating and instructing youth in all Universities, Colleges or Seminaries, in all schools, whether public or private, would be completely in accordance with Catholic teaching. Bishops and diocesan authorities, whose office binds them to defend the purity of Catholic teaching, to spread it, and to see that youth receives a Christian education, will in no

manner be impeded in carrying out these duties. They will be quite free to exercise the most careful supervision even over public schools, and to fulfill their pastoral duties with the maximum liberty.

(New diocesan boundaries.—Religious Orders.—Goods of the Church.—Agreements with other nations.)

EDUCATION UNDER THE TERMS OF
THE AUSTRIAN CONCORDAT

Consistorial Address, November 3, 1855.

(Concordat with Austria.—Juridical recognition of Jesus Christ, of the rights of the Pope and the bishops.)

Bearing in mind the tremendous importance, both for civil and religious society, of a timely formation of the young in piety and sound doctrine, provision has been made that in all public and private schools, the instruction given to Catholic youth will be fully in accordance with the doctrine of the Church. Thus, the bishops, in virtue of their ministry, will not only have to direct the religious instruction of youth everywhere, but will have to take care that nothing contrary to the Catholic religion and morals infiltrates into any part of this instruction. For this reason, elementary schools will be visited by an ecclesiastical inspector. It has also been stipulated that bishops will be completely free (as the sacred canons prescribe) in the management, government and administration of seminaries for the clergy. The appointment and choice of the superiors, of the professors and the teachers of the arts and sciences, and the admission of the pupils, will be left to their prudence and discretion. But it will never be permitted to teach theology, Canon Law or the Catechism without the authority of the bishops. **21** **(19, 92)**

(Marriage.—Religious.—Goods of the Church.)

BISHOPS' NATURAL RIGHTS OVER TEACHING

Letter *Dees humanae salutis auctor,* November 3, 1855 —confirming the concordat with Austria.

(Desire to end disputes.—Rights of bishops in doctrinal matters.)

22
(19) We have diligently watched over the Christian education of youth, and We have sought to protect and strengthen the natural rights that the bishops have in this important matter. All schools, whether public or private, devoted to the education of Catholic youth, throughout the territory of the Austrian empire, are subject to the supervision of the bishops. The instruction imparted must be fully in accordance with Catholic teaching. The bishops are to decide what books should be given preference for the religious instruction of youth. Teachers and professors in high schools and in schools attended by Catholic youth must be Catholics. Whether publicly or privately, theology and sacred science will be taught only by those whom the bishops consider suitable because of their learning, faith and piety.

(Ecclesiastical goods.—Articles of the concordat.)

COMPLETE RELIGIOUS FORMATION

Encycl. *Singulari quidem,* March 17, 1856—to the bishops of Austria.

(Unity in interpreting the concordat.—Indifferentism, Rationalism.—Reform of the clergy.)

23
(69) Do not, beloved Sons and Venerable Brethren, neglect all the measures necessary to bring up the youth of your diocese, whatever their sex and condition in life, in as

Catholic a manner as possible. Exert yourselves to the full, so that these young people, filled with the fear of God and nourished with the milk of piety, may not only be instructed in the basic factors of the faith, but may also be led on to a more complete knowledge of our holy religion. (a) Train them in virtue, in pure habits, in a Christian life, and put them on their guard against all the temptations and dangers of perversion and corruption.

(Diocesan assemblies.—Preaching.—Clergy of the Oriental Rite.)

BASIS FOR THE PROSPERITY OF THE STATE

Encycl. *Cum nuper,* January 20, 1858—to the bishops of the Two Sicilies.

(Earthquake.—Occasion for an examination of conscience and reform: Clergy.—Duties of parish priests.)

You must, Venerable Brethren, be most careful to see that the youth of both sexes are educated in the fear and the law of God and formed to good morals. Hence, you must continually attend to the supervision of public and private schools and thus make sure that youth are protected from all dangers and assured of a full and healthy Catholic training. Your pastoral solicitude must be principally directed towards this, since, as you are well aware, the prosperity of the State depends in great measure on the proper education of Christian youth. Neither are you ignorant of

24
(19,
92,
93)

23a Cf. C.I.C., canon 1373 §1: In qualibet elementaria schola pueris pro eorum aetate tradenda est institutio religiosa. §2. Inventus, quae medias vel superiores scholas frequentat, pleniore religionis doctrina excolatur, et locorum Ordinarii curent ut id fat per sacerdotes zelo et doctrina praestantes.

the considerable and criminal efforts of the enemies of God and men, in these sad times, to pervert and corrupt the young, especially those who are inexperienced.

(Battle against error.—Bad books.—Diocesan adminis-tration.—Exhortation and Blessing.)

THE REAL AIMS OF THOSE
WHO OPPOSE THE TEMPORAL POWER
OF THE POPES

Consistorial Address, December 17, 1860.

(Errors regarding the power and rights of the Church. —Schismatic publication of Cayla in Paris.)

25
(101, 102)
Thanks to the detestable publication which We have just mentioned, We have come to know, almost as if a mask had been removed, the real intentions of the author and of all those who try to deprive the Holy See of its temporal sovereignty. What they want, and this is the aim of all their schemes, is the complete destruction of our most holy religion. This is what they are seeking to achieve, by the most treacherous means, in the provinces which they have unjustly wrested from Our dominion, and in all the regions of Italy. This is what makes Us cry out in anguish. This is the purpose behind the perverse interpretations of the Holy Scriptures, spread everywhere in order to corrupt the faith, this torrent of libellous publications diffused everywhere to corrupt the morals of the young, this unbridled licence which cannot be restrained, this scorn for the power of the Church. This is the objective of that violation of sacred immunity, of the audacity with which they remove the education of youth from the authority and vigilance of the bishops, the teaching of doctrine and the

direction of morals, in order to entrust these tasks to men holding irreligious opinions.

(Measures against the clergy and religious.—Persecutions in the East.)

SECULARISM IN EDUCATION

Apost. Letter *Quum non sine,* July 14, 1864—to the Archbishop of Fribourg in Brisgovia.

(Congratulations for his resistance to the new scholastic legislation.)

It is undoubtedly a fact that the pitiful, the deplorable condition of modern society has its root cause in the wicked artifices employed in every walk of life to separate the holy Faith, the religion of Christ, His teaching of salvation, from public education and family life, and to hinder Christ's influence so as to render it powerless. These diabolic artifices are necessarily the product of all these detestable doctrines which, in these times, We are grieved to see being diffused everywhere and slowly gaining ground, to the great detriment of Christian and civil society. When God's revealed truths are barefacedly denied or when one presumes to submit them to the test of human reason, or to assert the subservience of the supernatural order to the natural, men are further removed than ever from their eternal reward while their thoughts and actions are limited to the material and to the passing things of this world. Those who propagate perverse doctrine spare no effort to deprive ecclesiastical authority of all its power with regard to human society, precisely because the Church was founded by her divine Author, the pillar and foundation of truth, to teach the divine Faith to all men, to defend the integrity of the faith entrusted to it, to direct society and human actions, and to inculcate in them irreproachable be-

**26
(5,
11,
26,
94)**

havior and integrity of life. They do not miss a single occasion in their attempts to restrict or abolish completely all ecclesiastical authority and the lifegiving activity which the Church, by its divine foundation, has always exercised and always ought to exercise over social activities. What is more, these strive by every means to submit human society to the absolute control of the civil and political power, a power guided by the changing opinions of the times.

Secularism in education

27
(26,
70,
92,
102,
105,
107)
It is not surprising that this destructive work is carried out above all in educating the young; but there can be no doubt that the greatest misfortune to society is when the public and private education of the young, which has so great an influence on the prosperity of religious and civil society, has been taken away from the controlling power of the Church and its salutary action. In this way, indeed, society little by little loses the true Christian spirit which is the only element that can give stability to the basis of public order and peace, that can achieve and guide the true and useful progress of civilization and that can procure for mankind the means needed to reach the final goal, namely eternal salvation. An education whose sole interest lies in knowledge of natural things and in the aims of human society, and which, moreover, departs from the truths revealed by God, inevitably falls under the yoke of error and falsehood; an education which, without the aid of Christian dogma and moral law, claims to form the spirit and the hearts of the young, whose nature is so sensitive and susceptible of taking evil form, must necessarily result in a generation completely under the influence of its evil passions and its intellectual pride; and the generations so formed cannot help but bring ever greater disaster on families and on the State.

But if this detestable method of instruction, severed **28** as it is from the Catholic faith and the Church's authority, *(69,* is the source of evil for the individual and for society, when *103,* it is a question of the arts and sciences, and of the educa- *107)* tion which the better classes of society obtain, who will fail to see that this method will produce much worse results if it is applied to schools for the children of the people? It is especially in these schools that, right from their tenderest years, working class children must be instructed in the mysteries and the commandments of our holy religion and must be taught to form good habits and to fulfill their religious and civil duties; and in these schools religious instruction must occupy first place in the teaching, and must stand out in such a way that other ideas taught to the children seem to take the place of extras. (a) In these schools when education is not clearly combined with religious instruction, youth are left exposed to the gravest of dangers.

As the schools for working class children are estab- **29** lished chiefly with a view to imparting a religious training, *(16,* of bringing the children to a sense of devotion and truly *69,* moral discipline; so it is that the Church has always *101-* watched over these schools with greater care than over *103,* others. The idea of wresting these schools from the atten- *110)* tion of the Church and the attempts already made to do this, are therefore, clearly inspired by a spirit that is inimical to the Church and by the desire to extinguish the divine light of our holy Faith amongst the people. The Church has founded these schools with so much care and has upheld them so zealously that she considers them as the choicest part of her authority and ecclesiastical influence;

28a Cf. C.I.C., canon 1372 §1: Fideles omnes ita sunt a pueritia instituendi ut non solum nihil eis tradatur quod catholicae religioni morumque honestati adversetur, sed praecipuum institutio religiosa ac moralis locum obtineat.

and every measure that is aimed at separating these schools from the Church, causes her, as it does the schools themselves, the greatest harm. Those who expect the Church to suspend or abdicate her governing power and salutary action over State schools are, in reality, asking her to violate the instructions of her Divine Author, and to renounce the fulfillment of the duty which has been divinely imposed on her to watch over the salvation of all men.

30
(114,
116)
In all places, in every country where this pernicious plan to deprive the Church of her authority over schools is formulated and, worse still, put into effect, and where youth will consequently be exposed to the danger of losing their faith, it is the serious duty of the Church to make every effort not only to obtain for youth the essential instruction and Christian training, but even more so to warn the faithful and to make it clear to them that they cannot frequent such schools as are set up against the Catholic Church.

31
(72,
102,
103)
We greatly rejoice with you, Venerable Brother, for the wisdom and energy with which you have remained so deeply attached to the teaching of the Catholic Church in all matters regarding the education and instruction of the young, and for your writings on the subject by which you have combated all the opinions in circulation and all the measures planned in the grand-duchy of Baden for the reform of the State schools—measures that would cause the greatest damage to Christian education and would absolutely destroy the venerable rights of the Church in so important a matter. We are certain that you will not overlook any opportunity to defend fearlessly the right of the Church and carefully to keep the training of the young free from everything that might in the slightest manner endanger the firmness of their faith, debase the purity of their religious conscience or blemish the uprightness of their

habits, that uprightness that only our holy faith can produce, reserve and develop.

(Blessing.)

HIGHER EDUCATION

Apostolic Letter *Maximae quidem,* August 18, 1864, to the Bishop of Bavaria.

(Congratulations for the meeting at Bamberg.—Defence of the freedom of the Church.—Congratulations for having defended the schools for working class children in the sense expressed in the Papal letter to the Bishop of Fribourg. [a] *)*

We appreciate the value of your reasons for having defended the rights of the Church over the State schools in these days. So, on this occasion, We cannot do less than to urge you to continue the courageous and zealous task of making these rights of the Church over the schools of higher learning in arts and sciences known and observed. As you are well aware, these schools are not under the authority and vigilance of the Church, a state of affairs which may give rise to vast and numerous evils; in fact, the errors and false doctrines affect the men of the highest classes who have government responsibilities on their shoulders and who have so much influence in the forming of the spirit and atmosphere of civil society.   **32** *(19, 103)*

(Studies of the clergy.—Exhortation for the continuation of the episcopal conferences.)

32a See above, No. **26** *(26)*

SOCIALIST AND COMMUNIST HOSTILITY

Encycl. *Quanta cura,* December 8, 1864.

(Preceding acts of Pius IX.—Naturalism.—Modern freedom.)

33
(93,
94,
101,
102,
109)

In teaching and professing the most fatal error of *Communism* and *Socialism,* they declare that "domestic society, that is, the family, derives all its reason for existence solely from civil rights, and consequently only from the civil law do the rights of all fathers over their sons derive and depend, and above all, the right to provide instruction and education." By such impious opinions and artifices do these most false teachers endeavor to eliminate the salutary teaching and influence of the Catholic Church from the instruction and education of youth and to infect and deprave by every pernicious error and vice the tender and pliant minds of the young. All those who endeavor to throw into confusion both religious and public affairs, to destroy the good order of society, and to annihilate all Divine and human rights, have always directed all their criminal schemes, attention, and efforts upon the manner in which they might, above all, deprave and delude unthinking youth; as We have already pointed out, it is upon the corruption of youth that they place all their hopes. Thus they never cease to attack the Clergy, both secular and regular, in every way, irrespective of the fact that historical records testify that very considerable benefits have been bestowed by them upon Christian and civil society, and upon the world of letters; they assert, moreover, of the Clergy in general, that "they, being the enemies of the useful sciences, of progress and of civilization, ought to be excluded from all paricipation in the work of teaching and training the young."

(Submission of the Church to the State.—Bad press. The true religion: happiness of men and of States.—A Jubilee of one month.—Prayer.)

SYLLABUS

Syllabus of the principal errors censured in the documents of Pius IX, December 8, 1864.

XLV. The entire system of public schools in which **34** the youth of a Christian State are educated, (excepting *(109)* only for certain reasons diocesan seminaries), may and ought to appertain to the civil authority, and belong to it to the extent that no other authority whatsoever shall be recognized as having any right to interfere in the discipline of the schools, the organization of the studies, the conferring of degrees, and the choice or approval of the teachers. (a)

XLVII. The good of civil society requires that schools **35** for the working class children and, in general, all public *(102)* institutes intended for instruction in the arts and more profound studies and for the education of youth, should be free from all ecclesiastical authority, control and interference, and should be fully subjected to the civil and political power at the pleasure of the rulers, and according to the standard of the prevalent opinions of the age. (a)

XLVIII. Catholics may approve of this system of edu- **36** cating youth severed from the Catholic faith and the *(114)* power of the Church, and which regards the knowledge of merely natural things, and only, or at least primarily, the aim of earthly social life. (a)

34a All. *In Concistoriali,* Nov. 1, 1850.—All. *Quibus luctuosissimis,* Sept. 5, 1851.—Denziger 1745.
35a Epistle to the Archbishop of Freiburg, *Quum non sine,* July 14, 1864.—Denziger 1747.
36a Epistle to the Archbishop of Freiburg, *Quum non sine,* July 14, 1864.—Denziger 1748.

THE CONSEQUENCES OF LAICISM IN FRANCE

Apost. Letter *Inter teterrima*, June 27, 1872, to H. Abeille and H. Bergasse.

37
(103, 106, 107, 110)
Among the numerous evils which in our days gives Us sorrow, the one which preoccupies Us the most is that which is injurious to the young, and is actually aiming at the destruction of every human hope for a restoration of religious and civil society. Impiety has taken control of authority and wealth, and so as to infect children and adolescents with its poison, persecutes, oppresses and destroys all the institutions in which those of tender age would otherwise have been able to receive a sane and religious education and a training in virtuous ways; when the children become youths, it entrusts them, against the will of their parents, to wicked teachers who under the deceitful appearances of knowledge, separate them from God, render them slaves to earthly things and encourage them to be proud, contemptuous of all authority, and thirsty for ephemeral attractions and pleasure. There is no more disastrous a corruption for humanity. According to the means at Our disposal, We oppose such evils, by means of schools in which the young may be trained in a sense of devotion and consequently may receive a sound and safe education; wherever possible We have supported similar moves; in every manner We have favored, exhorted and praised the Catholic societies dedicated to this end.

Therefore, dear Sons, you will understand with how much pleasure and with what joy We learned of your resolution to labor in every way for the defense and the progress of the Catholic religion, and especially to watch over the sound education of children and adolescents.

38
(4, 107,
And this is much more necessary among you as the evil has been at work over a longer period in your country to divert the minds from everything of a supernatural na-

ture, to arouse a contempt for religion, to spread the most *116)* harmful errors, to pervert habits, to give free rein to cupidity and to submerge the people in this mire. These are inevitably the causes of the violent conflict of opinions, the almost constant changes in the forms of government, the political unrest and frequent sedition, the application of the mind more to individual interests than to those of the nation and the outburst of violence which has led to recent terrible disasters.

The plan which you have embarked upon does not confine itself to furthering the good of religion and the spiritual benefit of the young; it also aims at restoring unity of minds, at creating a solid defense against the enemy, at recreating social order and leading your country back to its previous position of pre-eminence.

*(The clergy ought to be the first to work for this end.—
The recipients of this letter intend also to launch a counter-
attack against the bad press and to assist all Catholic
activities.)*

If you take such good care in educating the young, **39** you are going to the very roots of the evil and you may be *(4)* said to be constructing a new society which will benefit the future and which will take the place of corrupt society; further efforts of yours will help to throw off, check and heal the present evils of society.

*(Approbation of the Pope and the assurance of God's
assistance.)*

CHARITABLE INSTITUTIONS

Apost. Letter *Propositum a te,* December 19, 1872—
to Rev. Albert Cucito.

We are very grateful to you, dear Son, for the book on **40** "The Protection of the Children of the People," presented *(96,* by you to the first Italian Catholic Congress. We are well *107)* aware of the dangers to which these poor children are exposed, abandoned to themselves so that they are able to insult one another, to fight, to corrupt one another, on Sundays and holidays and during free time on ordinary weekdays; and we know what punishment is being prepared for society, both civil and religious. Indeed they are wanting in all religious and moral education; courtesy and good manners do not sufficiently restrain them, while the conversation and the example of their elders, in the office, in the home or in the street, has vitiated them to the lowest level: there rests to them only to grow up and to do harm to themselves and to others.

41
(113) Therefore nothing could be more in keeping with Christian charity, more useful to the Church and to human society, nothing more necessary to the children themselves, than the attentive and generous zeal that will bring these poor little ones to unite spontaneously in the places prepared for them: being attracted by honest recreations and by prizes, they will receive quite voluntarily from priests and serious lay people, a healthy and religious training, a sound education and the ideas which they so far lack, all for their greater advantage and that of the nation.

(Congratulations on having expounded the method to be followed and for having shown that it can be done.)

THE DIVINE MISSION
RESERVED TO THE CHURCH

All. to the German Literary Society, January 12, 1873.

(The Pope replies as did Christ to the servant of Caiphas: "If I have spoken well, why do you strike me?"—The powers of the world are not carrying out their duty of acting as protectors of the Church.)

Nor is that all: they want to destroy not only all those **42** great things that belong to the Church, but also what be- *(10,* longs to morality; they want to have public teaching in *20,* their own hands so that youth will be formed as they wish. *93)* But I say to them that as Jesus Christ has commanded that the power given by God to the Civil Authority be respected, likewise He ordered the Church and her minis- ters, and not the kings, nor the emperors, nor the sover- eigns, no; but He ordered the Church and her ministers: *Ite, docete omnes gentes.* (a) To the Church He has said that she must go and teach all nations, that God's ministers must travel the length and breadth of the earth, there to preach the word of truth; *baptizantes,* they must administer the sacraments; they must edify by their word and exam- ple: instruction, I repeat, belongs entirely to the Church.

(Exhortation to constancy.—Blessing.)

WORSE THAN HEROD

All. to the Rectors of colleges, June 29, 1873.

(Ecclesiastical training is more useful to the Church than artistic training.)

In our days, We see clearly why the enemies of God **43** wage such a fierce war against Catholic institutions: be- *(101,* cause the war against the colleges is a war against youth, *102)* and consequently a war directed against religion, against the faith and against Christian living, since *adolescens juxta viam suam, etiam cum senuerit, non recedet ab ea.* (a) In this they go even further than that cruel king, many centuries ago, who ordered the massacre of so many thousands of innocent children: these, at least, once be-

42a Matt. 28:19.
43a Prov. 22:6.

headed, had no greater evil to fear, while in the moral slaughter which is being committed today, the evil is much greater, as the aim is to kill the souls by extinguishing the faith that lives in them.

44
(79, 116)
Because of this, it is necessary to make greater sacrifices, to oppose our enemy so as to avoid worse evils, and consequently more tragic ones. Let your students know of the infamous snares employed by these corruptors; put them on their guard; make them aware of the fact that the wicked use infamous disguises, and of the goal they intend to attain; instruct them on the errors and the lies they propagate, and arm them with arguments that will serve them in combating and refuting these errors; so that these dear youths will always preserve the faith unsullied, and so become its future apostles in the world.

45
(69, 84, 85)
I beseech God to give you the strength to put into practice what I have counselled; but I implore Him most particularly to give you sufficient wisdom and understanding to know well the different kinds of characters there are, so as to lead them with all possible prudence to what is good. For example, there are among youth those who are of a weak and excessively cold character: something can be done with them by treating them with some severity. On the other hand there are those whose character is inclined rather to liveliness and sensitiveness: a moderate gentleness will serve much better with these than severity. These are the means employed by you in the past, but which you must continue to use if you desire to form youth who will work for the good of society, and the Church, and for the glory of God.

(Blessing.)

YOUTH AND REVOLUTION

All. to some Roman students, March 29, 1874.

Whenever there has occurred in society some upset, **46** some revolution, an overthrowing of public order, youth *(93)* has always been a target; by some to recall them to what is good, by others to corrupt them, first in heart and then in mind. You yourselves have witnessed it. In recent years I myself have seen University professors incite the impressionable minds of the young in an attempt to drive them to all kinds of disorders, under the pretext of breaking their chains, of honoring the nation and of rendering it free and independent, without noticing that they were only making it poor, disordered and contemptible.

Through a divine miracle and the intercession of the Blessed Virgin Mary, in the years preceding the unfortunate breach, the University of Rome has remained uncontaminated and has turned a deaf ear to the hissings of poisonous serpents or the voice of alluring sirens. It was indeed a marvel that young hearts were rendered docile, the eye of the guardians farsighted, and the conduct of the professors wise.

Now, I repeat, in every revolution, whether caused by the work of an irrepressible Conqueror, or the workings of sedition, the aim has always been to corrupt youth. There are many examples, both in ancient and modern times, which prove the assertion in both its alternatives.

Old and new examples

Nabucodonosor, having conquered Jerusalem and **47** established his supremacy, brought away with him among *(101)* his prisoners many youths whom he handed over to the surveillance of severe masters, so that they would conform to the morals of the Gentiles and so abandon their national traditions.

The young Daniel opposed this wicked plan and was joined by other youths who courageously declared that they intended to remain faithful to the laws of their fatherland. (a)

At the beginning of this century, another arrogant Conqueror (b), a persecutor of the Church and of the Supreme Pontiff, desired to band together in the capital a group of youths belonging to families of rank, of which there were many in Rome, so that they could serve the vanity of this Sovereign.

48-49
(94,
107)   Let us take the book of Machabees. In Jerusalem the spirit of faith was beginning to weaken. A not far distant King welcomed with great interest the complaints of the wicked and stirred up their perverse passions; in Scripture this King is known as the *radix peccatrix* (a), and bears the name of Antiochus; he encouraged those wicked people, *surrexerunt impii ex Israel* (b), and made them instruments of his ambitions and his avarice. It was then that a Gymnasium was opened in Jerusalem according to the custom of the Gentiles. The already corrupt Hebrews said, and they insinuated as much to others, that they would never be a great nation should they not live according to the morals and customs of the infidels; and so they prepared themselves and exposed themselves to God's curses. The Greek Gymnasiums served as meeting places and for certain activities for the young; they began in a praiseworthy manner, but then they degenerated into mere infamous assemblies. Under these abominable omens, the Gymnasium was opened in Jerusalem under the protection of the evil King who fed himself on the lowest form of corruption.

47a Daniel 1.
47b Napoleon I.
49a 1 Machabees 1:11.
49b Cf. 1 Machabees 1:12.

The spirit of the seditious is manifested today almost   **50**
in the same manner; and behold We see certain incredu-   *(94,*
lous professors occupying the Chairs in schools; it is pre-   *102,*
cisely because of this that We witness, in the Universi-   *107)*
ties and in the other so-called institutes of education, the
exclusion of every religious element; it is because of this,
We see it all too clearly, that they tend in a thousand ways
to set a trap for youth, exaggerating all that can lead to
vice, and belittling, (what am I saying?), and trying to
cause the total disappearance, if that were possible, of
everything that can elevate the spirit towards God: faith,
religion, and its Ministers.

The safe way

In the midst of these great evils, therefore, which have   **51**
paved the way for the insolent conquerors and the wicked   *(95,*
seditious, the only way to protect the young against such   *116)*
dangers is to rally around those youths who were mentioned in the Gospel this morning, those who accompanied
Jesus Christ on His triumphal entry into Jerusalem and
greeted Him calling out: *Hosanna filio David; Benedictus
qui venit in nomine Domini.* (a) Blessed is He Who comes
to the assistance, and comfort of the Church so despoiled
by its enemies, to encourage its Ministers so unjustly per-
secuted, to inspire the young with the spirit of faith against
the poison of incredulity, with the spirit of devotion and
recollection against the spirit of dissipation, which is fed in
a thousand diabolical forms. Christ comes again, carrying the scales of justice in His hands and, as a King, marks
out from this moment those who are destined to experience
in due course the effects of His rightly irritated justice.

As for us, dear Youth, let us follow His way. As He
very rightly stated: *Ego sum via.* (b) Follow in the foot-

51a Matt. 21:9.
51b John 14:6.

steps of the Divine Master and you will find yourselves, without realizing it, keen on your school work, assiduous in your religious duties, and constant in your good resolutions.

I beg God to bless you and to remove the difficulties and the unjust oppositions of those who set themselves up to deny *the freedom of teaching* which We wish to remain in its entirety; because if it is true that those who come among us, come with freedom on their lips and with deceiving expressions—"let us break away from their bondage, rid ourselves of the toils"—(c) it is incomprehensible that side by side with so much freedom, preached with such impudence, there should be so much slavery.

FREEDOM OF TEACHING

All. to Italian Youth, January 6, 1873.

(The Church and the Popes have been through other persecutions.—Practical directives: There are too many marriages being contracted between blood-relations as a result of the laws regarding civil marriage.—Military service for the Clergy.)

52
(95,
117)
While I demand both the freedom of the two sacraments (Matrimony and Orders) and of their effects, that does not mean that I overlook the claims for freedom of education. And when I say that I claim the freedom of education, I claim it as a real necessity.

(Prayer before Our Savior's crib.)

51c Ps. 2:3.

THE SPIRIT OF REVENGE

All. to the Pilgrims from Laval, September 8, 1875.

(Jesus Christ received bad for good; the same happens today to those who represent Christ.—Anti-religious laws and persecutions in Italy and elsewhere.)

We must concentrate all our efforts so that an end may be put to scandal in the timid, excessive fear in the weak, and misplaced hopes of friendly accord in the disillusioned. Speak out, therefore, so that the Church be given freedom in the choice of her Ministers and that no obstacle be placed in the path of the young Levites who desire to serve at the Altar. Speak out so that the attitude taken by the Church may seem reasonable, so that she can freely exercise her right to teach, a right given to her by Christ. Speak out so that a stop may be put to the licentiousness of the press which has everywhere become a school of immorality and corruption. Speak out so that injured rights may be repaired, so that they may once again be freely exercised. **53 (111, 112, 117)**

All this calls for perseverance, *welcome or unwelcome* (a) so that, by means of divine assistance, the freedom of the Church may be achieved. You have before you the example of Daniel O'Connell, whose venerated memory was celebrated only last month in a solemn manner in Ireland. He never slackened in keeping alive in the people this spirit of petition, and his perseverance was crowned by the great victory which brought his country near to freedom.

(Unity in the face of the enemy, and united prayer, never letting yourselves be overcome by difficulties.)

God has protected the first attempts of agreement in France for the attainment of freedom of education; this **54 (111,**

53a 2 Tim. 4:2.

112) fosters the hope that this success will bind ever more closely that famous and Catholic nation in uniformity of doctrine with the Holy See!

(Appeal for the Divine Blessing.)

ATTENDANCE AT NON-CATHOLIC SCHOOLS

Instructions of the Holy Office to the Bishops of the United States, November 24, 1875.

(Instructions confirmed by the Holy Father on November 24.)

55
(105,
107)
The first subject it was intended to discuss was the particular method of education of youth proper to these schools. To the Sacred Congregation, this method has appeared intrinsically dangerous and absolutely contrary to Catholicism. Indeed because the special program adopted by these schools excludes all religious instruction, the pupils cannot grasp the elements of the faith, nor are they instructed in the precepts of the Church, and therefore they are deprived of that which is most essential for man to know and without which it is impossible to live in a Christian manner. In these schools the young are trained right from their tender infancy, the age in which, as is well known, the seeds of virtue or vice take firm root. It is, therefore, an enormous evil that from this formative age they should grow up without any sense of religion.

56
(106)
What is more, in the above-mentioned schools which elude the Church's authority, the professors are chosen from all sects without distinction, while on the other hand no measures are taken to impede such pernicious influence as they might exercise on youth, so that they are able to disseminate error and vice amongst the young.

The fact that in these schools, or at least in the major-   **57**
ity of them, the adolescents of both sexes are grouped to-   *(98)*
gether in the same classrooms to attend lesson, and boys
and girls must sit together on the same benches, exposes
them to corruption to a certain extent. The result of all this
is that youth is unfortunately in danger of losing its faith,
while its good morals are threatened.

General principle

If this danger, which borders on perversion, is not   **58**
averted, these schools cannot be attended with peace of   *(114,*
mind. The divine and natural laws themselves proclaim it.   *116)*
This was clearly defined by the Holy Father when on
July 14, 1864, he wrote to the Archbishop of Fribourg: "In
all places, in every country where this pernicious plan to
deprive the Church of its authority over schools is formulated, and worse still, put into effect, with the result that
the young will be exposed to the danger of losing their
faith, it is the duty of the Church to make every effort not
only to take steps to obtain the essential instruction and
religious training for youth, but even more so to warn the
faithful and to make it clear to them that they cannot frequent such schools which are set up against the Catholic
Church." (a)

These words, founded on the natural and divine law,
state definitely a general principle, have a universal bearing, and apply to all countries where this injurious method
of instructing youth will unfortunately be introduced.

Need for Catholic schools

It is, therefore, absolutely necessary that all bishops   **59**
should make every effort to see to it that the flock entrusted   *(111,*

58a Apostolic Letter *Quum non sine.*—Cf. above No. 30.

112,
117,
118)
to them may avoid every contact with the public schools. To obtain this desired end, what is generally cônsidered most necessary is that, in all places, Catholics should have their own schools and that these should not be inferior to the public ones. Every effort must, therefore, be made to set up Catholic schools where they do not yet exist and to increase the number of and improve the organization of those that already exist so that instruction and training, on the same level as that of the public schools may be ensured. So that this plan, that is so sacred and necessary, may be put into effect, the bishops think it suitable and useful to appeal to the members of religious congregations of men and women; and so that the means for such a vast plan may come from the faithful more spontaneously and abundantly, when the occasion presents itself, it is absolutely necessary that they be reminded by pastoral lettters, at meetings or in private, that they would be falling short of their duty to a serious extent if they were not to guarantee that these schools could rely on all their care and resources. This appeal applies more to the Catholics who are known for their wealth, their influence over the people, and who are members of legislative assemblies. (a)

60
(92,
117)
In your states, no civil law prevents Catholics, if they deem it necessary, from educating their children in all the sciences and in the spirit of religious devotion in their own schools. It is up to the Catholics themselves to avoid the disaster that, with the establishment of public schools, menaces Catholicism. And all ought to realize that the pres-

59a Cf C.I.C., canone 1379, 1: Si scholae catholicae ad normam can. 1373 sive elementariae sive mediae desint, curandum, praesertim a locorum Ordinariis, ut condantur.
  2. Itemque si publicae studiorum Universitates doctrina sensuque catholico imbutae non sint, optandum ut in natione vel regione Universitas catholica condatur.
  3. Fideles ne omittant adiutricem operam pro viribus conferre in catholicas scholas condendas ut sustentandas.

ervation of religion is a matter of the greatest importance, not merely for every citizen and every family but more so for the flourishing American nation in which the Church places such great hopes.

Reasons and conditions
of non-Catholic schools

The Sacred Congregation is, moreover, aware of the **61** fact that there can be given circumstances in which Cath- *(114)* olic parents can, with a clear conscience, send their children to public schools, but in order to do so an adequate motive is needed and it must be left to the conscience of the bishops whether there exists sufficient motive or not in any given case; according to what has already been said, sufficient reason will exist if there are no Catholic schools or if those which already exist are not adapted to train adolescents according to their condition in life. So that these public schools can be attended with a clear conscience, however, the danger of perversion, which is always more or less inherent in the very system of these schools, must be warded off with suitable precautions. It must be ascertained whether, in the school to be attended, the danger of perversion is of such a nature that its evil effects are unavoidable, if the daily things that are taught and done are contrary to Catholic teaching and morality and cannot fail to cause spiritual injury. Such a danger must, quite obviously, be absolutely avoided, at the cost of any sacrifice whatsoever, even that of life.

Religious formation of the pupils
of non-Catholic schools

So that children may, with a clear conscience, be en- **62** trusted to the public schools, they should receive the *(114,* necessary Christian instruction and education in the most *116)* suitable manner outside school hours. Remembering, therefore, what the Council of Baltimore very prudently decided on this matter, parish priests and missionaries will teach the Catechism with great attention and will take special care to explain the truths of the Faith and of morals that are being opposed by the incredulous and the heterodox, and they will make careful and zealous efforts to impart strength to the young people who are exposed to so many dangers and will spur them on without respite to preserve their religion by means of the frequent approach to the Sacraments and by special devotion to the Blessed Virgin Mary. Parents, or those taking their place, should guard their children most carefully and should question them on the lessons they have attended; they should examine the books that have been issued and, if they find in them anything that is injurious, they should counteract its effects; finally, they should separate them absolutely and preserve them from all familiarity and intimacy with fellow-students who are capable of endangering their Faith or habits, and from those whose behavior is depraved.

Warning to parents

63   This instruction and this necessary Christian education
(114) of their children is often neglected by those parents who allow their children to frequent schools where it is impossible to avoid the loss of souls or who, notwithstanding the existence of a well-organized neighboring Catholic school or the possibility of having their children educated elsewhere in a Catholic school, entrust them to public schools without sufficient reason and without having taken the necessary precautions to avoid the danger of perversion; it is a well-known fact that, according to Catholic moral teaching, such parents, should they persist in their attitude, cannot receive absolution in the Sacrament of Penance.

LEO XIII
1878-1903

STUDIES AT THE SERVICE OF REVELATION

Encycl. *Inscrutabili*, April 21, 1878.

(Evil of the world: the rejection of the Church.—Merits of the Church.—Salvation of the world: in the Church, her teaching.)

It is then your duty, Venerable Brethren, to dedicate yourselves assiduously so that the seed of heavenly doctrine be sown generously in the field of the Lord, and so that, the teaching of the Catholic faith may be instilled in the minds of the faithful from their most tender years, may become deeply-rooted, and so preserve them from the contagion of error. The more the enemies of religion strive to teach the ignorant, and especially the young, doctrines which obscure the mind and corrupt the heart, so much greater must be the effort to see that not only the method of teaching be reasonable and serious, but, more important, that this same teaching be healthy and fully in accordance with the Catholic faith—whether it be in literature or the sciences, and, still more in philosophy. For on this latter depends, to a great extent, progress in other sciences; while it should aim not at attacking divine revelation, but instead, should take delight in smoothing out the way for it and defending it against attack, as the great Augustine, the Angelic Doctor and other masters of Christian wisdom have taught us by their example and writings.

64
(62, 66, 70, 82, 93, 116)

But the sound education of the young, if it is to safeguard their faith, religion and morals, must start from the most tender years in the family itself, which, in our times is in a miserable state of unrest, and cannot be recalled to

65
(28)

its dignity except by subjecting itself to the laws with which it was instituted in the Church by its divine Author.

(Christian marriage.—Union of bishops with the Holy See.)

SUPPRESSION OF THE CATECHISM IN SCHOOLS

Letter *In mezzo*, June 26, 1878—to the Cardinal Vicar.

(Sufferings at the commencement of the Pontificate: unrestrained Press, Protestant propaganda. . . .)

66
(101,
105)
... Here (in the city of Rome) there are schools, homes and hospices which unsuspecting youth may enter and whose seemingly philanthrophic aim is to help them in the cultivation of their mind and in material needs, but whose true aim is to form a generation hostile to Religion and the Church of Christ. And as if this were not enough, through the artifices of those who owe it to their office to promote the real interests of the Romans, a ban has now been imposed on the Catholic Catechism in municipal schools. It is an act worthy of reproof, which thus removes even this defence against heresy and growing unbelief and paves the way for a new sort of hostile encroachment, which is so much the more disastrous and dangerous than the old insofar as it tends directly to wrest from the hearts of the Romans the precious treasure of the faith and of the fruits which they derive from it. This fresh attempt against Religion and the piety of Our people fills Our soul with a deep-felt grief and forces Us to write this letter to you, Your Eminence, who take Our place in the spiritual government of Rome, on this painful subject, in order to recall its importance before God and man.

67
(22,
30,
And here, right at the beginning, in virtue of Our pastoral ministry, We must remind every Catholic of his very serious duty—obliging him by natural and divine law—

to instruct his children in the supernatural truths of the   *107)*
faith, and of the obligation that binds, in a Catholic city,
those who rule its destinies to facilitate and promote the
fulfillment of this duty. And while We raise Our voice,
in the name of Religion, to safeguard its sacred rights, We
wish likewise to bring out how much this rash decision is
contrary to the true well-being of society itself.

Benefits of religious teaching

Certainly, one is hard put to conceive of the pretext   **68**
that might have recommended such a measure—unless,   *(69,*
perhaps, it be that irrational, pernicious indifference to   *92,*
religion, in which nowadays it is hoped to make people   *94,*
grow up. Up to now, both reason and even ordinary com-   *107,*
mon sense have taught men to reject as useless those things   *116)*
which in practice have not proved themselves worth while,
or because of changed circumstances have become useless.
But who can say that the teaching of the Catechism has not
so far been worth while? Was it not religious education
that renewed the world, that sanctified and made more
human the mutual relations among men, which rendered
moral sense more delicate and trained that Christian conscience in a code that restrains excesses, reproves injustice
and exalts those who are loyal above all others? Might it
perhaps be said that the social conditions of the present
age have made it old-fashioned and harmful? But the well-
being and prosperity of a people has no sure protection
without truth and justice, for which present-day society
feels such an urgent need, and whose rights are fully protected by the Catholic Catechism. In recognition, therefore,
of the precious fruits, already gathered and rightly hoped
for from this teaching, one should, far from banning it from
public schools, promote it with every means in one's power.

And this is likewise a need which is innate in the very   **69**
nature of the child and the peculiar conditions in which we   *(60,*

71)   live. On no account may we call down once again on the
child the judgment of Solomon, and split him by an irrational and cruel rupture of intelligence and will: while the
former is to be taken in hand and cultivated, the latter
must be prepared so as to practice virtuous habits and
attain the final goal. Anyone educating the young who
neglects the will, concentrating all his efforts on the cultivation of the mind, makes instruction a dangerous weapon
in the hands of the wicked. It is the argument of naked
reason, added to an evil intent and often, to power, against
which no remedy is possible.

70   And the matter is so clear that these very people who
(60,   wish to exclude religious teaching from schools, recognize
69,   it,—naturally, at the price of contradiction; they do not
94,   limit their efforts to the intelligence alone, but extend them
97)   also to the will, ordering that in the schools there be taught
a system of ethics which they call "civil" and "natural," preparing youth for the acquisition of the social and civic
virtues. But, besides the fact that such a morality cannot
guide man to the supreme end destined for him by divine
Goodness in the beatific vision of God, it does not even
have sufficient effect on the soul of the child to lead him
along the path to virtue and to keep him resolute in good.
Neither does it respond to the real and deeply felt needs
of man, who is a religious animal just as he is a social animal, and no scientific progress can ever eradicate from his
heart the deep roots of religion and faith. But then, in order to educate the hearts of the young to virtue, why not
avail oneself of the Catholic Catechism, in which we find
the most perfect method and the most fertile seeds of a
healthy education?

71   The teaching of the Catechism ennobles and raises
(69,   man up in his own estimation, leading him always to re-
72)   spect himself and others. It is unfortunate that many of
those who decree the exclusion of the Catechism from the
schools, have chosen to forget, or do not consider, what

they themselves learned from the Catechism in their infancy. Otherwise it would be quite easy for them to understand what teaching should be given to the child, that he comes from the hands of God, the result of the love which He freely gave him; that all about him is constituted by God, King and Lord of creation; that he is so great and of so much value that the Eternal Son of God did not disdain to be made flesh in order to redeem him; that his forehead is bathed with the blood of the Man-God in baptism; that his spiritual life is nourished by the flesh of the divine Lamb; that the Holy Spirit residing in him as in a living temple fills him with divine life and virtue; all this is like giving the child a very powerful incentive to keep his glorious character of a child of God and to honor it by virtuous behavior.

They would likewise understand that it is only proper to expect great things from a child who during catechism class learns that he is destined for a very high end in the vision and love of God; who is made capable of keeping continual guard over himself and is given every sort of help to sustain the battle which implacable enemies wage against him; who is trained to be docile and submissive, learning to respect in his parents the image of the Father Who is in heaven, and in the Head of the State the authority that comes from God, and from God only derives the reason of its being and majesty; who is drawn to respect in his brothers the divine similarity which shines on his own brow and to recognize under the apparent misery of the poor the Redeemer Himself; who is saved in time from doubt and uncertainty, because of this Catholic teaching, which carries engraved on it the marks of infallibility and authenticity: in its divine origin, in the tremendous fact of its establishment upon earth, in the abundance of sweet and saving fruits which it produces. Finally, they would realize that Catholic morality, fortified by the fear of punishment and of the certain hope of the highest re-

72
(11, 69, 72, 74, 75)

ward, does not suffer the same fate as the "civil ethics" which people want to substitute for religious ethics; neither would they have made the disastrous resolution to deprive the present generation of so many and such precious advantages, by banning the teaching of Catechism from schools.

Optional religious instruction

73
(102,
105,
106,
115)
And We say, *ban*, since the mentality which is willing to furnish religious instruction only to those children whose parents expressly request it, is wholly illusory. We just cannot understand how the authors of this ill-fated directive were not aware of the dangerous impression produced in the mind of the child to see religious education given a place so different from that of other subjects. The child needs to realize the importance and necessity of what he is taught if he is to be stimulated to diligent study. But what respect can he have for a subject matter towards which the school authorities show themselves either indifferent or hostile, tolerating it unwillingly? And if there be (as it is not hard to find) parents who, either out of wickedness of heart, or, as is more probable, out of ignorance and negligence, do not think of asking that their children benefit by religious instruction, a great proportion of the young would remain deprived of very necessary means to salvation—with grievous harm not only to those innocent souls, but to civil society itself. And, in such sorry conditions, should it not be the duty of the directors of the school to remedy the malice or negligence of others? Hoping for advantages, which are certainly less important, they have now thought of making elementary instruction obligatory by law, thus forcing many parents under threat of fines to send their children to school: but then, how can they have the heart to take away from Catholic youth that religious instruction which undoubtedly forms the strongest guarantee for a wise and virtuous direction of life?

Is it not cruelty to presume that these children can **74** grow up without religious ideas and sentiments, until, *(107,* caught up in the storms of adolescence, they find them- *115)* selves face to face with seductive and violent passions, disarmed, without the ability for restraint, with the certainty of being dragged down the slippery path of crime? Our paternal heart is grieved to see the lamentable consequences of that unwise move: and Our suffering grows more bitter when We see that today, more than ever, provocation to every sort of vice is both strong and on the increase. Your Eminence, who by your high office as Our Vicar, follow closely the progress of the battle which, in our own city of Rome, is being waged against God and the Church, know quite well, without need for Us to speak much about it, which and how many are the dangers of perversion which the young have to face, such as dangerous doctrines which undermine all lawfully-constituted order, bold and violent proposals to condemn and discredit all legitimate authority, and finally immorality which, without any reserve, proceeds quite openly by a thousand paths to contaminate the eye and corrupt the heart.

In the face of these and like attacks on faith and morals, every one can see for himself just how opportune has been the moment chosen to throw out religious education from public schools.

(Do they perhaps want to pervert Christian Rome?)

Substitute for religious education

But, so long as the adorable dispositions of Providence **75** allow this trial to last, if it is not in Our power to change *(116)* the state of things, it is Our duty, however, to make every effort to mitigate the evil and reduce the damage, Hence, it is necessary, not that the parish priests redouble their diligence and zeal in the teaching of the Catechism, but that new and efficacious methods be applied to remedy the defect that has been caused by the fault of others. We have no doubt that the Roman clergy, as on other occasions, will not fail to fulfill the sacred duties of their priestly ministry, and will devote themselves with most affectionate care to the preservation of the youth of Rome from the dangers which threaten its faith and morality. We are likewise certain that the Catholic associations, flourishing in this city with so much benefit to religion, will collaborate with all the means in their power in this holy enterprise—to prevent this dear city from losing her sacred and venerable religious character and her enviable boast of being the Holy City, and from becoming a victim of error and a theater of unbelief. And We ask Your Eminence, with the wisdom and firmness you possess, to promote oratories and schools, where young people may be gathered together for instruction in the holy Catholic religion in which they have been born by a very special grace from heaven.

76
(43,
44,
116)
Seek, as is already being done with good fruit in some Churches, for virtuous and charitable laymen, who, under the guidance of one or more priests, offer to help teach the Catechism to children. See that parents are also exhorted by parish priests to send their children, and that they are reminded of the duty which is theirs, of demanding religious instruction for their children at school.

(Catechisms for adults.—Exhortation to pray.)

ANTI-CATHOLICISM IN ROME

Letter *Nel giugno,* March 25, 1879.—to the Cardinal Vicar.

(Reference to the letter "In mezzo." [a] *)*

77
(93,
It is well known by sad experience that, in the war now directed against the Church, the enemy concentrates

77a See above No. 66.

especially on the young, with the clear intention of forming *102)*
the growing generations according to their own plans and
to win them over at an early age to their cause. Having,
therefore, denied the Church any say in public affairs, and
having conceded equal rights to any sort of religion and
cult, they want to deprive public instruction of the watchfulness and the authority of the Church, who has always
been the promoter and teacher of every sort of knowledge.
They have everywhere granted free entrance to any kind
of teaching, even though atheist or infected with heresy.

Your Eminence is well aware that this way of instructing youth, removed from the beneficial influence of the
Church, has been introduced even in the States of the Holy
See, as these were gradually wrested away from the legitimate rule of the Pope; furthermore, without taking any
notice of the very special conditions and the peculiar character which invests Rome in the eyes of all, being the See
of the Vicar of Christ and the center of Catholicism, here
too they have opened the gates of the widest liberty to
error. Hence the situation, that, within these venerable
walls, where formerly was furnished no other teaching than
the pure teaching which the Church desired, now, instead,
in public schools the Catholic Catechism is barely tolerated
for some periods; furthermore, in those schools, opened
and conducted by non-Catholics, the tender minds of the
boys and girls are imbued with evil doctrines, conforming
to the heretical spirit of those who teach. Many well-known
facts reveal clearly the plan conceived by the enemies of
the Catholic religion, to spread widely in Rome the false
principles of Protestantism; and, profiting by the liberty
granted by the law, to direct especially against Rome all
the forces that until now were used in the various cities of
the peninsula, and to establish here a sort of center of un-
orthodox propaganda in Italy, under the influence of and
with the powerful help that comes to them from outside.
They desire to carry their scheme into effect particularly in

the schools and through the schools; which, therefore, far from diminishing with time, are growing in number from year to year through the efforts and with the money of foreigners, who, having come here, often open new schools, seeking by every art to attract many of the young.

78
(101, Hence they offer much monetary assistance to those
107) who feel in a greater degree the sting and the suffering of poverty, making it easier to provide for the necessities of life; with others they are liberal with promises, rewards, allurements and attractions of all kinds.—Neither can We disregard the fact, that, with characteristic audacity, they have gone so far as to open anti-Catholic schools even under Our very eyes, right up to the gates of the Vatican, venerable See of the Bishops of Rome.—On the contrary, while so much licentious liberty is granted to these heretical schools, they try to impede the increase and development of Catholic schools by indirect—yet extremely effective—ways. There is, indeed, no lack of sinister insinuations against them, nor of particular hardships, nor of threats in order to dissuade parents from entrusting their children to teachers who are sincerely Christian.

We will not here, Your Eminence, prove how contrary also to the public well-being and the common advantage, is the sort of instruction that is desired at the present moment, purged, as it is, of the spirit of Christianity. For everybody sees to what extremes a society will be led when in its midst there is allowed to grow up a generation deprived of Christian teaching, indifferent to the practice of religion and without firm moral principles. The lamentable proofs, which we already have, are a sinister omen for the future.

(It is particularly serious and unpleasant that these things happen in Rome.—Creation of a Commission of vigilance over schools.—A call for help to the aristocracy, clergy and the Roman people.)

AN INEVITABLE FIGHT

Letter *Les Conditions Internes,* November 4, 1879— to Leopold II, King of the Belgians.

(The law of 1842, even though not perfect, at least respected principles.—The present law upsets peace and renders the future alarming.)

This new Belgian education law, my Lord, proposed by people who have little affection for the Church and the Catholic religion, must of necessity grieve the Supreme Pontiff, who is custodian of truth and the defender of justice. Practically, the new law pays no heed to the authority given by God to the Bishops, with regard to the religious and moral education of youth. It does not grant that the teaching of our most holy religion should be the basis for public education. It tends, instead, to form future teachers of elementary schools removed from every religious guidance and influence. In this way, because of the principles which inspire the law, it paves the way—for the present and the future—to unbelief and the corruption of heart in the midst of the believing and upright people whom God has placed under your royal scepter.

The Bishops could not help but be profoundly moved in the face of so great an evil. They could not avoid protesting and seeking a remedy against the danger which threatens the souls confided to them. We ourselves, obliged to fight the same dangers in Italy and in the very Rome of the Popes, have given them an example by opening truly Catholic schools for the children.

Notwithstanding this, We, mindful of that divine charity taught us by our Redeemer and desiring to preserve His spirit even in defense of the most sacred rights, will not neglect any opportunity that offers itself—just as We have not failed to do so in the past—to urge the Pastors of Belgium to show the utmost evangelical kindness towards the erring

79
(16,
22,
102,
103,
105-
107,
110-
112,
117)

and the deceived, even when they find themselves forced by duty and necessity to offer a firm resistance to error.

However, Your Majesty, We believe that the struggle which has started in your Kingdom cannot cease, nor can peace be re-established, until the troublesome cause that is disturbing the peace has been removed. Every Bishop who wishes to carry out the work of his pastoral ministry, even using circumspection and moderation, necessarily finds himself at every moment in continual and inevitable conflict with the spirit, the tendencies, and the terms of this law, because it is too far removed from Catholic doctrine. This is why the Bishops of Belgium, in spite of differences in temperament and character, were all in unanimous agreement when they decided on the measures to be adopted to fight the consequences they feared from this new legislation. We recognize the seriousness of the disturbance that such events have produced in Belgium: We are profoundly affected and preoccupied by them. But We nourish the hope that the men who have the honor to be ministers of Your Majesty and the Crown's chief counsellors will, from their elevated office, consider the requirements of public affairs, not by insisting upon the adoption of a certain system, but by considering the common good of the entire nation—and reaching the conclusion that "les raisons d'Etat," as well as equity, counsel the spontaneous withdrawal of a law which is not the result of any real need and which has grievously wounded a very great portion of the subjects of Your Majesty.

NEUTRAL SCHOOLS

All. to Cardinals, August 20, 1880.

(Offenses to the Holy See by the Belgian Government. —Proposal to withdraw the Embassy to the Holy See.—Law on primary education.)

You are well aware, Venerable Brethren, of the char- **80**
acter and nature of this law. Its principal aim was un- *(102,*
doubtedly to remove youth from the influence of the Cath- *105,*
olic Church and to entrust their education solely to the *106,*
State. This law, in fact, excludes from public schools all *111)*
intervention of the sacred Pastors and any kind of vigilance
by the Church. Making a complete separation between religion and learning it desires to eliminate every sort of
religious education from the instruction of children in its
rulings on discipline of the public schools. It is easy to see
how great a danger this constitutes both for the faith and
the behavior of the growing generations. This danger appears more serious still, because, by the same law, all
religious instruction is banned even from those schools
which are called "normal schools," where, by means of
precepts and practical work, those who will later wish to
dedicate themselves to the teaching of boys and girls are
being trained.

Such a law, so contrary to the teachings and rights of
the Church, so dangerous for the eternal salvation of the
young, could not, according to the demands of their conscience, receive the approval of the Bishops, who are
placed by God Himself to watch faithfully over the salvation of souls and the defence of the faith.

And they, knowing full well what the times and the **81**
pastoral office demanded of them, have carefully studied *(117)*
how to keep the young away from these public schools,
and to open others, under their auspices, where the tender
minds of the children may grasp at one and the same time
the first elements of letters and the rudiments of religion. In
this regard, it is to the great merit of the Belgians that they
have given willing and generous cooperation to such opportune and salutary work. Having understood in how
great a danger religion was because of that law, they
strove, in the best possible manner, to defend their hereditary faith; and they did so with such fiery zeal that the

greatness of their work and of the expenses incurred
evoked the admiration of all those who heard of it.

82   And We, to Whom by Our most high office of Su-
(106, preme Pastor and Teacher, pertains the obligation of pre-
114) serving the faith in absolute purity, of guarding the sacred
rights of the Church and affronting the dangers which
threaten the faithful, could not let pass uncondemned a
law which Our Venerable Brethren have already rightly
condemned. Hence, in the letters We wrote to Our dear
Son, Leopold II, King of the Belgians (a), We openly
stated that the law of the first of July was very much in
contrast with the teachings of Catholic doctrine and fatal
to the eternal salvation of the young and to the true well-
being of the Belgian people themselves. As such, therefore,
We disapproved of and condemned it, and now again, in
your presence, and for the same reasons, We reprove and
condemn it. In doing so, We are only following the practice
and traditions of the Apostolic See, which has always
censured those schools without religion, which are called
neutral, and which, by their very nature, end up by not
recognizing God at all. Neither has the Holy See ever tolerated the attendance of Catholic youth at similar schools,
except in special cases, when necessity and force of circumstances demand it, and not without having first taken care
that the danger of perversion be at least kept at bay.

83   In any case, animated by the spirit of Christian charity
(110) and because We did not want to furnish any excuse to provoke a conflict, We have always warmly urged Our Venerable Brethren, who are fighting a difficult battle, to
show benevolent moderation in the application of the
directives already given, as and when occasion arises; and
that, when they have to punish, to do so mildly. Thus, the
Christian zeal, which stirs in them because of so serious

82a See above No. 79.

and justifiable a motive, may be tempered by a paternal benevolence, which embraces in charity all those who err.

(Protest on account of the expulsion of the Nuncio from Belgium and the calumnies against the Holy See.— In praise of the Belgian people for their affection to the Apostolic See.)

RIGHTS OF BISHOPS OVER SCHOOLS

Apost. Const. *Romanos Pontifices,* May 8, 1881—on the relations between the Bishops and the Regular Clergy in England.

(Difficulties regarding: exemption; the presence of the Regular Clergy at Synods; the ministry of the Regular Clergy.)

The questions dealt with above are closely related to the problem of deciding if schools for the children of the masses whether called elementary, primary or kindergarten, are dependent upon the authority of the Bishop. The imparting of instruction is in fact a very holy ministry and the schools where this instruction is given come immediately after places of worship. (a) Their very name indicates the sphere of action of these schools; they have as their aim the training of little children in the best manner possible, giving them the elementary notions of learning, of the truths of faith and moral principles. This institution is necessary to every period of time and to every sort of place or way of living, and is very important for the salvation of

**84
(3,
4,
19,
45,
52,
64,
69,
74)**

84a Quaeriter an Episcopis subesse debeant scholae pauperum quae elementares etiam, primariae, puerorum nuncupantur; est enim sanctissimum docendi ministerium et proximum piis locis ordinem tenent scholae de quibus agendum est.

the whole of human society as also for every man in particular. In fact, from the way the child is formed depends in
great measure the conduct of a man for the rest of his life.
For this reason, Pius IX has wisely indicated what those
who teach should especially aim at: "It is especially in these
schools that, right from their tenderest years, the working
class children must be instructed in the mysteries and the
commandments of our holy religion and must be well
formed in good habits and in the fulfilling of their religious
and civic duties; and in these schools religious instruction
must occupy first place in teaching, and must stand out in
such a way that other ideas taught to children seem to take
the place of extras." (b) Everybody therefore can see that
in this manner the instruction of the child falls within the
duties of Bishops and that the schools of which We speak,
whether they be in thickly-populated cities or in small villages, are included among those matters which especially
concern the government of the diocese.

85
(16,
19)
These points are further confirmed by history. There
has been practically no age in which the councils have not
taken special care to draw up rules for and to protect these
schools, concerning which they have issued very many and
wise directives. These decrees have laid down that the
Bishops should look after the re-establishment and development of these schools in cities and villages, and that
children be admitted free of charge, if possible. The same
authority has drawn up rules which the children should
follow in their application to religion and piety; it has defined the prerogatives and moral qualities which teachers
should possess, and has enjoined upon them to take an
oath according to the Catholic formula and profession.
Finally, it has laid down that inspectors should visit the
schools and see if they can find anything blameworthy or
unsuitable, and whether anything is being omitted of what

84b Cf. above No. 28.

the diocesan regulations have prescribed regarding the discipline of these same schools.

And for this reason, the Fathers of the Councils, understanding perfectly that parish priests also participate in the pastoral ministry, have reserved for them an important role in schools for children, whose care is closely connected with the care of souls. It was therefore judged suitable to set up in each parish primary schools, called "parochial." Parish priests were ordered to undertake teaching, calling on schoolmasters and schoolmistresses for help; they were given the responsibility of directing and administering these schools with diligence: and if they did not fulfill all this in a faithful and irreproachable manner, they were blamed for not having performed their duty and were considered therefore worthy of punishment by their Bishop. **86** *(16, 44)*

And so, the arguments of reason and the testimony of history lead to the same conclusion: that the schools for working class children must be included—and for very solid reasons—among the diocesan and parochial institutions. Hence, the Bishops of England have, up to the present time, been in the habit of visiting them with full authority in Missions under both secular and regular clergy. We also approve of that, declaring that the Bishops have the right thus to visit all these schools in Missions and parishes entrusted both to the regular and secular clergy. (a) **87** *(19)*

(The permission of the Holy See and the Bishop must be asked to open new Colleges of Regular Clergy.—Property of the Missions.—A plea for harmony.)

87a Cf. C.I.C., canon 1382: Ordinarii locorum sive ipsi per se sive per alios possunt quoque scholas qualibet, oratoria, recreatoria, patronatus, etc., in iis quae religiosam et moralem institutionem spectant, visitare; a qua visitatione quorumlibet religiosorum scholae exemptae non sunt, nisi agatur de scholis internis pro professis religionis exemptae.

SECULARIZATION OF SCHOOLS IN FRANCE

Letter *Les événements,* May 12, 1883—to the President of the French Republic.

(The Holy See's attitude toward France.—Measures against religious orders.)

88
(92,
107,
119)
Our grief and the damage to the Catholic Church were further increased by the passing of the law which excludes indispensable and traditional religious instruction from schools, and which, for the long period of its duration, produced such useful and abundant fruits for the very civilization of the country. In vain did the entire French hierarchy express its sorrow; in vain did fathers of families make legal appeals that their rights be preserved; in vain did disinterested men, quite openly members of the Republican Party—and among them political figures of exceptional intelligence—show the government how grievous it would be for a nation of thirty-two million Catholics, if a law were introduced that banned from schools that religius education in which man finds the most generous impulses and the most perfect rules for bearing the difficulties of life, respecting the rights of authority and justice and acquiring the virtues indispensable for domestic, political and civic life. No consideration was able to reverse the decision taken, and the law was promulgated and put into effect in the entire French territory.

(Exclusion of religion from all State institutions.—Law on marriage; on military service for the clergy.—Suppression of episcopal allowances because of a prohibition of school textbooks.)

89
(105,
107)
We cannot but note that the disturbance produced in consciences is not the result of the publication of the decrees of the Congregation of the Index. It goes back to preceding causes, among which must, in the first place, be

recalled the fact of having excluded religious instruction from schools, to the immense detriment of the faith of the budding generations, in spite of the protest of the entire hierarchy and of fathers of families, and of having introduced into school textbooks principles contrary to our holy religion. The government itself, which had foreseen this, had hastened to promise that never, in the schools, would anything contrary to religion be taught, nothing which could offend the consciences of the young and of their parents. But it is Our duty to say frankly, in accordance with Our Apostolic ministry, that these promises were not kept.

This fact—painful, yet irrefutable—will explain certain acts or certain expressions of some members of the clergy about whom the government thinks it has the right to complain. In the presence of the moral damage which youth suffers because of the suppression of religious education in schools—damage that has been increased by the reading of books which have been declared hostile to the principles of religion by the only authority competent to do so—it is easy to understand how the heart of a Bishop, to whom belongs the burden and responsibility of souls, must overflow with grief and bitterness.

**90
(12,
92,
107,
111)**

Is it against these shepherds that there should be need to be armed with defensive weapons, as if the attack and the offensive came from their side? One could understand this necessity if the Bishops, abandoning their sphere of religion, were to inculcate principles contrary to public order. But, as long as they, keeping to the field of conscience, exert themselves on behalf of the nation, to conserve whole and unstained the faith and morals taught by the gospels, to which the great majority of the French people rightly attribute the most vital importance, We do not think there exist sufficient motives to warrant general precautions on a scale which could only serve to alarm and offend all Catholics and especially the whole French episcopacy, which is well-deserving of both religion and country.

(Hope that the government will recognize the rights of God and the Church and the interests of the country.)

HISTORICAL STUDIES

Letter *Saepenumero*, August 18, 1883—to Cardinals de Luca, Pitra and Hergenroether.

(Distortion of history by the enemies of the Church.)

91
(102,
106,
108)
Still more serious, however, is the fact that this way of treating history should have found its way into the schools themselves. Very often, the textbooks provided for the children are full of falsehoods, which they are bound to absorb, especially when to these is added the teaching of a corrupt or superficial teacher; and thus they easily imbibe a proud aversion for what deserves veneration and an impudent scorn for the most sacred persons and things. Upon leaving the first classes, they frequently encounter even graver dangers, the reason being that in higher studies, the narration of facts is followed by a study of their root causes. From these causes are deduced at will laws and historical theories which very frequently are quite openly opposed to revealed doctrine, (a) and whose only aim is to dissemble and conceal the great and beneficial influence which Christian institutions have had on social life and on the entire course of human events. And this method is used by very many, who then have no scruples about being inconsistent or contradictory or about obscuring the philosophy of history. In short—not to enter into details—the entire teaching of history is directed to this end: to make the Church suspect, the Popes an object of

91a Nam in majorem disciplinarum meditationibus ad eventuum narratione ad rerum preceditur causas; a causis vero exaedificatio legum petitur ad iudicia temere ficta, quae saepius cum doctrina divinitus tradita aperte dissentiunt.

disapproval, and above all, to make the people believe that the civil authority of the Pope is detrimental to the safety and the greatness of Italy.

(The achievements of the Papacy for Italy and Europe.)

Meanwhile, however, it is incredible what immense harm is caused by this warping of history, when it is put to the service of parties and the various types of human greed. Undoubtedly, history will not then be the teacher of life nor the light of the truth which the ancients quite rightly judged it should be, but a flatterer of vice and a servant to corruption, and this, particularly to the detriment of youth, whose minds it will fill with unwholesome ideas, leading their souls far from uprightness and every ingenuous sentiment.

92
(64, 102, 108)

The study of history irresistibly captivates the vivid and ardent imagination of the young—the depiction of antiquity and the figures of those personalities which history brings to life make a warm appeal to youth and remain firmly fixed in their minds. And therefore, once the poison has been swallowed in the early years of life, it is impossible later on to find a suitable remedy. There is little hope that, with the passage of time, they will acquire a clearer power of discernment and unlearn what they have learned at the beginning: since few dedicate themselves to a profound and calm study of history, and when they attain a more mature age, they will, in the ordinary run of things, meet with occasions that tend to confirm rather than correct the errors.

It is therefore of the greatest importance to avoid so pressing a danger and to see that, at any cost, the study of history—in itself so dignified—should no longer be twisted so as to become a cause of such grave damage to society and private individuals. Honest men, then, well-versed in this branch of study must set themselves the task of writing history with the firm resolve and the intention of mak-

93
(64, 118)

ing truth known in all its integrity, and of replying, with skillful and timely refutation, to the insulting accusations which have far too long been piled up against the Popes of Rome. Against the bare recital of facts, let them offer painstaking and patient investigation; against a superficial expression of opinion, let them oppose maturity of judgment; against mere whim, the prudence of sound criticism. With regard to facts that have been misrepresented or merely presumed, let them do everything possible to put them in their true light by going back to the sources. In this connection, writers, in a special manner, would do well to remember that *the first law of history is neither to say anything false, nor to keep silent about the truth, so that no hint of favor or disfavor may appear in its recording.* (a)

There is, further, an urgent need to prepare comprehensive manuals for use in schools, without prejudice to the truth or danger to the young, and with advancement of historical studies themselves. For this, once the main work has been done on the testimony of the more reliable documents which exist, nothing more is required than to pick out the most edifying points and develop them clearly and with brevity. This work is certainly a bit difficult, but it is very advantageous and therefore calls for the diligent work of even the most gifted people.

(Famous historians.—The Vatican archives are available to historians.—Teachings of history about Divine Providence, the Church, the Papacy.)

NEUTRAL CHILDHOOD

Encycl. Letter *Nobilissima Gallorum Gens,* February 8, 1884—on the religious question in France.

93a Primam esse historiae legem ne quid falsi dicere audeat; deinde ne quid veri non audeat; ne qua suspicio gratiae sit in scribendo, ne qua simultatis. Cicero, *De Oratore,* 1. 2, 62 (Thes. Leipzig).

*(Elder daughter of the Church.—The eighteenth cen-
tury.—Religion is necessary for the good of the family and
of the State.)*

In regard to what primarily concerns domestic society, **94**
it is of the greatest importance that children born of Chris- *(14,*
tian marriages be instructed early in the precepts of re- *43,*
ligion, and that the methods usually adopted to educate *69,*
children in culture, go hand in hand with religious instruc- *106,*
tion. To separate one from the other is, really, to want to *114)*
keep the minds of children neutral in their duties towards
God. This is a false training and is particularly disastrous
in the tender years of childhood, since it is a way that leads
directly to atheism and excludes religion. Good parents
must be firm in seeing that their children, as soon as they.
reach an age when they can learn, should be instructed in
the precepts of religion, and that, in the schools, there
should be nothing which offends the integrity of faith and
morals. This care, which is required for the instruction of
children, is demanded by both divine and natural law, nor
can parents, under any pretext, consider themselves dispensed from it.

It is, therefore, the duty of the Church, guardian and
defender of the integrity conferred upon her by her divine
Founder, to call all people to Christian wisdom and at the
same time to observe carefully by what sort of principles
and institutions the youth growing up under her jurisdiction are informed. She has always openly condemned those
coeducational schools likewise known as "neutral," recom-
mending with repeated insistence to fathers of families
that they be on their guard in a matter of such vital importance.

Obedience to the Church in these matters will, at the **95**
same time, procure great advantages and further public *(47,*
welfare in the best possible manner. Those whose tender *69,*
years are not formed in religion, grow up without any *107)*
knowledge of the most important things, which alone can

nourish in men a love of virtue and control those desires which are contrary to reason; these things include the notions about God the Creator, God the Judge and Rewarder, the reward and punishment to be expected in the next life, the heavenly help conferred by Jesus Christ in order to fulfill these duties in a diligent and holy manner. Where there is ignorance of these, any education of the mind will be unhealthy: young people, not accustomed to the fear of God, will have no idea how to follow the rules of honest living, and, like those who have never known how to deny their passions anything, will easily be incited to create chaos in their countries.

(Church and State.—All agreed to defend Catholic principles.)

FREEMASONRY AND YOUTH

Encycl. *Humanum genus*, April 20, 1884.

(Dangers of Freemasonry.—Doctrine.—Rejection of God and Church.)

96
(94,
97) A God, Creator and providential Ruler of the world; an eternal law which commands respect and prohibits the violation of the natural law; the ultimate end of man, situated beyond created things, outside this earth: these are the sources and principles of justice and morality. If these principles are abolished—as is done by Naturalists and Freemasons—natural ethics no longer have any support nor can they be sustained. The only morals which the Freemasons admit and in which alone they would like to educate the youth, are those they call "civil and independent," and which have nothing to do with any religious notions.

97
(97) But the lamentable fruits which have already appeared demonstrate how wretched, uncertain and exposed to every wind of passion is such a system of morals. In

fact, wherever it has begun to have free reign, with the resultant rejection of a Christian education, there has been a decline in moral standards; detestable and monstrous opinions raise their heads and crime makes bold progress in a frightening manner. Everybody laments and deplores this, and often, in the face of the truth, many of those who would have preferred a different state of affairs are compelled to admit it.

(Secularization of matrimony.)

The Masons, with unanimous tenacity, concentrate on obtaining control of the education of the young. They understand only too well that that tender and flexible age lends itself to be moulded at will, and that, therefore, there is no better device for forming in the State the sort of citizens they want. Hence they give no chance to the ministers of the Church to direct or watch over the task of educating and instructing children. In many places the situation has already so deteriorated that the education of youth is entirely in lay hands, and any notion of the great and sacred duties that bind man to God is eliminated from moral instruction. **98**
(94, 101, 102)

(Remedies for the evil.)

In the fourth place, in order to accomplish our purpose more easily, We most warmly commend to your faith and vigilance the young people who are the hope of human society. **99**
(4, 33, 111)

Let their good education occupy a very great part of your ministry and do not ever think that you have watched or done enough in order to keep youth far from those schools and teachers whose teaching may be marked by sectarian ideas. See that parents, spiritual directors, parish priests, in the teaching of Christian doctrine, do not weary of giving timely warning to their sons and pupils about the iniquitous nature of these lodges, so that they may learn the many fraudulent tricks used by the propagandists of the lodges to ensnare people. Better still, those who prepare children for their First Holy Communion would do well to induce them to resolve and promise not to become members of any society without the prior knowledge of their parents or without consulting their parish priest or confessor.

(The good must join together in a great union of prayer and action.)

THE FREE SCHOOL AND THE NATION

Letter *Spectata Fides*, November 27, 1885—to the Bishops of England.

(Decisions regarding the education of children submitted to the Holy Father.)

100
(117,
119)
It is very consoling for Us to see, Venerable Brethren, that, in a matter so important, you are not working alone. We are well aware of what your clergy has achieved in this field. Urged on by a burning charity and a courage that refuses to yield to difficulties, they have been brave enough to open schools for children. These same priests, who have taken on the responsibility of teaching, devote themselves with diligent and praiseworthy endeavor to form youth in Christian virtue and to initiate them in the rudiments of learning. In the measure, then, in which Our words can be of encouragement and well-merited praise, We wish that your priests may continue to earn the gratitude of the children. Let them accept the assurance of Our esteem and Our special pleasure, hoping for a much greater reward from Our Lord, in Whose service they are working.

Furthermore, We affirm that Catholics in this matter are not less worthy of praise. We know that they continually and generously provide for whatever is necessary to preserve their schools. And not only the rich, but also those of modest means and even the poor. Indeed it is a moving and a noble sight to see these latter finding in their very poverty the gift they generously offer for the education of children.

Now, in our times and with the customs prevalent to-day, when so many and so various are the dangers which, on all sides, threaten the tender age and innocence of children, there is no better plan than to impart knowledge in conjunction with education in faith and morals. For this reason, We have said so more than once, We willingly approve of schools of the sort called "free schools," which have been founded by the assistance and generosity of private individuals in France, Belgium, America and in the colonies of the British Empire, and We desire to see them increase and prosper as much as possible, by increased attendance. On Our part, bearing in view the crowded cities here, We have not neglected—with very real concern and at great expense—to provide for many such schools to be placed at the disposal of the children of Rome.

101
(4,
69,
92,
107,
114,
117,
119)

It is in these schools and in virtue of these same schools that We can preserve intact the magnificent heritage which we have received from our forefathers, namely, the integrity of the Catholic faith. By means of these schools the freedom of parents is still assured. Furthermore —and this is something that has been made very necessary, particularly on account of the unbridled licentiousness in thought and action—a noble lineage of citizens is formed for the country, for none is superior to the one who has embraced the Christian faith with conviction from his childhood and has lived it. The sources, and, so to say, the seeds of all the culture that Jesus Christ has divinely brought to the human race, are to be found in the education of children: for, in practice, adult citizens cannot have a moral make-up that is very much different from that received at the time of the child's first education. The pernicious error of those who prefer children to grow without any religious education destroys all the wisdom of our forefathers and threatens the very roots of civil society. This shows you, Venerable Brethren, that fathers of families must not send their children to elementary schools where no religious instruction is given.

102
(92,
115)
As regards what concerns Great Britain, We realize that not only yourselves, but, in general, very many of your fellow-citizens, have a great interest in the religious education of the young. Without being fully in agreement with Us, they know how important it is, both for private and the public order, not to lose that patrimony of Christian wisdom received by your forefathers from Our Predecessor, St. Gregory the Great, through St. Augustine, and which the violent storms that followed have not completely dissipated. We know that today there are many well-disposed people who are striving as diligently as possible to preserve their hereditary faith and that they produce abundant fruits of charity. Our thoughts of you are full of emotion, because We feel a paternal tenderness for what was justly called the Island that nourished saints. In this spirit we firmly hope and foresee a guarantee of salvation and prosperity for Great Britain. Continue then, Venerable Brethren, to pay special attention to youth, continue your work with zeal in every corner of your dioceses, and, with earnest confidence, cultivate whatever seems good seed to you, in order that God, Who is aboundingly rich in mercy, may give it growth.

(Blessing.)

INSUFFICIENT REMEDIES

Encycl. *Quod multum,* August 22, 1886—to the Bishops of Hungary.

(Preservation of the Catholic faith.—Rationalism, naturalism, socialism.—Liberty of the Church in the State; the family; Education.)

It will be of great benefit to the nation to provide for the education of children from their infancy, with righteousness and wisdom.

The times and customs are such today, that many, and at the price of great effort, are striving to wrest school-going youth from the vigilance of the Church and the salutary influence of religion. On all sides there is a demand for the sort of school called "neutral," "mixed," or "lay," whose aim is to bring up pupils in complete ignorance of the most sacred things and without the slightest thought of religion. This evil is much more widespread and powerful than its remedy, and so we are faced with the vision of a rising generation that is indifferent to the good of the soul, ignorant of religion, and often, downright impious. Venerable Brethren, We exhort you to keep your beloved Hungary far from so terrible an evil and to exert yourselves to the full and with all your zeal to this end. Train the young, from their tenderest years, in Christian living and Christian wisdom, for today, more than ever, this is a task that concerns not only the Church, but the State as well.

All upright people understand this perfectly, and therefore, in many regions we find not a few Catholics who take the education of youth seriously and constantly devote the greater part of their energies to this task, without letting themselves be over-awed by the greatness of the sacrifice or the pressure of work. We know that in Hungary there are many making the same sacrifices; however, permit Us, Venerable Brethren, to stimulate your episcopal zeal in this matter a little further.

Considering the importance of the question, We must certainly pray and hope that, in the education of youth, full liberty may be granted to the Church to accomplish the duty placed on her, and We cannot but entreat you to concentrate all your energies diligently to this end. At the same time, do not cease from warning fathers of families

103
(4,
5,
102,
107,
111)

104
(10,
19,
53,
114,
117)

and insisting that they must not allow their sons to attend schools where, it is to be feared, their faith may be in danger. See also that there is no lack of schools, singled out for the excellence of the training and the high standards of the teaching staff; let such schools be set up through your initiative and be placed under the vigilance of the clergy. We should like what We have said to apply not only to elementary schools but also to those schools where the arts and higher studies are pursued.

(*Clergy.—Missions.—Press.—All invited to serve the Church.*)

UNIVERSITY TEACHING

Letter *Quod in novissimo,* April 10, 1887—to the Archbishop of Baltimore.

105
(16,
17)
The joint letter addressed to Us, dated October the 25th of last year, informs Us that you and the other Pastors of the Church in North America, intend now to begin the erection of a University as was decided by the collective vote of the bishops of the region during the last Assembly held at Baltimore in 1864. We felt an immense joy over this testimony of your faith and sincere attachment to the Apostolic See, to which, right from the beginning, you have committed the patronage and protection of this Academy. It has always been the glory of the Pastors of the Church, but above all, of the Supreme Pontiffs, constantly to promote the acquisition of a knowledge worthy of its name, and carefully to watch over the teaching—especially theological and philosophical—imparted, so that it may be in keeping with the principles of faith. This union between the teaching of revelation and that of reason constitutes an indestructible bulwark of the faith. And this is why Our Predecessors, very anxious about the education of the Christian people, have never, in the past, spared attempts

and sacrifices to set up, in the chief European cities, famous centers of learning, or, in other words, Universities, which, both in the Middle Ages and in successive centuries, have given to Christian and civil society an imposing series of cultured men.

After the duty of governing the Church was conferred on Us, our chief aim has been to reform the pursuit of knowledge. In particular, We have devoted Our attention and energies to revive the excellent doctrine of St. Thomas Aquinas to its legitimate place and splendor. It was Our intention that, in the pursuit of the higher branches of learning, taking into account the recent achievements in the field of learning and the results of near-contemporary wisdom, philosophy should be revised according to the wisdom of the ancients and should closely follow the method of the Angelic Doctor. We think it certain and quite evident that, once this reform has been achieved, the very study of literature and other branches of human learning—together with the practice of a sincere piety—can be a source of many benefits to civil society. **106** *(70, 92)*

There is no need to demonstrate the value and importance of this work, in the midst of the disasters which today threaten the youth of European countries: you yourselves have clearly observed it, in the light of the North American situation. Indeed, the unbridled liberty of thought and of the press, which is for you, as for Europe, the consequence of false and widely diffused notions about divine and human realities, is the root and fountain-head of immoral opinions. Religion having been in the majority of cases exiled from schools, criminal men are boldly laboring to extinguish, by the deceits of a false wisdom, the Christian faith in the souls of adolescents, and to enkindle impiety. It is therefore necessary to imbue youth as best we can, with a more virile doctrine, and, especially, to arm these adolescents, who are the hope of the Church, with **107** *(116)* every weapon that can equip them to defend the cause of Catholic truth.

108
(19,
62)
Very willingly, then, We welcome and approve of this plan, by which, prompted by your concern for the common good and the desire to achieve the well-being of your country, you propose to found a University. But, in order that this most worthy proposal be successfully carried out and developed from day to day, it must always remain under the authority and direction of all the prelates of your country. Thus, its administration should be in the hands of those Bishops selected for the purpose. These should have the task of drawing up the syllabus, preparing the rules of procedure and discipline, choosing professors and other collaborators for the University, and organizing everything which will render its direction most efficient. It would be well to submit all decisions in this matter to the examination of the Holy See so that it may sanction them by its authority. Regarding the choice of the city in which the University will have its seat, We desire you to communicate your proposals to the other Bishops of the United States and make a final decision only after having heard their individual opinions.

(Encouragement and Blessing.)

COMMON DUTIES AND INTERESTS

Encycl. *Officio sanctissimo*, December 22, 1887—to the Bishops of Bavaria.

(History of the Church in Bavaria.—Present difficulties.—Formation of the clergy.)

109
(5,
16,
To this brief outline on the manner of educating young clerics, we should like to add—and it is quite appropriate to do so—some indications about youth in general. We are

very anxious that they should be educated in a completely   55,
irreproachable and correct manner, both as regards the   92)
cultivation of the intellect and as regards spiritual perfection.

    The Church has always surrounded children with ma-
ternal tenderness. With great love, she has devoted much
effort to their protection and has procured for them help
of every kind. Among other things, many religious congregations have been instituted to instruct adolescents in
letters and arts, but above all, to ground them in prudence
and Christian virtue. This is what assures these young souls
of the beneficial and easily acquired influence of piety
towards God. With these foundations, the timely instruction of man's duties towards himself, his neighbor and his
country, inspires great and early hopes.

Rights of the Church

    Actually however, the Church has good reason to com-   **110**
plain when she sees that her children are torn away from   (12,
her even at a tender age, and are forced to enter those ele-   25,
mentary schools where they are told absolutely nothing   106)
about God, or perhaps hear some casual blasphemous reference to Him. Nothing is done to stem the tide of error,
there is no belief in divine teaching, no chance given for
truth to defend itself. Now, this exclusion of the authority
of the Catholic Church from these places of learning and
the arts, is very harmful, and so much the more because
God has committed to the Church the office of teaching
religion, which all men need to reach eternal salvation. No
other society has received this mandate and no other society can appropriate it. When the Church duly affirms
and vindicates this her often unheeded right, she is within
her proper and personal rights.

    We must especially be on our guard and strictly see   **111**
to it that in these schools which have rejected totally, or in   (111,

115, part, the authority of the Church, the youth do not run
116) any risk or suffer any harm to their Catholic faith or to the
integrity of their morals.

In this field, the labors of both the clergy and men of good will can be very effective—on the one hand, if they strive not only to prevent the banning of religious education from schools, but also to see that it continues to retain the importance it deserves and is entrusted to capable teachers of proved virtue; on the other hand, if they find other means to ensure this teaching for youth in a practical and an irreproachable manner.

Duties and rights of parents

112   The united recommendations and activities of the fa-
(8, thers of families will carry great weight. Hence, they must
30, be warned, with all possible insistence, about their obliga-
42, tion to realize the grandeur and the sanctity of their duties
96, to their children before God. They are bound to educate
111) their children in the knowledge of religion and good habits, and must teach them piety towards God. They are courting disaster, when, with great peril, they entrust their children, easily deceived and defenseless as these are, to teachers who are suspect. Let fathers of families remember that, to these duties, which they assumed together with that of the procreation of children, there correspond rights, according to nature and equity, rights which not even they can surrender, nor any human power usurp; and this, because a man cannot be deprived by another of the duties which bind him to God. Hence, let parents reflect that, while they are under the grave obligation to support their children, they have also the other much more important duty of bringing them up in the nobler life that concerns the soul. If they themselves cannot ensure this, they must allow themselves to be substituted, but in such a manner

that the children receive and learn the necessary religious doctrine from approved teachers.

And it is no rare sight to see the beautiful example of faith and generosity set by Catholics, who, in regions where no other public school, besides the so-called "neutral" schools, existed, have opened their own schools at the cost of great self-sacrifice and expense, and support them with equal resolution. It is very, very desirable that these admirable and safe refuges for youth rise up wherever there is need, according to place and circumstance. **113** *(117)*

In the interest of the State

There is no need to conceal the fact that the Christian education of youth is for the greater good of the State itself. It is quite clear that many serious evils are to be feared for a society in which the program and method of instruction do not include religion, or, what is worse, oppose it. Once we neglect and despise that supreme and divine authority, which teaches respect for the authority of God and confirms the certainty of our faith in divine revelation, human science moves to swift destruction, deteriorating into pernicious errors, beginning with naturalism and rationalism. **114** *(92, 103, 107)*

As a result, everyone will claim the right to judge and decide what he should believe, and worse, what he should do, thus immediately weakening and shaking the public authority of the rulers. It would be surprising if those in whom the harmful conviction has been inculcated that they are not subject to the authority and dominion of God should respect and be subject to human authority. Once you destroy the foundations on which all authority rests, the social bond that binds men is broken and destroyed; there will be no longer any public well-being and all will be subject to the tyranny of force and crime.

115   But perhaps, cannot society, relying on its own
(110, strength, avert so horrible a calamity? Can she do so if
112)   she rejects the assistance of the Church, if she be in conflict with the Church? That, surely, is clear and manifest to
anybody. Civil prudence itself recommends that we leave
to the Bishops and the clergy their part in the education
and instruction of youth, and take care that men of indifferent religion or no religion at all, or openly hostile to the
Church, should not be entrusted with the noble duty of
teaching. And it would be appalling if that sort of person
were made to teach sacred doctrine, which is the queen
of all sciences.

(*Freemasonry.—Freedom of the Church.—Agreement
with the State.—Conclusion.*)

CHRISTIAN PATRIOTISM

An Address to French pilgrims, April 13, 1888.

(*Union of France with the Holy See.—Her Christian
vocation.*)

116   You have just recalled, and with reason, that the re-
(92)   ligious education of children and youth, the founding of
schools where pious and well-instructed teachers impart
knowledge of religious truths and precepts, together with
human sciences can be regarded as great achievements.
This is, in truth, the starting point for all progress and civilization and the sole font from which springs the real well-
being of peoples. This, then, dearest children, We offer as
an example for you to emulate with holy generosity: to
prepare Christian generations for your country, subject to
God and His Church; to mould heroes ready to sacrifice
all to the call of duty.

(*Blessing.*)

THE FORTUNE OF A COUNTRY

An Address to Belgian pilgrims, April 19, 1888.

(Close ties between Belgium and the Supreme Pontiff. —The Belgians have known how to defend their religious freedom.)

The instruction and religious education of youth, as you know, forms the object of the ceaseless and most tender solicitude of the Church. We know what great zeal and care your Bishops exercise in this regard. Nevertheless, We cannot fail to remind you how important it is that the young, whether in schools, colleges or the family, should everywhere receive an education free from error and profoundly Christian. To form, in this manner, the mind and heart of new generations, is to work in the most efficacious manner possible for the real good of your country.

We should like to say a word about the Catholic University of Louvain. To further its glory and success, We have advised the Bishops to found special Chairs for higher training in philosophy, which should be steeped in the doctrine of the Angelic Doctor, St. Thomas. We are certain that this will result in abundant and valuable fruit, and intellectuals of the highest calibre will be formed, who will revive the glory of the ancient University of Louvain, the pride of Belgium.

(Blessing.)

117
(5,
48,
92)

VILLAGE SCHOOLS

Address to Dutch pilgrims, April 29, 1888.

(Attacks of the enemies of the Church.—Firmness of Dutch Catholics.—Restoration of the hierarchy.)

In order to make victory surer, We strongly recommend you to multiply and promote schools wherever there

118
(117)

is a Catholic population, even in the most humble villages and hamlets, to see that youth are preserved from all erroneous doctrine and everywhere receive an instruction and a training in conformity with the teachings of Catholic faith and morals.

(Blessing.)

FREEDOM OF EDUCATION

Encycl. *Libertas,* June 20, 1888.

(Christian freedom; psychological freedom; moral freedom.—Liberalism: rejection of divine authority.—Modern freedoms: of worship and of the Press.)

119
(63, 95) There can be no doubt that truth alone should imbue the minds of men; for in it are found the well-being, the end and the perfection of every intelligent nature; and therefore nothing but truth should be taught (a) both to the ignorant and the educated, so as to bring knowledge to those who have it not and to preserve it in those who have. For this reason, it is plainly the duty of all who teach to banish error from minds and to arm them against it by means of efficacious arguments.

120
(95, 107) From this it follows, as is evident, that the freedom of which We have been speaking is greatly opposed to reason, and tends absolutely to pervert men's minds, inasmuch as it claims for itself the right of teaching whatever it pleases —a freedom which the State cannot grant without failing in its duty. And the more so, because the authority of teachers has great weight with their hearers, who can

119a Cum dubium esse non possit quin imbuere animos sola veritas debeat, quod in ipsa intelligentium naturarum bonum est et finis et perfectio sita, propterea non debet doctrina nisi vera praecipere.

rarely decide for themselves as to the truth or falsehood of the instruction given to them. Wherefore, this freedom, in order that it may deserve the name, must be kept within certain limits, lest the office of teaching be turned with impunity into an instrument of corruption.

Natural and supernatural truth

Now, truth, which must be the only object of teaching, is of two kinds, natural and revealed. Natural truths, which are the first principles and whatever reason derives therefrom, form a kind of common patrimony of the human race, in the order of ideas. And because on these truths, as on a most firm foundation, rest morality, justice, religion, and the very bonds of human society, to allow this sacred heritage to be squandered with impunity would be most impious, most foolish and unreasonable. **121** *(12, 13, 95)*

But with no less care must we preserve that great and sacred treasure of truths which God Himself has taught us. Through many convincing proofs, as those often used by the Apologists, certain most basic facts have been established, namely, that some truths have been revealed by God; that the only-begotten Son of God was made flesh, to bear witness to the truth; that a perfect society was founded by Him—namely, the Church, of which He is head and with which He has promised to abide till the end of the world. He entrusted to this society all the truths which He taught and ordered it to have custody of them, to defend them and with lawful authority explain them; and at the same time He commanded all nations to believe and obey the voice of the Church, as if it were His own, threatening with everlasting perdition those who would not listen. **122** *(11, 12)*

Thus it is manifest that man's best and surest teacher is God, the source and principle of all truth; and the only-begotten Son, Who is in the bosom of the Father, the Way, the Truth and the Life, the true Light which enlightens every man, and to whose teaching all must submit: "And they shall all be taught of God." (a)

Infallible teaching authority

123
(10,
11,
16,
18)
In faith and in the teaching of morality, God Himself made the Church a partaker of His divine authority, and through His heavenly gift, she cannot be deceived. She is therefore the greatest and most reliable teacher of mankind, and in her dwells an inviolable right to teach men. Sustained by the truth received from her divine Founder, the Church has always sought to fulfill in a holy manner the mission entrusted to her by God; undeterred by the difficulties surrounding her on all sides, she has never ceased to assert her freedom to teach, and in this way the wretched superstition of paganism being dispelled, the world was renewed and became Christian.

The Church and science

124
(13,
17,
62,
69,
70,
95)
Now, reason itself clearly teaches that the truths of divine revelation and those of nature cannot be opposed to one another. Because every doctrine that contradicts revealed truth must necessarily be false, it follows that the divine teaching of the Church, so far from being an obstacle to the pursuit of knowledge and the progress of science, or in any way retarding the advance of civilization, in reality confers upon them the sure guidance of shining light. And for the same reason it is of no small advantage for the perfecting of human liberty, since Our Savior Jesus

122a John 6:45.

Christ has said that by truth is man made free: "You shall know the truth and the truth shall make you free." (a)

Therefore there is no reason why genuine freedom should grow indignant, or true science feel aggrieved, at having to bear the just and necessary restraint of laws by which, in the judgment of the Church and of reason itself, human teaching has to be controlled. The Church, indeed— as facts have everywhere proved—looks chiefly and above all to the defence of the Christian faith, while careful at the same time to foster and promote every kind of human learning. For learning is in itself good and praiseworthy and desirable; and further, all erudition which is the fruit of sound reason, and in conformity with the truth, serves not a little to confirm what we believe on the authority of God. The Church, truly, to our great benefit, has carefully preserved the monuments of ancient wisdom; has opened everywhere centers of science, and has promoted intellectual progress by fostering most diligently the arts by which the culture of our age is so much advanced.

Matters left to be freely treated

Lastly, we must not forget that a vast field lies freely open to man's industry and genius, containing all those things which have no necessary connection with Christian faith and morals, or as to which the Church, exercising no authority, leaves the judgment of the learned free and unconstrained. **125** *(13)*

From all this may be understood the nature and character of that freedom which the followers of Liberalism so eagerly advocate and proclaim. On the one hand they demand for themselves and for the State a license which opens the way to every perversity of opinion; and on the **126** *(95)*

124a John 8:32.

other, they hamper the Church in various ways, restricting her liberty within the narrowest limits, although from her teaching not only is there nothing to be feared, but in every respect very much to be gained.

(*Freedom of conscience.—Tolerance.—Summary of doctrine on liberalism.—Separation of Church and State.*)

Adaption and intransigence

127
(*110*)
Lastly, there remain those who, while they do not approve the separation of Church and State, think nevertheless that it would be well if the Church adapted herself to the times and conformed to what is required by the modern system of government. And they are not wrong, if they mean some equitable adjustment consistent with truth and justice, namely, that the Church, in the hope of some great good, which she foresees as certain should show herself indulgent, and should conform to the times insofar as her sacred duties permit. But it is not so in regard to practices and doctrines which a perversion of morals and a warped judgment have unlawfully introduced. Religion, truth, and justice must ever be maintained; and as God has entrusted these great and sacred matters to the care of the Church, she can never be so unfaithful to her office as to dissemble in regard to what is false and unjust, or to connive with what is hurtful to religion.

128
(*95,
117*)
From what has been said, it follows that it is quite unlawful to demand, to defend or to grant unconditional freedom of thought, of speech, of writing, or of worship, as if these were so many rights given by nature to man. For if nature had really granted them, it would be lawful to refuse obedience to God, and there would be no restraint on human freedom. It follows, likewise, that freedom in these things may be tolerated wherever there is a just cause; but only with such moderation as will prevent its

degenerating into licence and excess. And where such freedoms are in use, men should employ them in doing good,
and should estimate them as the Church does; for freedom
is to be regarded as legitimate only insofar as it affords
greater facility for doing good, but not otherwise. (a)

*(Different forms of government.—The Church, protec-
tor of true civil freedom.)*

FREEDOM WHICH CORRUPTS

Letter *È giunto,* July 19, 1889—to the Emperor of
Brazil.

*(Liberty of worship; an error that is not tolerance at
all, but the legalized apostasy of society.—Religion, foundation of social order.)*

Not less productive of sorry results in the social field **129**
itself is the so-called freedom of education. This permits *(2,*
an unrestrained liberty in schools to enlarge upon theories *13,*
and doctrines of all sorts—even if they are quite opposed *17,*
to both natural and revealed truths. Under the lying pre- *76,*
text of science, to whose true progress faith has never *95,*
proved harmful but has always contributed very extensive- *101ff)*
ly, they trample upon and openly oppose those fundamental principles on which morality, justice and religion are
founded.

Thus, teaching deviates from its noble ideal, which
is to give to society not only well-instructed members, but
honest men, who, by the scrupulous fulfillment of their
duties towards their fellowmen, their families and the
State, work towards obtaining the happiness of all. Instead

128a Omnis enim libertas legitima putanda quatenus rerum
honestarum majorem facultatem afferat, praeterea nunquam.

of subjugating in these young hearts the germs of passion, whence come egoism, pride and greed, and instilling sentiments and virtues which characterize the good son, the good father, the good citizen, it becomes an instrument of corruption, leading inexperienced youth along the path of scepticism, error and unbelief and sowing in their hearts every destructive inclination.

These results are all the more inevitable when we see that, on the one hand, the way is paved for every sort of monstrous error, and on the other, having proclaimed the principle of free education, the liberty of the Church and her rightful influence in the education of the youth is obstructed in a thousand ways.

(Save Brazil from the consequences of a similar mistake.)

THE CRADLE OF CIVIL SOCIETY

Encycl. *Sapientiae christianae,* January 10, 1890—on the chief civic duties of Christians.

(Hierarchy between service of the Church and service of State.—War against the Church.—Attitude of Catholics.—Church-State relations.—Submission to ecclesiastical superiors.—Regulation of whole life according to Christian teaching.)

130
(7,
28,
29,
31,
34,
53,
93,
106,
111,

This is a suitable moment for Us to exhort especially heads of families to govern their households according to these precepts, and to educate their children from their earliest years. The family may be regarded as the cradle of civil society, and it is in great measure within the circle of family life that the destiny of the State is fostered. Consequently they who would break away from Christian discipline are working to corrupt family life and to destroy it utterly, root and branch. From such an unholy purpose they are not deterred by the fact that they are inflicting

a cruel outrage on parents, who have the right from nature *112,*
to educate those whom they begot, a right to which is *114,*
joined the duty of harmonizing instruction and education *117)*
with the end for which they were given their children by
the goodness of God. It is then incumbent upon parents to
make every effort to resist attacks on this point and to vindicate at any cost the right to direct the education of their
offspring, as is fitting, in a Christian manner; and first and
foremost to keep them away from schools where there is
risk of their being imbued with the poison of impiety.

Where the right education of youth is concerned, no
amount of trouble and labor is too much. In this matter
there are many Catholics of various nations who deserve
to be praised and who incur great expense and exhibit
much zeal in opening schools for the education of children.
It is desirable that this noble example be followed according to the needs of the times. However, let everyone be
firmly convinced, first of all, that the minds of children are
best trained above all by the teaching they receive at home.
If in their growing years they find in their homes the rule
of an upright life and the exercise of Christian virtue, the
salvation of society will be in great part assured.

(Exhortation to apply this teaching.)

THE WATCHWORD OF MASONRY

Encycl. *Dall'alto,* October 15, 1890—to the Bishops,
clergy and people of Italy.

(Present evils caused by Masonry.—The plan of action.)

The foundation and religious constitution of the family   **131**
have been removed by the proclamation of what is called *(101,*
"civil matrimony" and by introducing an instruction which *102,*
is entirely secular from elementary studies to the higher *106,*
education of the Universities. Thus, the coming genera-   *107)*

tions, insofar as the State is concerned, are almost obliged to develop without any idea of religion, deprived of the primary and essential notions of their duties towards God. Truly, this is to put the axe to the roots, nor can a better and more widespread system be imagined to remove from the influence of the Church and of the faith, society itself, the family and the individual. "Use every possible means to root out clericalism (or rather, Catholicism) from its foundations and in its very sources of life, namely, in the school and the family"—this is the authentic masonic policy as declared by its writers.

(Catholic resistance.—Social and political repercussions of anti-clericalism.—Benefits of a return to the Church.)

THE LIGHT OF CHRISTIAN WISDOM

Letter *Volenti laetoque*, October 24, 1890—to Card. Mermillod.

(Zeal of the Bishops of Switzerland for the University of Fribourg.)

132
(17,
19,
70,
103)
In the midst of the evil which is daily spreading its dark shadows, while, in places which boast of their humanism and scientific knowledge, the Church is deprived of the right to educate, and her achievements in the field of human culture are ungratefully forgotten; while a wave of unclean and nefarious error is sweeping over everything because the light of truth has been extinguished, it is a relief to see traditional Christian wisdom gradually triumphing over difficulties and reasserting itself. In this, We must acknowledge a very special favor of Divine Providence. For, We are quite sure of it, thanks to this same wisdom which brings faith and reason into harmony, the hearts of men are raised to God, the sole principle of the one and the other, in the clear light of truth; and men, rec-

ognizing the path that leads to life, will follow it, without care for the sons of darkness who are in conflict with this light because they hate the truth.

This is why, conscious of Our very high office of teaching all nations, an office divinely committed to the Church and primarily, to the Apostolic See, We, recalling at the same time and in the light of history, the traditional achievements of the Church and the Roman Pontiffs, who civilized a Europe devastated by barbarians, with the cult of learning and the arts, will spare no effort in order to continue and accomplish this noble mission, so closely connected with Our ministry. This mission, We repeat, carries with it the obligation of promoting and encouraging learning and other branches of higher studies, with particular solicitude; of assisting those who cultivate them, and of showing the greatest benevolence to the illustrious men who support them by their labors and offerings.

(The favor of the Holy See is assured to the University.)

ST. ALOYSIUS GONZAGA

Letter *Opportune quidem,* January 1, 1891.
(Third centenary of his death.)

In fact, We can propose no better model to Catholic youth, no one more filled with those virtues which we commonly expect to see flourishing among young people. From the life and doings of Aloysius, young people can find many examples to follow, from which they can learn with what careful vigilance they must preserve the integrity and innocence of their lives; with what constancy the body must be mortified to dominate the vehemence of passion; how to despise riches and not bother about honors; with how much diligence they must pursue their studies and fulfill the other duties and offices proper to their age; and,

133
(88)

what is of special and the highest importance in these
times, with what loyalty and filial love they must be attached to the Church and to the Apostolic See.

Whether in his father's house, or as page boy in the
royal Court of Spain, or in the pursuit of sanctity and
learning, or, having renounced his title and entered the
Society of Jesus, where, as was his ardent desire, he was
happy to be cut off from honors and to spend himself entirely and solely for the salvation of his neighbor—the angelic youth was an example in every walk of life, earning
far higher praise than others and leaving an outstanding
testimony of holiness. For this reason, those in charge of
the education and instruction of Christian youth, are wont,
and very wisely, to hold up Aloysius as a most noble model
to imitate, and this in conformity with the mind of Our
Predecessor Benedict XIII, who declared Aloysius the chief
heavenly Patron of all young people engaged in study.

(Celebration of the Centenary.—Indulgences.)

PUBLIC SCHOOLS AND THE TAXPAYER

Letter *Quae coniunctim,* May 23, 1892—to the Bishops of the Province of New York.

(Controversy regarding two parochial schools.)

134
(19,
48,
106,
114)

Among the revered Prelates of your region, whose very
great devotion to the Holy See We have known and had
proof of in their visits to Us, none of them, without exception, showed the least doubt about the doctrine issued by
the Holy See regarding schools, in which Catholic children
have to be educated.

All agree unanimously that they cannot approve of
the schools called "neutral," namely, those deprived of religious instruction, and declare the need for private, reli-

gious schools (as is the case in regions populated by faithful mixed with non-Catholics), schools, that is, in which the children are suitably instructed in religion by those whom the Bishops consider fit for the task.

It is, therefore, most important, Venerable Brethren, that, together with all the other prelates of the region, you should endeavor wisely and zealously to see that Catholic children do not attend scholastic institutions in which their religious education is omitted and their morality laid open to danger. Therefore, We earnestly desire—as has been notified by the Congregation of Propaganda—that, during the coming meetings of Bishops, you should diligently study the concrete means to be adopted in order to achieve this end.

We wish, further, that you should do your utmost to see to it that those in charge of the administration in individual cities, recognizing that there is no greater help to public welfare than religion, may, by means of wise legislation, take care that the Department of Education, to which everyone, and therefore Catholics, too, contribute their money, may enact nothing that will offend conscience or religion. And We have no doubt that your co-citizens, who happen to be separated from Us, by that strength of intelligence and prudence which distinguishes them, will easily throw off all suspicion and prejudice against the Catholic Church, and recognize her great merits in having dissipated pagan barbarism with the light of the Gospel, and in generating a new society, excelling in Christian virtues and every branch of human civilization. **135 (18, 25, 106)**

This being so, We think that nobody there will tolerate an obligation on the part of Catholic parents to protect and promote primary and secondary schools which they cannot make use of to educate their own children.

(Close union with the Holy See and with the other Bishops.)

FACE TO FACE WITH FREEMASONRY

Letter *Custodi di quella fede,* December 8, 1892—to the Italians.

(War against the religion which has been the cause of Italy's greatness.)

136
(94,
95,
97,
102)
Our country has seen and suffered great evils in a very short space of time.

The religion of our fathers has been the object of all sorts of persecution, which, with diabolic intent, seek to replace Christianity by naturalism, the cult of faith by the cult of reason, Catholic morality by a so-called independent morality, spiritual progress by material progress. It has dared oppose the holy precepts and laws of the Gospel by laws and precepts which can be called a Code of Revolution, and Christian learning and the arts by an atheistic instruction and a despicable sophistry in schools.

(Church possessions.—Military service for the clergy.— Civil matrimony and burial.)

Though they have not yet succeeded in wresting the education of the young and the direction of charitable institutions from the hands of the Church, they continue with dogged perseverance to secularize everything, which means obliterating all traces of Christianity from everything.

(Press.—The Religious.—Realizations and Plans of Freemasonry.)

The social order, it may be said, is torn up by its roots, Books and newspapers, schools and professorial chairs, literary circles and theaters, monuments and political speeches, photography and the fine arts—all conspire to pervert the mind and corrupt the heart.

(Freemasonry, the enemy of God, of the Church and of the country.—Attitude of Catholics.)

We should like parents, educators, employers and all **137**
those who are in a position of authority to remember that *(33)*
a strict obligation binds them to prevent, as far as possible,
the entrance of those under them into this tainted sect, or,
if they are already members of it, continuance in it. It
is urgent that in so important a question, where it is so
easy to be seduced, the Christian should be on guard from
his earliest years, fear the slightest dangers, avoid every
occasion, take the most careful precautions, and, in short,
according to the advice of the Gospel, be as guileless as
doves and as wise as serpents. (a)

Fathers and mothers of families should guard against
receiving into their homes and into the intimacy of the
family, unknown persons or persons whose religious background is not sufficiently known. Instead, they should
first endeavor to ascertain whether, under the mantle of
a friend, or teacher, or doctor or other well-wisher, there
is not concealed a shrewd enlister of the sect. Oh, in how
many families has the wolf penetrated under the guise
of a lamb!

(Avoid suspicious company and persons.)

Freemasonry has obtained control of the public **138**
schools: you strike back by instructing and educating Chris- *(94,*
tian children and youth in private schools, in the home, *102,*
in schools run by zealous clerics and the religious of both *112,*
sexes. Above all, let Christian parents not entrust the edu- *114,*
cation of their children to schools that are doubtful. *117)*

(Press.—Various activities.)

What more? That sect strives to subjugate the Church,
to reduce her to the condition of a humble servant-maid
under the foot of the State! And, you, do not cease to ask,
and, within legal limits, to demand, the liberty and independence owed to her.

(Union and courage.)

137a Matt. 10:16.

THE MOST IMPORTANT DUTIES
OF PARISH PRIESTS

Encycl. *Constanti Hungarorum,* September 2, 1893—
to the Bishops of Hungary.

(Wrongs already suffered by Catholicism.—How to behave.—Mixed marriages.—Catholic Congress.—Legislative elections.—The Press.)

139
(19,
44,
45,
92)
In a very special way, Venerable Brethren, We should like you to direct your attention to and bestow every care on the education of children and adults. We have no intention of repeating the recommendations already put forward in the same letter which We mentioned at the beginning; (a) nevertheless We cannot do less than touch upon a few questions of very great importance.

Regarding primary schools it is necessary to insist and to urge parish priests and other directors of souls, Venerable Brethren, to watch continually over them with the greatest attention and give to the instruction of their pupils in Christian doctrine a special part of their pastoral office. Neither should they want to entrust such a noble and important task to others, but should take up the work lovingly, (b) in the certainty that a healthy and pious education of the child is, in great part, responsible not only for the safety of the family, but of the State as well.

Do not imagine that you can show any particular sort of diligence or industry greater than that which must be

139a Encycl. *Quod multum,* August 22, 1886.—See above No. 103 ss.
139b De primordiorum scholis, instandum urgendumque est, Venerabiles Fratres, ut curiones ceterique animarum curatores summo in eas studio continentur evigilent, maximasque ponant officii sui partes in alumnis sacra doctrina erudiendis. Tale vero munus, nobile atque grave, ne alienae procurationi permittant, sed ipsi sibi assumant habeantque carissimum.

used for schools of this kind, in order, daily, to obtain satisfying results.

Furthermore, it would be useful to appoint inspectors of schools in every diocese—one for the whole diocese and others for the deaneries—together with whom, every year, the Bishops may make plans about the state and conditions of the schools, and especially, about what concerns faith, morals and the care of souls. And, if it be necessary to build new schools, according to the localities, or to extend those already existing, We have no doubt, Venerable Brethren, that your ready generosity, already so often experienced, will come to the rescue, as also that of Catholics in every walk of life.

For high schools and schools for higher studies, the greatest care must be taken that the good seed, so to say, sown in the minds of the children, may not perish in adolescence. And therefore, Venerable Brethren, exert yourselves as much as possible, by word and deed, to see that these dangers are removed or diminished, and, above all, be extremely attentive in choosing learned and honest men for religious classes, and thus remove those causes which too often prevent the same classes from bearing good fruit. **140** *(19, 62, 68, 106, 111)*

Finally, though We are well aware of the interest manifested by you to see that those Chairs, which their founders desired should stay in the hands of the Church and the Bishops, remain so; nevertheless, We further exhort you to let no opportunity slip by to pursue this end, by common consultation and according to your rights and duties. For, what is granted to the enemies of Catholicism is as repugnant to equality and justice as that which is denied to Catholics: the common good demands that the God-fearing and wise institutions of our forefathers be always used, not to the detriment of the Church and the Catholic faith, but for their protection and defense, and still more, for the good of the State itself.

(Clergy.—Episcopal Meetings.)

SIMULTANEOUS PROGRESS OF
RELIGIOUS AND SECULAR TEACHING

Encycl. *Caritatis providentiaeque*, March 19, 1894—to the Bishops of Poland.

(Merits of Catholic religion.—Church and civil society. —Domestic society.)

141
(39,
114)
... that parents provide for the care and benefit of their offspring, above all for their education, for which they themselves should pave the way by the example of their conduct, there being nothing as efficacious or as important. They should not think that they can give their children any sort of a correct and decent education without being extremely watchful. For they must avoid not only those schools and colleges, where the teaching is deliberately infected by religious error, or where impiety practically reigns supreme, but also those in which there exists no course or special form of instruction in Christian doctrine and morals.

142
(24,
69,
101)
It is absolutely necessary that those who study sciences and letters should receive timely instruction in the knowledge and cult of religion, since nature both obliges and binds them not only to serve the country, but also, and in a far greater degree, to serve God. This is why they were created, in order that, serving the nation, they might direct their steps towards that country which awaits them in Heaven, and make every effort to reach the goal.

And as they grow up, this instruction must never stop, but must go hand in hand with civil culture: if anything, it must be insisted upon even more, both because, in these times of feverish study the passion for knowledge fires youth increasingly from day to day, and because this passion is full of ever greater perils for the faith, which has already had to deplore considerable losses in so serious a matter.

When also, the Church thinks of issuing certain warn- **143** ings, of defining certain methods regarding the manner of *(12,* imparting sacred doctrine, the moral integrity and skill of *19,* the teachers, or the choice of books, she does so with full *45,* right: neither can she dispense herself from doing so, since *116)* she is bound by the obligation of preventing the infiltration of anything contrary to the integrity of faith or morals or detrimental to the Christian people. Let the Church, then, draw up and put into effect a course of sacred instruction to be given in schools, which may be held, in certain circumstances and according to certain rules, in the curiae and churches where the seeds of faith and charity may be cultivated and developed abundantly, as on their proper soil.

(Clergy.—Question of workers.—Advice to the Poles subject to Russia, Austria, Germany.)

DUTIES OF THE STATE

Letter *Ante vestrum,* May 1, 1894—to the Bishops of Austria.

(Congratulations for their union with the Supreme Bishop.—Education, theme of the conference of Bishops.)

Nothing is more disastrous and harmful to the State **144** than the opinion that there must necessarily be disagree- *(25,* ment between the civil authority and the Church. Certainly *103)* both the one and the other have limits beyond which they must not pass. But, since earthly prosperity depends, above all, on justice and honesty, the civil authority has need to be helped by religion, whose function it is to guide souls in the practice of all the virtues. Religion, on the other hand, which does not deal with pure spirits but with men, and with men joined in society, requires the friendly support of the civil authorities. Hence those who seek to separate Church from State are wrong; it is necessary instead that they be united by a mutual treaty, which, if essential in other matters, is even more so as regards the proper education of youth. (a) Thus, the temporal authority, inculcating the young with the sciences and the knowledge necessary for the common welfare, must also interest itself in their religious and moral education, and must do this through and under the surveillance and direction of the Church. We hope that the new Minister for Public Educaton will see to it that, in the educational institutions of Austria, the clergy is given its rightful place, and that nothing is introduced which can induce diffidence of, and aversion to, the Catholic faith in the minds of children.

(Blessing.)

THE SEED OF PRIESTLY AND
RELIGIOUS VOCATIONS

Motu Proprio *Auspicia rerum,* March 19, 1896.

(Special situation of Catholicism in the East.—Union of Bishops is a means to make it profitable.—Seminaries.)

145
(55,
62,
69,
83)
The other means, not less worthy of attention than the first, relate to the conserving and multiplying of primary schools. It is self-evident that it is most important to take care that those of tender age do not receive, together with the first elements of learning, anything contrary to Catholic

144a Nihil sane deterius reique publicae nocentius quam ut opinio sit, civilem inter auctoritate et Ecclesiam necessario dissidium esse.... Hinc statum et Ecclesiam ab altero separandos contenditur perperam: sed illos mutuo conjungi foedere necesse est, quod quidem si in ceteris, at in juventute probe instituenda vel maxime.

truth and morals, and all the more so in that the children of darkness, strong in their cunning and wealth, are striving daily more and more to inflict losses on us in this field.

It is necessary that the principles of right doctrine and love of religion be instilled in these pliable souls so as to influence and prepare them to profess the Catholic faith. No other task certainly will be of greater merit or more profitable than that of Congregations dedicated to the welfare of children.

Furthermore, by the very fact that the teachers entrusted with religious and moral education teach more by example than by precept, the result will naturally be that the better pupils receive at an early age the seeds of the priestly or religious vocation and develop them in good time. And it is a very useful and desirable thing that many children of either sex should reach this goal.

(Press.—Missions.—Sympathy for the traditions of the East.)

LEARNING AT THE SERVICE OF THE FAITH

Encycl. *Militantis Ecclesiae,* August 1, 1897.

(Third centenary of the death of St. Peter Canisius.)

Present times, in fact, resemble to some extent those **146** in which Canisius lived, when the lust for novelty and the *(116)* wave of the most liberal doctrines were followed by a weakening of faith and a corruption of morals.

To ward off this two-fold pest from all, but especially from youth, was the labor of the second apostle of Germany, second that is, after Boniface; and he did so not only by appropriate preaching and subtle arguments, but especially by the foundation of schools and the printing of good books.

(The labor of the Saint: learning placed at the service of Christian truth.—Battle against the Lutheran heresy: scholastic teaching; catechism.—Follow his example.)

Learning, the weapon of today

147
(18,
65,
70)
If ever there was a time in which the defense of Catholicism demanded much learning and erudition, it is the present one, in which rapid progress in all branches of civilization sometimes provides the enemies of Christianity with an excuse to attack the faith. We must repel their attack with the same weapons; we must be the first to acquire strategic positions and wrest from their hands those weapons with which they strive to break every bond between divine and human reality.

To fortified and well-prepared Catholics full permission will be granted to demonstrate that divine faith is not only in no wise hostile to culture, but rather is the crown and climax of culture. Even in those matters where there seems to be opposition or contradiction, it can be harmonized very easily with philosophy, to their reciprocal illumination, for nature is not the enemy but the companion and handmaid of religion. Strengthened by religion, all knowledge is enriched and the letters and the arts acquire greater splendor and vigor.

148
(65,
69)
How much profane studies contribute to the adornment and dignity of sacred doctrines is apparent to anybody with a knowledge of human nature, inclined as this is to those things which allure the senses. Hence the more cultured peoples do not readily accept a rudely-presented wisdom, and the learned especially are not interested in things which are not presented in pleasing and refined form. Now, we are debtors to the wise no less than to the unwise (a) and we must stand by the former in the battle and help and succor them if they fall.

148a See Rom. 1:14.

Science in the history of the Church

And here a vast field opens up for the Church. When, **149**
after the period of persecution had passed, she recovered *(17,*
her strength, learned men rose up who, by their genius *64,*
and learning expounded that faith for which strong men *65)*
had previously shed their blood. The first to exalt the faith
were the Fathers and they did so with a vigor that has
never yet been surpassed; they did so generally in a refined style, that in no way offended Roman and Greek
ears. Spurred on and stimulated by their teaching and eloquence, many that followed gave themselves to the ardent
study of sacred truths and thus accumulated a rich patrimony of Christian wisdom in which all men of succeeding
generations in the Church have found weapons to root out
the old superstitions and combat the new errors. This rich
harvest of learned men was perfected at every period, even
during those times when all that was most precious was
exposed to the avidity of barbarians and ran the risk of
being neglected and forgotten. If, however, those ancient
prodigies of the mind and human skill, if those things
which, once upon a time, were held in the highest esteem
among Greeks and Romans, were not completely destroyed,
it was due to the labor and watchfulness of the Church.

Since the study of the sciences and the arts throws **150**
so much light on religion, it is certain that those who are *(50,*
entirely dedicated to study must not confine their activity *65)*
to mere speculation, but must pass on to action, so that
their knowledge may not remain closed in itself and sterile.
Educated men, therefore, should place their studies at the
service of the Christian community and devote their free
time to the common welfare. In this way their knowledge
will not be ineffectual but will be accompanied by concrete action. This action is best seen in the education of
young people—a task important enough to demand a major
part of their labors and cares.

Teaching without religion

151
(*19*,
112)   For this reason, We earnestly exhort you, Venerable Brethren, above all, to keep your schools firm in the integrity of the faith, or even to watch carefully over and remind them of this integrity, if necessary. Devote your attention both to schools of long standing, and to those only recently opened; to schools for children and to high schools and University colleges. The other Catholics of your region should, in the first place, seek to safeguard the rights proper to parents and the Church, in the education of adolescents.

152
(*72*,
80,
106,
107,
117)   In this matter special care must be paid to these points. First of all, Catholics should not frequent "mixed" schools, especially those for little children. They should everywhere have their own schools and should choose excellent, trustworthy teachers. An education which contains religious errors or which bans all religion, is full of dangers: and this often happens in the schools we have called "mixed." (a) Let nobody easily persuade himself that piety can be separated from instruction with impunity. In fact, if in no period of life, whether in public or in private affairs, can religion be dispensed with, much less can that inexperienced age, full of life, yet surrounded by so many corrupt temptations, be excused from religious obligations. Whosoever, therefore, organizes education so as to neglect any point of contact with religion is destroying beauty and honesty at their very roots, and instead of helping the country, is preparing for the deterioration and destruction of the human race. For, once God is eliminated, who can

152a The word "mixed" here and elsewhere mentioned in connection with schools, does not mean schools composed of both sexes, but a school which receives pupils of different religious beliefs, Catholic and non-Catholic.

make young people realize their duties or redeem those who have deviated from the right path of virtue and fallen into the abyss of vice?

Education imbued with religion

Religion must not be taught to youth only during certain hours, but the entire system of education must be permeated with the sense of Christian piety. If this is lacking, if this holy spirit does not penetrate and inflame the souls of teacher and pupil, small benefit will be derived from any other sort of education; instead damage will be done. Almost every sort of training has its dangers, and only with difficulty will these be averted from growing youth, especially if the divine controls are lacking which restrain their minds and wills. Great care must therefore be taken so that what is essential, namely, the pursuit of justice and piety, may not be relegated to a second place, confining youth to the visible world and thus leaving their vital potentiality for virtue to rot; so that, again, while teachers, with painful exertion, drill on boring subjects and analyze syllable and accent, they may not neglect that true wisdom, whose *beginning is the fear of the Lord* (a) and whose precepts demand obedience in every circumstance of life. A wide knowledge should go hand in hand with care for spiritual progress; religion must permeate and direct every branch of knowledge whatever be its nature, and by its sweetness and majesty must make so great an impression on the minds of youth as to be an incitement to better things.

Since it has always been the Church's intention that every branch of study be of great service in the religious formation of youth, this particular subject matter not only must have its place, and the principal place at that, but nobody should be entrusted with so important a teaching

153
*(19,
70,
72,
106,
107,
115)*

153a Ps. 110:10.

role who has not first been declared suitable for the purpose in the judgment and by the authority of the Church.

But religion does not clamor for its rights only in schools for children.

154
(67,
72)
Times were, when, in the statutes of every University, and principally in that of Paris, the entire scheme of studies centered round theology, so that no one was considered to have attained a very high degree of learning who had not taken his doctorate in that subject. When the war was waging against religion, the restorer of the Augustan age, Leo X, and after him other Popes, Our Predecessors, wanted the Roman Athaeneum and other so-called Universities to be solid fortresses, where youth would be instructed under the light and authority of Christian wisdom. This program of studies, which gave first place to God and sacred things, bore excellent fruit, and made sure that the young people so instructed were more faithful to their duties. You, too, will obtain these same good results if you make the necessary effort to preserve the rights of religious education in secondary schools, in colleges and Universities.

155
(111)
Let it, however, never happen that good advice be reduced to naught and so much labor go to waste because oneness of mind and unity of action are wanting. For what can the divided forces of the good do against the combined assault of the enemy? Of what use is the courage of individuals if there is no united plan of action? Therefore, We earnestly appeal to you all to eliminate from your midst all undesirable controversy, which can only serve to sow division, and to agree among yourselves in order to serve the good of the Church. In thus uniting your energies and wills, you must have but one aim, namely, to be "endeavoring to keep the unity of the Spirit in the bond of peace." (a)

155a Eph. 4:3.

The memory and commemoration of a great Saint has **156** moved Us to issue these warnings. May Heaven grant that *(65,* his shining example imprint itself in hearts, moving them *71,* to that love for wisdom which he possessed, a wisdom *92)* which never ceased from laboring for the salvation of men and from defending the dignity of the Church.

We are confident that you, Venerable Brethren, who devote special attention to this matter, will find many learned men to collaborate with you in a labor so full of joy. This noble task, however, can be accomplished especially by those to whom Providence has given the magnificent office of instructing youth.

If these remember, as the ancients liked to observe, that learning separated from justice must be called astuteness rather than wisdom, or better, if they meditate the words of Holy Scripture: "All men are vain in whom there is not the knowledge of God" (a) they will learn to use the weapons of learning not to further personal interests, but for the salvation of all. They will be able to hope to obtain from their labors and exertions the same results that Peter Canisius once obtained in his colleges and institutions, namely, meek and virtuous youth, of good morals, who shun the example of the wicked and who are as keen about virtue as about knowledge. When piety has taken deep roots in these young people, the dangers of their being infected by perverse opinions and of being deflected from their natural virtue is practically eliminated. In them, both the Church and civil society place their fondest hopes, as illustrious citizens of the future; their advice, their prudence and their learning will be able to assure social order and untroubled family life.

(Conclusion.)

156a Wisdom 13:1.

EDUCATIONAL JUSTICE

Encycl. *Affari vos,* December 8, 1897—to the Bishops of Canada.

(Bonds between Canada and the Church.—Zeal to conserve Catholicism.—Support of the Holy See for the foundation of numerous educational institutions.—Particularly the University of Quebec.—Manitoban affairs.)

157
(107) The question under discussion is really very important and of exceptional weight. We intend to speak of the decision regarding schools taken, about seven years ago, by the Parliament of Manitoba. The act of union with the Confederation had assured Catholic children of the right to be educated in public schools according to the dictates of their consciences; now the Parliament of Manitoba has abolished this right by means of contrary legislation. It is a harmful law.

Catholic requirements

158
(114) Consideration is not given to the fact that our children are not permitted to seek the benefit of the instruction given in schools which ignore the Catholic religion or positively combat it, schools in which her doctrine is despised and her fundamental principles repudiated. If the Church has allowed it in some places, she has done so unwillingly and with sorrow and after having surrounded the children with many means of defense, which, however, elsewhere, have often proved inadequate to offset the damage caused. Likewise, we must avoid at all costs those unfortunate schools where religious beliefs are indifferently admitted with equal treatment, as if, in the things that regard God and divine affairs, it matters little to have or not to have the right doctrine, or to embrace truth or error. You, Venerable Brethren, are well aware that all such schools have been condemned by the Church, because nothing is more per-

nicious, nothing more calculated to destroy the purity of faith and mislead young minds from the path of truth.

There is another point on which We might easily be in agreement even with those who disagree with Us on all other points: namely, that Catholic children will not leave school in the state the country wishes and desires of them if they are given a purely scientific education or merely vague and superficial notions about virtue. To make them good Christians, upright and honest citizens, they must be given much more solid and nourishing food: their formation must be the result of principles, which, deposited in the depths of their conscience, will influence their lives as natural consequences of their faith and religion. Without religion there is no moral education worthy of the name; neither can it be truly efficacious, considering the fact that the very nature and the force of every duty derive from those special duties which bind man to God, to God Who commands and forbids, Who places a sanction on good and on evil. For this reason, to want to have souls steeped in good morals, and at the same time to leave them deprived of religion, is as absurd as asking somebody to live virtuously after having undermined the foundations.

159
(5,
47,
69,
74,
92,
97,
100,
105)

Now, for the Catholic, there is only one true religion: the Catholic religion; hence, in doctrinal, moral or religious matters, he cannot accept or recognize anything which does not spring from the very sources of Catholic teaching.

Therefore, justice and reason demand that our pupils find not only scientific instruction in schools, but also a knowledge of moral principles which, as We have said, should be in harmony with the principles of their religion— a knowledge without which all education, instead of being profitable, will only be disastrous. Hence the necessity to have Catholic teachers, reading books and textbooks approved by the Bishops, and to have the freedom to organize schools so that the teaching may be fully in accordance with the Catholic faith and its consequent duties.

160
(42,
43,
106,
111)
For the rest, to decide in what colleges the children will be educated, what teachers will be commissioned to teach them their moral duties, is a right inherent in parental authority. Therefore, when Catholics ask, and it is their duty to ask and demand, that the education given by teachers be in accordance with the religion of their children, they are using their right. And no greater injustice can be done to parents than to place them in the dilemma of either letting their children grow up in ignorance, or of putting them in surroundings which constitute a clear danger for the higher interests of their souls.

These principles of judgment and right behavior, which are based on truth and justice and which safeguard both public and private interests, may not be called into question or rejected under any circumstances.

Furthermore, when the new law came to strike at Catholic education in the province of Manitoba, it was your duty, Venerable Brethren, to make open protest against the injustice and the blow that was inflicted upon you. The manner in which you fulfilled this duty has been a magnificent proof of your united watchfulness and of your very worthy episcopal zeal. And although, on this point, every one of you has been sufficiently recompensed by the testimony of your consciences, We should nevertheless like you to know that We add Our assent and approval. For these are sacred matters which you have striven and are still striving to protect and defend.

Discord: a great weakness

161
(111,
112)
For the rest, the difficulties produced by the legislation in question were by themselves a warning that to procure a suitable remedy for the evil, perfect understanding is necessary. So strong was the Catholic cause that all good and honest citizens should have found themselves in agreement and closely united to defend it. It has been to the

great detriment of the cause itself that the contrary has happened. It is still more deplorable that the Canadian Catholics themselves could not, as they should have done, agree among themselves to defend interests that are the concern of all, being of so great importance and gravity that the interest of political parties, which are so much inferior, should have been silenced. (a)

We are not unaware that something has been done to change the law. The men at the head of the federal and provincial governments have already taken decisions in order to lessen the evident wrong done to the Catholics of Manitoba. We have no reason to doubt that these decisions have been inspired by a desire for fair play and with a praiseworthy intention. We cannot, however, hide the truth: the law which has been formulated as a remedy is defective, imperfect and inadequate. Catholics ask much more, as nobody doubts, they have a right to. Furthermore, the very amendments that are planned have the defect that they can easily be nullified in practice according to changes in local circumstances. To put it in brief, sufficient provision has not been made for the rights of Catholics and the education of our children in Manitoba. Now, in this matter, everything requires, in accordance with justice, that full provision be made, namely, that practical acceptance of the unchangeable and sacred principles We have set forth above be assured. This is what must be sought, this is the end that zeal and prudence must obtain.

Nothing is more contrary to this than discord: unity of mind and harmony of action is absolutely necessary. Nevertheless, since the end which is proposed and which must be attained does not fix a rigid and exclusive line of action,

---

161a Dolendum illud etiam magis, catholicos ipsos canadenses sententias concorditer, ut oportebat, minime in re tuenda junxisse, quae omnium interest plurimum: cujus prae magnitudine et pondere silere studia politicarum rationum quae tanto minoris sunt, necesse erat.

but on the contrary admits many, as ordinarily happens in such matters, it follows that there may be, regarding the line of action to adopt, different opinions, all good and plausible. However, nobody must lose sight of the rules of moderation, kindness and fraternal charity; nobody must forget the respect he owes to others; rather all must weigh well what the circumstances demand and, having decided on the best course of action, follow it with cordial agreement, after hearing your opinion.

162
(110,
117) As regards what especially concerns the Catholics of Manitoba, We are confident that, with God's help, they will one day have full satisfaction. This hope is based above all on the justice of their cause, then on the sense of fair play and wisdom of those who hold the reins of the government of the State, and finally, on the good will of all honest men in Canada. While they wait, and until they obtain the vindication of all their rights, they should not refuse partial satisfaction. Hence, where the law or custom or well-disposed persons offer some mitigation of the evil, and in order to stave off the damage longer, it is quite proper and useful to profit by them and get the fullest possible benefit. Everywhere, instead, where the evil has no other remedy, We exhort and beseech them to provide the remedy by generously redoubling their liberality. They can do nothing more profitable or more favorable to the prosperity of their country than to contribute to the maintenance of their schools with all the resources at their command.

163
(19,
23,
50,
62,
70,
118) There is still another matter which calls for your united attention. It is necessary, with your authority and the collaboration of those who direct educational institutions, that the whole program of studies be elaborated diligently and wisely and that special care be taken to see that men not endowed with all the necessary natural or acquired qualities be excluded from teaching. It is appropriate that Catholic schools should hold their own with

the best, both in the excellence of methods of formation
and in the quality of the teaching. From the point of view
of intellectual formation and the progress of civilization,
one cannot but find good and noble the plan conceived by
the Canadian provinces to develop public instruction, to
raise its standards and to bring it closer to perfection by
constant improvement. Now, there is no kind of study, no
progress in human knowledge which may not fully harmonize with Catholic doctrine.

Those Catholics, engaged in press work, especially the **164**
daily press, are in a good position to explain and defend *(111)*
what We have said till now. They should be mindful
of their duty. They should defend, religiously and courageously, whatever concerns the truth, the rights, the interests of Church and Society, and do so in a dignified
manner, respecting other persons, always restrained. They
should be respectful and be particular about showing
themselves deferential to the authority of the Bishops and
to all legitimate authority. The more difficult the times,
the greater becomes the harm caused by division, and a
greater effort must be made to inculcate unity of thought
and action, without which there is little or no hope of ever
obtaining the object of our common interests.

(Blessing.)

LEVEL OF CATHOLIC INSTRUCTION

Encycl. *Caritatis studium*, July 25, 1892—to the Bishops of Scotland.

*(A call to dissidents: merits of the teaching authority
of the Church.—Duties of Catholics: prayer, Christian life.)*

It is a good thing, also, to use every effort to preserve,   **165**
to render more stable and to fortify with every possible   *(64,*
defense the Catholic education of youth. We are well   *117,*

118) aware that you have institutions for public instruction endowed with everything that can prove useful to young people desirous of learning, nor is there any lack of excellent methods of study. But an effort must be made to see that Catholic schools are in no way inferior to others; nor must we fall into the defect of seeing our adolescents endowed with less literary culture and specialized formation than others: the Christian faith demands these things as very useful to defend her and be an honor to her. Love of our religion and affection for our country require Catholics to increase the efficiency and number of Catholic institutions, whether they be for elementary education or for higher studies. This they must do to the best of their power.

(*Formation of the clergy.*)

OUTSTANDING WORK OF CHARITY

Letter *Pergratum Nobis*, April 10, 1900—to the Baron of Vittinghoff-Schell.

(*Congress of charitable associations.*)

166
(4,
52,
80)
It gives Us pleasure to recommend a work that is above all others dear to you and to Us: the work on behalf of youth, which your zeal should not neglect. Because this time of life is very much at the mercy of the deceits of the wicked and the fire of passion! It is therefore the most important and most beneficial duty of charity to make zealous provision for the need of adolescents: for all that is done for them, in the line of self-denial and care, redounds not only to their advantage but to the benefit of the people and the country.

(*Blessing.*)

THE FIRST TECHNICAL SCHOOLS
AND TRAINING COLLEGES FOR TEACHERS

Letter *Antequam Christus,* May 24, 1900—on the occasion of the canonization of Bl. John Baptist de la Salle.

(Life of the Blessed.—Evolution of the process going on in Rome.—Act of Canonization.—Conclusion.)

He was filled with the fullness of God, so that a divine **167** instinct moved him to provide for the needs of the future, *(16,* and he neglected no institution that might be useful to the *59,* education and instruction of youth. *118)*

Thus, not satisfied with multiplying schools for the poor and with perfecting educational methods, he first founded technical schools for skilled labor and for business; at the same time he conceived the idea and founded colleges for the formation of teachers, a most beneficial accomplishment and deserving of the highest praise. Guided by faith, by zeal for souls and love for the Roman Church, he drew up for these colleges excellent statutes and rules, which have since been applied with profit by numberless similar ventures stimulated by his example.

He should be taken as a model by those who deserve the holy name of teacher, and they should strive to imitate him in their teaching; here is the intercessor, through whose good offices you must pray God that the schools of Christian nations escape the snares and tyranny of Satan and his satellites.

ULTIMATE AIM OF EDUCATION

Letter *Per hosce dies,* May 30, 1900—to Monsignor Guibert.

(Congratulations for his life of St. John Baptist de la Salle.)

168   May your readers learn the art of imparting intellec-
(59,   tual culture, and above all, spiritual culture, to those of
80)   tender and inexperienced age, who are the hope of both
the family and of civil society. And since this time of life
is so much exposed to the seductions of the world, may
they understand that all possible care must be used that
children may be preserved and not become unworthy of
that high purpose for which they were brought into the
world.

(*Blessing.*)

THE CHRISTIAN CLASSICS

Letter *Ea disciplinae*, May 20, 1901—to the Bishop
of Namur.

169   That method of education which, for the literary for-
(64)   mation of the youth, especially in ecclesiastical seminaries,
wishes to add to the assiduous study of the ancient Greek
and Latin classics, the knowledge and correct appreciation
of the most famous Christian writers is not without merit.
The Apostolic See has already said so when the occasion
presented itself. (a)

Your letter informs Us that a learned member of your
diocese, Canon L. Guillaume, spurred on by this, has, for

169a Pius IX, already, in the Encyclical, *Inter Multiplices* of
March 21, 1853, said: "Let clerics learn the elegance of
style and eloquence both of the works full of wisdom of
the Holy Fathers, and of the famous profane authors,
purged of all dangerous elements" (A.P. IX, 1, 443). And
in the letter, *Quo libentius* of April 1, 1875, to Mgr.
d'Avanzo: "The written monuments of every century of the
Church, which you have reviewed, bring before our eyes
the origins, the progress and the high quality of a new
form of Latin, and at the same time they teach that it was
always the custom of the Church to teach Latin to the
young through the reading of both sacred and profane
authors" (AAS. 8, 560).

a long time, together with some collaborators, dedicated much care and labor to the preparation and publication of a series of volumes in which for every literary form he puts our writers face to face with pagan authors.

They have sent Us this collection. We have received it with pleasure and are grateful for their filial homage. Regarding the initiative in itself, We hope—and this is precisely the scope to which it tends so earnestly—that it may be of benefit in the intellectual, and, especially, moral formation of youth.

Here, however, the tutor and guide needs prudence which will certainly not be lacking, thanks to your watchful care. And the succèss will be more certain and widespread when the students have learned the art of writing and acquired a refined taste. This they will learn from the teachings and examples of those who, from the testimony and practice of the Holy Fathers and the well-known fruits they have always produced, are rightly considered to be the best teachers of humanity. (a) **170** *(64, 69)*

Thus, by means of prudent application, the candidates for the altar will be assured, in the written and oral exposition of religious matter, of the double advantage, always desirable, of a fully persuasive truth together with the dignity suitable to subject matter of such importance.

(Blessing.)

170a Tunc enim certius uberiusque res proficiet cum alumni jam sibi facultatem scribendi et judicii elegantium paraverint, ex eorum scilicet praeceptis atque exemplis qui, probe nosti, ipso testimonio usuque Sanctorum Patrum explorataque fructuum perpetua copia, omnis humanitatis jure habentur magistri optimi.

ST. PIUS X
1903-1914

THE UNJUST FRENCH LEGISLATION

All. to Cardinals, March 18, 1904.

(Returning thanks.—Battles of the Church.—Events in France.)

We find it necessary to confess that while the continual demonstrations of devotion and solidarity coming to Us from that Catholic people gladden Our paternal heart greatly, We are deeply grieved by the measures already adopted and others that are in the process of being adopted in the legislative sphere against the religious Congregations —Congregations which, in that country, with their extraordinary works of charity and Christian education, contribute to the glory of the Catholic Church and no less to that of the nation. Just as if what has taken place up to now, causing damage to religious Congregations, had not been an immensely grievous and deplorable affair, it was decided to go still further, notwithstanding Our efforts to avoid such, by presenting and putting forward a project whose aim is not only to interdict, by an unjust and hateful exception, any teaching whatsoever to members of religious Institutes, even authorized ones, solely because such Institutes are religious, but also to suppress the same Institutes approved for the precise purpose of teaching and to liquidate their goods. **171** *(102, 104)*

As everyone well understands, such measures will have the sad result of, to a very great extent, destroying Christian teaching, the main foundation of every civil society, a teaching prepared and nourished by Catholics under the protection of the law and at the cost of the most numerous sacrifices. By these means, contrary to their parents' will, **172** *(92, 102, 104, 107)* innumerable children will be educated without the aid of faith or Christian morality and with incalculable injury to their souls; also, once again there will arise the pitiful and discouraging spectacle of thousands of religious men and women, not having in the slightest merited these penalties and deprived of all their resources, forced to go roaming throughout the French territories and even to become refugees in foreign countries.

173
(104) We strongly deplore and reprove such severity which is contrary to the essentials of well-founded freedom and to the basic laws of the country, to the rights inherent in the Catholic Church and to the rules of civilization itself— rules which forbid interfering with peaceful civilians, who, under the protection of the law dedicate themselves to the work of Christian education, and who never failed in the duties or burdens imposed on other citizens. Nor, while on this subject, can We omit expressing Our sorrow for the practice of submitting to the State Council, as abusive, certain respectful letters sent to the Supreme Tribunal of the Republic by some responsible Pastors, three of whom are members of the Sacred College, the Senate of the Holy See; these letters were sent in an attempt to make the Head of the State realize how closely the above arguments were connected with the more urgent duties of conscience and public welfare.

(Exhortation to confidence and courage.)

RELIGIOUS LIFE AND TEACHING

Apost. Letter *Quum propediem,* April 23, 1905—to the Superior General of the Brothers of the Christian Schools.

(The coming general chapter.—The persecution of the Church in France.)

As you have not hesitated to undergo exceptional as- **174**
saults from the enemy and, hence, have won the esteem *(110)*
and admiration of the people, We exhort you to lift up your
hearts on high and, as long as the rigors of the times do
not render it impossible, to preserve the very reason for
your Institute's existence.

We have heard that an opinion is being diffused which
claims that for you the education of children should take
first place and the religious profession second place; this is
what the spirit and the needs of these times would have.
We absolutely do not want to find this opinion gaining
even the slightest credit in your Institute or in other religious Institutes, which, like yours, have as their end the
education of youth. Without doubt, insofar as it is possible,
it is necessary to offer some practical remedy for such
grave evils from which society suffers, and consequently,
it may be necessary to yield in many things because of the
exigencies of the times but without going to the extent of
injuring the holy religious Institutes which would be to
injure the holy patrimony of doctrine itself.

Let it be very clear then that in many things the re- **175**
ligious life stands above the lay life, and that, if you are *(57)*
gravely bound to your neighbor by the duty to teach, much
more serious are the obligations that bind you to God. On
the other hand it goes without saying that, up till the present day, you have been the noted teachers and educators
of youth, even to the extent of being set up as objects of
public praise, a fact due to the formation that you have
received from the Rules of your Institute. Continue prac-
tising and loving these rules, trusting unconditionally in
your superiors and remaining united with them and among
yourselves. For the rest, you know your duties; carry them
out and trust in God.

(Apostolic Blessing.)

STUDENTS' STRIKES

Encycl. *Poloniae populum,* December 3, 1905—to the Bishops of Poland.

(Love for Poland.—Damage caused by the terrorists and the radical nationalists.—Remedies: fidelity of the Catholics, respect for the civil authority, the labor problem.)

176
(4,
19,
30,
42,
48)
We maintain that it is a worthy matter which deserves the special attention of Catholics; as you cannot have good and useful citizens without first having them educated right from childhood, it is therefore the duty of all to employ every means and legal assistance that young Catholics will have schools where they will be taught Catholic morality and where they will be trained in good habits. On this point, Venerable Brethren, once again We would like to stimulate your care and diligence, which has already made itself evident to Us in times of trial. Indeed, on you, because of your office, as on parents, is imposed the obligation to procure the Christian education of children.

177
(87)
But here, as We are speaking of schools, We must add some serious advice to adolescents who are engaged in studies; they should never interrupt these studies and cease to frequent the schools simply because they have set their mind against school for political reasons. As Our Venerable Brother, the Archbishop of Warsaw, so admirably pointed out, many serious losses, both public and private, are the result of this interruption of the scholastic course.

(The formation of young clergy.—Freedom of conscience granted in Russia.—Advantage should be taken of the rights granted.)

SCHOOLS FOR RELIGION

Encycl. *Editae saepe*, May 26, 1910.

(Third centenary of the canonization of St. Charles Borromeo.—Intervention of Divine Providence in difficult times.—The Pseudo-Reform.—The genuine restoration: the faith, the school.)

Let fathers of families and schoolteachers remember with how much zeal the holy Bishop constantly advised them about the teaching of Christian doctrine to children and servants; their position is not just that of supplying the means but of making it a duty. The seminarians must not forget that they must assist the parish priest in this teaching; and the latter should see to it that these schools be multiplied according to the number and necessity of the faithful, and that these schools be commendable for the impeachable character of their teachers, who should have assistants, either men or women, of proven integrity, in the manner that has been prescribed by the said Archbishop of Milan. (a) **178 (34, 44, 69, 116)**

The necessity of such Christian instruction seems to have increased, both because of the progress of the times and of modern ways, and as a result of those public schools, where all religion is neglected and where it is considered amusing to deride everything holy. **179 (106, 109, 113, 116)**

To remedy, as much as it was in our power, such a grave evil caused by the very ones who, while demanding profound obedience from others, deny it to the supreme Master of all things, We recommended the setting up of religious schools in cities. And though, thanks to your efforts, this work has made great progress so far, nonetheless it is greatly to be desired that it be propagated more widely, **180 (50)**

178a Prov. Council V, Part 1.

that is, that these schools be opened everywhere and in greater numbers, and have teachers that are commendable for their knowledge of doctrine and integrity of life.

(Preaching.—Restoring virtue.—Civil powers acting as persecutors.—The battle against truth.—The intercession of St. Charles.)

FIRST HOLY COMMUNION

Decree *Quam singulari,* August 8, 1910.

(Alterations of the ecclesiastical customs regarding the age required for the reception of the First Holy Communion.—The abusive demand for an older age for Communion than for Confession.)

181
(73) This custom, by which, under the plea of safeguarding the august Sacrament, the faithful were kept away from the same, was the cause of many evils. Consequently the innocence of childhood, deprived of the embraces of Christ, had no interior life, so that youth, destitute of this strong help, surrounded by so many snares, having lost its candor, fell into vice before ever tasting of the sacred mysteries. Even though a more thorough preparation and an accurate sacramental confession precede First Holy Communion—which is not the case everywhere—yet the loss of first innocence is always to be deplored and might have been avoided by the reception of the Holy Eucharist at a more tender age.

(The influence of Jansenism.—The Eucharist is a remedy and not a reward.)

182
(73) Neither does it appear reasonable that, while formerly even sucklings received the remnant of the sacred particles at present special preparation should be required from the children who are in the happy state of innocence and can-

dor, and greatly need this heavenly food on account of the many temptations and dangers of our times.

The abuses We condemn may be traced to the fact **183** that those who demand a certain age for Penance and an- *(73)* other for Holy Eucharist have neither wisely nor rightly defined the required age. The Lateran Council requires one and the same age for both sacraments, since it imposes a joint obligation of Penance and Communion. (a)

Therefore, since the age of discretion required for **184** Penance is that at which right can be distinguished from *(73)* wrong, namely when one comes to the use of reason; so also for Holy Communion that age is required which can distinguish the Eucharistic bread from the common; which age indeed is that at which a child attains the use of reason.

(Such is the teaching of the interpreters of the Lateran Council, of Saint Thomas, of the Council of Trent, of the Roman Council held under Benedict XIII and of the Roman Catechism.)

(Practical rules.)

(III).—The knowledge of religion required in the **185** child that would enable him to prepare himself sufficiently *(73)* for his First Communion, is that which makes him realize, according to his capacity, what are the mysteries of the faith, and which enables him to distinguish the Eucharistic Bread from the ordinary material bread, so that he may approach the Blessed Eucharist with the devotion which his age allows.

(IV).—The obligation of the precept of Confession **186** and Communion, which concerns the child, devolves on *(34,* those who are responsible for his education—the parents, *44,* the confessor, the teacher, and the parish priest. According *73)* to the Roman Catechism, it pertains to the father, or who-

183a Cf. Denzinger, 437.

soever acts on his behalf, and to the confessor, to permit the child to make his First Holy Communion.

187
(69,
73)
(VI).—Those who have care of children must see to it with the greatest diligence that, after their First Communion, children often approach the Sacred Table—daily, if possible—as desired by Jesus Christ and Our Holy Mother the Church; and that they do so with the devotion compatible with their age. Moreover, let those who have care of the education of children remember that they are obliged to see to it that the same children frequent the catechism classes; when this is impossible, they should see to it that their religious instruction is supplemented in other ways.

These decisions, decreed by the Most Eminent Cardinals in this Sacred Congregation, were approved by His Holiness Pope Pius X in an audience on the seventh of the present month, when he commanded the publication and promulgation of the present decree. He commanded that each Ordinary make it known not only to the parish priests and the clergy but also to the faithful, to whom, every year during the season of the Paschal precept, it must be read in the vernacular.

THE FUTURE OF SOCIETY

Apost. Letter *Quod hierarchia,* June 6, 1911—to the Bishops of Brazil.

(Increase of the Brazilian hierarchy.—A reminder of the duties of Bishops.—Care of emigrants.—Preaching, etc.)

188
(44)
Finally, permit Us to encourage you to direct your zeal towards the field where, rightly, already your best attention has been given—We refer to the instruction and education of children. It is imperative that you continually

watch over the children of the rich as of the poor and that
you apply great care that religion may be their guide and
that they may be instructed in the truth and trained to
live an honest life. This is of capital importance for Christian society and the common good: the future depends
upon the impressions created at a tender and delicate age.

(Conclusion.—Blessing.)

THE FREEDOM OF THE CHURCH

All. to the pilgrims who came on the occasion of the
sixteenth centenary of the Edict of Constantine, February 13, 1913.

*(Freedom essential to the Church which is a society
over and above human society.)*

The Church has from God Himself the right to teach, **189**
and Her word ought to penetrate the conscience of all *(10,*
without any obstacles and without check. Christ did not *14)*
say: let your words be directed towards the poor, the ignorant and the masses; but rather to all without distinction
because, in the spiritual order, you are superior to all the
sovereignties of the earth.

*(Rights of administering the Sacraments, of teaching
the evangelical counsels and of holding possessions.)*

These rights are so sacred that the Church has always **190**
maintained and defended them, well aware that if she *(16,*
yielded even a fraction to the claims of her enemies, she *110)*
would fall short of her heavenly mandate and fall into
apostasy. History thus sounds a warning, presenting us
with a series of protests and claims made by the Church
against the numerous attempts to enslave her. Her first
words to Judaism, spoken by Peter and the Apostles:

"God has more right to be obeyed than men" (a), have been repeated by their successors and will continue to be repeated till the end of the world, even if they have to be confirmed by a baptism of blood.

191
(92,
95,
109)
Even our enemies are so aware of this that they repeat to the letter that every kind of freedom is to be found under the standard of their flag; indeed freedom, or more correctly licence, can be had by all, but freedom of the Church is to be excluded.

(Freedom of worship and thought.)

Freedom of education, but subject to the monopoly of governments, which permit the spread and defence of every system and error in schools, and even prevent children from studying the catechism.

(Freedom of the press, etc.)

You will firmly devote every effort to the achievement of a fruitful apostolate, persuading adversaries and dissenters that the freedom of the Church will admirably provide for the well-being and tranquillity of her peoples, because by exercising the teaching power divinely entrusted to her, she will preserve intact and in their true vigor the principles of truth and justice, on which order of every kind rests and from which is born peace, honesty and every civil culture.

(Encouragement and Blessing.)

190a Acts 5:29.

THE TRADITIONAL PEDAGOGY
OF THE CHURCH

Letter of Cardinal Merry del Val—to Canon Lahargou, November 6, 1913.

(Gift to the Holy Father of summaries of 26 congresses.)

The Holy Father rejoices with you in that your main preoccupation is the religious formation of the young, a formation based on a profound knowledge of the faith, and supported by an active and well-guided sense of devotion; indeed there is no education superior to that which raises the child above himself and carries him closer to God. **192 (26, 69)**

(Frequent Communion.)

In spite of the obstacles raised by official programs, the "Association of the Institutes of Christian Education" has the magnificent record of constant attempts to preserve the methods approved by the traditional pedagogy of the Church. The Church has always been the refuge and protector of learning and, it can be said with certainty, that the classical culture that is still flourishing in the world is due to the present Christian teaching. **193 (17, 118)**

This same teaching is also praiseworthy in that it arms children against the seduction of false systems so deleterious to the understanding of a sound philosophy.

(Blessing.)

BENEDICT XV

1914-1922

NEVER PLACE THE CATHOLIC SCHOOL
IN DANGEROUS CIRCUMSTANCES

Apost. Letter *Commisso divinitus,* September 8, 1916—
to the Bishops of Canada.

*(Serious difference of opinion between French and
English-speaking Catholics; in the bilingual provinces each
side claims the right to use its own language in the pastoral
ministry and the Catholic schools.—Motives.—Appeal for
agreement.—The Bishops ought to come together to decide.)*

The Catholic Bishops of your country ought to remem- **194**
ber that it is of the greatest importance to avert placing *(69,*
the Catholic schools in a state of danger for any reason *117)*
whatsoever; they should see to it that, though receiving a
literary training, the children should learn also to preserve
the Catholic Faith, to profess openly the Church's teaching
and faithfully to obey its law. The love of children, the
good of religion and the cause of Christ all demand this.

(Exhortation to union.)

SAINT JOSEPH CALASANCTIUS

Apost. Letter *Compluribus quidem,* February 10, 1917
—to the Superior General of the Piarist Fathers.

We can witness to the constant and violent attacks **195**
against the Church with the use of weapons such as laws, *(102,*
writings, institutions, etc.; but we can be sure of one *106,*
thing, that no kind of weapon is better adapted for evil- *107)*
doing than the so-called lay-education of children and ado-

lescents. It is this education, claiming to be extraneous to religion, under the pretext of safeguarding freedom, which in reality is meant to do harm and is contrary to religion.

If those of tender and inexperienced age, fully receptive to the formation imparted them by their teachers, do not learn from them to honor God, but on the contrary, form the habit of neglecting and despising everything which refers to God, who will be able to hold them to their duty when the ardor of passions drags them toward vice? Moreover, once the foundation of duty has been destroyed, what value will the term, "virtue," have yet in the mind of youth? In fact, experience has shown that since this brand of education began to be spread, the moral standard of the people has become tremendously lower, surprisingly so among the young: instead of obedience towards parents, a general spirit of revolt is apparent; reformatories for children are continually being opened; too numerous are those youths, at times more depraved than adults, who are serving sentences in public prisons; and finally, we are daily faced with many suicides of young people who are disgusted with life before they have even enjoyed it.

196
(119)   Such are the many misdeeds of the wicked, but there would be greater reason to complain if holy men, inspired by God's grace, had not dedicated themselves to the education of children and continue to do so through those who have taken their place in the Institutes which they founded.

197
(17,
59,
65,
69,
71,
107)   Among them stands out one, Joseph Calasanctius, whose memory is soon to be celebrated with the occasion of the third centenary of the founding of the Congregation of Christian Schools. Among those who have a right to universal esteem for having contributed to the progress of instruction of the children of the masses who can be compared to this man, who, in the very work to which he had dedicated himself with his sons, had to undergo many trials, even to the extent of imitating the patience of Job? Before all others, he was the first to pave the way for Chris-

tian charity and, in an epoch when the rudimentary elements of learning were generally taught to the children of
the upper classes, he ventured into the field of free education for the children of the poor so that they would not be
deprived of all learning because of their lack of means. If,
following these, he opened schools for the rich, he never
demanded their fees. His example, leaving others aside,
proves quite well that those who claim that they are propagators of the light while, at the same time spreading calumny against the Church, saying that she carried with her
darkness and left the people in complete ignorance, do so
because of their bias and hate. But contrary to the manner
of acting of these teachers of youth, he never attended
exclusively to the inculcation of the rudiments of education
to the extent of overlooking what is of capital importance—
the training carried out according to sound traditions; well
understanding that one thing is incomplete without the
other, however, he diligently instructed their intelligence,
while he even more diligently cultivated their souls. Practically speaking, it is much more important, in the interest
of the individual as well as of society in general, to know
how to live a good life than it is to know a great deal.

*(Trials and prosperity of the Institute.—The desire that
it should grow, and also that other similar Institutes be
created with the task of repairing the damage wrought by
lay education.)*

LEGAL VINDICATION

Apost. Letter *Litteris apostolicis,* June 7, 1918—to the
Canadian Bishops.

*(Reference to a previous exhortation for an agreement
between different races and languages. (a)—The scholastic
law for bilingual schools.)*

198a See above, No. 194.

198
(19,
112)
Without overstepping the limits of justice, French Canadians can demand the government's explanation of the so-called scholastic legislation and at the same time they can strive for the granting of other concessions in their work, for example: their own nomination of Catholic school inspectors for private schools; the right to use the mother-tongue in the early years of the child's schooling, at least in the teaching of some of the more fundamental subjects such as Christian Doctrine; the authorization for Catholics to set up their own training colleges for teachers.

199
(111,
112)
If they prove useful, these and other concessions ought to be sought after by Catholics but in such a manner as not to resemble open revolution with the use of violent and illegal means; they ought to be demanded peacefully and with moderation, using, for example, the rights of every citizen and invoking the legal application and protection of the law. In the present case, We confirm this all the more surely and firmly as the civil authority itself has recognized and stated that the scholastic legislation passed by the Ontario government is lacking in clarity, thus rendering it difficult to determine its limits with precision.

In this field and with these measures, the French Canadians are free to seek all the clarifications and amendments they judge necessary in the scholastic laws. However in the future, when such affairs involve the Catholics as a group, let no one dare approach the civil court with his own case without first having sought the authorization of his Bishop. Further, the Bishop will not decide anything without having first sought the opinions of the other Bishops with whom the question is immediately concerned.

(Repeated exhortation to mutual charity.)

SERVING THE COMMON GOOD

Apost. Letter *Exeunte altero,* January 27, 1919—to the Superior General of the Brothers of the Christian Schools.

(The second centenary of St. John Baptist de la Salle.—His aim: to teach religion to children while at the same time educating them in the rudiments of knowledge.)

In these days the education of children is lacking to an incredible extent in the true Christian spirit: many are attempting to snatch the schools from the Church's maternal care and so to introduce the so-called "lay" training, which even lacks the slightest religious atmosphere. In so acting they are substituting a home of virtue for a den of vice. Once the principle has been abolished, that "learning is vain without the fear of God" (a), what will be left to save those of a defenseless age from the burning desires of the passions? **200** *(4, 102, 107)*

It should, therefore, be obvious to all that the most effective way to serve the common good is to educate children, who are the hope of the future, according to Christian teaching and morals.

(Exhortation.—Indulgences.)

FREEDOM OF EDUCATION
IN THE UNITED STATES

Apost. Letter *Communes litteras,* April 10, 1919—to the Bishops of the United States.

(Approval of the Episcopal conferences.—Commissions for the social question and for education.)

200a Ps. 110:10.

201
(16,
47,
49,
92,
95,
102,
109)

The Catholic education of children and of youth is of the greatest importance as it effectively protects the integrity of faith and morals. You know only too well, Venerable Brethren, that God's Church has never ceased to promote this training with all possible attention, and to defend and to protect it, according to its means, against every attack. And even if We had no special reason, the most effective argument is the conduct of the enemies of Christianity among continental peoples. The enemy here would like to vindicate their exclusive right to teach, thus excluding the Church's possibilities of safeguarding the Christian Faith, and impeding the work of the private schools established under her maternal care successfully to combat the anti-religious schools. The enemy tramples underfoot and violates the natural rights of the fathers of families. While an unbridled liberty unworthy of such a name everywhere reigns supreme, they attempt to restrict and abolish by all possible means the freedom proper to the religious and to Catholics to teach the young. Your nation has not experienced this deplorable state of affairs; and We well know how you have devoted all your resources with great liberality and attention to the founding of Catholic schools. We rejoice also with the parish priests and with the religious of both sexes who, under your guidance, have not spared either expense or sacrifice in order to retain the prosperity and efficiency of their schools throughout the entire United States. Nevertheless, you yourselves ought to be convinced that a clear vision of the future could be obscured by the present prosperity and that the lot of the Church and the State depends absolutely on scholastic conditions. You will have no Christians other than those instructed and educated by you.

(Congratulations for the progress of the Catholic University of Washington and for the construction of a Church dedicated to Mary Immaculate.)

PHYSICAL AND SPIRITUAL MOTHERHOOD

An Address to the Women of Italian Catholic Action, October 22, 1919.

(Congratulations to the Catholic Women's Association. —Their natural sphere of action.)

We applaud the confirmed proposal "to dedicate our- **202** selves to the education of the young and to the improve- **(7)** ment of family conditions and the school." We do not wish to stress the right, guaranteed in the name of freedom, to educate children, as it would be a barbarous thing if those who are involved in the formation of the less noble part of their children were to abstain from giving any care to the development of their more noble part.

(Fashions.—Action to be taken.)

With gratitude We have heard that the Catholic Wom- **203** en's Association "promises to dedicate itself in a special **(4,** manner to the forming of the young, to the improvement **25,** of family conditions and the school." It is mainly in this **43,** that We feel the joy of having Our desires anticipated, for, **111)** if We had had to draw up a program of action for women, We would not have laid down rules other than these of yours, directed toward the good of the family, youth and the school. However it is not solely the aims that We praise but also the means chosen for their fulfillment "as has been said, by introducing a clear vision of justice and charity into national life." Oh! If only the coming generations were brought up in these virtues, and what is more, if only justice and charity were spoken of less in theory and more often put into practice, then the somewhat frightening social problems of today would be solved quickly and most effectively.

To achieve this desired effect the Catholic woman ought to appeal to the parents whose duty it is to provide a religious education for their children; she ought to appeal

to the civil authorities who are at least under the obligation of not hindering them; but above all she ought to be
convinced of the necessity of seeking the most opportune
line of action and of putting it boldly into practice.

*(Hope of a sound women's organization in Italy, and
of social reform.)*

CHRIST IN THE BISHOP

Apost. Letter *Libenter quidem,* October 15, 1921—to
the Apostolic Delegate of the East Indies.

*(Directives to Catholics.—Everybody must submit to
the Bishops.—Powers and duties of the Bishops.)*

204
(11,
19,
69)

Bishops, using their threefold authority, namely, that
of teaching, ministering, and governing, ought to maintain
and direct authoritatively the following (a): *the Church's
possessions...; the Catholic education of the young,* which
must never be separated from religious instruction. Actually—since the Savior affirmed of Himself, "You have but
one Master: Christ" (b), and since He continues His teaching through the Bishops, according to the saying: "He who
hears you, hears Me" (c),—it belongs to the Bishops to
establish the legitimate rules which Catholic teachers
ought to follow with great attention in all that pertains to
Catholic schools and the training of seminarians in major
and minor seminaries; and finally, *the relations between
the faithful and non-Catholics in civil life....*

(Native clergy.—Agreement.)

204a Episcopi triplici sua potestate utentes, *magisterii* scilicet, *ministerii* atque *rigiminis,* tueri debent et auctoritative
moderari quae sequuntur: tum administrationes ecclesiasti-
cas ... tum catholicam juventutis educationem ... tum re-
lationes fidelium cum acatholicis in vita civili.
204b Matt. 23:8, 10.
204c Luke 10:16.

PIUS XI

1922-1939

HUMAN KNOWLEDGE AND FAITH

Apost. Letter *Con vivo compiacimento,* April 22, 1922
—to Rev. Fr. Gemelli.

*(The progress of the University of the Sacred Heart in
Milan.—Hopes placed in it.)*

Precisely because you are dealing with an Athenaeum **205**
which boasts that it is Catholic, the untiring and most per- *(62,*
fect submission to pontifical directives will always form *68,*
for it the indispensable condition for maintaining its stan- *119)*
dard high and esteemed, the standard which carries the
motto: *In scientia religio et in religione scientia.* To live
up to this motto, which is the synthesis of your didactic
and moral program and in which religion and learning are
harmoniously united, it must, in what regards religion, attend with the greatest care to the moral formation and the
spiritual training of youth, so as to prepare the coming
generations to cooperate effectively in the religious and
moral rebirth of society and in the setting up of God's
Kingdom on earth.

With regard to doctrine itself, it must maintain its au- **206**
thority in the scientific field: and so dedicate itself with *(17,*
keen and unrelenting care and with persevering labor to *68,*
the study of the human sciences and so validly compete *70)*
in that wise progress of science which prepares man for
new victories and still more glorious conquests.

And so from the evidence of facts, once again it will
be demonstrated that "the Church is far from attempting
to hinder the cult of arts and sciences, but rather in many
ways favors and promotes it. The Church does not ignore
nor despise the advantages that are derived from this com-

bination; rather it holds that, as the arts and the sciences come from God, the Seat of Wisdom, so when man rightly deals with them, with the help of His grace, they lead directly to God." (a)

In fact it is human reason that has the task of paving the way for faith, a task so well described by St. Augustine opposing the incredulous of his time: "There are those who are of the opinion that Christianity ought to be derided rather than professed, as it does not contain something that can be seen, but man is asked to have faith in things that are not seen. We, therefore, in refuting the argument of those who think that they are acting wisely in not believing in what cannot be seen, even though we cannot show to mortal eyes the divine things in which we believe, nevertheless we will show to human minds that belief must be given also to what cannot be seen." (b)

Further, the Holy Doctor, who gave human reason so great a part to play in the defense of the Catholic doctrine, beautifully synthesized the duty of human reason itself in connection with faith by asserting that from the study of human things *fides saluberrima ... gignitur, nutritur, defenditur, roboratur.* (c)

If the new Catholic University with the help of that Heart "in quo sunt omnes thesauri sapientiae et scientiae"

206a Vatican Council, sess. 3, De fide catholica.—Cf. Denzinger 1799.
206b St. Augustine, *De fide rerum quae non videntur,* I.— "Sunt qui putant christianam religionem propterea.ridendam esse potius quam tenendam, quia in ea non res quae videatur ostenditur, sed fides rerum quae non videntur hominibus imperatur. Nos ergo ad hos repellendos, qui prudenter sibi videntur nolle credere quod videre non possunt, etsi non valemus humanis adspectibus monstrare divina quae credimus, tamen humanis mentibus etiam illa quae non videntur credenda esse monstramus."
206c St. Augustine, *De Trinitate,* I, 14, ch. I.—Migne P.L. 42, 1037.

(d) will combine to the extensive and profound study of the human sciences a no less extensive and profound devotion for Catholic truths, it will contribute greatly to the dissipation of the evil errors of those who find a contradiction between science and faith; as the Vatican Council has said, "this error has its foundations either in the fact that the dogmas of the faith were not understood and expounded according to the mind of the Church, or that false and fantastic principles are employed as postulates of reason." (e)

Following these rules, even though like all great things the difficulties and obstacles to overcome will be numerous and heavy, the new Catholic Institute will resume the glorious traditions of the Universities founded throughout all ages by Our predecessors; these Universities, which in the darkness of the Middle Ages were the only beacons transmitting to us the beneficial rays of divine and human knowledge, will illustrate with a new light the salutary doctrines of Catholicism for the benefit and joy of human society. **207 (16)**

(Blessing.)

LEARNING AND MARIAN DEVOTION

Letter *Quandoquidem probe,* April 25, 1922—to the Bishops of the United States.

(Gratitude for the Catholic University at Washington.)

Everywhere there are signs of a general attempt to consolidate order in human society. It is clear indeed that no such restoration is possible without a solid formation **208 (4, 45,**

206d Litany of the Sacred Heart.
206e Vatican Council, Sess. 3.—Cf. Denzinger 1797.

73, of the young; this formation is not obtainable with just any
88, kind of education; indeed, this is to be realized only in an
107, education that has at the root of its scientific instruction
119) religion and virtue, the two essentials that the Church unceasingly recommends in numerous ways.

It is extremely important that youth be inflamed with
an equal liking for learning and religious devotion, and
that for this reason, they have a special devotion to the
Blessed Mother, who is both the seat of wisdom and the
fount of piety. Hence the American Bishops have decided
to erect the national church dedicated to the Immaculate
Conception next to the Catholic University; it is only natural that next to the temple of knowledge there be erected
the temple of prayer because "holiness is all-availing" (a),
and without holiness "knowledge breeds self-conceit." (b)

*(Reminder of the rules laid down by Leo XIII: an elect
Catholic society must be created.)*

209 For your seminaries, colleges and schools, always and
(50, unceasingly prepare teachers who are equipped not only
58, with a generally complete education but with one that is
68) deeply penetrated with a really genuine Catholic spirit.
Especially in America, where methods of education are
subject to such precise and unchanging principles that all
institutes seem identical, it is an achievement of great importance to come to a perfect understanding and unison
as regards the method of education of children. Certainly
We understand how, not one, but many Universities are
needed for the immense territory of your country; however
it would be to the detriment of the country to have new
foundations that would be left wanting in any manner, be
it in facuties or in the necessary development of the indi-

208a 1 Tim. 4:8.
208b 1 Cor. 8:1.

vidual faculties. It is preferable to have one well-equipped University than many imperfect ones.

(All the Bishops must agree regarding the program to be drawn up.)

THE WAR IS AN ABOMINABLE FRUIT OF ATHEISM

Encycl. *Ubi arcano,* December 23, 1922.

(The first sorrows and the first joys of the Pontiff.— Present evils.—Causes.)

God and Jesus Christ, as well as His doctrines, were banished from schools. As a sad but inevitable consequence, schools became not only secular and non-religious, but openly atheistic and anti-religious. In such circumstances it was easy to persuade poor ignorant children that neither God nor religion are of any importance as far as their daily lives are concerned. God's name, moreover, was scarcely ever mentioned in such schools, unless perchance it were to blaspheme Him or to ridicule His Church. Thus schools, forcibly deprived of their right to teach anything about God or His law, could not but fail in their efforts really to educate, that is, to lead children to the practice of virtue, for the schools lacked the fundamental principles which underlie the possession of a knowledge of God and the means necessary to strengthen the will in its efforts toward good and in its avoidance of sin. And so there was no possibility of preparing for the family and society true elements of order, peace and prosperity. **210** *(103, 105, 107)*

With the light of Christian spirituality so hidden and even extinguished, the invading materialism set itself in recent times to prepare the ground for an extensive propaganda of anarchy and social unrest. Finally came the world war, which threw nations and peoples one against the other; **211** *(107)* long pent up dissension and hatred were let loose, while men became accustomed to violence and blood, and sealed with blood the initial dissension and hatred.

(Remedies.—The peace of Christ.—Means of attaining it.—Catholic unity.)

THE STATE REAPS WHAT IT SOWS

All. to the Sacred Consistory, March 24, 1924.

(Conclusion of the question of the Diocesan Associations.—Attachment of the Catholics to the Holy See.—Persecutions in Russia.—The return to unity.—Alleviating misery.—American charity.—New American Cardinals.)

212
(5,
49,
80,
111,
112,
114)
Looking around Us We are most certainly consoled to see that the Crucifix, the symbol and most expressive reminder of the Redemption, has returned to the classrooms; We are even more consoled at the return of religious instruction to primary schools, the place where these favorites of the Redeemer and Divine Master receive the first directives for life and the first elements of knowledge. However there are still certain preoccupations; and while entrusting them to the necessary preparation, to the fidelity and the didactic conscience of those whose task it is to arrange and impart such teaching, We consider it the duty of the Apostolic Ministry to charge, as We do "in visceribus Christi," Our Venerable Brothers the Bishops of Italy and their clergy, as also Our beloved children, the mothers and fathers of families, not to neglect their rights and duties of cooperation and vigilance. For this is a matter which is of the highest importance and therefore of the gravest responsibility. On it depends not so much the fate of the Church, which is spread throughout the world and has divine promises for all times, as the fate of the family, society and the nation, which tomorrow will inevitably reap the crop sown today: truth or error, true and genuine

Christianity or paganism, that is to say, civilization in the true sense of the word or barbarism, dreadful and dishonorable, even if clothed in the splendor of exterior and material progress.

(Fascist violence.—Arrangements that are consoling.—Dispossession of the Pontifical State.—Plenary Council in China.—Religious centenaries.—Missionary exhibition.)

SOCIAL RESTORATION AND GIRLS

Homily for the Canonization of Blessed Mary Magdalen Postel and Blessed Madeleine Sophie Barat, May 24, 1925.

(Saint Mary Magdalen Postel during the Revolution.)

What was wanting in France was certainly a genuine **213** restoration, a restoration from the very foundations, in fact. *(4,* Among the people, many had lost even the conscience of *59)* duty; after the shortages and sufferings of a long exile, if not all, at least a part of the nobility that had its possessions returned were demoralized by the past difficulties and abandoned themselves to an easy life. So it was that Mary Magdalen Postel and Madeleine Sophie Barat saw that the only useful action was to consecrate their lives to the sound education of growing children of the coming generation.

(Foundation of the Christian schools of mercy for the children of the people.—Saint Madeleine Sophie Barat.)

Although she added next to every institution a school open to the poor, she wanted particularly to dedicate her work to the education of the children of the nobility and the rich.

It is a fact of experience, and one which did not escape the notice of this wise woman, that people of distinguished birth surrounded by wealth are frequently in more miserable circumstances than the poor; their craving of heart and spirit is camouflaged by a worldly attitude and by finery. If on the other hand, among the upper classes, the mothers of families are formed from childhood to a holy life, it will naturally come about that by their words and especially by their example they will lead to the faithful practice of religious duties not only their own children but aso the ordinary people who come in contact with them.

(*Apostolate of the two religious families.*)

The apostolate for the holy education of girls is a present-day necessity: it is urgently needed to awaken the Christian spirit among the masses and to assist women to be for humanity, with the gifts they have from nature and grace, instruments not of ruin but of conversion and salvation.

(*The intercession of the two Saints.*)

ST. ALOYSIUS GONZAGA

Letter *Singulare illud*, June 13, 1926—to the Superior General of the Society of Jesus.

214
(5,
88)
A singular note in the life of the Divine Master is His special love for the young. He attracts and draws to Himself the innocent children. (a) He severely rebukes, and threatens with heavy punishments those who would corrupt them (b); and to the unblemished young man He holds out as both allurement and reward the complete and perfect ideal of sanctity. (c)

The Church and youth

215
(5,
The Church, having imbibed this very spirit from her Founder Whose mission and work she has inherited, from

214a Cf. Mk. 10:13-16.
214b Matt. 18:6.
214c Mk. 10:21.

the beginning of the Christian era has shown herself to be
inflamed with similar ardent love for the young.

She began, therefore, to provide for the physical and
moral welfare of the little ones; to open schools and Universities, and instruct her children from the first elements
of knowledge to the highest; and to approve and encourage the founding of religious Orders and Congregations
which, by opening Academies, Colleges and Schools, and
by starting various Associations, might attend to the proper
education of youth. The Church has always claimed that
to impart such education was her own inviolable right. She
could not fail to teach, before the whole human race entrusted to her care, that she alone possesses the true doctrine of morality, and that she is the only safe teacher of
the most difficut art of forming the true character of man
on Christian principles.

We greatly rejoice in Our days to see everywhere
numberless young men and women from all ranks of society gathering around the Priests and Bishops, eager to
perfect themselves in every point of Christian doctrine and
life, and to help the Church to carry on her work of re-
forming and saving mankind.

And remembering the many groups of young people
that during the Holy Year came to Us from all parts, We
feel once again the joy We then felt, when We thought
that with such groups organized in all countries, it would
be possible one day to form a strong, yet peaceful, army
which the Holy See could employ for the reformation of
a decadent world. The love We bear for the young strikes
deeper root in Our heart when We consider the many and
execrable snares laid for their innocence and faith. In this
warfare against their entire spiritual life, it often happens
that the strength of the body and soul of many, who otherwise would have been useful to the Church and to society,
grows weaker or is even totally impaired.

14,
16,
80,
88)

Followers of St. Aloysius Gonzaga

216
(88)
The Second Centenary, therefore, of the Canonization of St. Aloysius Gonzaga, which will be completed on the last day of this year, brings with it so many advantages for the spiritual advancement of youth, that We most willingly turn Our thoughts and words to Our younger children who, all the world over, represent the hope of the Kingdom of Christ. As they must have recourse to this strong and powerful protector in the battles and dangers of life, so must they follow him as a wonderful model of every virtue. If they study his life carefully, they will clearly see which is the way to perfection, which are the fittest means they must use to attain it, and which are the priceless fruits of virtue they will reap, provided they follow in the footsteps of St. Aloysius. Let them see him in his true light and such as he really was, and not as the enemies of the Church have falsely represented him or even unwise writers portrayed him, and they will find in him a unique model of all youthful virtues, even now after so many recent examples of sanctity.

217
(88)
Glancing through the pages of the Church's history, one easily discovers that a large number of the youths and men who are most worthy of admiration for their innocent life, and whom the Holy Ghost has raised up since the death of St. Aloysius to our own day, have been modelled on his example. To give but a few instances, We would mention St. John Berchmans, who, while a student in the Roman College, resolved to copy Aloysius in every detail; Nunzio Sulprizio, a young workman, who did likewise from his childhood to his death; Contardo Ferrini who, rightly called by his companions a second Aloysius, had the tenderest devotion for the Saint, taking him as the model for and guardian of his chastity; Bartholomea Capitanio who, in her life and in her death, perfectly reproduced Aloysius to whom she was greatly devoted and through whom, in this Centenary year, she seems to have received in return

the grace to share his glory, with her enrollment in the list of the Blessed.

It may safely be affirmed that Aloysius also helped not a little in the conversion and sanctification of St. Gabriel of our Lady of Sorrows, who, in spite of the levity and carelessness of his youthful years, never ceased to recommend himself to him whom he had been taught to revere as the Patron of Youth. And to mention one at least of the most recent educators and teachers of the young, Don Bosco not only had a tender devotion to St. Aloysius, but he strongly recommended it also to the boys whom he undertook to train in holiness, and left it as a kind of inheritance to his children. Of the former, the one most advanced in the imitation of St. Aloysius was Dominic Savio, a very pure and holy boy, whom God allowed the world to see and admire for so brief a period.

The lesson of St. Aloysius Gonzaga

It was certainly a mysterious dispensation of God's Providence that Aloysius should die at a very early age, when his eminent qualities of mind and heart, his resolute and active will, and his singular and almost superhuman prudence combined with zeal for religion and souls, gave promise of an exceedingly fruitful apostolate. It pleased God, however, that young people should learn from an angelic youth, whom similarity of age would naturally make them love and follow, what was their special and principal duty—to prepare themselves for the battle of life by the solid practice of the Christian virtues. We deem that those who lack the interior virtues which so splendidly shone in Aloysius are neither fit nor equipped to face the dangers and battles of life or undertake apostolic work. Having become "as sounding brass or a tinkling cymbal," (a) they will be of no use to the cause they mean to promote and

218
(79,
88)

218a 1 Cor. 13:1.

defend. They will even do harm, as experience has more than once demonstrated in the past. The Centenary celebrations of St. Aloysius, therefore, come opportunely and at the right time. By the example of his life, the Saint recommends to young men, already too much inclined by nature to worldly matters, and only too eager to live a life of action, not to think of working for others before they have made progress in the study and practice of the interior virtues.

219
(72,
88)
First of all, Aloysius shows the young that the fundamental basis of true Christian education is the spirit of a living Faith, enlightened by which, as by "a lamp that shineth in a dark place," (a) they may know the nature and importance of this life. Having determined to order his life, not according to worldly principles, but in the light of eternal ones, from which whosoever departs ceases to be a spiritual man, the Saint was accustomed to consider such motives—all taken from divine revelation—in the solitude of the retreats to which, first in his tender years in the world, and later on as a Jesuit, he was devoted, to the great profit and consolation of his soul. Under the guidance of Aloysius it should be deeply impressed on the mind of every young person that man's life is not to be debased in such a way as to be confined to the care and enjoyment of perishable things, by which the mind and the senses are often carried away. It should be rather looked upon as a training ground in which, while serving Christ alone, we strive to attain eternal happiness.

Young people will easily develop this true view of life if, following the example of St. Aloysius, they sometimes wholly withdraw from the tumult of the world to make a retreat of a few days since these, as long experience teaches, are admirably fitted to win over their tender and docile souls.

219a 2 Pet. 1:19.

Illumined by the splendor of the eternal truths, having **220**
resolved to use all possible means in order to live a spot- *(76,*
less life, Aloysius adhered so strongly to his resolution as *77,*
to be free, during the whole of his life, from every stain *78)*
of mortal sin. In particular, so diligently did he preserve
the flower of his purity from the slightest blot, that among
his companions he went by the name of Angel—by which
name the Christian world has ever since been accustomed
to honor him; and Blessed Robert Bellarmine, a Spiritual
Father of great experience, considered that he was confirmed in grace. Nor did St. Aloysius attain to such a high
degree of sanctity because he was, by God's special favor,
exempted from those battles which, within and without our
souls, we must fight against in our fallen nature. From impure temptations he was indeed freed through a similar
grace, but he was not exempt from the fire of anger and
the tingling of pride. With a determined will, however, he
not only repressed such inclinations, but subjugated them
entirely to the rule of reason.

Prayer—Sacraments—Mortification

Moreover, well knowing man's innate weakness, and **221**
placing no trust whatever in himself, he sought to gain the *(72,*
help of divine grace by praying day and night, even for *73,*
many hours together, at the same time begging for the in- *76,*
tercession of the Virgin Mother of God, in whose devotion *77,*
he greatly excelled. Above all, he approached the Holy Ta- *88)*
ble which he understood to be the fount and support of all
spiritual life, as often as was allowed in those days, to benefit by its ever-renewing strength. As, however, man's
cooperation must go hand in hand with divine grace, to
maintain his innocence and purity, Aloysius added to a fervent devotion to the Blessed Sacrament and to the Mother
of God a detachment from all worldly things and such
mortification of his senses as most men may well admire

but can never equal. It is a marvellous fact and hardly credible that, amidst so great a corruption of morals, Aloysius could vie with the Angels in purity of soul; that in such a keen seeking after pleasure he should distinguish himself for his extraordinary abstinence and for the austerity and rigor of his life; that in such eagerness for honors, he should despise and loathe them, so as to renounce willingly the Principality which by hereditary right was to be his, and desire to join that religious Order wherein a special vow shuts the door even to sacred dignities; that in the excessive worship of the ancient culture of Greece and Rome, so assiduous should be his study and application to heavenly things, that both by a particular gift of Heaven and by his own wonderful industry, he lived so entirely absorbed in God as to suffer no distraction whatever in his prayer. These are singular heights of sanctity, inaccessible even to men of consummate virtue. Let this, however, be a warning to our youths as to the true means by which their most excellent grace and ornament, that is to say, their innocence and purity of morals, must be preserved.

The method of Christian education

222
(77,
88,
118)
Concerning this matter, We are not unaware that many educators of the young, frightened by the moral corruption of our day, through which so many youths plunge into ruin to the deepest detriment of soul, and desirous of removing from civil society such a serious calamity and loss, are all intent on thinking out new systems of education. We wish they could properly understand that they will be of no service to the State, if they neglect those methods of action and that discipline which, derived as they are from the fountain of Christian wisdom, and tested by the long experience of centuries, Aloysius found in himself extremely effective—a living faith, flight from seduc-

tions, self-control, operative love of God and the Blessed Virgin, and a life frequently refreshed and strengthened by the Bread of Angels.

Disciplining the spirit

If young men attentively consider Aloysius as a perfect model of chastity and of sanctity, not only will they learn to check sensuality, but they will also avoid the snares into which those fall who, imbued with the dictates of a certain teaching that despises the doctrine of Christ and of the Church, allow themselves to be led astray by an immoderate thirst for liberty, by pride of mind and independence of will. Aloysius, conscious though he was of being the heir to a Principality, willingly allowed himself to be guided in his studies and his spirit by the teachers assigned to him. Later on, as a member of the Society of Jesus, he submitted himself so perfectly to the commands and directions of his superiors as not to depart, even in the most insignificant duties of religious life, from what the Institute prescribes. No one fails to see how this conduct of the Saint is so greatly opposed to that of so many young men, who, deceived by appearances and chafing under every restraint, despise the advice of their elders. Everyone who wishes to serve under the banner of Christ must hold it as certain that once the yoke of discipline is shaken off, he will reap shameful defeats instead of victories, nature having so providentially arranged that young people cannot make intellectual or moral progress or shape their lives according to Christian principles unless they are guided by others. And if great docility is required in every branch of knowledge, how much more so in all that concerns an active apostolate! Such duties being closely connected with the office entrusted by Christ to the Church, they cannot possibly be done holily and profitably,

223
(86,
88,
95,
97)

unless they are performed with submission to those whom the Holy Ghost has placed as Bishops to uphold the Church of God. (a)

As once in the Garden of Eden, by promising great and incredible things as a reward for their disobedience, Satan led our first parents to rebel against God, so nowadays, by the bait of independence, he corrupts and drags into the mire many youths who are swollen with empty pride, whereas their true greatness lies in submission to lawful authority.

Though Aloysius, on account of his special prudence, was admired by his fellow-countrymen, who hoped for great things from his future government, and later was looked upon by his Jesuit brethren as quite fit to be eventually raised to the Generalship of the Order, he despised himself with a submission at once most humble and most noble, and obeyed all those who held the place of his eternal Lord and King in his regard.

The ideal perfection of youth

224
(60,
72,
88)
Aloysius reaped the sweetest and choicest fruits of a most holy conduct of life, led according to the light and rule of faith. So well, indeed, did gifts of nature and grace blend in him that he presents himself to us as a perfect model of a young man. Do not the excellence of his mind and the maturity of his judgment, the nobility and strength of his soul, the polish and pleasantness of his manners make him such? Proof of the high intellectual power of this in-

223a Quodsi magnam ad ceteras disciplinas, ad maiorem profecto ad actionis atque apostolatus officia animi docilitatem afferant opportet: quae quidem officia, cum munus Ecclesiae a Christo mandatum attingant, sancte utiliterque expleri nequeant, nisi demissis erga eos animis, quos *Spiritus Sanctus posuit episcopus regere Ecclesiam Dei.*—Acts 20:28.

nocent youth who, free from all inordinate passions, was wholly given to contemplation and perfect knowledge of what is true and good, is afforded by the success with which he went through his course of studies, the universal applause with which he held philosophical debates, and finally his writings, especially his letters, which, though few on account of the short span of his life, are worthy of admiration as showing a profound knowledge and appreciation of things.

Aloysius showed clearly his sound judgment and acuteness by the manner in which he transacted and brought to a successful conclusion the most difficult affairs entrusted to him by his father; and after the death of his father by the no less difficult feat of effecting a reconciliation between his brother and the Duke of Mantua, thus putting an end to feuds and hatred. The nobility of his heart and the gentleness of his manners were universally lauded by all who came in touch with him, in everyday life or in the splendors of the court, whether they were citizens or servants, princes or courtiers; but especially by the superiors and members of the Society of Jesus, who greatly admired him. We know, however, that strength of character and firmness of will were most peculiarly evident in St. Aloysius.

Having from childhood resolved to become a saint, he was with such strength and courage faithful to his resolution till death as never to hinder or delay the spiritual ascent which he began with the first use of reason.

Can there be, then, any more timely and fit model for the love and imitation of the young and especially of students? Besides minds and hearts filled with sound and solid culture, they require a wise, calm and balanced criterion in order to judge and to feel rightly about men and events, so as not to let themselves be led astray by false impressions, by unruly and enfeebling passions, or by public opinion. They must distinguish themselves by kindness and amiability in order to maintain peace in their

225
(60,
63,
88)

families and in society, and by strength and constancy of
will in order to direct themselves and others on the path
of goodness.

226
(79,
88)

We find, likewise, in Aloysius the admirable diligence
and alacrity in helping his fellowmen which forms the essence of the apostolate that often attracts young people
so powerfully. Though his main and constant occupation
was to meditate on the things of Heaven and to converse
intimately with God, so that his life could be said to be
"hidden away with Christ in God," (a) still there often
burst from his heart sparks of apostolic zeal, which fore-
casted in some way the ardent flames of later years. Thus
we see him, when still a boy, edifying all with whom he
came into contact by his good example and pious conversation, and on occasion stirring them up to the practice
of virtue. As he advanced in years and longed for greater
things, we see him looking forward to the highest and the
hardest duties for the salvation of souls, and turning his
thoughts to the conversion of heretics and pagans in foreign lands.

Rome saw Aloysius, when a student in the Roman College, go through the squares, the streets and the alleys of
the city to teach the children and the poor the elements of
Christian Doctrine. She was witness of the heroic charity
with which, when Rome was ravaged by an epidemic, he
served those infected with it, and caught himself the first
germs of that disease which a few months after was to
bring him to the grave when barely twenty-four.

Here, then, lies a very wide field open to all our youth,
in which they may strenuously work under the leadership
of Aloysius. They should imitate him in leading an exemplary life, in doing good through speech, in zeal for missionary work, in teaching Christian Doctrine, and in
devoting themselves to various works of charity. If groups of

226a Col. 3:3.

Catholic youths were to devote themselves to works such as these, they would revive and fittingly adapt to our times, the Aloysian Apostolate which, far from ceasing with the death of Aloysius, continues its salutary efficacy from Heaven.

The patron of Christian youth

As a matter of fact, from his heavenly throne, where the Carmelite Virgin, Mary Magdalen di Pazzi, in one of her visions saw him reigning, and where, two centuries ago, Our Predecessor of happy memory, Benedict XIII, declared that he was seated among the elect and had been solemnly enrolled in the list of the saints, Aloysius has never ceased to shower his favors on all his followers, but especially on the young. Hence it is that there are so many sodalities named after him, and proud of being under his protection. Hence it is that there are so many youths, boys and girls alike, who in following his example interlace the thorns of self-denial with the lilies of purity. Hence it is that St. Aloysius and Christian youth seem to vie with one another—he in pouring on them heavenly gifts, they in invoking him as their celestial Patron. What wonder, then, if the Popes have chosen Aloysius as the model and patron of youth?

227
(88)

Pondering, therefore, once more on all these things and moved by that anxious care that We, more than all men, feel for a thoroughly good education of the young and for their salvation in these times of unusually grave dangers, and, moreover, as a token of gratitude for past favors, and to obtain even greater favors from Aloysius, following the example of Our Predecessors, and in particular of Benedict XIII and of Leo XIII, We solemnly confirm, and, if need be, by Our Apostolic authority declare that St. Aloysius Gonzaga is the heavenly patron of all Christian youth. And while We entrust these choicest offspring of the Catholic family to the charge and faithful protection of Aloysius, that they may grow and flourish more profusely; and that, while openly professing the Christian faith, they may lead a more innocent life, We entreat them with all Our heart to keep Aloysius before them as a model, to honor and invoke him constantly, by means also of those pious exercises, such as the practice of the Six Sundays, which, as from long experience We know, bring many great blessings.

(Youth Congress in Rome as a part of the Centenary celebrations.)

St. Stanislaus Kostka

228
(88)

As it happens, on the very same day as Aloysius there was canonized a saint who had lived and died in the Society of Jesus, but a few years previous to him, namely Stanislaus Kostka; so it is fitting that on this auspicious occasion, youth should raise their minds and hearts to this saintly Polish youth to whom Our Lord, "in the lavishness of his wisdom," conceded "the grace to reach a mature saintliness at an even more tender age."

He also was born of a noble family, and was of strong and generous spirit, a flower of angelic purity. Seeking the highest ideals, he had to strive for a long time with his brother, who led a worldly life of pleasure; he also won over a heretical, evil-living family, and dissipated companions. Thence, consoled and strengthened by the Eucharistic Bread, more than once offered to him by the hands of Angels, he undertook long trips on foot with the sole intention of following the voice of God, which was calling him to greater things, and of the Blessed Virgin, who was urging him to enter the Society of Jesus. He came here to Rome, but only it seems to ascend from here, a short while later to the eternal Jerusalem—the youngest of the confessor saints, consumed by the internal fire of charity when only eighteen years of age and still a novice. It would appear that God desired to reward in a special way the courage and constancy of Stanislaus, by attributing to this most innocent young man such glorious splendor that through his patronage, he offered an impregnable defense to his nation, and even more to Christianity as a whole, against the more formidable danger of that time, the Turkish invasions. His prodigious intervention in the dangerous divison of the fatherland was so evident to all, that the great Christian Caesar, John Sobieski, who liberated Vienna from the terrible siege, did not hesitate to affirm that the victories were due to Stanislaus' protection rather than the force of arms.

May God, through the joint supplications of both Saints, grant to our youth the grace to follow their example, striving with a greater love and advancing much more rapidly towards the conquest of the only true Christian greatness, which is the most beautiful ornament of purity and sanctity.

(Blessing.)

THE FLOURISHING OF SACERDOTAL VOCATIONS

Letter *Caritatem decet*, March 4, 1929—to the Bishops of Czechoslovakia.

(The thousandth anniversary of St. Wenceslas.—His life.—The growth of Catholicism.—The heritage of the Saint.)

Above all, care must be taken that the best boys enter the seminaries. However this would be rendered impossible if the Christian education offered in the family and in the public schools were not absolutely sound and well-founded. Therefore, Venerable Brethren, do not tire of insistently warning Catholic parents that it is their serious duty to train their children in holiness and that they have the right

229
(30,
35,
79,
114,
117)

from the natural law freely to found Catholic schools or to demand, according to their means, that even in the public schools the faith of their children be preserved from all dangers, and that their minds and wills be formed according to the rules of Christianity.

230
(79) Moreover, frequent communion greatly attracts the young towards the priesthood. In this, therefore, it is advisable that all those associations, such as the Marian Congregations, which encourage frequent reception of the Blessed Eucharist, be multiplied. Steps must also be taken in order that young people may be encouraged to join the ranks of the association commonly known as the Knights of St. Wenceslas who, following the example of their patron, promise that they will frequently approach the Eucharistic Table.

(Czechoslovakian clerics.—The return of the dissidents. —St. Wenceslas, model of rulers and citizens.)

THE DUTY OF THE STATE

All. to the students of the Mondragone College, May 14, 1929.

(The day after a Fascist speech.)

231
(14,
16) We are bound to witness in this Institute, (a) a noble example and testimony of that great mission of Christian education which, together with the mission of saving souls, God has entrusted to the Church. Indeed, it must be asked to whom does Christian education belong if not to this Mother and Teacher who is the depositary of Divine Revelation and, as the Poet says, the "eternal preserver of the incorruptible Blood," (b) to this Mother and Teacher of

231a The Cavanis Institute of Venice.
231b Manzoni, *La Pentecoste*, v. 3-4.

Christian life and holiness. Of this mission the Church has always made a right and a duty; it could not be otherwise.

(Number of religious houses of education throughout the world.)

The work of the Church in history

We are indeed struck with a deep sense of admiration when we realize that all this is not only a reality of today but that the Church has always attended to education and instruction, according to the possibilities of the times, even in the Middle Ages which some still insist on calling "dark," but which produced many splendid cathedrals, from sunny Sicily to snowy Scandinavia, many works of philosophy, theology, medicine and all branches of learning—works which, we must admit, we find difficult to read in our day— and all this with so few means. This is explainable by the fact that right back in those far-off Middle Ages when there were so many (some have even said too many) monasteries, convents, churches, collegiate-churches, cathedral chapters, etc., there was attached to each a home of study, of teaching, of Christian education. To these we must add all the universities, spread over every country and always by the initiative and under the protection of the Holy See and the Church. That grand spectacle, which today we see better, as it is nearer to us and more imposing because of the conditions of the age, was the spectacle of all times; and they who study and compare historical events remain astounded at what the Church has been able to do in this matter, and marvel at the manner in which she has succeeded in fulfilling her God-given mission to educate generations of men to a Christian life, producing everywhere a magnificent harvest of fruitful results. But if we wonder that the Church in all times has been able to gather about her and educate hundreds, thousands, millions of students, no less wonderful is it to bear in mind what she has done not only in the field of education, but in that also of true

232
(14,
16,
17)

and genuine erudition. For, if so many treasures of culture, civilization and literature have escaped destruction, that is due to the action by which the Church, even in times long past and uncivilized, has shed so bright a light in the domain of letters, of philosophy, of art, and in a special manner of architecture. He who looks to the past, not for the invention of arguments for his own use and benefit but in order to discover the truth, cannot but be convinced that this is true history.

233
(7,
9,
10)
Your presence here suggests to Us another obvious and beautiful fact, the explanation of your being here, namely it shows Us with what great gratitude and earnestness the fathers and mothers of families—Christian families —have responded to this activity of the Church. Right from the most ancient times Christian parents have always understood that it was their duty and also to their interest to profit from that treasury of Christian education that the Church puts at their disposition. Thus at all times Christian families, fathers and mothers, came knocking on behalf of their children on the doors of the schools and the educational institutions offering Christian instruction. These most beautiful truths eloquently demonstrate two facts of great importance: that of the Church placing at the disposal of families her office of mistress and educator, and of the families eager to profit by the offer, and entrusting their children to the Church in hundreds and thousands. And these two great facts recall and proclaim a striking truth of the greatest significance in the moral and social order. They declare that the mission of education regards before all, above all, primarily the Church and the family, and this by natural and divine law, and that therefore it cannot be slighted, cannot be evaded, cannot be supplanted.

The State assists, supplements and completes

234
(20-
The State is obliged to take a vital interest in the education of its citizens; however it does so only in that it

aids the individual and the family in all that they cannot
do of themselves. The State is not made to absorb, to en-
gulf and to annihilate the individual and the family; that
would be ridiculous, it would be contrary to nature in that
the family precedes the State and society. The State cannot neglect the question of education but must contribute
and procure what is necessary and sufficient to help, to cooperate and to perfect the efforts of the family, to correspond entirely with the desires of the father and mother and
above all to respect the divine right of the Church. To a
certain extent it can be said that it is called to complete
the work of the family and the Church, because the State,
better than all other institutions, is provided with the
means which are placed at its disposal for the needs of
all; and it is right that it use them for the benefit of the
very ones from whom they come.

22,
25,
109)

It is clear then that, in the educational field, the State
can offer professional and conscientious wage earners, but
it can never offer vocations, lives consecrated to education
by an entire and complete dedication.

235
(54,
109)

We do not say that, to carry out its work in the educational field, it is necessary and opportune that the State
should train groups of conquerors, fitted for conquest.
What is done in one State could be done throughout the
world. And if all the States were educated for conquest,
where would things end? This manner of educating would
contribute to a general conflagration rather than to a general pacification. Unless there was an intention of asserting
(and perhaps it is precisely this that was intended), that
the training is meant to conquer truth and virtue, in which
case We would be in perfect accord.

Intransigency of the Church

But We can never be in accord with all that wants to
restrain, to diminish and to deny the right that nature and

236
(9,

16, God have given to the family and the Church in the field
100, of education. We do not wish to say that We are intractable
110) on this point, for one reason because intractableness is not
a virtue, but only intransigent, just as We must be intransigent when asked what is the sum of two plus two. It is
four and it is not our fault that it is not three, or five, or six,
or fifty. When it is a question of the salvation of some soul
or of preventing greater evils from befalling souls, We feel
courageous enough to deal with the devil in person. And it
has been precisely to impede a greater evil that, as all have
been able to observe, We have at a certain moment nego-
tiated, when it was a question of deciding the fate of Our
Catholic explorers; We have made great sacrifice to avoid
greater evils, but We have put on record all the grief We
felt in being forced to do so.

As you see, beloved sons, you have come at a very
propitious moment, one of those that Divine Providence
supplies so opportunely. We have spoken to you about in-
transigence when principles and rights that are beyond
discussion are being dealt with. We must add that we do
not dispose of the material means to sustain this intransi-
gence. Nor, on the other hand, does this displease Us, for
truth and justice have no need of material forces, as they
have their own irrefutable, irreplaceable and irresistible
qualities.

STATE, LEARNING AND
CHRISTIAN EDUCATION

Letter *Ci si è domandato*, May 30, 1929—to Cardinal
Gasparri.

*(Discussions following the signing of the Lateran Trea-
ty.—Yet again the nature of Christianity and the rights of
the Church have been questioned.)*

237 Logically it should be recognized that the full and
(10, perfect task of teaching belongs not to the State but to the

Church, and that the State cannot prevent her from ful-   *18,*
filling this duty nor can it reduce it to a tacit teaching of   *24,*
the religious truths.   *103)*

No damage can be done in this way to the true and
proper rights, or rather, the duties of the State, as regards
the education of its citizens.

• The State has nothing to fear from the education given
by the Church and under her directives; it is this education
that has given substance to modern civilization insofar as
concerns what it now possesses of good.

The family at once realized that such is the case, and
from the Church's very first days right through the ages to
our times, fathers and mothers, even if weak or non-
believers, sent their sons by the millions to the educational
institutions founded and directed by the Church.

Science, the scientific method and research have less   **238**
still to fear, if such be possible, than the State itself from   *(13,*
future and higher developments of religious teaching.   *68)*

The Catholic Institutions, to whatever grade of teaching and learning they belong, do not need any apology.
The respect they command, the praise they receive, their
scientific achievements and, more than all else, the graduates they have fully and perfectly prepared and given to
the magistrature, the professions, teaching and to all walks
of life, justify them more than sufficiently.

Dangerous authors imposed by the curriculum

But We cannot join in that praise, whether merited or   **239**
not, that would seem to be attributed to the Catholic Uni-   *(64,*
versity of Milan and its professors, most dear to Us, as re-   *108)*
gards studies and written works concentrating on the historical personality and doctrine of Kant and of others opposed to good scholastic philosophy and Catholic teaching,
as if this were an effect and a sign of a leaning toward

such doctrines, and not rather the result of a scrupulous teaching conscience which does not permit the refutation of that which is not first well understood, and the unavoidable necessities of imposed programs—a necessity which suffices and must suffice to explain and justify the inclusion (though not without reasonable precaution) in the scholastic series, published by the well-deserving Salesians, of certain authors and texts which St. John Bosco, so profoundly understanding with regard to men and things, and so eminent an apostle of classical and professional culture and above all of wise education, most certainly would not have numbered among those adapted to the attainment of these aims, especially in a country and among a people as here in Italy which he knew so well. To Us, from that small personal experience which We have had in teaching and among books, We often think and fear that there is in store for our young the damage already pointed out by St. Augustine: *necessaria non norunt, quia superflua didicerunt.*

(The perversion of the Concordat.—The connection between the Concordat and the Treaty.)

EDUCATION OF THE REDEEMED MAN

Encycl. *Divini illius Magistri,* December 31, 1929.

Introduction

240
(5)   As the Representative on earth of that Divine Master Who, while embracing in the immensity of His love all mankind, even unworthy sinners, showed nevertheless a special tenderness and affection for children, and expressed Himself in those singularly touching words: "Suffer little children to come unto me," (a) We also, on every occa-

240a Mk. 10:14.

sion, have endeavored to show a wholly paternal predilection towards them, particularly by our assiduous care and timely instructions in regard to the Christian education of youth.

And so, in the spirit of the Divine Master, We have directed a helpful word, now of admonition, now of exhortation, now of direction, to young people and to their educators, to fathers and mothers, on various points of Christian education, with that solicitude which becomes the common Father of all the Faithful, with an insistence in season and out of season, demanded by Our pastoral office and inculcated by the Apostle: "Be insistent in season, out of season; reprove, rebuke, exhort with all patience and doctrine." (b) Such insistence is called for in these our times, when, alas, there is so great and deplorable an absence of clear and sound principles, even regarding the most fundamental problems.

Now this same general condition of the times, this ceaseless agitation in various ways of the problem of educational rights and systems in different countries, the desire expressed to Us with filial confidence by not a few of yourselves, Venerable Brethren, and by members of your flocks, as well as Our deep affection for the young referred to above, move Us to turn more directly to this subject, if not to treat it in all its well-nigh inexhaustible range of theory and practice, at least to summarize its main principles, throw full light on its important conclusions, and point out its practical applications.

Let this be the record of Our Sacerdotal Jubilee which, with altogether special affection, We wish to dedicate to our beloved youth, and to commend to all those whose office and duty is the work of education.

Indeed never has there been so much discussion about education as nowadays; never have exponents of new peda- **241** (94)

240b 2 Tim. 4:2.

gogical theories been so numerous, or so many methods and means devised, proposed and debated, not merely to facilitate education, but to create a new system infallibly efficacious, and capable of preparing the present generations for that earthly happiness which they so ardently desire.

242
(2, 94)
The reason is that men, created by God in His image and likeness and destined for Him Who is infinite perfection, realize today more than ever, amid the most exuberant material progress, the insufficiency of earthly goods to produce true happiness either for the individual or for nations. And hence they feel more keenly in themselves the impulse towards a perfection that is higher, and which is implanted in their rational nature by the Creator Himself. This perfection they seek to acquire by means of education. But many of them with, it would seem, too great insistence on the etymological meaning of the word, expect to draw education out of human nature itself and put it into practice by its own unaided powers. Such people easily fall into error, because, instead of fixing their attention on God, the first principle and the last end of the entire universe, they fall back upon themselves, becoming attached exclusively to the passing things of this earth; and thus their restlessness will never cease till they direct their attention and their efforts to God, the goal of all perfection, according to the profound saying of St. Augustine: "Thou didst create us, O Lord, for Thyself, and our heart is restless till it rests in Thee." (a)

The essence and importance of Christian education

243
(1, 2,
It is therefore as important to make no mistake in education, as it is to make no mistake in the pursuit of the last goal, with which the whole work of education is intimately

242a *Confessions*, I, i: Fecisti nos, Domine, ad Te, et inquietum est cor nostrum donec requiescat in Te.

and necessarily connected. In fact, since education consists   26,
essentially in preparing man for what he must be and for   94)
what he must do here below, in order to attain the sublime
goal for which he was created, it is clear that there can be
no true education which is not wholly directed to man's
last end, and that in the present order of Providence, since
God has revealed Himself to us in the Person of His only-
begotten Son, Who alone is "the Way, the Truth and the
Life," (a) there can be no ideally perfect education which
is not Christian education.

Hence the supreme importance of Christian educa-   **244**
tion, not merely for each individual, but for families and   (2-4,
for the whole of human society, whose perfection comes   26,
from the perfection of the elements that compose it. From   80,
these same principles, the excellence, we may well call it   92)
the unsurpassed excellence, of the work of Christian education becomes manifest and clear; for after all it aims at securing the Supreme Good, that is, God, for the souls of
those who are being educated, and the maximum of well-
being possible here below for human society. And this it
does as efficaciously as man is capable of doing it, namely
by cooperating with God in the perfecting of individuals
and of society, inasmuch as education imprints upon the
soul the first, the most powerful and lasting impression for
life, according to the well-known saying of the Wise Man:
"Raise up a child in the way he should go, and even when
he is old, he will not depart from it." (a) Quite rightly,
therefore, did St. John Chrysostom say, "What greater work
is there than training the mind and forming the habits of
the young?" (b)

But nothing reveals to us the supernatural beauty and
excellence of the work of Christian education more than

243a John 14:6.
244a Prov. 22:6.
244b Hom. 60, in ch. 18 Matt.

the sublime expression of love of our Blessed Lord, identifying Himself with children, "Whosoever shall receive one such child as this in My Name, receiveth Me." (c)

Now in order that no mistake may be made in this work of utmost importance, and in order to conduct it in the best manner possible with the help of God's grace, it is necessary to have a clear and definite idea of Christian education in its essential aspects, viz., those who have the mission to educate, those who are the subjects to be educated, what are the necessary concomitant circumstances, what is the object and aim proper to Christian education according to God's established order in the economy of His Divine Providence.

Those who must educate

245
(2,
6,
8,
15,
20,
21,
60)
Education is essentially a social and not merely an individual activity. Now there are three essential societies, distinct one from the other and yet harmoniously combined by God, into which man is born: of these two, namely the family and civil society, belong to the natural order; the third, the Church, to the supernatural order. In the first place comes the family, instituted directly by God for its particular purpose, the procreation and the formation of offspring; for this reason it has priority of nature, and therefore of rights, over civil society. Nevertheless, the family is an imperfect society, since it does not in itself possess all the means for its own complete development; whereas civil society is a perfect society, having in itself all the means for its own special end, which is the temporal well-being of the community; and so, in this respect, that is, in view of the common good, it has pre-eminence over the family, which finds its own suitable temporal perfection precisely in civil society.

244c Mk. 9:36.

The third society, into which man is born when through Baptism he reaches the divine life of grace, is the Church; a society of the supernatural and universal order; a perfect society, because it has in itself all that is required for its own purpose, which is the eternal salvation of mankind; hence it is supreme in its own domain.

Consequently education which is concerned with man as a whole, individually and socially, in the order of nature and in the order of grace, necessarily belongs to all these three societies, in due proportion, corresponding, according to the disposition of Divine Providence, to the coordination of their respective ends.

The Church

First of all education belongs pre-eminently to the Church, by reason of a double title in the supernatural order, conferred exclusively upon her by God Himself; absolutely superior therefore to any other title in the natural order. **246** *(10-12, 14)*

The titles of the Church

The first title is founded upon the express mission and supreme authority to teach, given her by her divine Founder: "All power is given to Me in Heaven and on earth. Go ye therefore and teach all nations, baptizing them in the name of the Father, and of the Son, and of the Holy Ghost, teaching them to observe all things whatsoever I have commanded you, and behold I am with you all days, even to the end of the world." (a) Upon this magisterial office Christ conferred infallibility, together with the command to teach His doctrine. Hence the Church "was set by her divine Author as the pillar and ground of truth, in order to teach the divine Faith to men, and keep whole and inviolate what was entrusted to her; to direct and

246a Matt. 28:18-20.

fashion men, in all their actions, individually and socially, towards purity of morals and integrity of life, in accordance with the revealed doctrine." (b)

The second title is that of supernatural motherhood, in virtue of which the Church, spotless spouse of Christ, generates, nurtures and educates souls in the divine life of grace, through her Sacraments and her doctrine. With good reason then does St. Augustine maintain: "He has not God for Father who refuses to have the Church as mother." (c)

The rights of the Church

247
(10-
13,
15,
62)
Hence it is that in this very objective of her educational mission, that is, "in faith and morals, God Himself has made the Church sharer in the divine magisterium and, by a special privilege, granted her immunity from error; hence she is the mistress of men, supreme and absolutely sure, and she has inherent in herself an inviolable right to freedom in teaching." (a) Consequently the Church is independent of any sort of earthly power whether it be in her origin or in the exercise of her mission as educator, not merely in regard to her proper end and object, but also in regard to the means necessary and suitable to attain that end. Hence with regard to every other kind of human learning and instruction, which is the common patrimony of individuals and society, the Church has an independent right to make use of it, and above all to decide what may

246b Pius IX, Letter *Quum non sine,* July 14, 1864: Columna et firmamentum veritatis a Divino suo Auctore fuit constituta, ut omnes homines divinam edoceat fidem, eiusque depositum sibi traditum integrum inviolatumque custodiat, ac homines eorumque consortia et actiones ad morum honestatem vitaeque integritatem, iuxta revelatae docrinae normam, dirigat et fingat. Cf. Nos. 26-31.

246c De Symbolo ad catech., XIII: Non habebit Deum patrem, qui Ecclesiam noluerit habere matrem.

247a Encycl. *Libertas,* June 20, 1888. Cf. No. 123.

help or harm Christian education. And this must be so, because the Church, as a perfect society, has an independent right to the means conducive to her end, and because every form of instruction, no less than every human action, has a necessary connection with man's last end, and therefore cannot be withdrawn from the dictates of the divine law, of which the Church is guardian, interpreter and infallible mistress.

This is clearly set forth by Pius X, of saintly memory: "Whatever a Christian does even in the order of earthly things, he may not overlook the supernatural; indeed he must, according to the teaching of Christian wisdom, direct all things towards the supreme good as to his last end; all his actions, besides, insofar as they are good or evil in the order of morality, that is, in keeping or not with the natural or divine law, fall under the judgment and jurisdiction of the Church." (a) **248 (2, 10)**

It is worth noting how a layman, an excellent writer and at the same time a profound and conscientious thinker, has been able to understand well and express exactly this fundamental Catholic doctrine: "The Church does not say that morality belongs purely, in the exclusive sense, to her; but that it belongs wholly to her. She has never maintained that outside her fold and apart from her teaching, man cannot arrive at any moral truth; she has, on the contrary, more than once condemned this opinion because it has appeared under more forms than one. However she does say that because she was instituted by Jesus Christ, because the Holy Ghost was sent to her in His name by the Father, she alone possesses what she had directly from God and can never lose, the whole of moral truth, *omnem veritatem*, in which all individual moral truths are included, as **249 (12)**

248a Encycl. *Singulari quadam*, September 24, 1912.

well those which man may learn by the help of human reason, as those which form part of revelation or which may be deduced therefrom." (a)

250
(13,
15,
61)
The Church, therefore, is fully entitled to promote letters, science, and art insofar as is necessary or helpful to Christian education, in addition to her work for the salvation of souls; founding and maintaining schools and institutions adapted to every branch of learning and degree of culture. (a) Nor may even physical culture, as it is called, be considered outside the range of her maternal supervision, for the reason that it also is a means which may help or harm Christian education.

251
(18,
20,
110)
This work of the Church in every branch of culture is of immense benefit to families and nations which, without Christ, are lost, as St. Hilary correctly points out: "What can be more fraught with danger for the world than the rejection of Christ?" (a) Nor does it in the least interfere with the regulations of the State, because the Church in her motherly prudence is not unwilling that her schools and institutions for the education of the laity be in keeping with the legitimate measures of the civil authorities; she is in every way ready to cooperate with these authorities and to make provision for a mutual understanding, should difficulties arise.

252
(13,
14,
18,
19,
Again it is the inalienable right, as well as the indispensable duty of the Church, to watch over the entire education of her children, in all institutions, public or private, not merely in regard to the religious instruction given there, but in regard to every other branch of learning

249a A. Manzoni, *Osservazioni sulla Morale Cattolica*, ch. III.
250a Codex Iuris Canonici, can. 1375: Ecclesia est ius scholas cuiusvis disciplinae non solum elementarias, sed etiam medias et superiores condendi.
251a Commentar. in Matt. Ch. 18: Quid mundo tam periculosum quam non recepisse Christum?

and every regulation insofar as religion and morality are
concerned. (a)

Nor should the exercise of this right be considered as
undue interference, but rather as the maternal care on the
part of the Church in protecting her children from all grave
danger of doctrinal and moral evil. Moreover this watchfulness of the Church not merely can create no real in-
convenience, but must, on the contrary, confer valuable
assistance in the right ordering and well-being of families
and of civil society; for it wards off from youth the moral
poison which at that inexperienced and changeable age
most easily penetrates the mind and most readily spreads
its baneful effects. For it is true, as Leo XIII has wisely
pointed out, that without proper religious and moral instruction "every form of intellectual culture will be injurious; for young people not accustomed to respect God will
be unable to bear the restrictions of a virtuous life, and
never having learned to deny themselves anything, they
will easily be incited to disturb public order." (b)

The extent of the Church's mission in the field of education is such as to embrace every nation, without excep-

24,
25,
69,
80,
107)

252a Codex Iuris Canonici, canon 1381, °1. Religiosa iuven-
tutis institutio in scholis quislibet auctoritati et inspectioni
Ecclesiae subiicitur.
2. Ordinarium locorum ius et officium est vigilandi ne in
quibusvis scholis sui territorii quidquam contra fidem
vel bonos mores tradatur aut fiat.
3. Eisdem similiter ius est approbandi religionis magistros
et libros; itemque, religionis morumque causa, exigendi
ut tum magistri tum libri removeantur.
Canon 1382. Ordinarii locorum sive ipsi per se sive per
alios possunt quoque scholas quaslibet, oratoria, recreatoria, patronatus, etc., in iis quae religiosam et moralem institutionem spectant, visitare; a qua visitatione quorumlibet religiosorum scholae exemptae non sunt, nisi agatur de
scholis internis pro professis religionis exemptae.
252b Encycl. *Nobilissima Gallorum gens,* February 8, 1884.
Cf. No. 95.

tion, according to the command of Christ: "Teach ye all nations;" (c) and there is no power on earth that may lawfully oppose her or stand in her way.

The work carried out by the Church

253
(14,
16,
18)
In the first place, it extends over all the Faithful, of whom she has the same anxious care as a tender mother. For these she has throughout the centuries created and promoted an immense number of schools and institutions in every branch of learning. As We said on a recent occasion: "Right back in the far-off Middle Ages when there were so many (some have even said too many) monasteries, convents, churches, collegiate churches, cathedral chapters, etc., a center of study, of teaching, and of Christian education was attached to them. To these we must add all the universities, existent in every country and always by the initiative and protection of the Holy See and the Church. That grand sight, which today we see better, as it is nearer to us and more imposing because of the circumstances of the era, was the spectacle of all times; and those who compare and study historical events remain astounded at·what the Church has been able to do in this matter, and marvel at the manner in which she has succeeded in fulfilling her God-given mission to educate generations of men to a Christian life, producing everywhere a magnificent harvest of fruitful results.

254
(17,
18)
"But if we wonder that the Church in all times has been able to gather about her and educate hundreds, thousands, millions of students, it is no less wonderful to bear in mind what she has done not only in the field of education, but also in that of true and genuine erudition. For, if so many treasures of culture, civilization and literature have escaped destruction, this is due to the action by

252c Matt. 28:19.

which the Church, even in times long past and uncivilized, has shed so bright a light on the domain of letters, of philosophy, of art and, in a special manner, of architecture." (a)

The Church has been able to do all this because her mission to educate extends equally to those outside the Fold, seeing that all men are called to enter the kingdom of God and reach eternal salvation. Just as today when her missions scatter schools by the thousand in districts and countries not yet Christian, from the banks of the Ganges to the Yellow River and the great islands and archipelagos of the Pacific Ocean, from the Dark Continent to the Tierra del Fuego and to frozen Alaska, so in every age the Church, by her missionaries, has educated to Christian life and to civilization the various peoples which now constitute the Christian nations of the civilized world. **255 (10, 14, 18, 103)**

Hence it is evident that both *de jures* and *de facto* the mission to educate belongs pre-eminently to the Church, and that no one free from prejudice can have a real reason for opposing or impeding the Church in this her work, the precious advantages of which are now enjoyed by the world.

The harmony existing between the rights of the Church and those of the family and of the State

This is all the more true because the rights of the family and of the State, even the rights of individuals regarding fair liberty in the pursuit of learning, of the methods of learning and all sorts of lay culture, are not only not opposed to the pre-eminence of the Church, but are in complete harmony with it. The fundamental reason for this harmony is that the supernatural order, to which the Church owes her rights, not only does not in the least de- **256 (18, 24)**

254a Address to the students of the Mondragone College, May 14, 1929. Cf. No. 232.

stroy the natural order, to which pertain the other rights mentioned, but elevates that order and perfects it, each affording mutual aid to the other, and completing it in a manner proportioned to its respective nature and dignity. The reason is because both come from God, Who cannot contradict Himself: "The works of God are perfect and all His ways are judgments." (a)

This becomes clearer when we consider more closely and in detail the mission of education proper to the family and to the State.

The family

257
(7-
9,
40)
In the first place the Church's mission of education is in wonderful agreement with that of the family, for both proceed from God, and in a remarkably similar manner. God directly communicates to the family, in the natural order, fecundity, which is the principle of life, and hence also the principle of education for life, together with authority, the principle of order.

The inviolable right that precedes that of the State

The Angelic Doctor, with his wonted clearness of thought and precision of style, says: "The father according to the flesh has in a particular way a share in that principle which in a universal manner is found in God. . . . The father is the principle of generation, of education and discipline and of everything that bears upon the perfecting of human life." (a)

The family holds, therefore, directly from the Creator the mission, and hence the right, to educate the young, a

---

256a Deut. 32:4.
257a S. Thomas, Summa Theologica, 2a. 2ae, q. 102, a. I: Carnalis pater particulariter participat rationem principii, quae universaliter invenitur in Deo . . . Pater est principium et generationis et educationis et disciplinae, et omnium quae ad perfectionem humanae vitae pertinent.

right inalienable because inseparably joined to a strict obligation, a right anterior to any right whatever of civil society and of the State, and therefore inviolable on the part of any power on earth.

That this right is inviolable St. Thomas proves as follows: "The child is naturally something of the father ... so by natural right the child, before reaching the use of reason, is under the father's care. Hence it would be contrary to natural justice if the child, before arriving at the use of reason, were removed from the care of its parents, or if any arrangement were made concerning him against the will of the parents." (a) And as this duty on the part of the parents continues up to the time when the child is in a position to provide for itself, this same inviolable parental right of education also endures. "Nature intends not merely the generation of offspring, but also its development and advancement to the perfection of man considered as man, that is, to the state of virtue" (b) as St. Thomas himself says.

The wisdom of the Church in this matter is expressed with precision and clearness in the Code of Canon Law, can. 1113: "Parents are under a grave obligation to see to the religious and moral education of their children, as well as to their physical and civic training, as far as they can, and moreover to provide for their temporal well-being."(c)

258
(2,
7,
29,
30,
109)

258a St. Thomas, *Summa Theologica*, 2a, 2ae, q. 10, a. 12: Filius enim naturaliter est aliquid patris ... ; ita de iure naturali est quod filius, antequam habeat usum rationis, sit sub cura patris. Unde contra iustitiam naturalem esset, si puer, antequam habeat usum rationis, a cura parentum subtrahatur, vel de eo aliquid ordinetur iuvitis parentibus.
258b St. Thomas, Suppl., 3 p., q. 41, a. 1: Non enim intendit natura solum generationem prolis, sed etiam traductionem et promotionem usque ad perfectum statum hominis in quantum homo est, qui est virtutis status.
258c C.I.C., 1113: Parentes gravissima obligatione tenentur prolis educationem tum religiosam et moralem, tum physi-

259
(8,
24,
30,
109)
On this point the common sense of mankind is in such complete accord, that they would be in open contradiction with it those who dared to maintain that the children belong to the State before they belong to the family, and that the State has an absolute right over their education. Untenable is the reason they adduce, namely that man is born a citizen and hence belongs primarily to the State, not bearing in mind that before being a citizen man must exist; and existence does not come from the State, but from the parents, as Leo XIII wisely declared: "The children are something of the father, and as it were an extension of the person of the father; and, to be perfectly accurate, they enter into and become part of civil society, not directly by themselves, but through the family in which they were born." (a) "And therefore," says the same Leo XIII, "the father's power is of such a nature that it cannot be destroyed or absorbed by the State; for it has the same origin as human life itself." (b)

260
(2,
7,
9,
29,
30,
111,
112,
114)
It does not, however, follow from this that the parents' right to educate their children is absolute and despotic; for it is necessarily subordinated to the last end and to natural and divine law, as Leo XIII declares in another memorable encyclical, where he sums up the rights and duties of parents: "By nature parents have a right to the training of their children, but with this added duty that the education and instruction of the child be in accord with the end for which, by God's blessing, it was begotten. Therefore it is the duty of parents to make every effort to pre-

cam et civilem pro viribus curandi, et etiam temporali eorum bono providendi.

In canon 1372, °2, there is added: Non modo parentibus ad normam can. 1113, sed etiam omnibus qui eorum locum tenent, ius et gravissimum officium est curandi Christianam liberorum educationem.

259a Encycl. *Rerum novarum,* May 15, 1891.
259b Encycl. *Rerum novarum,* May 15, 1891.

vent any invasion of their rights in this matter, and to make absolutely sure that the education of their children remain under their own control in keeping with their Christian duty, and above all to refuse to send them to those schools in which there is danger of imbibing the deadly poison of impiety." (a)

It must be borne in mind also that the obligation of the family to educate children, includes not only religious and moral education, but physical and civic education as well, (b) principally insofar as it touches upon religion and morality.

Recognition by a sane civil jurisprudence

This incontestable right of the family has at various times been recognized by nations anxious to respect the natural law in their civil enactments. Thus, to give one recent example, the Supreme Court of the United States of America, in a decision on an important controversy, declared that it does not lie within the powers of the State to fix any uniform standard of education, by forcing children to receive instruction exclusively in public schools, and it bases its decision on the natural law: the child is not the mere creature of the State; those who nurture him and direct his destiny have the right, coupled with the lofty duty, to educate him and prepare him to carry out his duties. (a)

261
(7,
109)

The tutelage of the Church

History bears witness how, particularly in modern times, the State has violated and does violate rights con-

262
(9,

260a Encycl. *Sapientiae Christianae*, January 10, 1890. Cf. No. 129.
260b C.I.C., canon 1113. Cf. No. 258.
261a *"The fundamental theory of liberty upon which all governments in this Union repose excludes any general power*

102) ferred by God on the family. At the same time it shows magnificently how the Church has ever protected and defended these rights, a fact proved by the special confidence which parents have in Catholic schools. As We pointed out recently in Our Letter to the Cardinal Secretary of State: "The family has instinctively understood this to be so, and from the earliest days of Christianity down to our own times, fathers and mothers, even those of little or no faith, have been sending or bringing their children in millions to places of education under the direction of the Church." (a)

It is paternal instinct, given by God, that turns them with confidence to the Church, certain of finding in her the protection of family rights, thereby illustrating that harmony which God has ordered in all things. The Church is indeed conscious of her divine mission to all mankind, and of the obligation which all men have to practise the one true religion; and therefore she never tires of defending her right, and of reminding parents of their duty, to have all Catholic-born children baptized and brought up as Christians. On the other hand, so jealous is she of the family's inviolable natural right to educate the children, that she never consents, save under peculiar circumstances and with special cautions, to baptize the children of infidels, or provide for their education against the will of the parents, till such time as the children can choose for themselves and freely embrace the faith. (b)

of the State to standardize its children by forcing them to accept instruction from public teachers only. The child is not the mere creature of the State; those who nurture him and direct his destiny have the right coupled with the high duty, to recognize, and prepare him for additional duties." U. S. Supreme Court Decision in the Oregon School Case, June 1, 1925.

262a Letter to the Cardinal Secretary of State, May 30, 1929 Cf. No. 237.

262b C.I.C., canon 750, §2.—St. Thomas, *Summa Theologica* 2a 2ae, q. 10, a. 12.

We have therefore two facts of supreme importance, **263** as We said in Our above-mentioned discourse: The *(7,* Church places at the disposal of families her office as mis- *10,* tress and educator, and families, eager to profit by the *18)* offer, entrust their children to the Church in hundreds and thousands. These two facts recall and proclaim a striking truth of the greatest significance in the moral and social order. They prove that the mission of education, above all, primarily concerns the Church and the family, and this by natural and divine law, and that therefore it cannot be slighted, cannot be evaded, cannot be supplanted. (a)

The State

From such priority of rights on the part of the Church **264** and of the family in the field of education, most important *(20,* advantages, as we have seen, accrue to the whole of so- *24,* ciety. Moreover, in accordance with the divinely estab- *92)* lished order of things, no damage can follow from it to the true and just rights of the State in regard to the education of its citizens.

For the common temporal good

These rights have been conferred upon civil society by the Author of nature Himself, not because of fatherhood, as in the case of the Church and of the family, but in virtue of the authority which it possesses to promote the common temporal welfare, which is precisely the purpose of its existence. Consequently education cannot pertain to civil society in the same way in which it pertains to the Church and to the family, but in a different way, corresponding to its own particular end and object.

263a Address to the students of the Mondragone College, May 14, 1929.—Cf. No. 233.

265
(20,
21)

    Now this end and object, the common welfare in the temporal order, consists in that peace and security in which families and individual citizens are freely able to exercise their rights, and at the same time to enjoy the greatest spiritual and temporal prosperity possible in this life, by the mutual union and coordination of the work of all. The function, therefore, of the civil authority residing in the State is twofold, namely, to protect and to foster, but by no means to absorb the family and the individual or to substitute itself for them.

Protecting the family and the individual

266
(9,
21,
22,
24)

    Consequently, in the matter of education, it is the right, or to speak more correctly, it is the duty of the State to protect by means of its legislation, the prior rights, already described, of the family as regards the Christian education of its offspring, and consequently also to respect the supernatural rights of the Church in this same realm of Christian education.

    It is also the duty of the State to protect the rights of the child itself when the parents are found wanting, either physically or morally in this respect, whether by default, incapacity or misconduct, since, as has been shown, their right to educate is not an absolute and despotic one, but dependent on the natural and divine law, and therefore subject to the authority and jurisdiction of the Church, and to the vigilance and administrative care of the State in view of the common good. Besides, the family is not a perfect society, that is to say, it has not in itself all the means necessary for its full development. In this case, an exceptional one no doubt, the State does not take the place of the family, but merely makes provision for its deficiencies, and provides suitable means, always in conformity with the natural rights of the child and the supernatural rights of the Church.

In general, then, it is the right and duty of the State to protect, according to the rules of right reason and faith, the moral and religious education of youth, by removing public impediments that stand in the way.

Promoting education and instruction

In the first place it pertains to the State, in favor of the common good, to promote in various ways the education and instruction of youth. It should begin by encouraging and assisting, of its own accord, the initiative and activity of the Church and the family, whose successes in this field have been clearly demonstrated by history and experience. It should, moreover, supplement their work whenever this falls short of what is necessary, even by means of its own schools and institutions. For the State, more than anyone else, is provided with the means put at its disposal for the needs of all, and it is only right that it should use these means to the advantage of those who have contributed thereto. (a)

Over and above this, the State can exact, and take measures to secure that all its citizens have the necessary knowledge of their civic and political duties, and a certain degree of physical, intellectual and moral culture, which, considering the conditions of our times, is really necessary for the common good.

267
(21,
23,
25)

However, it is clear that in all these ways of promoting education and instruction, both public and private, the State should respect the inherent rights of the Church and of the family concerning Christian education, and should moreover have regard for distributive justice. Accordingly, monopoly, whether educational or scholastic, which, physically or morally, forces families to make use of government

268
(22,
24,
109)

267a Address to the students of the Mondragone College, May 14, 1929. Cf. No. 234.

schools contrary to the dictates of their Christian conscience, or contrary even to their legitimate preferences, is unjust and unlawful.

The branch of education reserved to the State

269
(23,
97,
101,
109)
This does not prevent the State from making due provision for the right administration of public affairs and for the protection of peace, within or without the realm. These are things which directly concern the public good and call for special aptitudes and special preparation. The State may therefore reserve to itself the establishment and direction of schools intended to prepare for certain civic duties and especially for military service, provided it be careful not to injure the rights of the Church or the family in what appertains to them.

Physical training and the military spirit

It is well to repeat this warning here; for in these days a spirit of nationalism which is false and exaggerated, as well as dangerous to true peace and prosperity is spreading its influence. Excesses are committed in giving a military turn to the so-called physical training of boys (sometimes even of girls, contrary to the very instincts of human nature); or again in usurping unreasonably on Sunday the time which should be devoted to religious duties and to family life at home. It is not, however, Our intention to condemn what is good in the spirit of discipline and legitimate bravery promoted by these methods; We condemn only what is excessive, as for example violence, which must not be confounded with courage nor with the noble sentiment of military valor in defense of country and public order; or again exaltation of athleticism which even in classic pagan times marked the decline and downfall of genuine physical training.

Civic education

In general it also appertains to civil society and to the State to provide what may be called civic education, not only for youth, but for all ages and classes. This consists in the practice of presenting publicly, to groups of individuals, information with an intellectual, imaginative and emotional appeal, calculated to draw them towards what is upright and honest, and to urge its practice by a sort of moral compulsion, in the positive sense by disseminating such knowledge, and in the negative sense by suppressing what is opposed to it. This civic education, so wide and varied in itself as to include almost every activity of the State aimed at the public good, ought also to comply with the rules of rectitude, and therefore cannot conflict with the doctrines of the Church, which is the divinely appointed teacher of these rules.

270
(23,
66)

Relations between Church and State

All that We have said so far regarding the activity of the State in educational matters, rest on the solid and irremovable foundation of the *Catholic doctrine of the Christian Constitution of States* set forth in such masterly fashion by Our Predecessor, Leo XIII, notably in the Encyclicals *Immortale Dei* and *Sapientiae Christianae*. He writes as follows: "God has divided the government of the human race between two authorities, ecclesiastical and civil, establishing one over things divine, the other over things human. Both are supreme, each in its own domain; each has its own fixed boundaries which limit its activities. These boundaries are determined by the peculiar nature and the proximate end of each, and describe as it were a sphere within which, with exclusive rights, each may develop its influence. As, however, the same subjects are under both authorities, it may happen that the same matter, though from a different point of view, may come under

271
(20,
24)

the competence and jurisdiction of each of them. It follows that Divine Providence, whence both authorities have their origin, must have traced with due order the proper line of action for each. The powers that are, are ordained by God." (a)

272
(12,
20,
23,
24)

Now the education of youth is precisely one of those matters that belong both to the Church and to the State, "though in different ways," as explained above. "Therefore," continues Leo XIII, "between the two powers there must reign a well-ordered harmony. Not without reason may this mutual agreement be compared to the union of body and soul in man. Its nature and extent can only be determined by considering, as We have said, the nature of each of the two powers, and in particular the excellence and nobility of the respective ends. To one is committed directly and specifically the charge of what is helpful in worldly matters; while the other is to concern itself with the things that appertain to heaven and eternity. Everything therefore in human affairs that is in any way sacred, or has reference to the salvation of souls and the worship of God, whether by its nature or by its end, is subject to the jurisdiction and discipline of the Church. Whatever else is comprised in the civil and political order, rightly

271a Encycl. *Immortale Dei,* November 1, 1885: Deus humani generis procurationem inter duas potestates partitus est, scilicet ecclesiasticam et civilem, alteram quidem divinis, alteram humanis rebus praepositam. Utraque est in suo genere maxima: habet utraque certos, quibus contineatur, terminos, eosque sua cuiusque natura causaque proxime definitos; unde aliquis velut orbis circumscribitur, in quo sua cuiusque actio iure proprio versetur. Sed quia utriusque imperium est in eosdem, cum usuvenire possit ut res una atque eadem quamquam aliter atque aliter, sed tamen eadem res, ad utriusque ius iudiciumque pertineat debet providentissimus Deus, a quo sunt ambae constitutae, utriusque itinera recte atque ordine composuisse. Qua autem sunt, a Deo ordinatae sunt (Rom. 13:1).

comes under the authority of the State; for Christ commanded us to give to Caesar the things that are Caesar's, and to God the things that are God's." (a)

Good results of the accord

Whoever refuses to admit these principles, and hence to apply them to education, must necessarily deny that Christ has founded His Church for the eternal salvation of mankind, and maintain instead that civil society and the State are not subject to God and His law, natural and divine. Such a doctrine is manifestly impious, contrary to sound reason, and, especially in this matter of education, extremely harmful to the proper training of youth, and disastrous not only to civil society but also to the well-being of all mankind. On the other hand, from the application of these principles, there inevitably result immense advantages for the right formation of citizens. This is abundantly proved by the history of every age. Tertullian in his *Apologeticus* could challenge the enemies of the Church in the early days of Christianity, just as St. Augustine did in his; and we today can repeat with him: "Let those who

273
(12,
92,
103,
105)

272a Encycl. *Immortale Dei,* November 1, 1885: Itaque inter utramque potestatem quaedam intercedat necesse est ordinata colligatio: qua quidem coniunctioni non immerito comparatur, per quam anima et corpus in homine copulantur. Qualis autem et quanta ea sit, aliter iudicare non potest, nisi respiciendo, uti diximus, ad utriusque naturam, habendaeque ratione excellentiae et nobilitatis causarum; cum alteri proxime maximeque propositum sit rerum mortalium curare commoda, alteri caelestia ac sempiterna bona comparare. Quidquid est igitur in rebus humanis quoque modo sacrum, quidquid ad salutem animorum cultumve Dei pertinet, sive tale illud sit natura sua, sive rursus tale intelligatur propter causam ad quam refertur, id est omne in potestate arbitrioque Ecclesiae: cetera vero, quae civile et politicum genus complectitur, rectum est civili auctoritati esse subiecta, cum Jesus Christus iusserit, quae Caesaris sint, reddi Caesari, quae Dei, Deo.

declare that the teaching of Christ is opposed to the welfare of the State, furnish us with an army of soldiers such as Christ says soldiers ought to be; let them give us subjects, husbands, wives, parents, children, masters, servants, kings, judges, taxpayers and taxgatherers who live up to the teachings of Christ; and then let them dare assert that Christian doctrine is harmful to the State. Rather let them not hesitate one moment to acclaim that that doctrine, rightly observed, is the greatest safeguard of the State." (a)

274
(24,
92,
94)
While discussing education, it is not out of place to point out here how an ecclesiastical writer, who flourished in more recent times, during the Renaissance, namely the saintly and learned Cardinal Silvio Antoniano, to whom the cause of Christian education is greatly indebted, has set forth most clearly this well-established point of Catholic doctrine. He had been a disciple of that wonderful educator of youth, St. Philip Neri; he was teacher and Latin secretary to St. Charles Borromeo, and it was at the latter's suggestion and under his inspiration that he wrote his splendid treatise on *Della educazione cristiana dei figliuoli*. In it he argues as follows:

"The more closely the temporal power of a nation aligns itself with the spiritual power, and the more it fosters and promotes the latter, so much the more does it contribute to the conservation of the commonwealth. For it is the aim of the ecclesiastical authority, by the use of spiritual means, to form good Christians in accordance with its own particular end and object; and in doing this it helps

273a Letter 138. Proinde qui doctrinam Christi adversan dicunt esse reipublicae, dent exercitum talem, quales doc trina Christi esse milites iussit; dent tales provinciales, ta les maritos, tales coniuges, tales parentes, tales filios, tale dominos, tales servos, tales reges, tales iudices, tales deni que debitorum ipsius fisci redditores et exactores, quale esse praecipit doctrina christiana, et audeant eam dicer adversam esse reipublicae; imo vero non dubitent eam cor fiteri magnam, si obtemperetur, salutem esse reipublica

at the same time to form good citizens, and prepares them
to meet their obligations as members of a civil society.
This is a necessary consequence because, in the City of
God, the Holy Roman Catholic Church, a good citizen and
an upright man are absolutely one and the same thing.
How grave is therefore the error of those who separate
things so closely united, and who think that they can produce good citizens by ways and methods other than those
which make for the formation of good Christians. For, let
human prudence say what it likes and reason as it pleases,
it is impossible to produce true temporal peace and tranquillity by things repugnant or opposed to the peace and
happiness of eternity." (a)

Christian education and science

What is true of the State, is also true of science, scientific methods and scientific research; they have nothing to
fear from the full and perfect mandate which the Church
holds in the field of education. Our Catholic institutions,
whatever their grade in the educational and scientific
world, do not need to be defended. The esteem they enjoy, the praise they receive, the learned works which they
promote and produce in such abundance, and above all,
the men, fully and splendidly equipped, whom they provide for the magistracy, for the professions, for the teaching career, in fact for every walk of life, more than sufficiently testify in their favor. (a) **275 (13)**

These facts, moreover, present a most striking confirmation of the Catholic doctrine defined by the Vatican
Council: "Not only is it impossible for faith and reason to
be at variance with each other, they are on the contrary **276 (13, 17, 70)**

274a Dell'educaz. crist., lib. I, ch. 43.
275a Letter to the Cardinal Secretary of State, May 30, 1929.
   Cf. No. 238 above.

of mutual help. For while right reason establishes the foundations of Faith, and, by the help of its light, develops a knowledge of the things of God, Faith on the other hand frees and preserves reason from error and enriches it with varied knowledge. The Church, therefore, far from hindering the pursuit of the arts and the sciences, fosters and promotes them in many ways. For she is neither ignorant nor unappreciative of the many advantages that flow from them to mankind. On the contrary she admits that just as they come from God, Lord of all knowledge, so too, if rightly used, with the help of His grace, they lead to God. Nor does she prevent the sciences, each in its own sphere, from making use of principles and methods of their own. Only while acknowledging the freedom due to them, she takes every precaution to prevent them from falling into error by opposition to divine doctrine, or from overstepping their proper limits, and thus invading and disturbing the domain of Faith." (a)

277
(62, This rule of a just freedom in things scientific, serves also as an inviolable rule for a just freedom in didactic

276a Vatican Council, Session 3, Ch. 4. Neque solum fides et ratio inter se dissidere nunquam possunt, sed opem quoque sibi mutuam ferunt, cum recta ratio fidei fundamenta demonstret eiusque lumine illustrata rerum divinarum scientiam excolat, fides vero rationem ab erroribus liberet ac tueatur eamque multiplici cognitione instruat. Quapropter tantum abest, ut Ecclesia humanarum artium et disciplinarum culturae obsistat, ut hanc multis modis iuvet atque promoveat. Non enim commoda ad iis ad hominum vitam diminantia aut ignorat aut despicit; fatetur immo, eas, quemadmodum a Deo scientiarum Domino profectae sunt, ita, si rite pertractentur, ad Deum iuvante eius gratia perducere. Nec sane ipsa vetat, ne huiusmodi disciplinae in suo quaeque ambitu propriis utantur principiis et propria methodo; sed iustam hanc libertatem agnoscens, id sedulo cavet, ne divinae doctrinae repugnando errores in se suscipiant, aut fines proprios trangressae ea, quae sunt fidei, occupent et perturbent.—Denzinger 1799.

matters or for rightly understood liberty in teaching; this 95) should be observed, therefore, in whatever instruction is imparted to others. Its obligation is all the more binding in justice when there is question of instructing youth. For in this work the teacher, whether public or private, has no absolute right of his own, but only such as has been communicated to him by others. Besides every Christian child or youth is entitled to instruction in keeping with the teaching of the Church, the pillar and ground of truth. And whoever disturbs the pupil's Faith in any way, does him grievous wrong, inasmuch as he abuses the trust which children place in their teachers, and takes unfair advantage of their inexperience and of their natural craving for unrestrained liberty, at once illusory and false.

II

The subject of Christian education

It should never be forgotten that the subject of Chris- **278** tian education concerns man as a whole, soul united to *(1,* body by nature, together with all his faculties, natural and *26,* supernatural, such as right reason and revelation show him *36,* to be; man, therefore, fallen from his original estate, but *60,* redeemed by Christ and restored to the supernatural con- *72,* dition of adopted son of God, though without the preter- *76)* natural privileges of bodily immortality or perfect control of appetite. There remain, therefore, in human nature the effects of original sin, the chief of which are weakness of will and disorderly inclinations.

"Folly is bound up in the heart of a child and the rod of correction shall drive it away." (a) Disorderly inclinations then must be corrected, good tendencies encouraged and regulated from the tender age of childhood, and above all the mind must be enlightened and the will strengthened

278a Prov. 22:15.

by supernatural truth and by the means of grace, without which it is impossible to control evil impulses, impossible to attain the complete and full perfection of education intended by the Church, which Christ has endowed so richly with divine doctrine and with the Sacraments, the efficacious means of grace.

Pedagogic naturalism

279
(85,
87,
94,
97)

Every form of pedagogic naturalism which in any way excludes or weakens supernatural Christian formation in the teaching of youth, is therefore false. Every method of education founded, wholly or in part, on the denial or forgetfulness of original sin and of grace, and which relies on the sole powers of human nature, is unsound. Such, generally speaking, are those modern systems bearing various names which appeal to a claim to self-government and to unrestrained freedom on the part of the child, and which diminish or even suppress the teacher's authority and action, attributing to the child an exclusive primacy of initiative, and an activity independent of any higher law, natural or divine, in regard to his education.

If any of these terms are used, less properly, to denote the necessity of a gradually more active cooperation on the part of the pupil in his own education; if it is intended to banish despotism and violence from education, which, by the way, are not to be confused with just punishment, this would be correct, but in no way new. It would mean only what has been taught and reduced to practice by the Church in traditional Christian education, in imitation of the method employed by God Himself towards His creatures, of whom He demands active cooperation according to the nature of each; for His Wisdom "reacheth from end to end mightily and ordereth all things sweetly." (a)

279a Wisdom 8:1.

But alas! It is clear from the obvious meaning of the   **280**
words and from experience, that what is intended by not   *(94,*
a few, is the removal of education from every sort of de-   *97,*
pendence on the divine law. So today we see, strange sight *101,*
indeed, educators and philosophers who spend their lives   *107)*
in searching for a universal moral code of education, as if
there existed no decalogue, no gospel law, no law even of
nature impressed by God on the heart of man, promulgated by right reason, and revealed by God Himself in the
Ten Commandments. These innovators are wont to refer
contemptuously to Christian education as "heteronomous,"
"passive," "obsolete," because it is founded upon the authority of God and His holy law.

Such men are miserably deluded in their claim to
achieve what they call the emancipation of the child, while
in reality they are making him the slave of his own blind
pride and of his disorderly affections, which, as a logical
consequence of this false system, come to be justified as
the legitimate demands of a so-called autonomous nature.

But what is worse is the claim, not only vain but   **281**
false, irreverent and dangerous, to submit to research, ex- *(74,*
periment and conclusions of a purely natural and secular *99)*
order, those matters of education which belong to the
supernatural order; as for example, questions of priestly or
religious vocation, and in general the secret workings of
grace which indeed elevate the natural powers, but are
infinitely superior to them, and may be nowise subjected
to physical laws, for "the wind breathes where it will." (a)

Sex-education

Another very grave danger is that naturalism which   **282**
nowadays invades the field of education in that most deli- *(76,*
cate matter of purity of morals. Far too common is the   *94,*

281a John 3:8.

99)   error of those who with dangerous assurance and under
an ugly term propagate a so-called sex-education, erroneously imagining that they can arm youths against the
dangers of sensuality by purely natural means, such as
foolhardy initiation and precautionary instruction for all
indiscriminately, even in public; and, worse still, by exposing them at an early age to the opportunity, in order to
accustom them, so it is argued, and as it were to harden
them against such dangers.

Such persons grievously err in refusing to recognize
the inborn weakness of human nature, and the law of
which the Apostle speaks, warring against the law of the
mind; (a) and also in ignoring what is taught by facts,
from which it is clear that, particularly in young people,
evil practices are the effect not so much of ignorance of
intellect as of weakness of a will exposed to dangerous
occasions, and deprived of the means of grace.

283   In this extremely delicate matter, if, all things con-
(38,   sidered, some private instruction is found necessary and
78,   opportune, on the part of those who hold from God the
99)   mission to teach and who are in a state of grace, every
precaution must be taken. Such precautions are well known
in traditional Christian education, and are adequately described by Antoniano, cited above, when he says:

"Such is our misery and inclination to sin, that often
in the very things considered to be remedies against sin,
we find occasions for and inducements to sin itself. Hence
it is of the highest importance that a good father, while
discussing with his son a matter so delicate, should be well
on his guard not to descend to details, nor refer to the
various ways in which this infernal hydra destroys with
its poison so large a portion of the world; otherwise it may
happen that instead of extinguishing this fire, he unwit-
tingly stirs or kindles it in the simple and tender heart of

282a Rom. 7:23.

the child. Speaking generally, during the period of childhood it suffices to employ those remedies which produce
the double effect of opening the door to the virtue of
purity and closing the door upon vice." (a)

Co-education

False also and harmful to Christian education is the
so-called method of "co-education." This too, according to
many of its supporters, is founded upon naturalism and the
denial of original sin; according to the majority, however,
it is upon a deplorable confusion of ideas that mistakes a
leveling promiscuity and equality, for the legitimate association of the sexes. The Creator has ordained and disposed
perfect union of the sexes only in matrimony, and, with
varying degrees of contact, in the family and in society.
Besides, there is not in nature itself, which fashions the
two quite different organisms, temperaments and abilities,
anything to suggest that there can be or that there ought
to be promiscuity, and much less equality, in the training
of the two sexes. These, in keeping with the wonderful
designs of the Creator, are destined to complement each
other in the family and in society, precisely because of
their differences, which therefore ought to be maintained
and encouraged during the years of formation, with the
necessary distinction and corresponding separation, according to age and circumstances. These principles, with due
regard to time and place, must, in accordance with Christian prudence, be applied to all schools, particularly in
the most delicate and decisive period of formation, that,
namely of adolescence; and in gymnastic exercises and de-
portment, special care must be devoted to the Christian
modesty of young women and girls, which is so gravely
impaired by any kind of exhibition in public.

284
(61,
78,
94,
98)

283a Silvio Antoniano, Dell'educazione cristiana dei figliuoli,
    lib. II, Ch. 88.

Recalling the frightening words of the Divine Master: "Woe to the world because of offenses!" (a) We most earnestly appeal to your solicitude and your watchfulness, Venerable Brethren, against these pernicious errors, which, to the immense harm of youth, are spreading far and wide among Christian peoples.

III

Environment of education

285
(27,
28,
39,
44)
In order to obtain perfect education, it is of the utmost importance to see that all those conditions which surround the child during the period of his formation correspond exactly to the end proposed—in other words the combination of circumstances which we call environment.

The Christian family

The first natural and necessary element in this environment, as regards education, is the family, and this precisely because it is so ordained by the Creator Himself. Accordingly, that education which is received in a well-ordered and well-disciplined Christian family will, as a rule, be more effective and lasting, and more efficacious in proportion to the clear and constant good example set, first by the parents, and then by the other members of the household.

It is not Our intention to treat formally the question of domestic education, nor even to touch upon its principle points. The subject is too vast and besides there is no lack of special treatises on this topic by authors, both ancient and modern, well known for their solid Catholic doctrine. One which seems deserving of special mention is the golden treatise already referred to, of Antoniano, "Della

284a Matt. 18:7.

educazione cristiana dei figliuoli," which St. Charles Borromeo ordered to be read in public to parents assembled
in their churches.

Nevertheless, Venerable Brethren, and beloved chil-   **286**
dren, We wish to call your attention in a special manner to   *(44,*
the present-day lamentable decline in family education.   *96,*
The offices and professions of a transitory and earthly life   *101,*
which are certainly of far less importance, are prepared   *102)*
for by long and careful study; whereas for the fundamental
duty and obligation of educating their children, many parents have little or no preparation, immersed as they are in
earthly cares. The declining influence of domestic environment is further weakened by another tendency, prevalent
almost everywhere today, which, under one pretext or another, for economic reasons, or for reasons of industry,
trade or politics, causes children to be more and more
frequently sent away from home even in their tenderest
years. There is even a country where the children are actually being torn from the bosom of the family, to be
formed (or, to speak more accurately, to be deformed and
depraved) in godless schools and associations, in the pat-
tern of irreligion and hatred, according to the theories of
advanced socialism; and thus is renewed in a real and
more terrible manner the slaughter of the Innocents.

For the love of Our Savior Jesus Christ, therefore, We   **287**
implore pastors of souls, by every means in their power,   *(40,*
by instructions and by catechisms, by word of mouth and   *44,*
by widely distributed written articles, to warn Christian   *85,*
parents of their grave obligations. And this should be done   *86,*
not merely in a theoretical and general way, but with prac-   *92,*
tical and specific application to the various responsibilities   *93,*
of parents touching the religious, moral and civil training   *113)*
of their children, and with an indication of the methods
best adapted to make their training most effective, in addition to the influence of their own exemplary lives. The
Apostle of the Gentiles did not hesitate to descend to such

details of practical instruction in his epistles, especially in his Epistle to the Ephesians, where among other things he gives this advice: "And you, fathers, provoke not your children to anger." (a) This fault is the result not so much of excessive severity, as of impatience and of ignorance of the means best calculated to effect the desired correction; it is also due to the all-too-common relaxation of parental discipline which fails to check the growth of evil passions in the hearts of the younger generation. Parents, therefore, and all who take their place in the work of education, should be careful to make right use of the authority given them by God, whose vicars in a true sense they are. This authority is not given for their own advantage, but for the proper upbringing of their children in a holy and filial "fear of God, the beginning of wisdom," (b) on which foundation alone all respect for authority can rest securely; and without which, order, tranquillity and prosperity, whether in the family or in society, will be impossible.

The Church

288
(1,
9,
14-
16,
29,
41,
45)
To meet the weakness of man's fallen nature, God in His Goodness has provided the abundant help of His grace and the countless means with which He has endowed the Church, the great family of Christ. The Church, therefore, is the educational environment most intimately and harmoniously connected with the Christian family.

This educational environment of the Church embraces the Sacraments, the divinely efficacious means of grace, the sacred ritual, so wonderfully instructive, and the material structure of her churches, whose liturgy and art have an immense educational value; but it also includes the great number and variety of schools, associations and institutions of all kinds, established for the training of youth

287a Eph. 6:4.
287b Ps. 110:10.

in Christian piety, together with literature and the sciences, not omitting recreation and physical culture. And in this inexhaustible fecundity of educational works, how marvellous, how incomparable is the Church's maternal providence! So admirable, too, is the harmony which she maintains with the Christian family, that the Church and the family may be said to constitute together one and the same temple of Christian education.

The school

Since, however, the younger generations must be trained in the arts and sciences for the benefit and prosperity of civil society, and since the family of itself is unequal to carry out this task, it was necessary to create that social institution, the school. But let it be borne in mind that this institution owes its existence to the initiative of the family and of the Church, long before it was undertaken by the State. Hence, considered in its historical origin, the school is by its very nature an institution subsidiary and complementary to the family and to the Church. It follows logically and necessarily that it must not be in opposition to, but in positive accord with those other two elements, and form with them a perfect moral union, constituting one single sanctuary of education, as it were, with the family and the Church. Otherwise it is doomed to fail in its purpose, and to become instead an agent of destruction.

289
(21,
46,
47,
106,
107)

This principle We find recognized by a layman, famous for his pedagogical writings, though these, because of their liberalism, cannot be unreservedly praised. "The school," he writes, "if not a temple, is a den." And again: "When literary, social, domestic and religious education do not go hand in hand, man is unhappy and helpless." (a)

289a Nic. Tommaseo, *Pensieri sull'educazione*, Part 1, 3, 6.

Neutral, lay, mixed, "unique" schools

290
(102,
106,
109,
114)

From this it follows that the so-called "neutral" or "lay" school, from which religion is excluded, is contrary to the fundamental principles of education. Such a school, moreover, cannot exist in practice; it is bound to become irreligious. There is no need to repeat what Our Predecessors have declared on this point, especially Pius IX and Leo XIII, at times when laicism was beginning in a special manner to infest public schools. We renew and confirm their declarations, (a) as well as the Sacred Canons in which the frequenting of non-Catholic schools, whether neutral or mixed, those namely which are open to Catholics and non-Catholics alike, is forbidden to Catholic children, or at the most is tolerated, on the approval of the Ordinary alone, under determined circumstances of place and time, and with special precautions. (b) Neither can Catholics admit that other type of mixed schools, (least of all the so-called "école unique," obligatory to all), where the students are provided with separate religious instruction, but receive other lessons in common with non-Catholic pupils from non-Catholic teachers.

The Catholic school

291
(48,

The mere fact that a school gives some religious instruction (often extremely stinted), does not bring it into

290a Pius IX, Letter *Quum non sine,* July 14, 1864; No. 26; *Syllabus,* Prop. 48: No. 36; Leo XIII, Allocution August 20, 1880: No. 80; Encycl. *Nobilissima,* February 8, 1884, No. 44; Encycl. *Quod multum,* August 22, 1886, No. 103; Encycl. *Officio sanctissimo,* December 22, 1887, No. 109; Encycl. *Caritatis,* March 19, 1894, No. 141; etc.

290b C.I.C., Can. 1374: Pueri catholici scholas acatholicas, neutras, mixtas, quae nempe etiam acatholicis patent, ne frequentent, Solius autem Ordinarii loci est decernere, ad normam instructionum Sedis Apostolicae, in quibus rerum adiunctis et quibus adhibitis cautelis, ut periculum perversionis vitetur, tolerari possit ut eae scholae celebrantur.

line with the rights of the Church and of the Christian   72,
family, or make it a fit place for Catholic students. To be   106,
this, it is necessary that all the teaching and the whole or-   107,
ganization of the school, its teachers, syllabus and text-   115)
books of every kind, be regulated by the Christian spirit, under the direction and maternal supervision of the
Church; so that religion may be in very truth the foundation and crown of youth's entire training; and this applies
to every grade of school, not only the elementary, but the
intermediate and the higher institutions of learning as
well. To use the words of Leo XIII: "It is necessary not
only that religious instruction be given to the young at
certain fixed times, but also that every other subject taught
be permeated with Christian piety. If this is wanting, if
this sacred atmosphere does not pervade and warm the
hearts of masters and scholars alike, little good can be
expected from any kind of learning, and considerable harm
will often be the consequence." (a)

A nation of divided faith

Let it not be said that in the case of a nation where   **292**
there are different religious beliefs, it is impossible to pro-   (22,
vide for public instruction otherwise than by neutral or   106)
mixed schools. In such a case it is the duty of the State—
indeed it is the easier and more reasonable method of procedure—to leave free scope to the initiative of the Church
and the family, while giving them such assistance as justice demands. That this can be done to the full satisfaction
of families, and to the advantage of education and of public peace and tranquillity, is clear from the actual experience of some countries comprising different religious
denominations. There the school legislation respects the
rights of the family, and Catholics are free to follow their

291a Encycl. *Militantis Ecclesiae*, August 1, 1897.—Cf. No.
153.

own system of teaching in schools that are entirely Catholic. Nor is distributive justice lost sight of, as is evidenced by the financial aid granted by the State to the several schools demanded by families.

293
(112,
117)
In other countries of mixed creeds, things are otherwise, and a heavy burden weighs upon Catholics, who under the guidance of their Bishops and with the indefatigable cooperation of the clergy, secular and regular, support Catholic schools for their children entirely at their own expense; to this they feel obliged in conscience, and with a generosity and constancy worthy of all praise, they are firmly determined to make adequate provision for what they openly profess as their motto: "Catholic education in Catholic schools for all the Catholic youth." If such education is not aided from public funds, as distributive justice requires, certainly it may not be opposed by any civil authority ready to recognize the rights of the family, and the irreducible claims of legitimate liberty.

Where this fundamental liberty is thwarted or interfered with, Catholics will never feel, whatever may have been the sacrifices already made, that they have done enough, for the support and defense of their schools and for the securing of laws that will do them justice.

Catholic action in favor of the schools

294
(52,
92,
111,
117)
Whatever Catholics do in promoting and defending Catholic education for their children, is always a genuinely religious work and therefore an important task of "Catholic Action." For this reason the associations which in various countries are so zealously engaged in this work of prime necessity, are especially dear to Our paternal heart and are deserving of every commendation.

Let it be loudly proclaimed and well understood and recognized by all, that Catholics, no matter what their nationality, in agitating for Catholic schools for their children, are not mixing in party politics, but are engaged in a religious enterprise demanded by conscience. They do not intend to separate their children either from the body of the nation or its spirit, but to educate them in a perfect manner, most conducive to the prosperity of the nation. Indeed a good Catholic, precisely because of his Catholic principles, makes the better citizen, attached to his country, and loyally submissive to constituted civil authority in every legitimate form of government.

The Catholic program

In such a school, in harmony with the Church and **295** the Christian family, the various branches of secular learn- **(48,** ing will not enter into conflict with religious instruction **50,** to the manifest detriment of education. And if, when oc- **62,** casion arises, it be deemed necessary to have the students **64,** read authors propounding false doctrine, for the purpose **82)** of refuting it, this will be done after due preparation and with such an antidote of sound doctrine, that it will not only do no harm, but will be an aid to the Christian formation of youth.

In such a school, moreover, the study of the vernacular and of classical literature will do no damage to moral virtue. There the Christian teacher will imitate the bee, which takes the choicest part of the flower and leaves the rest, as St. Basil teaches in his discourse to youths on the study of the classics. (a) Nor will this necessary caution, suggested also by the pagan Quintillian, (b) in any way hinder the Christian teacher from gathering and turning to profit, whatever there is of real worth in the systems and methods of our modern times, mindful of the Apostle's advice:

295a Migne, P.G., 31, 570.
295b Inst. Or., 1, 8.

"Prove all things: hold fast to that which is good." (c) Hence in accepting the new, he will not hastily abandon the old, which the experience of centuries has found expedient and profitable. This is particularly true in the teaching of Latin, which in our days is falling more and more into disuse, because of the unreasonable rejection of methods so successfully used by that sane humanism, whose highest development was reached in the schools of the Church.

296
(62,
64,
66,
70,
82)
These notable traditions of the past require that the youth committed to Catholic schools be fully instructed in the letters and sciences in accordance with the exigencies of the times. They also demand that the doctrine imparted be deep and solid, especially insofar as concerns sound philosophy, avoiding the muddled superficiality of those "who perhaps would have found the necessary, had they not gone in search of the superfluous." (a) In this connection Christian teachers should keep in mind what Leo XIII says in a pithy sentence: "Greater stress must must be laid upon the employment of apt and solid methods of teaching, and, what is still more important, on bringing into full conformity with the Catholic faith, what is taught in literature, in the sciences, and above all in philosophy, on which depends in great part the right orientation of the other branches of knowledge." (b)

Good teachers

297
(10,
Perfect schools are not so much the result of good methods as of good teachers, teachers who are thoroughly

295c 1 Thes. 5:21.
296a Seneca, Epist. 45: Invenissent forsitan necessaria nisi et superflua quaesiissent.
296b Leo XIII, Encycl. *Inscrutabili*, April 21, 1878.—Cf. No. 64 above.

prepared and well-grounded in the subject they have to
teach; who possess the intellectual and moral qualifications required by their important office; who cherish a
pure and holy love for the youth confided to them, because
they love Jesus Christ and His Church, of which these are
the favorite children; and who have therefore sincerely at
heart the true good of family and country. Indeed it fills
Our soul with consolation and gratitude towards the Divine
Goodness to see, side by side with religious men and wom-
en engaged in teaching, such a large number of excellent
lay teachers, who, for their special spiritual advancement,
are often grouped in special sodalities and associations,
which are worthy of praise and encouragement as most excellent and powerful auxiliaries of "Catholic Action." All
these labor unselfishly with zeal and perseverance in what
St. Gregory Nazianzen calls "the art of arts and the science
of sciences," (a) the direction and formation of youth. Of
them also it may be said in the words of the Divine Master: "The harvest indeed is great, but the laborers few." (b)
Let us then pray the Lord of the harvest to send more
such workers into the field of Christian education; and let
their formation be one of the principal concerns of the
pastors of souls and of the superiors of Religious Orders.

50,
52,
56,
58,
80,
81)

Necessary vigilance

It is no less necessary to direct and watch the education of the adolescent, "soft as wax to be moulded into
vice," (a) in whatever other environment he may happen
to be, removing occasions of evil and providing occasions
for good in his recreations and social intercourse; for "evil
communications corrupt good manners." (b)

**298
(33,
80,
91,
97,
111,**

297a Horace II, Migne, P.G., 35, 426.
297b Matt. 9:37.
298a Horace, Art. poet. v. 163: cereus in vitium flecti.
298b 1 Cor. 15:33.

113)   More than ever nowadays a far-reaching and careful
vigilance is necessary, inasmuch as the dangers of moral
and religious shipwreck are greater for inexperienced
youth. Especially is this true of impious and immoral
books, often diabolically circulated at low prices; of cinema
shows and broadcasts. These most powerful means of
publicity, which can be of great utility for instruction and
education when directed by sound principles, are only too
often used as an incentive to evil passions and greed for
gain. St. Augustine deplored the passion for circus shows
which possessed even some Christians of his time, and he
dramatically narrates the infatuation for them, fortunately
only temporary, of his disciple and friend, Alipius. (c) How
often today must parents and educators bewail the corruption of youth brought about by the modern theater and
vile books!

Worthy of all praise and encouragement, therefore,
are those educational associations whose aim is to point out
to parents and educators, by means of suitable books and
periodicals, the dangers to morals and religion that are
often cunningly disguised in books and theatrical entertainments. In their spirit of zeal for the souls of the young,
they endeavor at the same time to circulate good literature
and to promote plays that are really instructive, going so
far as to put up at the cost of great sacrifices, theaters and
cinemas, in which virtue will have nothing to lose and
much to gain.

299   This necessary vigilance does not demand that young
(116) people be removed from the society in which they must
live and save their souls; but that today more than ever
they should be forewarned and forearmed as Christians
against the seductions and the errors of the world, which,
as Holy Writ admonishes us, is all "concupiscence of the

298c *Conf.,* 6, 8.

flesh, concupiscence of the eyes and pride of life." (a)
Let them be what Tertullian wrote of the first Christians,
and what Christians of all times ought to be, "sharers in
the possession of the world, not of its error." (b)

This saying of Tertullian brings us to the topic which
we propose to treat in the last place, and which is of the
greatest importance, that is, the true nature of Christian
education, as deduced from its proper end. Its consideration reveals with noon-day clearness the pre-eminent educational mission of the Church.

IV

The aim of Christian education

The proper and immediate aim of Christian education **300**
is to cooperate with divine grace in forming the true and *(26,*
perfect Christian, that is, to form Christ Himself in those *60,*
regenerated by Baptism, according to the emphatic expres- *88)*
sion of the Apostle: "My little children, of whom I am in
travail in birth again, until Christ be formed in you." (a)
For the true Christian must live a supernatural life in
Christ: "Christ Who is your life," (b) and display it in all
his actions: "That the life also of Jesus be made manifest
in our mortal flesh." (c)

For precisely this reason, Christian education takes in
the whole of human life, physical and spiritual, intellectual
and moral, individual, domestic and social, not with a view
of minimizing it in any way, but in order to elevate, regulate and perfect it, in accordance with the example and
teaching of Christ.

299a 1 John 2:16.
299b *De Idolatria*, 14: Compossessores mundi non erroris.
300a Gal. 4:19.
300b Col. 3:4.
300c 2 Cor. 4:11.

301
(26,
75,
76,
92)

Hence the true Christian, product of Christian education, is the supernatural man who thinks, judges and acts constantly and consistently in accordance with right reason illumined by the supernatural light of the example and teaching of Christ; in other words, to use the current term, the true and finished man of character. For, it is not every kind of consistency and firmness of conduct based on subjective principles that makes true character, but only constancy in following the eternal principles of justice, as is admitted even by the pagan poet when he praises as one and the same "the man who is just and firm of purpose." (a) And on the other hand, there cannot be full justice except in giving to God what is due to God, as the true Christian does.

The authentic Christian in this world

302
(60,
117)

The aim and end of Christian education as here described, appears to the worldly as an abstraction, or rather something that cannot be attained without the suppression or dwarfing of the natural faculties, and without a renunciation of the activities of the present life, and hence inimical to social life and temporal prosperity, and contrary to all progress in letters, arts and sciences, and all the other elements of civilization. To a like objection, raised by the ignorance and the prejudice of even cultured pagans of a former day, and repeated with greater frequency and insistence in modern times, Tertullian replied as follows: "We are not strangers to life. We are fully aware of the gratitude we owe to God, our Lord and Creator. We reject none of the fruits of His handiwork; we only abstain from their immoderate or unlawful use. We are living in the world with you; we do not shun your forum, your markets, your baths, your shops, your factories, your stables,

---

301a Horace, Od. I. III, od. 3, v. I: Iustum et tenacem propositi virum.

your places of business and trade. We sail and fight with you, we cultivate the land and we exchange skilled labor and display our works in public in your service. How we can seem useless to you with whom we live and of whom we are, I know not." (a) The authentic Christian does not renounce the activities of this life, he does not stunt his natural faculties; but he develops and perfects them, by coordinating them with the supernatural. He thus ennobles what is merely natural in life and secures for it new strength in the material and temporal order, no less than in the spiritual and eternal.

The fact is proved by the whole history of Christianity and its institutions, which is nothing else but the history of true civilization and progress up to the present day. It stands out conspicuously in the lives of the numerous Saints, whom the Church, and she alone, produces, in whom is perfectly realized the purpose of Christian education, and who have in every way ennobled and benefited human society. Indeed, the Saints have ever been, are, and ever will be the greatest benefactors of society, and perfect models of every class and profession, for every state and condition of life, from the simple and uncultured peasant to the master of sciences and letters, from the humble artisan to the commander of armies, from the father of a family to the ruler of people and nations, from simple maidens and matrons of the domestic hearth to queens and em- **303**
(4,
18,
88)

302a Apol., 42: Non sumus exules vitae. Meminimus gratiam nos debere Deo Domino Creatori; nullum fructum operum eius repudiamus; plane temperamus, ne ultra modum aut perperam utamur. Itaque non sine foro, non sine macello, non sine balneis, tabernis, officinis, stabulis, nundinis vestris, caeterisque commerciis cohabitamus in hoc saeculo. Navigamus et nos vobiscum et militamus, et rusticamur, et mercamur, proinde miscemus artes, operas nostras publicamus usui vestro. Quomodo infructuosi videamur negotiis vestris, cum quibus et de quibus vivimus, non scio.

presses. What shall We say of the immense work which has been accomplished even for the temporal well-being of men by missionaries of the Gospel, who have brought and still bring to barbarian tribes the benefits of civilization together with the light of the Faith? What of the founders of so many charitable and social institutions, of the vast numbers of saintly educators, men and women, who have perpetuated and multiplied their life work, by leaving behind them prolific institutions of Christian education, in aid of families and for the inestimable advantage of nations?

Conclusion

304
(14, 88)
Such are the fruits of Christian education. Their price and value are derived from the supernatural virtue and life in Christ which Christian education forms and develops in man. Of this life and virtue Christ Our Lord and Master is the source and dispenser. By His example He is at the same time the universal model, accessible to all, especially to the young, in the period of His hidden life, a life of labor and obedience, adorned with all virtues, personal, domestic and social, before God and men.

Now all this array of priceless educational treasures which We have barely touched upon, is so truly a property of the Church as to form her very substance, since she is the Mystical Body of Christ, the Immaculate Spouse of Christ, and consequently a very admirable mother and an incomparable and perfect teacher. This thought inspired St. Augustine, the great genius, the fifteenth centenary of whose blessed death we are about to celebrate, with accents of tenderest love for so glorious a mother. "O Catholic Church, true Mother of Christians! Not only dost thou preach to us, as is meet, how purely and chastely we are to worship God Himself, Whom to possess is life most blessed; thou dost moreover so cherish neighborly love and charity, that all the infirmities to which sinful souls are subject, find their most potent remedy in thee. Childlike thou art in moulding the child, strong with the young man, gentle with the aged, dealing with each according to his needs of mind and body. Thou dost subject child to parent in a sort of free servitude, and settest parent over children in a jurisdiction of love. Thou bindest brethren to brethren by the bond of religion, stronger and closer than the bond of blood.... Thou unitest citizen to citizen, nation to nation, yea, all men, in a union not of companionship only, but of brotherhood, reminding them of their common origin. Thou teachest kings to care for their people, and biddest people to be subject to their kings. Thou teachest assiduously to whom honor is due, to whom love, to whom reverence, to whom fear, to whom comfort, to whom rebuke, to whom punishment; showing us that whilst not all things nor the same things are due to all, charity is due to all and offence to none." (a)

304a De moribus Ecclesiae catholicae, lib. I, ch. 30: Merito Ecclesia catholica Mater christianorum verissima, non solum ipsum Deum, cuius adeptio vita est beatissima, purissime atque castissime colendum praedicas; sed etiam proximi dilectionem atque caritatem ita complecteris, ut variorum morborum, quibus pro peccatis suis animae aegrotant, omnis apud te medicina praepolleat. Tu pueriliter pueros, fortiter iuvenes, quiete senes prout cuiusque non corporis tantum, sed et animi aetas est, exerces ac doces. Tu parentibus filios libera quadam servitute subiungis, parentes filios pia dominatione praeponis. Tu fratribus fratres religionis vinculo firmiore atque arctiore quam sanguinis nectis.... Tu cives civibus, gentes gentibus, et prorsus homines primorum parentum recoratione, non societate tantum, sed quadam etiam fraternitate coniungis. Doces Reges prospicere populis; mones populos se subdere Regibus. Quibus honor debeatur, quibus affectus, quibus reverentia, quibus timor, quibus consolatio, quibus admonitio, quibus cohortatio, quibus disciplina, quibus obiurgatio, quibus supplicium, sedulo doces; ostendens quemadmodum et non omnibus omnia, et omnibus caritas, et nulli debeatur iniuria.

Let us then, Venerable Brethren, raise our hands and our hearts in supplication to heaven, "to the Shepherd and Bishop of our souls," (b) to the divine King "Who gives laws to rulers," (c) that in His almighty power He may cause these splendid fruits of Christian education to be gathered in ever greater abundance "in the whole world," for the lasting benefit of individuals and of nations.

As a pledge of these heavenly favors, with paternal affection We impart to you, Venerable Brethren, to your clergy and your people, the Apostolic Benediction.

CHIEF AIM OF MATRIMONY

Encycl. *Casti connubii*, December 31, 1930.

(Divine institution of matrimony.—The "benefits" of matrimony.—Offspring: bonum prolis.)

305
(7,
28,
29,
32)
The blessing of offspring implies more than the begetting of it; its proper education is also required. (a) God, for all His wisdom, would have made insufficient provision for the begotten child (and therefore for the whole human race) if those who have received from Him the power and the right to beget had not also received the right and the duty to educate the child. Clearly, even in the matter of its natural life, the child is not self-sufficient; it is still less so in regards to supernatural life. For many years it will need to be helped by others, to be instructed and educated. And there can be no doubt that, by natural and divine law the right and duty of educating offspring belong primarily to those who, having begun the work of nature by begetting children, are absolutely forbidden to

304b Cf. 1 Peter 2:25.
304c Deut. 10:17, 1 Tim. 6:15, Apoc. 19:16.
305a Procreationis autem beneficio bonum prolis haud sane absolvitur, sed alterum accedat oportet, quod debita proli educatione continetur.

leave the work they have begun and so expose it to inevitable ruin. For this most necessary task of education the best possible provision has been made in marriage, where the indissoluble bond between the parents ensures that their collaboration and mutual help in that work will be always available.

Since We have dealt at length elsewhere with the Christian education of youth (b) We may confine Ourselves to summarizing the matter here in the words of St. Augustine, which We have already quoted: "Offspring signifies that children shall be lovingly welcomed . . . and religiously educated." (c) As the Code of canon law succinctly expresses it: "The primary end of matrimony is the procreation and education of offspring." (d)

(Conjugal fidelity; the Sacrament.—Errors concerning marriage.—Remedies.)

SEX-EDUCATION

Decree of the Holy Office, March 21, 1931.

Question: May the method called "sex-education" or even "sex initiation" be approved?

Answer: No. In the education of youth the method to be followed is that hitherto observed by the Church and the Saints as recommended by His Holiness the Pope in the encyclical dealing with the Christian education of youth, promulgated on December 31, 1929. (a) The first place is to be given to the full, sound and continuous in-

306
*(69,
72,
73,
77,
99,
118)*

305b Cf. Nos. 240-304.
305c *De Genesi ad litt.*, 1. IX, c. 7, No. 12: In prole (attenditur), ut amanter suscipiatur . . . , religiose educetur.
305d C.I.C., canon 1013, 1: Matrimonii finis primarius est procreatio atque educatio prolis.
306a Encycl. *Divini illius Magistri*, December 31, 1929. Cf. above Nos. 282-283.

struction in religion of the youth of both sexes. Esteem, desire and love of the angelic virtue must be instilled into their minds and hearts. They must be made fully alive to the necessity of constant prayer, and assiduous frequenting of the Sacraments of Penance and the Holy Eucharist; they must be directed to foster a filial devotion to the Blessed Virgin as Mother of holy purity, to whose protection they must entirely commit themselves. Precautions must be taken to see that they avoid dangerous reading, indecent shows, conversations of the wicked, and all other occasions of sin.

Hence no approbation whatever can be given to the advocacy of the new method even as taken up recently by some Catholic authors and set before the public in printed publications.

(Condemnation of the Eugenic method.)

OPPOSITION, IN PRACTICE, BY THE STATE

Letter *Dobbiamo intrattenerla,* April 26, 1931, to Cardinal Schuster.

(Discourse to Jurists at Milan.)

307
(12,
25,
61,
97,
101,
102,
111)
It is claimed that the intention is to educate youth in their fathers' religion, and so far all is well; We have not hesitated to recognize how much good has been effected by proceeding and acting in this manner. Never can it be regarded as superfluous to observe that the very competence and the proper and specific authority in this field belong to the Church, and that the State has the duty not merely of following this divinely entrusted Magisterium but even of seeing that it is carried out. However, it is certainly not this that is being effected but rather the contrary, exposing youth to sentiments of hatred and irreverence, rendering the practice of religious duties difficult

and almost impossible because of other simultaneous activities, permitting public competitions of women's athletics of which even paganism showed it had understood the drawbacks and dangers.

On Our part, if We have not left and will never leave anything untried to save Catholic Action, it is also and principally in order to provide as extensively and efficaciously as possible for the salvation of youth, the predilection of the Divine Heart, by ensuring that they should not only have that *minimum* of Christian and supernatural life but also that greater abundance of life to bring which the Divine Redeemer proclaimed to have come: *Ego veni ut vitam habeant et abundantius habeant.* (a)

(Totalitarian corporative regime and Catholic Action.— Catholic, fascist regime.)

THE CHURCH AND LEARNING

Apost. Const. *Deus scientiarum Dominus,* May 24, 1931—regarding the Universities and Faculties of ecclesiastical studies.

When God, Lord of all knowledge (a), entrusted His Church with the divine task of teaching all nations (b), He set it up beyond all doubt as the infallible teacher of divine truth and, in so doing, the very patron and protector of all human knowledge. **308 (13, 17, 70)**

It is the inalienable duty of the Church to teach all men the sacred doctrines which she herself has evolved and drawn from Divine Revelation; however, since faith and human reason "cannot ever contradict one another," but rather, considering their perfect harmony, "help and complete one another," the Church has always protected

307a John 10:10.
308a 1 Sam. 2:3.
308b Matt. 28:19; Mark 16:15.

and guarded its office of instituting and assisting the teaching of the arts and sciences (c); this has always been testified to by the numerous historical documents of undeniable evidence.

In ancient Christianity

309
(16,
18)
After the primitive epoch of the Church in which the Holy Ghost, with the abundance of His charismata, directly provided the faithful with the learning which they might not have otherwise obtained; already in the second century after Christ, we find foundations of Christian learning flourishing at Smyrna, Rome, Alexandria and Edessa. Towards the end of the second century and during the third, there grew up those illustrious Universities (Athenaei) of Alexandria, Caesarea and Antioch, from which Clement of Alexandria, Origin, Saint Dionysius the Great, Eusebius of Caesarea, Saint Athanasius, Didymus the Blind, Saint Basil the Great, Saint Gregory Nazianzen, Saint Gregory of Nyssa, Saint Cyril of Alexandria, Saint John Chrysostom and Theodoret, to mention the better known, drew their knowledge. These Fathers and Ecclesiastical writers along with Saint Ephrem, Saint Hilary (of Poitiers), Saint Ambrose, Saint Jerome, Saint Augustine and other innumerable Doctors and Teachers of the Church were regarded by all members of the Civil Society as the Aristocrats of knowledge.

With the setting of the sun on the period of the Great Fathers, there sprung up numerous schools especially through the efforts of the monks and Bishops, who, in turn, were ably aided by the rulers of that time. It is undeniable that it was from these schools, built alongside Cathedrals and monasteries, that secular education and ecclesiastical teachings, during those centuries, were liberally diffused for the common good.

308c Vatican Council, *De fide catholica,* Ch. 4.

At the time of the barbarian invasions

During that period of the Middle Ages, normally **310** termed the Dark Ages, while the fine arts and letters were *(17)* being threatened with destruction by the new Barbarian invasions and being abandoned by all and left to a miserable state, they found a safe shelter and refuge, the only one left to them, in the churches and monasteries of Catholicism. The Roman Councils of 826 and 853 sanctioned the law, emerging as a *light in the darkness*, that "in every episcopacy and among the subject peoples and wherever there is need, take all care and diligence to establish masters and doctors who will impart with assiduity a training in letters and arts." Had the Roman Church in that tempestuous age not protected the ancient documents of human culture, certainly the human race would have lost forever the literary treasures passed down from antiquity.

The universities

The University of Studies, that glorious medieval in- **311** stitution, then called "Studium" or "Generale Studium," *(16,* came into contact with the Church as a most liberal mother *118)* and patron, right from its very first appearance. Indeed, even though not every university took its origin from the Catholic Church, it is, however, beyond all doubt, that almost all the Athenaei of ancient times were either the result of the direct initiative of the Roman Pontiffs or at least experienced the aid and leadership of the Popes.

In this connection, everyone is amazed when they realize exactly how much the Apostolic See has contributed to the development and progress of the sacred and secular sciences, even within the space of one century.

Of the fifty-two universities founded before 1400, no less than twenty-nine of them were created solely by the Roman Pontiffs and ten others were constituted by means of an emperor's or a prince's decree together with a papal bull. The most famous Universities which include, among others, those built at Bologna, Paris, Oxford, Salamanca, Toulouse, Rome, Padua, Cambridge, Pisa, Perugia, Lisbon, Siena, Grenoble, Prague, Vienna, Cologne, Heidelberg, Leipzig, Montpellier, Ferrara, Louvain, Bale, Cracow, Vilna Graf, Valladolid, Mexico, Alcalà de Henares, Manila, Santa Fé, Quito, Lima, Guatemala, Cagliari, Leopolis, and Warsaw, are indebted to the Roman Church for their origin, or at least for their development.

Quite often, it is true, the leaders of public affairs have gradually alienated the Church's direction and control of the Universities and schools; but, though deprived of her liberty and once-abundant means, the Church has not, by the innate exigencies of her nature, slackened for a moment in setting up and maintaining these sources of knowledge and seats of learning. On account of this innate exigency which the Church has from God, the heralds of Catholicism go to the furthest extremes in order that schools may be opened side by side with the chapels built in almost barbarous country; there sacred and secular subjects are taught, and even modern scientific means supplied so as to educate those almost primitive peoples in the first elements of letters and in the art of farming. And if one day those boasters of falsely-termed progress (on arriving in those regions made famous by the messengers of Jesus Christ), should dare to secularize the schools founded there, they will not be able to deny that these scholastic institutions, which they have snatched away, owe their origin to the Church.

Nor can it be said that the Church takes an active interest in culture only in mission countries; she does likewise, in fact more intensely, in the nations where she has been more often despoiled of her temporal inheritance.

Thus We witness great universities rising in Our days thanks to her, such as that dedicated to the Sacred Heart at Milan, the Catholic Institute of Paris, the Athenaei of Lille, Angers, Lyons, and Toulouse in France, the University of Nimega in Holland, of Lublin in Poland, of Beirut in Syria. at Washington in the United States, of Quebec, Montreal and Ottawa in Canada, of Santiago in the Republic of Chile, of Shanghai and Peking in China, of Tokyo in Japan and many others.

Preservation of books, deposits of knowledge

Another glorious proof which demonstrates how the Church has greatly favored human knowledge and culture is found in the great care taken in the continual founding and bettering of libraries. From the library of Caesarea to the Ambrosian and Vatican libraries, nobody could give even a rough estimation as to the number of manuscripts and books the Holy Mother Church has collected. It is well known that from the very first centuries of Christianity, the pastors of souls, in the fact of imminent danger, were undisturbed at the loss of all their possessions, but went to the utmost extremes to save along with the sacred vessels, these very volumes. Certainly there is not a calumny more unfounded than the claim that the Church encourages ignorance. While Catholicism does not fear persecutors, or the heresies which bring out more clearly the value of sacred teaching, there is only one thing that she does fear: ignorance of the truth. Certainly the Church's enemies will alter their attitude if they diligently study with an open mind her precepts and reasonings; as Tertullian said in the second century of those who hated the very name of Christian: "Those who put an end to ignorance will also put an end to their hate." (a)

312
(79,
116)

312a Tertullian, *Ad Nationes*, I:I Desinunt odisse qui desinunt ignorare.

Today's duties

313   Although in the past centuries Our Predecessors did
(13, not spare their efforts and their work to enrich and develop
68)   the study of the sciences and liberal arts and to set up in
many places seats of learning, they were particularly concerned with the spread of the divine doctrine as that which
is more directly connnected with the divine mission of the
Church. (a)

It is here, to the very subject of the sacred sciences,
that, well aware of the serious duty entrusted to Us by Our
Lord, We wholeheartedly turned Our thought, sincerely hoping that the Universities and Ecclesiastical Faculties, being the highest in dignity, may also shine among
other Athenaei as regards seriousness of studies and
splendor of learning.

For this reason, hardly had We been raised to the
cathedra of Supreme Pontiff, when We deemed it Our duty
to prepare a law directed to those institutes of higher studies spread throughout the world—and there are more than a
hundred of them—so that they should outline more clearly
their aims, delineate more accurately the method to be
used in training and stabilize organization in a uniform
manner; of course at the same time without impeding their
natural adaptability in different environments and in a
manner that would entirely fulfill the exigencies of these
modern times.

314   Every kind of error, to gain a wider credence, espe-
(65, cially in our times, is generally hidden under a covering
101) of knowledge, as a result of fascination that its light as
doctrine exerts over many souls. It is necessary, therefore,
that Christ's faithful, and especially these students for the
Holy of Holies, with prayers to the Father of light, (a)
and keeping in mind that sentence that "never yet did wis-

313a St. Thomas, *Summa Theol.*, p. 1, q. 1, a. 5.
314a James 1:17.

dom find her way into the schemer's heart," (b) go deeper into the sacred subjects and those that are nevertheless connected with them and so gain control of them in such a manner that, when the occasion presents itself, they may be able to teach the Catholic truth and defend it strenuously against the attacks and the sophisms of the adversary.

Certainly, on Our part We will not omit anything within Our power so that sacred subjects, as in earlier times, when they held primacy in the public Universities, will now also have the primacy, as demanded by the rich treasury of truth they impart and the influence which by their very nature they exert in confirmation of the Catholic faith, wipe out the darkness of error and bring the morals of all into keeping with the principles of the Gospel. In this manner all men, called from darkness to the marvelous light of the faith, (c) will arrive at a knowledge of the truth, (d) and every intellect, with the help of the grace of God, will be directed to the homage of God. (e)

(Norms for the ordering of the studies.—Command to observe them.)

THE STATE'S MONOPOLY OF EDUCATION

Encycl. *Non abbiamo bisogno,* June 29, 1931.

(Gratitude for the sympathy of the Bishops, of Catholic Action and of the whole world.—Previous protests against the violent measures regarding Italian Catholic Action.—Recent attacks in a public broadcast.)

We dare say that even Catholic Action itself is only **315** a pretext. That which was desired and that which was *(102)* attempted was to tear away the young from Catholic Ac-

314b Wis. 1:4.
314c 1 Pet. 2:9.
314d 1 Tim. 2:4.
314e 2 Cor. 10:5.

tion, and, consequently from the Church, and every young person at that. So true is this that, after all the talk about Catholic Action, action was taken only against the Youth Associations. Nor were these attacks limited to the Youth Associations affiliated to Catholic Action. Rough hands were laid also upon Associations of a simply devotional character, upon works of pure piety and of a primary catechetical nature, such as sodalities of the Children of Mary and Oratories. So far did this go that in many cases the grossness of the acts was recognized by the perpetrators themselves as a blunder.

(The rights of the Church and of the faithful to receive and communicate the treasures of the Redemption.)

The divine mandate of the Church

316
(5,
10,
102)
Besides, there is involved another right of the Church, equally inviolable—the right to fulfill the imperative divine mandate entrusted to her by her Divine Founder, to bring to souls, to bring to every soul, all the treasures of truth and of goodness, doctrinal and practical, which He Himself brought to the world. "Going, therefore, teach ye all nations . . . teaching them to observe all things whatsoever I have commanded you." (a)

How great is the importance of childhood and adolescence in this absolute universality and totality of the divine mandate to the Church has been shown by the Divine Master Himself, the Creator and Redeemer of souls, by His example, and particularly by those memorable words which are also so formidable: "Suffer little children and do not forbid them to come to Me.". . ."who believe in Me, for of such is the Kingdom of Heaven.". . ."whose angels always behold the face of the Father Who is in Heaven. Woe to that man who shall scandalize one of these little ones!" (b)

316a Matt. 28:19-20.
316b Matt. 19:13 ff; 18:1 ff.

Impediments placed by the state

And here We find Ourselves confronted by a mass of authentic affirmations and no less authentic facts, which reveal beyond the slightest possibility of doubt the resolution (already in great measure put into effect) to monopolize the young completely, from their tenderest years up to manhood and womanhood, to the exclusive advantage of a party and of a régime based on an ideology which clearly resolves itself into a really pagan worship of the State—the "State idolatry"—which is no less in contrast with the natural rights of the family than it is in contradiction with the supernatural rights of the Church. To propose and to promote such a monopoly—to persecute for this reason Catholic Action, as has been done for some time more or less openly or under cover; to reach this end by striking at the Catholic Associations of Youth, as has lately been done—all this is truly and literally to "forbid little children to go to Jesus Christ," since it impedes their access to His Church, and, where His Church is, there is Jesus Christ. This usurpation goes so far as to snatch the young from Christ and His Church even with violence.

317
(39, 101, 102, 109)

The precedence of the supernatural order

The Church of Jesus Christ has never contested the rights and the duties of the State concerning the education of its citizens. Indeed, We Ourselves have recalled and proclaimed them in Our recent Encyclical Letter on the Christian Education of Youth. (a) Such rights and duties are unchallengeable, as long as they remain within the limits of the State's proper competence—a competence which, in its turn, is clearly indicated and determined by the role of the State, a role which, though certainly not confined to

318
(10, 12, 14, 20, 24, 94)

318a Encycl. *Divini illius Magistri*, December 31, 1929. Cf. above Nos. 240-304 and especially No. 264 ff.

mere bodily and material things, is by its very nature limited to the natural, the terrestrial and the temporal. The universal and divine mandate with which the Church of Jesus Christ has been incommunicably and exclusively commissioned by Jesus Christ Himself, extends to the supernatural, the celestial, the eternal, and to that order of things which on the one hand, calls for the strictest obligation from every rational creature, and which, on the other hand, must, by the very nature of things, subordinate and coordinate all else to itself.

The extension of the Church's mandate

319
(15) The Church of Jesus Christ is certainly acting within her mandate, not only when she puts into souls the first indispensable beginnings and elements of supernatural life, but also when she watches over the growth of this supernatural life according to the opportunities, the capacities, and the ways and means which she deems suitable, even to the extent of preparing capable and efficient collaboration with the Apostolic Hierarchy. It was Jesus Christ Himself Who made the solemn declaration that He came in order that souls might have not only some beginning or some element of supernatural life, but that they might have it in abundance. "I have come that they may have life, and may have it more abundantly." (a) It was Jesus Christ Himself Who laid the first foundations of Catholic Action, by choosing and educating the Apostles and disciples as fellow-workers in His Divine Apostolate. And His example was at once followed by the first Holy Apostles, as Sacred Scripture itself proves.

320
(19) Therefore, it is an unjustifiable pretension, and is, indeed, irreconcilable with the name and the profession of Catholicism, to claim to teach the Church and her Head

319a John 10:10.

what is sufficient, and what must be sufficient for the education and Christian formation of souls, and for promoting,
especially among the young, the application of the principles of the Faith in social life.

To this unjustifiable presumption is added the very
clear evidence of the absolute incompetence of those who
claim these rights and their complete ignorance of the matters under discussion. Recent events must have opened the
eyes of the public since they have shown beyond dispute
that, instead of saving true religion and saving Christian
and civil education, their work has ended rather in disrup-
tion and destruction.

The insufficiency of the simple lessons
of religious instruction

You know, Venerable Brethren, Bishops of Italy, from **321**
your pastoral experience, that it is a grave and disastrous *(102,*
error to believe, and to make believe, that the work of *106,*
the Church done by Catholic Action, and through Cath- *115)*
olic Action, is superseded and made superfluous by the
religious instruction given in schools, and by the presence
of chaplains in the Youth Associations of the (Fascist)
Party and of the régime. Both are certainly necessary.
Without them the schools and the Associations would inevitably and quickly become, by logical and psychological
necessity, pagan things. Necessary, therefore, indeed they
are; but they are not sufficient. As a matter of fact, by such
religious instruction and such ecclesiastical assistance from
the chaplains, the Church of Jesus Christ can develop only
a minimum of her spiritual and supernatural efficacious-
ness and even this minimum is attained amid surroundings
and in an environment which do not depend on the Church
but are engrossed in many other kinds of teaching matters
and by many other activities in obedience to immediate
superiors, who are often little, or not at all, favorably dis-

posed towards religion, and who sometimes exercise a directly contrary influence both by their words and by the example of their lives.

Religion on paper—persecution in fact

322
(103)   We have said that recent events have proved beyond any shadow of doubt that a few years have been sufficient to cause the loss and the destruction of true religious feelings and education.

We have seen in action a kind of religion which rebels against the directives of the higher religious authorities and enjoins or encourages the non-observance of these directives; an attitude towards religion which becomes similar to persecution and which tries to destroy all that the Supreme Head of religion is known to prize and cherish most; a feeling which permits itself, and provokes others, to utter insulting words and to do injurious things against the person of the Father of all the faithful, even to the extent of shouting, "Down with the Pope!" and "Death to him!" This is real teaching of parricide. Such a sham of religion cannot in any way be reconciled with Catholic doctrine and practice, but is something that must be considered contrary to both.

The contradiction is more serious and destructive in itself when it not only consists of external actions perpetrated and carried into effect, but when it also proclaims its principles and its maxims as the fundamentals of a social system.

Condemnation of the state's monopoly of youth

323
(103,
109)   A conception of the State which makes the rising generations belong to the State entirely, without any exception, from the tenderest years up to adult life, cannot be reconciled by a Catholic either according to Catholic doctrine or to natural family rights. It is not possible for a

Catholic to accept the contention that the Church and the Pope must limit themselves to the external practices of religion (such as Mass and the Sacraments), and that all the rest of education belongs to the State.

(The unlawful oath required by the [Fascist] Party.— Fears for the future.—Prayer and hope.)

The firm foundation of the demands of the Church

... The Church of God does not deprive the State of any of its privileges, the State must not deprive the Church of her privileges, namely the sphere of Christian formation and education of youth entrusted to her not by mere human approval but by divine mandate; so the Church always has and always will demand her rights and must necessarily do so precisely because it is not dependent on human philosophies of different times and places, but rather on its divine and inviolable calling. **324 (10, 16, 20)**

(Blessing.)

THE MOST VITAL INTEREST

All. to French pilgrims of Catholic Action, May 20, 1932.

(Gratefulness and congratulations.)

We have noted with paternal joy and pride what you have done in such a short time ... all these committees: the Teaching Committee, for example, which you have so rightly placed foremost is, particularly in France (everywhere, but in France above all) and in these times, of the greatest and most vital interest. **325 (52)**

(Other committees.—Exhortations for the apostolic spirit.—Congratulations on the work done by the Pilgrimages of Notre Dame du Salut.)

WORKING CLASS YOUTH

Encycl. *Acerba animi*, September 29, 1932—on the conditions of Catholicism in Mexico.

(The evils undergone by Catholics.)

326
(4, 44, 107)

To this is added not only that religious knowledge is legally prohibited in the primary schools, but frequently an attempt has been made to force those whose duty it is to educate the coming generations to spread irreligious and immoral doctrines, thus forcing parents to make extreme sacrifices in an attempt to protect the innocence of their children. And while We warmly bless these Christian parents and all those teachers who act as their auxiliaries, We strongly recommend you, Beloved Brothers, the secular and religious Clergy, and all the faithful, to pay close attention to the scholastic problem and formation of youth, especially the youth of the poorer classes all the more so that they are the more exposed to the dangers of atheistic, Masonic and Communist propaganda; you must realize that the future of your country depends on the manner in which your children are formed.

(Rules of conduct.—Worship.—Catholic Action.—Congratulations to those openly professing the faith.)

THE LAW AGAINST
RELIGIOUS TEACHING IN SPAIN

Encycl. *Dilectissima nobis*, June 3, 1933—concerning the unjust situation of Catholicism in Spain.

(Laws on religious [creeds] and religious Congregations.—The Church can be reconciled to every form of political power.—The error of desiring to separate the

Church from the State.—The new law persecutes the Church in its teaching, in its worship, in its properties and in its Religious.)

... With the recent law, it is desired to strike yet another very serious blow against the religious Orders and Congregations by prohibiting them the power to teach. With this ruling an act of deplorable ingratitude and open-faced injustice has been committed. Why, indeed, has a class of citizens guilty solely of having embraced a life of renunciation and perfection been deprived of a right to freedom which is granted to all, to exercise the right to teach? Does this imply that to be a religious, that is, to have abandoned and sacrificed all to dedicate oneself entirely to the teaching and education of youth as to an apostolic mission, constitutes a title of incapacity or of inferiority in the art of teaching itself? And yet experience has proved with what great care and competence the Religious have carried out their duties; what magnificent results have been achieved in the training of the intellect, surpassed only by the training of the heart's sentiment, the culmination of their patient work. It is brilliantly proved by the number of persons really noted in all fields of knowledge who have graduated from the schools under the control of Religious; it is demonstrated by the increase witnessed in Spain of these schools and by the encouraging concourse of students. It is confirmed, finally, by the trust placed in them by the parents who, having received from God the right and the duty of educating their own children, are at the same time free to choose whosoever they may desire to cooperate efficaciously with them in this educational task. **327
(7,
42,
55,
57,
104)**

But this very serious act was insufficient even as regards religious Orders and Congregations. The indisputable rights of property have in like manner been denied while the free will of founders and benefactors has been **328
(101,
102,
104)**

openly violated by taking possession of the buildings with the intention of converting them into lay schools or more correctly, into Godless schools, in spite of the fact that generous donors had specified that education of an entirely Catholic nature should be imparted therein.

It is only too clear from all this that the object of these moves is to educate the future generation to a spirit of religious indifference if not of anti-clericalism, and to wrench from the young souls the traditional Catholic sentiments so deeply rooted in the good people of Spain. In this way it meant to laicize all teaching which, until now has been inspired by religion and Christian morality.

329
(74,
111-
113)
In the face of a law which is so injurious to ecclesiastical rights and liberties, rights which We must defend and preserve in their entirety, We believe it to be the duty of Our Pontifical ministry to repudiate and condemn it. Therefore, We solemnly protest with all Our power against the law itself, declaring that it cannot ever be invoked against the imprescriptible rights of the Church.

And We wish here to reaffirm Our warm trust that Our beloved sons of Spain, involved in the injustice and injury of such measures, will enlist all legitimate means which they have at their disposal, whether by nature or by legal measures, in order that they may induce the legislators themselves to reform the laws, so contrary to the rights of every citizen and so hostile to the Church, substituting for them others reconcilable to the Catholic conscience. In the meantime, however, with all Our heart and soul as Father and Shepherd, We energetically exhort Bishops and Priests and all those who are in some manner dedicated to the education of youth, to further the religious training and the practices of the Christian life more intensively with every effort and means. This is all the more necessary in that the recent Spanish legislation, with its deleterious introduction of divorce, dares to profane the sanctity of family life, thus encouraging—with the attempted dissolution of domestic society—the germs of most painful destruction of civil society.

(The faithful to work in union with Catholic Action.— Trust in God.—Blessing.)

"THE REDEMPTION FROM IGNORANCE"

All. to the National Federation for Free Education in France, March 31, 1934.

(Easter Sunday, canonization of Don Bosco, and the visit of the Federation.)

To this is added words so warm, so modest and yet so **330** eloquent in the same time with which you have put before *(119)* Us a synthesis of the entire glorious history of education which you represent here before Us in such a solemn manner, in all its levels, primary, secondary and higher education, reminding Us of the great progress which goes from 1833 to 1875, those glorious stages and great conquests which your spokesman has just related to Us.

It would undoubtedly be a great result to have impeded the ruin which the lay schools impart! But what is more, what can We say of the great good that has been done by your teaching, dear sons and daughters, of the positive good effected in such a great number of minds which you have been able to reach with your teachings, rich with Christian thought! Let it be said and already you have had good right to say it, that because of this education the major part of France has been saved or has been reconverted to Christianity. We congratulate you and all those who have labored and have dampened the path with their sweat, indeed it can well be said with the blood of their souls; this is the work of the good laborers and of those who have been martyred for the glory of the good God and the salvation of souls.

331
(51,
52,
83)
We are really happy to have you here with Us towards the close of the Holy Year. You who desire to be and are the instruments and mediators in this Redemption of which we are now celebrating the XIX centenary, are in your right places. Your office as teachers is exactly the same office as that of the Redeemer: "euntes docete." (a) This is what He said when He sent His Apostles to bring His doctrine to the world. This is your task, this is your glory, this is your great and inestimable reward; indeed it ought to be very consoling to think that in this way you enter into the plan of Redemption. It is by your work that there is effected the first redemption, the redemption from ignorance; to which work of teaching, already very rich, you have known how to unite the example of your lives—lives that are truly Christian and enriched by the treasures of Redemption. This ought to be the fruit of the Jubilee Year.

(The Redeeming Sacrifice.—Its fruit: the Christian life.)

Our desire is that Our Blessing come down upon each one of you and upon all those dear to you; above all on your friends and collaborators in this Christian training, the redeeming of souls, which is the first and last of all works; and on all those who administer, direct and work for the continuance of your organization which has the merit of being such a vital part of the Church, having such close links with the hierarchy. It is a type of Catholic Action that is very close to Our heart. Now "action" itself is in proportion to the intensity of life.

(Blessing.)

SAINT JOHN BOSCO

Homily on the occasion of the canonization of Saint John Bosco, April 1, 1934.

(Joy over this canonization.)

331a Matt. 28:19.

Although his whole life was full of great and resplend- **332**
ent deeds, We desire to set before you for admiration and *(82)*
imitation what seem to be his chief glories. Entirely devoted to the honor of God and the salvation of souls, whatever our saint knew by some instinct from above to be
required by the will of God, that he strove to execute. It
did not matter whether the matter seemed foolhardy or
not; it did not matter whether others shook their heads or
not; the saint pursued his purpose undistractedly, courageously stepping onto new paths and methods in keeping
with the changing times.

Seeing troops of children roaming the streets of Turin, **333**
abandoned by their parents and entirely uncared for, he *(16,*
gathered them paternally about him and, by every sort of *91)*
enticement, won their hearts, imparted the truths of the
Catholic religion to them, and lovingly induced them to
spend their lives in a spirit of self-discipline, of virtue, and
of the frequent reception of the Sacraments. You know
well what immense advantage there accrued to the education of the young and to their redemption from the allurements of vice, by means of what were known as the Festive
Oratories. Don Bosco founded these Oratories not only in
Turin and in neighboring cities and towns, but wherever
he introduced his religious family.

Desiring, besides, to give his great companies of growing boys and youths the means of securing a decent livelihood so as to provide for themselves and their future
children, he established those technical schools in which
they could be received and prepared for the trade for which
each was especially suited. He extended his help also to
those dedicated to the study of letters and the humanities
and opened many colleges in which, if they so willed, they
could safely advance to higher spheres of learning and
grow up, well formed to be the hope of the Church and the
Nation.

334   In this respect it may be noted that the secret of Don
(60, Bosco's success in shaping and educating the minds of the
62,   young is to be sought in his Catholic principles. His work
69,   was crowned with the happiest fruits because he aimed
92)   with buoyancy of spirit and wonderful clear-sightedness
at nothing else but the sterling education which the
Church so much commends and which We Ourselves have,
as the occasion arose, so often commended. This is an education which is wholly imbued with the teachings of the
Gospel and the sublime examples of Jesus Christ. Through
it, under the guiding light of the religious faith and the
virtues of Christianity, youthful behavior is formed and
fashioned in such wise as to become altogether worthy of
the praise belonging to excellent citizenship in one's earthly homeland and also worthy of the final, imperishable
crown which is virtue's reward in our heavenly country.

This education does not overlook the training that
makes for physical well-being, but it especially strengthens
and fortifies the soul, curbing its impetuous and disorderly
movements and turning them towards virtue. It concerns
itself with all the branches of human knowledge calculated
to promote the refinement of this present life, yet it does
not neglect the chief concern of man but firmly inculcates
the doctrine of God, the Creator and Rewarder, and insists
on the laws of His Church.

*(His two religious families.—His successes, based on
God.)*

THE MOST APOSTOLIC ACTION

All. to the Friends of St. Francis, August 31, 1935.

*(Thanks rendered to the Franciscan Teaching Pil-
grimage.)*

335   It may be truly said that teaching is the most modern
(51, form of apostolate and is the most important aspect of it.
52)   We reflected before making this statement: it is truly the
most apostolic work, the most modern form of apostolate.

It is the most apostolic: never forget this! This thought is your greatest daily consolation, which gives you strength to undergo all sufferings. Our Lord, Our King, Jesus Christ said to His Apostles: "Go ye and teach." (a) This is what you are doing. You, therefore, take direct part, and this is not mere talk but a true fact, in the mission confided to the Apostles. "Go ye and teach." (b) Thus, you unite yourselves with the first Apostles. The greatest possibilities for the apostolate opens up before you when you consider the great number of youths whom the school, the meeting-place of souls, gathers together.

(Blessing.)

THE FAMILY AND CHRISTIAN SOCIETIES

Letter of Cardinal Pacelli, Secretary of State, to His Excellency, Bishop Killian, November, 1936.

(The Australian Congress of Catholic Education.)

Any thoughtful person realizes, and history proves it irrefutably, that the foundations of civil society necessarily collapse with the decadence of the Christian institutions and Christian standards; while, on the other hand, the renewal of the Evangelical spirit constitutes an adequate remedy even for inveterate evils, and leads to the attainment of the highest and fullest perfection of individual, family and civic conditions. This, in any case, is perfectly natural. **336 (92)**

Christianity and civilization

The Church, being the great Teacher of mankind, firmly and faithfully defends the integrity of those principles on which the duties of everyone, at all times, and everywhere, are based, suggesting the more effective rea- **337 (18, 92)**

335a Matt. 28:19.
335b Matt. 28:19.

sons for leading an honest life, and pointing out, as the goal of virtue, a happiness which lies outside the brevity and fragility of earthly life. Although the Church tends towards heavenly things, she by no means hinders or condemns the progress of those resources which lead to temporal well-being, and neither does she condemn that which develops natural talent, perfects manners, and strengthens the body so as to render it more capable of carrying out with greater perfection the good works of the spirit and that which supplies life's innocent pleasures; all that regards art and literature, the enterprises and institutions useful to human society, all that is honest and lawful has not only never found impediments of any kind in the Church but rather its beginning or valuable aid. It seems to be a fact established by a wonderful design of Divine Providence that at the moment when the divine flame—Christ crucified—shone from the torch, civilization and culture worthy of the name sprang up, like a precious herb entwined about the trunk of the Cross, a fruit ripening at the side of the Cross, a light surrounding the Cross, a dignity flowering in the life of mankind from the tree of life.

338
(2,
12,
26)
However, all these resources, falling within the confines of nature, though useful and praiseworthy, are insufficient to satisfy a soul created for higher things. Our soul, in fact, tends towards God, Who is not attained by material means, but by means of knowledge and love. This, the principal and necessary thing, is handed down to men by the Church only, which has been set up by divine will as the Holy City of the living God; the Church perfects minds with the truth received from Heaven, and she perfects wills by charity, in such a manner that she unites men to the Highest Truth, and the Highest Good, without in the slightest falling short of her purpose, for with the light of doctrine and the strength of grace the Church teaches by helping, and helps by teaching, disposing in a marvelous order the duties of the faithful to guide them, since the

fulfillment of the divine will and the observance of the law are the means for attaining the reward of eternal happiness.

The true Christian

Who is wiser, nobler and stronger than the follower of the Church, than he who is aware of his duties? He submits his mind to God, Ruler of the universe, and, allured by celestial promises, patiently resists the enticements of this perishable life, and does not permit his mortal body, destined to be the instrument and weapon of justice, to become the seal of sin; in such a manner he has a foretaste of heavenly things, since "man rejoices in peace and true liberty, when the flesh is subject to the spirit which judges, and when the spirit is subject to God Who controls." (a) In all that he thinks, in all that he says, in all that he does, be it in public or in private, he always regulates himself so as to have the truth as ruler, love as law and eternity as a goal. **339** *(92)*

The Christian family

Such being the Catholic formation, the great abundance of good derived for the formation of society and domestic life cannot fail to be realized by all. Matrimony is not contracted for the satisfaction of fleshly desires, but for the procreation and education of children, who are taken from God and for whom account will have to be rendered. The foundations of the domestic home cannot be undermined since, till the death of one of the couple, the matrimonial contract continues to hold good, so that the pledged faith, chastity and the fear of God keep impure wickedness at bay. Paternal power is suitably tempered in view of the dignity of the wife and children; children, moreover, consider sacred the homage of obedience to be **340** *(92)*

339a St. Leo the Great, Sermo I de quadrag., No 2: *Tunc est vera pax homini et vera libertas quando et caro animo judice regitur et animus Deo praeside gubernatur.*

rendered not because of threats and force, but as a duty of conscience—a duty born of the reflected authority of God in parents.

What is more beautiful, more joyful, greater than the peace of a home resting on the dictates of Catholic education! The offspring grow up happily, and their number is determined not by disgraceful calculations but by the providence of God Who blesses the nuptial bed. The married, loving one another reciprocally, are fully united in the love for their children, and as a reward for their care, are encouraged by signs of a virtue which proudly reflects ancestral habits. The father's hard work is softened by the thought that the children are amusing themselves at home, while not even the night brings with it a slackening of the care and attention of the mother. With what a smile, with what feeling, the mother, holding the little children on her knees as they babble their first words, made all the more sweet by the stumbling tongue, suggests for their inexpert lips the sublime and adorable name of Jesus! A family formed in the Catholic spirit does not complain of poverty, is not ungrateful in times of abundance, convinced that, whatever be their lot, favorable or otherwise, there is always constancy of soul to be practised; and even when faced by want, they always find something to give, never ceasing to desire only what is good.

Christian Society

341
(31,
92)   If these things contribute in such a great measure to the well-being of cities, individuals, too, when they dutifully and faithfully observe the rules of Catholic education, become excellent citizens, be it in time of war or of peace. The very precept of love of God, which is the peak of religious teaching, bears most excellent fruit and does so spontaneously of its very nature, namely, love of one's neighbor which is the nursery and source of all social virtues. Forgiveness of offenses, generosity, kindheartedness

and benignity are the characteristic virtues of the follower of the Gospel, virtues which once aroused such admiration among the pagans that they were almost enraptured by the new marvel, and very speedily embraced the Christian religion.

To this charity is added also respect for justice. Let every honest and competent person, then, who has civil prosperity and dignity at heart, reflect what great utility and tranquility is offered to the State by education taught according to the spirit and directives of the Church. In fact, for him who professes the Catholic religion, it is a sacred and inviolable matter to give everyone his due, to honor the nation and the authorities who rule it; to turn a willing ear to governors, to render them obedience, fidelity and devotion, not unlike that which is given by children to their parents; to respect the law; to avoid all revolts, zealously to defend public order; to devote oneself with unlimited diligence and dedication to the glory and prosperity of the nation.

... The Adelaide Congress which stands out so solemnly because of the number of holy Prelates and priests, the crowds of people, the holy ceremonies, the debates and conferences, should prove itself fruitful to Australia, and should serve as an example to the entire world, a warning to all peoples, reminding them that, by abandoning Christ they commit the worst of errors and plunge themselves into ruin, while those adhering to Him with unshakeable faith and hope will reap the most sublime benefits. Indeed Jesus Christ leads the way to a holy existence, the truth of a divine teaching, and a life of eternal happiness; the light of the world, the only Master of men Who, having set up the Church as a pillar and support of the truth, teaches us and outwardly trains us with the infallible teaching of the Church, while internally, in the intimacy of the heart, He instructs us by the secret light of grace every time that the whisper of His divine voice, which speaks without sound,

342

(92,
107)

is heard by a clear conscience, with a genuine faith and in the noble silence of the mind that meditates and prays.

(The Holy Father's blessings for the Congress.)

NAZISM AND YOUTH

Encycl. *Mit brennender Sorge,* March 14, 1937—to the Bishops of Germany, dealing with Nazism.

(The Concordat with the Reich.—Faith in a personal God, in Jesus Christ, in the Church.—Distorted Christian concepts.)

343   The number of those fools, who today attempt to sepa-
(94,   rate morality and religion, has become legion. They do not
107)   or will not see that by expelling confessional teaching, that is, clear and definite Christianity, from instruction and education, from the formation of social and public life, they are paving the way for spiritual impoverishment and decline. No coercive power of the State, no mere earthly ideals, though they be high and noble in themselves, will be able in the long run to replace the final and decisive influence that comes from belief in God and Christ.

(Moral.—The natural law.)

Force violates the law

344   Conscientious parents, aware of their duty in the mat-
(9,   ter of education, are entitled, in the spirit of the true faith
109)   and in conformity with its principles and its ordinances, to decide upon the education of the children given to them by God. Laws or other regulations concerning education that disregard the rights of parents guaranteed to them by the natural law, or that by threat and violence nullify those rights, contradict the natural law and are utterly and essentially immoral.

The Church, whose mission is to guard and interpret the natural law, cannot do otherwise than declare that the registrations which have just taken place in circumstances of notorious coercion are the result of violence and void of all legality.

An attempt to put the Church and the nation at variance

As the representative of Him Who said to the young **345** man of the Gospel: "If thou wilt enter into life, keep the *(116)* commandments," (a) We especially address fatherly words to young people.

By a thousand tongues today a Gospel is preached in your ears that is not revealed by your heavenly Father. A thousand pens write in the service of a sham Christianity of Christ. Day by day the press and radio overwhelm you with broadcasts that are hostile to your faith and Church and, with no consideration or reverence, attack what should be sacred and holy to you. We are well aware that many of you have had to undergo difficult periods of misunderstanding, suspicion, slander, accusations of anti-patriotism and many losses in your social and professional lives, all this because of your devotion to the faith and the Church and because of your membership in the religious associations protected by the Concordat. We also know that many of Christ's unknown soldiers are to be found in your ranks and that, with weary hearts but with heads held high, they readily carry their burdens, rejoicing in the thought that they had been found worthy to suffer in the Name of Christ. (b)

Today, when new perils and conflicts threaten, we say to these young people: "If anyone preach to you a gos-

345a Matt. 19:17.
345b Acts 5:41.

pel that is contrary to that which you have received, a curse
be upon him:" (c)

346   If the State founds a national youth association to
(25) which all are obliged to belong, then it is—without prejudice to the rights of Church associations—an inalienable
and obvious right of the young themselves, and of their
parents responsible for them before God, to demand that
this obligatory organization should be cleansed of all tendencies hostile to Christianity and the Church; these tendencies, from the recent past and even of the present, place
these faithful parents in a somewhat difficult conscientious
quandary, as they cannot give the State what it is asking
of them without depriving God of what belongs to Him.

National heroism—Christian heroism

347   No one has any intention of obstructing the youth of
(25, Germany on the road that is meant to bring them to the
95, realization of a real national unity and to promote a noble
117) love of liberty and an unshakable devotion to the fatherland. It is against an intentional and systematically fo-
mented opposition between these educational and religious
aims that We must necessarily protest. Consequently We
say to youth: sing aloud your songs of freedom, but do not
forget that true freedom is that of the sons of God. Do not
permit the nobility of this irreplaceable freedom to be en-
slaved in the servile chains of sin and lust. Those who sing
patriotic songs to the fatherland are not permitted to become traitors and to be unfaithful to God, the Church and
the Eternal Fatherland.

348   So much is spoken about the greatness of heroism,
(102, in designed and false contrast to evangelical humility and
109) patience; but why obscure the fact that heroism is possible also in the moral struggle, and that the preservation of

245c Gal. 1:9.

baptismal innocence constitutes a heroic action which ought to be calculated according to its merits both in the religious and natural spheres? Much is spoken about human frailty throughout the history of the Church; but why hide those great feats which occur in the Church throughout the centuries, the saints she has produced and the profit she has brought to Western culture by the vital union between the Church and your people?

Again, much is said of sport which, when used to a **349** reasonably moderate extent, is of great benefit to the *(61)* young. However today it has been extended so as to entail much that does not take into account the harmonious formation of the body and the spirit, nor the resultant care of family life nor the commandment to keep holy the Sabbath day. With a sense of indifference which borders on contempt, Sunday, contrary to the best German traditions, has been deprived of its holy and reserved character. We trustingly expect from German youth that in the difficult circumstances of obligatory State organization, they will openly vindicate their right to keep Sunday holy in a Christian manner and We trust that the attention given to the strengthening of their bodies will not make them neglect their immortal souls, that they will not let themselves be beaten by this evil and will strive to conquer it by good (a) and that they will attain their highest and most noble ideal—to win the crown of victory in the stadium of eternal life. (b)

(Priests.—Religious.—Faithful.)

Responsibilities of Christian parents

We address a particularly cordial greeting to Catholic **350** parents. At present their rights and duties as regards the *(112,*

349a Cf. Rom. 12:21.
349b Cf. 1 Cor. 9:24 ff.

115) education of the children entrusted to them by God are being attacked in a manner worse than which would be difficult to imagine. The Church of Christ cannot commence to complain and deplore only when the altars are already stripped and sacrilegious hands have burned down the sanctuaries. When it is sought with an anti-Christian education to profane the tabernacles of the children's souls sanctified by Baptism, when the light of faith in these temples of God is forcibly replaced by a false light as a substitute which has absolutely no connection with the faith of the Cross, then the spiritual profanation of the temple is near; then it is the duty of every professing Christian to separate clearly his responsibility from that of the other side as well as to keep his conscience clear of any culpable cooperation in such dreadful work and corruption. And the more the enemy attempts to deny or disguise his shameful aims, the more necessary is it to adopt an attitude of mistrust and suspicious vigilance, encouraged by bitter experience. The formal preservation of religious instruction, especially when controlled and shackled by incompetent people, in the atmosphere of a school which, in the teaching of other subjects, works systematically and invidiously against religion, can never be a justification for a believing Christian to give his free approval to such a school that aims at destroying religion.

351
(24,
29)
We realize, beloved Catholic parents, that there can be no question of such willingness on your part. We know that a free and secret ballot would in your case be equivalent to an overwhelming vote for the religious school. And therefore we shall not weary in the future of representing to responsible parties the injustice of the coercive measures so far adopted, and the obligation of allowing free expression of a free will. In the meantime, keep this in mind: no earthly power can release you from the divine responsibility which unites you to your children. None of those who, today, are suppressing your right in the matter

of education and pretending to free you from your duty in this matter, will be able to reply for you to God Almighty when He asks: "Where are those whom I have entrusted to you?" Let each one of you be able to reply: "I have not lost any of those whom You have entrusted to me." (a)

(Hope for better days.—Blessing.)

THE WAY OPEN TO COMMUNISM

Encycl. *Divini Redemptoris,* March 19, 1937—theme on Communism.

(Communist doctrine.—The Church's doctrine.—Remedies to be applied.—The duty of the clergy, the faithful and the State.)

Everywhere today there is an anguished appeal to **352** moral and spiritual forces; and rightly so, for the source *(107,* of the evil we must combat is primarily an evil of the *110)* spiritual order, and it is from this polluted source that the monstrous emanations of the communist system flow. Now, the Catholic Church is undoubtedly pre-eminent among the moral and religious forces of today. Therefore the very good of humanity demands that her work be allowed to proceed unhindered.

Those who act otherwise, and at the same time fondly pretend to attain their objective with purely political or economic means, are in the grip of a dangerous error. When religion is banished from the school, from education, and from public life, when the representatives of Christianity and its sacred rites are held up to ridicule, are we not really fostering that materialism which is the fertile soil of communism?

(The erring recalled.—Saint Joseph, model and patron.)

351a John 18:9.

CATHOLIC ACTION AND
THE FORMATION OF YOUTH

Encycl. *Firmissimam constantiam*, March 28, 1937—
on the conditions of Catholicism in Mexico.

*(Christian Restoration.—The Formation of Priests and
the Laity of Catholic Action.—Social Action.)*

353
(66,
69,
72,
90)
Catholic Action ... must carefully look after students
who one day, as professional men, will have great influence
on society and quite possibly will occupy public positions.
Together with the practice of the Christian religion and the
formation of a Catholic mind and conscience which form
the fundamental elements common to all the faithful, you
must also associate a very special and precise intellectual
training and formation, or in other words that which is
called a perennial philosophy. Today, in fact, a solid and
adequate religious instruction seems more than ever necessary because of the tendency, always more generalized of
modern life towards externals, the difficulty of and the repugnance toward reflection and meditation, indeed the pro-
pensity even in the spiritual life to allow oneself to be
guided by sentiment rather than by reason.

We ardently desire that the praiseworthy efforts on
the part of Catholic Action in other countries to see to it
that cultural and religious instruction occupy an intellectual pre-eminence among Catholic students and graduates,
be undertaken also by you, insofar as is possible, suiting the
instruction to the particular necessities, conditions and possibilities of your own country.

354
(90)
The University students who serve in the ranks of
Catholic Action give Us great hopes of a better future for
Mexico, and We have no doubt that they will prove themselves worthy of the hopes We place in them. It is quite
evident that they form an important part of Catholic Ac-

tion, which is so dear to Our hearts, no matter in what form it may be organized, as this depends in great part on local conditions and circumstances, which vary from one country to another. These University students not only offer Us great hopes for a better tomorrow, as We have stated above, but right now they can render effective service to the Church and to the Fatherland, whether it be by means of that apostolic work they carry out among their companions, or by means of the capable and enlightened leadership they give to the various branches and associations of Catholic Action.

Children

The particular conditions of your country oblige Us to remind you of the necessary, indispensable and fitting care that must be devoted to children whose innocence is in danger and whose Christian formation and education is undergoing such a severe trial. **355** *(97, 111- 114, 116)*

All Mexican Catholics have two grave obligations. The first, which is negative, is to keep the children far away from impious and corrupted schools; the second, which is positive, is to provide them with careful and seeming assistance and religious instruction. As regards the first obligation, which is so grave and so delicate, We had occasion only recently to make known Our thoughts about it. The second obligation, which deals with religious instruction, although We are aware that you yourselves have insistently brought it to the notice of both priests and people, We still desire to repeat it to you, since it is one of the most important and capital problems that confronts the Church today in Mexico. It is necessary that what has already been done in such a praiseworthy manner in certain dioceses be extended to all of them so that the priests and active members of Catholic Action may give themselves ardently and without counting the cost in order that these young children on whom our divine Savior showered many signs of predilection be kept safe for God and for the Fatherland.

The future of these coming generations—We repeat it with all the anguish of Our paternal heart—awakens in Us a great anxiety and a deep solicitude. We are aware of the great dangers to which young people are exposed, now more than ever, and most especially so in Mexico, where an immoral and anti-religious press sows in their hearts the seeds of apostasy from Christ. To remedy such grave evil and protect your young children from such dangers it is necessary to take every legal means and make use of every form of organization, such as the Association of "Fathers of Families," the morality and vigilance committees for publications and censorship of cinema.

356   As regards the personal defence of the individual, We
(111) are well aware, by means of the various testimonies We receive from many parts of the world, that service in the ranks of Catholic Action offers the best fortress against the wiles of the evil one, the most perfect school of virtue and of purity, the most efficacious training-ground of Christian fortitude. It is these very youths who, enraptured by the Christian ideal, succored by the divine Grace of which they are assured through prayer and the Sacraments, will dedicate themselves with ardor of spirit and with joy to win over the souls of their companions, harvesting thereby many consoling rewards of goodness.

(Civic activities.)

THE FIRST APOSTOLATE
OF CATHOLIC ACTION

Letter *Cor singular*, January 18, 1939—to the Bishops of the Philippine Islands.

(Recalling the XXXIII International Eucharistic Congress.—Dedication of the Clergy and Religious.)

We must nevertheless sorrowfully admit that despite your diligent and assiduous attention there is still being enacted to the loss of many souls in that region, as unfortunately in many others, a silent war and at times an open battle against what is most precious to Holy Mother Church, with great injury to souls. The safety of the family has been shaken to its foundations by the frequent attacks against the sanctity of marriage; the Christian education of youth, hindered here as in other nations today, and at times neglected, is now seriously compromised by errors against faith and morals and by calumny against the Church represented as the enemy of progress, freedom and the common good; civil society itself is threatened by the wicked propaganda of subversive theories of every social order. **357** *(97, 106)*

(Catholic Action is Catholic life; its fate depends on the clergy.—Defense of the family.)

Religious instruction

Since religious instruction is the essential prelude to the supernatural life, it ought to be the first apostolate to which Catholic Action will give its full co-operation. (a) **358** *(58, 89, 111)*

This catechetical apostolate appears more necessary and more urgent in view of the present condition of your

---

358a Siendo la instrucción religiosa como el preludio necesario de la vida sobrenatural, debe ser la primera actividad de apostolado, a que la Acción Catolica prestará su sincera cooperación.

country and others where various factors contribute to the lack of religious formation in city and country youth.

It rests on you, Venerable Brethren, to call on the able assistance of Catholic Action in the enormous task of religious instruction.

(Multiply catechists and catechism schools.)

This apostolate of Christian education, necessary also as a remedy, within limits, for the deficiencies of public schools in religious matters, will be more effective if regulated by a unity of directives; thus it will be necessary to establish co-ordinating centers for this activity as a whole in relation to the national bodies of Catholic Action.

Students

359
(68, 82, 90, 101)
University students, who are very numerous, deserve special attention on the part of Catholic Action. They, in fact, represent the future leaders of society in the various fields of culture, trade, industry and public affairs. But, unfortunately, during this formative period of their lives they are often exposed to grave dangers. It may seem a very difficult undertaking to try to penetrate and exercise a salutary influence on university life, but the very difficulty of the task should be an incentive to set out on this work with great generosity of heart and complete abandonment to the help of divine grace, which can triumph over all obstacles.

360
(79, 90)
Experience has shown Us that ardent youths with an apostolic spirit, even in the midst of a multitude of indifferent and sometimes ill-disposed persons, can, by their virtue and open profession of faith, little by little become centers of attraction to their fellow students and apt instruments for the salvation of souls.

It is therefore of great importance that associations of students shall be established in every center of higher studies, which will strive not only to form perfect Christians who will be faithful to Christian moral principles in the exercise of their profession, but likewise active apostles in their own sphere of life.

The pupils of secondary schools ought also to be the object of special assistance in the spiritual order: and, in regard to this, We repeat to you, also, Venerable Brethren, the recommendation made to others, namely, the establishment of groups of Catholic Action in colleges and Catholic schools for boys and girls, in cooperation with the respective directors. The considerable results obtained through these internal associations where they have existed for many years should be an incentive to establish them everywhere. We do not doubt that the religious men and women who direct the colleges and establishments of Catholic students with so much care will respond with perfect docility to Our appeal and yours. They will wish to add new merits to those already acquired. **361** *(90)*

(Urge the cultured also to play a part in Catholic Action.)

We believe it necessary here to re-emphasize the great importance of the annual retreat and the monthly recollection for the spiritual progress of university students and persons of culture, and for strengthening them in the spirit of the apostolate. We, therefore, repeat the earnest exhortations expressed in Our Encyclical *Mens Nostra*. **362** *(88)*

(The working class.)

The mass media

It is known that the enemy of all good, who has always many faithful followers in the world, has made of every scientific discovery an instrument of ruin and death for souls. **363** *(91, 97, 113)*

It is sufficient to point out the great spiritual slaughter caused by the anti-religious or simply neutral press, by film and by the radio, all of which ought to be means of education and enlightenment for the people.

Now, Venerable Brethren, in Our encyclical on the Christian education of youth of December 31, 1929, We earnestly exhorted Catholics to circulate "good literature and to promote performances that are really educational, even going so far as to put up, at the cost of great sacrifices, stage and motion picture theaters in which virtue will have nothing to suffer and much to gain." (a) What is more, always pay great attention to the growing ruin that is being caused by films; We have never doubted it and, as you know, We have made it the subject of an entire encyclical in *Vigilanti cura*, of June 29, 1936.

(Co-ordination of activities.)

363a Cf. above, No. 298.

PIUS XII
1939-1958

CHILDREN'S COMMUNION

All. to newly-weds, June 7, 1939.

*(The effects of the Blessed Eucharist in married life.—
Set the example of frequent Communion.)*

The children will arrive, those small sons and daughters, whom you will rear and educate in your faith, in the belief in and love of the Blessed Eucharist and, prepare them early for the reception of Holy Communion, convinced that there is no better means of safeguarding the innocence of your young ones. You will lead them with you to the altar to receive Jesus and your example will be their most eloquent and convincing lesson. **364 (34, 39, 73)**

(Blessing.)

A MOTHER FORMS A SAINT

All. to newly-weds, June 21, 1939.

(The children's happiness is the parents' happiness.)

Now, O beloved newly-weds, your children's joy and happiness rests mainly in your hands as it is connected with the education which you will impart to them in the home right from the very first hours of their lives. **365 (28, 36, 88)**

It is today that we are celebrating the feast of Saint Aloysius Gonzaga, Christian youth's most brilliant glory. Undoubtedly God's grace abundantly endowed this privileged soul with extraordinary gifts right from his very early years; but it is none the less certain that God found a responsive, gentle and industrious cooperator in Martha, the very fortunate mother of our lovable Saint. A mother who fully responds to the sublimity of her calling as educator is capable of so much!

366   To help you in the carrying out of this mission, We
(88) would like to point out this angelic youth as a model which
you ought to propose to the children God will bestow on
you, and as a Patron to whose care and protection you will
entrust these pledges of your love.

Certainly, times, customs and aspects and methods of
education have changed; but the real and genuine figure
of Aloysius Gonzaga remains and will always remain the
sublime model whose example and directives are adaptable
to the young of all times. It is on account of this that Our
Predecessor Pius XI, of venerable memory, confirming the
previous decrees of Benedict XIII and Leo XIII, wanted
again to proclaim solemnly that Aloysius Gonzaga is the
Patron of all Christian youth. (a) And reuniting this most
elect part of the human family under his guidance and protection, he strongly exhorted it and paternally besought it
to concentrate its attention on that marvellous youth, a
masterpiece of nature and grace, who, to the rapid achievement of a consummate sanctity, consecrated his natural
talent, strength of character, force of will, hard work, and
generous renunciation and was an authentic angel of purity
and a martyr of charity.

*(An invitation to pray before his relics in the Church
of Saint Ignatius in Rome.)*

FAITHFUL ADAPTATION TO THE IDEAL

All. to the Regular Canonesses of St. Augustine, of the
Roman Union, July 21, 1939.

(Welcome and Praise.)

367   You have remained, and doubtless intend to remain,
(30, faithful to the spirit of your founders: "I want," said Our

366a Letter, *Singulare illud,* June 13, 1926; see above Nos.
214-227.

Lord to His servant Alice le Clerc, "the little souls, which
are like little children abandoned by their mother, to have,
from now on, a mother in you." How many parents today,
even if they still think about the health and temporal future of their children, completely neglect their souls! It is
for these souls that you labor, treating, according to another phrase that you know, "the poor children as your sisters, and applying yourselves to the education of the rich,
in order to make them humble." Are these last phrases not
enough to show that yours is always a mission of current
interest: to give a Christian education to poor girls, to give
them the heart of a sister, free from class-hatred and national antagonisms; to give a Christian education to rich
girls, to teach them modesty of demeanor, of apparel, of
language, of their very feelings? *66,
77)*

But since a tradition of three centuries runs the risk of
remaining inert or deficient in its application, if it is not
revitalized by the breath of progress and adaptation, We
are glad to see that, while remaining substantially faithful
to the origins of the Institute, the Congregation of Our
Lady has assumed a new form in the twentieth century. In
a world thirsting for education and in the face of young
women threatened, in many countries, to be blinded by
the glare of an atheist education, you have seen the necessity of a unification of your different centers, in order to
coordinate and distribute with more profit your combined
intellectual resources, with the help of a general Superior. **368**
*(56,
58)*

*(Be like unto daughters of the Church.—A charming
nickname: Le Oiseaux.)*

EDUCATION AND CITIZENSHIP

Encycl. *Summi Pontificatus,* October 20, 1939.

*(The Reign of Christ in our times.—Origin of present-
day evils: rejection of all universal laws of morality; neg-*

lect of the natural law; total secularization; no heed paid to ties of necessity and charity existing among men.—The State before God and man.)

369
(8,
109)
There would even be a danger lest the primary and essential cell of society, the family, with its well-being and growth, should come to be considered from the narrow standpoint of national power and lest it be forgotten that man and the family are by nature anterior to the State, and that the Creator has given to both of them powers and rights and has assigned them a mission and a charge that correspond to undeniable natural requirements. (a)

The education of the new generation in that case would not aim at the balanced and harmonious development of physical powers and of all the intellectual and moral qualities, but at a one-sided formation of those civic virtues that are considered necessary for attaining political success, while the virtues which give society an air of nobility, humanity and reverence would be inculcated to a lesser extent, for fear they should detract from the pride of citizenship.

(Present-day family difficulties.—The State has the right to intervene still more for its good, but according to the order established by God.)

370
(21,
25,
30,
66,
94,
107,
109)
The charge laid by God on parents, to provide for the material and spiritual well-being of their offspring and to procure for them a suitable training, imbued with the true spirit of religion, cannot be wrested from them without grave violation of their rights. Undoubtedly, that formation should aim as well at preparing youth to fulfill with intelligence, conscientiousness, and pride those duties of noble patriotism, which gives to one's earthly fatherland all due measure of love, self-devotion and service. On the other hand, a formation which forgets or, worse still, deliberately

369a Encycl. *Divini illius Magistri;* cf. above No. 257 ff.

fails, to direct the gaze and the desire of youth to their heavenly fatherland would be an injustice to youth, an injustice to the inalienable duties and rights of the Christian family and an excess for which a remedy must be found in the interests of the people and of the State itself. Such an education might perhaps appear to those responsible for it, a source of increased strength and vigor; it would, in fact, be the opposite, as sad experience would prove. The crime of high treason against the "King of kings and Lord of lords" (a) perpetrated by an education that is either indifferent or opposed to Christianity, the reversal of "suffer the little children to come unto Me" (b) would bear most bitter fruits. On the contrary, the State which dispels the anxiety from the bleeding and torn hearts of fathers and mothers and restores their rights, only promotes its own internal peace and lays the foundations of a happy future for the country.

The souls of children, given to their parents by God and consecrated in baptism with the royal character of Christ, are a sacred charge over which the jealous love of God watches. The same Christ Who pronounced the words, "Suffer little children to come unto Me" (a) has, for all His mercy and goodness, threatened with fearful evils those who offend the ones so dear to His Heart. Now what greater harm can be done to generation after generation, than a formation of youth which is misdirected towards a goal that leads away from Christ "the way, the truth and the life" and leads to open or hidden apostasy from Christ? That Christ, from Whom they want to alienate the youthful generations of today and tomorrow, is the same Christ Who has received from His eternal Father all power in heaven and on earth. He holds in His omnipotent hand the **371** (5, 29, 107, 109)

370a 1 Tim. 6:15; Apoc. 19:16.
370b Mark 10:14.
371a Mark 10:14.

destiny of States, of peoples, of nations. His it is to shorten or prolong life: His to grant increase, prosperity and greatness. Of all that exists on the face of the earth, only the soul is immortal. A system of education that did not respect the sacred precincts of the Christian family, protected by God's holy law, that attacked its foundations, barred to the young the way to Christ, to the Savior's fountains of life and joy, (b) that considered apostasy from Christ and the Church as a proof of fidelity to the people or to a particular class would pronounce its own condemnation and experience in due time the inescapable truth of the prophet's word: "They that depart from Thee, shall be written in the earth." (c)

(Remedies in Catholic doctrine.—Conclusion.)

CHRISTIAN AND NATURALISTIC EDUCATION

Encycl. *Sertum laetitiae*, November 1, 1939—to the Bishops of the United States.

(The hundred and fiftieth anniversary of the constitution of the Hierarchy.—The first Bishop.—Progress of the Church.)

372
(92) It is with good reason that visitors from other lands admire the organization and system under which your schools of various grades are conducted, the generosity of the faithful upon whom they depend, the vigilant care with which they are watched over by the directors. From these schools comes forth a host of citizens, strong in heart and mind, who by reason of their reverence for divine and human laws are justly considered to be the strength and the flower and the honor of Church and country.

371b Is. 12:3.
371c Jer. 17:13.

(Missions and other works.—Prosperity alone no assurance of happiness if God is left out.—This is the cause of evil in the world.)

We raise Our voice in paternal lament that in many schools of your land Christ is often despised or ignored, the explanation of the universe and mankind is forced within the narrow limits of naturalism or of rationalism, and new educational systems are sought after which cannot but produce a sorrowful harvest in the intellectual and moral life of the nation. **373** *(94)*

(Abandoning of God's law in the family: marriage.— Remedies: everything that helps to teach divine truths.— The social question.—Appeal for unity.)

FAILURE OF NON-CHRISTIAN CULTURE

R.M. to Catholics of the United States, November 13, 1939.

(Jubilee of the Catholic University at Washington.)

The Christian education of youth was never of more decisive or vital importance than it is today, when we are faced with the bewildering errors of that naturalism and materialism which are plunging the world into war—evidence in themselves of the hollowness of a philosophy built on purely human standards. **374** *(67, 79, 93, 107, 119)*

As We see these calamities grow worse, We might well lose heart, were We not sustained by trust in the loving Providence of God, which gives strength and solace more abundantly as worldly confidence fails.

But our chief hope, after God, rests in the schools of Christian culture, old and new, among which stands your Catholic University as a typical example, assigning in its zeal for truth the correct place in its programs to natural sciences and metaphysics, to mind and heart, to past and present, to reason and revelation.

Thus, in the austere retirement of your schoolroom, by alternating reflection and study with prayer, you will continue to train the young men of tomorrow to face false teaching and its evil consequences as intrepid champions of those fundamentals of civilization which, enshrined in the Gospel of Christ and taught unerringly by the Church, are truly spirit and life.

(Greetings and Blessing.)

CONSEQUENCES OF A DEFECTIVE EDUCATION

All. to newly married couples, January 24, 1940.

(The Conversion of St. Paul.—First Lesson: never despair of the conversion of a sinner.)

375
(36,
85,
96)
But the story of Saul, the persecutor, teaches a second lesson that can be of great use to those united in Christian wedlock. Why was this young man, with his clear intelligence, sound judgment, firm will and enthusiasm, not among the first to follow Jesus? Why did he start off as an implacable enemy of all that, later, he was to love, preach and defend to death? Here again, he himself provides the answer. "A Pharisee, the son of Pharisees" (a), "more exceedingly zealous of the traditions" of his fathers (b), he "acted ignorantly in unbelief." (c) Saul's hatred was then the result of ignorance and error, and these in their turn were the fruit of a defective education. He had imbibed, first from his parents, then from his teacher Gamaliel (d), the narrow spirit of sectarian formalism which wizened old Pharisees had introduced, like a corroding poison, into the divine law and the sublime prophecies of the Old Testament. Thus he had become the heir to a patrimony of

375a Acts 23:6.
375b Gal. 1:14.
375c 1 Tim. 1:13.
375d Acts 22:3.

implacable hatred and prejudice against anything that seemed likely to threaten the carefully-designed fabric of their sophistry.

These are the fruits of an education that is warped, or even of an education whose roots are simply defective. Christian husbands and wives, ponder well your duties as educators. Gathered around you are hosts of children exposed to the dangers of bad literature, immodest shows, evil companions, because of a negligence that We must deplore. Look at that blind affection in which children are brought up in an exaggerated love of comfort and frivolity, in practical neglect, if not downright contempt, of moral law: the duty of prayer, the necessity of sacrifice and victory over passion, the basic obligation of justice and charity towards our neighbor.

(Third lesson: cooperation with grace.)

SAINT JOHN BOSCO, THE TEACHER'S MODEL

All. to newly-weds, January 31, 1940.

It is now more than a century since there lived a small boy with his two little brothers in a humble village of the Piedmont mountains. Having been orphaned at an early age by the death of his father, he who was later to become the father of orphans, received nothing but the cares and attentions of his mother. With what great wisdom this simple country woman, uneducated but guided by the Holy Ghost, brought up her son in the highest and most complete sense of the word; it can even be said that the Church has recognized her success in that her son, St. John Bosco, whose feast-day we celebrate today, has been raised officially to the altars of the Church. This humble priest, who was later to become one of the brighter glories of the Church and of Italy, was a marvellous teacher; it is in this, beloved sons and daughters, that his life offers you, future fathers and mothers, a very useful and valuable lesson.

376
(7,
36,
46,
59)

When God entrusts a child to Christian couples He seems to repeat to them what the daughter of Pharoah commanded the mother of the young Moses: "Take this child and bring it up." (a) According to the Divine Plan, the parents are the first educators of their children. Nevertheless it must be admitted that, in the actual conditions of daily life, at times, the urgent occupation of providing daily bread makes it difficult to fulfill such an essential duty.

This was also the situation when John Bosco dreamed of assisting parents and even of substituting for them, if the need arose, in this their grave duty. His heart told him that he was providentially destined for this very mission; his soul had a sort of revelation of this in a dream of his early life in which he saw wild beasts changed suddenly into gentle lambs that followed him docilely to pasture.

Don Bosco's formation

377
(32,
36,
45,
73)
To understand how he translated this dream into action, it is necessary to recall the education he received and the education he gave ... the one is connected with the other; the mother he had explains in great measure why he was the father of others.

Don Bosco, in founding his first educational institution, called it "non laboratorio, ma oratorio"—"not a laboratory, but an oratory"—as he himself said, because he intended making it first of all a place of prayer, "a little church wherein to gather the little ones." But it was also his idea that the oratory should become a sort of family circle for the children he brought there. Was it not perhaps because "Mamma Margherita" had made a kind of oratory for him of the little house of *Becchi?* Imagine the young widow with the three children kneeling there before her for morning and evening prayers! See them looking angelic in their Sunday suits, suits always carefully kept, going to

376a Ex. 2:9.

the market town of Murialdo to assist at Holy Mass. Picture
them clinging around her in the afternoon after the frugal
meal in which the only cake was a piece of blessed bread.
She calls to their mind the commandments of God and the
Church, the great lessons of the catechism, the ways of
eternal salvation; then, with the sweet poesy of simple
souls and of the imagination of the people, she narrates
the tragic story of the faithful Abel and the evil Cain, the
idyll of Isaac and Rebecca, the joyous mystery of Bethlehem, and the painful death of the good Jesus, nailed to the
cross for us on Calvary. Who can measure the profound
influence of that first maternal training! On becoming a
priest, Don Bosco attributed to these his tender and trusting devotion to Our Blessed Lady and the Divine Eucharist; actually a later dream was to show him these two
devotions as the two columns to which the souls of his
children, battered like fragile ships on the stormy seas of
the world, should tightly lash themselves to ensure salvation and peace.

Reason and faith in education

Religion is the cornerstone of a good education. But
Don Bosco associated reason with religion, reason illumined by faith. True reason, as the Latin word *ratio* would
indicate, consists above all in moderation and wisdom, balance and fairness. Would it, for example, be consistent to
correct a child for the same faults that you commit daily
in his presence? To want him to be obedient and submissive if, in his presence, you criticize ecclesiastical or civil
superiors, if you disobey the commandments of God or the
just laws of the State? Would it be reasonable to want
your children to be loyal when you are untruthful; patient,
if you are violent and ill-tempered? Example is always the
best teacher. In the little village of *Becchi*, "Mamma Margherita" did not continually exhort them to work. But, with
the death of the head of the family, the courageous widow

378
(40,
62,
83,
86,
87)

put her own hand to the plough, to the scythe, to the reins, and with her example, so we read, she even tired out the hands hired daily during the harvesting and threshing season. Formed in this school, the young John, at the age of four, already did his part in the common work of unraveling the stalks of hemp and, when old, devoted all his time to work, giving only five hours to sleep and even spending a whole night in prayer every week. However we must admit that, in this, he surpassed the just limits of human reason. But the supernatural reasoning of the saints permits these excesses of generosity, without imposing them on others, because their wisdom is inspired by an insatiable desire to please God, and their ardor is stimulated by a filial fear of displeasing Him and a very lively eagerness for good.

Displeasing his father or mother is the supreme grief of a child who is brought up well. John Bosco had experienced it in his home, where a little sign or a reproving look sufficed to check his childish jealousy right at the beginning.

The principal method of the educator

379
(40,
81)
For this reason he wanted the educator to adopt constant solicitude as his first principle, solicitude prompted by paternal affection. Parents should, therefore, give their children the best time they have at their disposal instead of wasting it far from them in dangerous recreations or in places where they would blush to take them.

With this love, guided by reason, and reason guided by faith, home education will not be subject to those deplorable extremes that so often imperil it: alternating weak indulgence with sharp severity, going from culpable acquiescence, which leaves the child unguided, to severe correction that leaves him helpless. On the other hand, the affection shown by parents, to which there is corresponding confidence on the part of the child, distributes due praise and merited correction with equal moderation, because it is master of itself, and with complete success, because it has the child's love. "Try to make yourself loved,' St. John Bosco used to say, "and you will be obeyed." Oh, newly-weds, the future fathers and mothers of families, may you also reproduce something of this saintly ideal in your homes!

THE EDUCATIONAL WORK OF THE JESUITS

Letter *Nosti profecto,* July 6, 1940—to the General of the Jesuits.

(Fourth centenary of the Society's foundation.—Circumstances in which it was founded.—Eulogy of its achievements.)

We have not the slightest intention of passing over in silence those outstanding achievements of your Society in providing a sound and first-rate education for youth during the past four hundred years. You are well aware of the urgency of this question. Not only the fate of the country, but that of the Church itself, depends, in very large measure, on the conditions and the training given in schools, since, for the greater part, the quality of both citizens and the faithful will correspond to the training they received in adolescence. We therefore congratulate you on the innumerable institutions for the study of letters and arts which you have opened, and in which you are moulding an impressionable youth in right doctrine and the practice of virtue, in order that these young people may be living examples of Christian life and offer great hopes for the future. With praiseworthy judgment, you give this youth for meditation and imitation, the examples of saintly young men: who like Aloysius Gonzaga, John Berchmans, Stanislaus Kostka, protected the virginal lily of their purity with the prickly thorns of mortification.

380
(4,
47,
49,
88)

But you have not restricted your attention to the education of youth. As your Founder and Father, anticipating

381
(59,

68) future needs, recommended in the Constitutions, you have in many places founded Institutes of higher learning, and Universities, and, what augurs well for the Church, you have undertaken the formation of the clergy in doctrine and piety—as in Our dear City and almost under Our very eyes you are doing in masterly fashion in the Pontifical Gregorian University and affiliated institutions. Together with this, you are working diligently to prepare citizens in all walks of life for the offices they will be called upon to occupy both in public and private life.

382
(90,
117)
You have, moreover, powerfully fortified this education by those training-schools in piety and apostolate, called Marian Sodalities, which provide the Church of Christ with a ready band of picked auxiliary troops in peaceful array under the banner of the Virgin Mary. Continue then to promote this most holy task with the zeal that characterizes all your labors, and never imagine that any of your efforts are strenuous enough to dispense of further effort. Till there are countries where the young are constrained to attend schools and educational institutions in which error, disguised as truth, shackles minds and corrupts hearts, no effort must be spared to ensure that no region shall suffer from a dearth of sound educational institutions in which students may imbibe solid doctrine together with the practice of Christian virtue.

(Other undertakings of the present day.—That the Society itself remain the same.)

AUTHORITY WITHOUT BITTERNESS

All to newly-weds, July 10, 1940.

(The Precious Blood of Christ recalls the forgiveness of injuries.—The pardon of injuries in the Old and New Testaments.—In family life.)

Between parents and children, if authority is to be of value, if it is to maintain its right to be respected, to protect them by giving advice, by correcting them, when necessary, by punishing them, how deplorable would be the slightest sign of resentment or of personal revenge on the part of either the father or the mother! Often in itself it is sufficient to shake or even destroy the confidence and filial affection in the heart of the child. **383 (40)**

(Example of St. John Gualbert [July 12].—Our Father.)

UNDERSTANDING THE YOUNG

All. to newly-weds, July 17, 1940.

(Models of Christian charity.—Camillus de Lellis, Vincent de Paul, Jerome Emiliani.)

Even irrational animals are instinctively solicitous for their young. How then could it be necessary to exhort you, Christian newly-weds to be solicitous for your children! However, it can happen that an excess of severity or a lack of understanding will raise a barrier between the heart of the child and that of its parents. Saint Paul said: "With the weak, I became as one who is weak...; I have been everything by turns to everybody, to bring everybody salvation." (a) It is a great quality that of knowing how to make yourselves little with the little, children among the children, without thereby compromising maternal or paternal authority. **384 (84, 85)**

(The aged and the sick.—The life of Saint Camillus.)

384a 1 Cor. 9:22.

READING MATTER FOR CHILDREN

All. to newly-weds, August 7, 1940.

*(Action of the Church against bad reading matter.—
The freedom to read everything.—Today, people are more
indifferent to immoral literature than to bad companions.)*

385
(32,
39,
80)

What is more, beloved newly-weds, seeing that you
are now preparing for your future and asking, among other
divine favors, the blessing of fecundity upon your union,
keep in mind that the souls of your children will be a reflection of your own souls. Undoubtedly you are intent on
educating them in a Christian manner and on instilling in
them only worthy principles. An excellent resolution, but
will it always be sufficient? Alas! At times it happens that
Christian parents, who have very carefully brought up their
sons or daughters, who have kept them away from dangerous pleasures and bad company, see them suddenly
become, towards the age of eighteen or twenty years, victims of wretched and even scandalous falls: the good seed
which they had sown was ruined by weeds. Who has been
the *inimicus homo,* the enemy, (a) responsible for such
evil? In the home itself, in this small paradise, the cunning
tempter has stealthily entered and has found the corrupting elements ready to offer to innocent hands: a book care-
lessly left on the father's writing table which has threatened
the faith of baptism in the son; a novel left on the sofa or on
the mother's fireside chair, which has darkened the purity
of the daughter's first communion. Once surprisingly discovered, the evil is all the more difficult to eradicate according to the penetrative nature of the stain tarnishing the
whiteness of the virgin soul.

*(Deceptive literature, at times more murderous than
aerial bombardments.—Living in the presence of God.)*

385a Matt. 13:28.

COLLABORATION OF PARENTS, PRIESTS AND TEACHERS

All. to newly-weds, January 15, 1941.

(Two states of life have their origin in a sacrament: marriage and the priesthood.—Harmony between them.)

In the Christian formation of the little souls whom Our Lord will entrust to you in creating them to vivify the bodies you beget, there is reserved to you a part, a teaching role. You are not permitted to be indifferent to this your role, nor can anyone satisfactorily substitute for you.

No doubt, in this sacred instruction, you will seek the assistance of zealous priests and catechists, of the unrivalled teaching abilities of religious men and women; but no matter how great and precious and beneficial these helps may be, they do not exonerate you from your duties and responsibilities. How often Christian teachers, in the training of their pupils, bewail the difficulty—and often, even the impossibility—which they encounter in offsetting and supplementing by their own efforts that which the family should have done, but omitted to do, or did badly!

Take good care of these little angels, heaven's gift to you. Guard them for the Lord, for His heavenly Jerusalem and for Holy Mother Church. Do not ever forget that beside the cradle there must be two fathers and two teachers, one natural, the other spiritual. And just as, in the ordinary Providence of God, souls cannot live in a Christian manner and be saved if they live outside the Church and are deprived of the ministry of priests ordained for the purpose by the Sacrament of Holy Orders, so, too, normally they cannot grow up in a Christian manner outside the home and without the ministry of parents blessed and united by the Sacrament of Matrimony.

(Appeal for the grace of Christ.)

386
(28,
34,
41,
43,
46)

THE EXAMPLE OF PARENTS

All. to newly-weds, March 19, 1941.

(The divine paternity in the Most Blessed Trinity, creation, grace.—Ministry of parents.)

387
(39,
42,
72)
Raise them in the faith and the fear and love of God. Imbue them with the knowledge of right living, which makes the Christian, sets him on the path of virtue and guides him amid the dangers of many insidious enemies of youth. Be an example to them in the pursuit of whatever is good. Always behave in such a manner that your children may only have to model their lives on yours and be esteemed merely for being as you are. In this way, you will adequately correspond to the designs of God, Who used you as an instrument in giving them a life like yours. Let the light of their lives be to observe you, to imitate you, to remember, some day when you are no longer at their side, your admonitions, exemplified and confirmed by a perfect fulfilling of all the obligations of a Christian life, by a refined and strong sense of duty without compromise, by an unshakable faith and confidence in God in the midst of the severest trials, by mutual affection grown stronger with the passage of years, by a charitable attitude to every sort of misery.

Your children will expect a great deal from the care with which you watch over their infant steps and the first reawakening and blossoming of their minds and hearts. And later on, when you entrust them to teachers worthy of your confidence as Christian parents, you will not cease to assist them even more by advice and encouragement. But your example will serve more than your words. For a long period of years, they will have before their eyes continually the example of your way of life in the free intimacy of the home, and, with the penetrating vision and disconcerting sharpness of youth, they will judge the example set before them.

(Example of Tobias.—You cannot assure your children of worldly goods; you must assure them of higher treasures.)

THE MOTHER'S PLACE IS IN THE HOME

All. to newly-weds, September 10, 1941.

(God has subjected the wife to the husband.—The modern way of life tends to upset this order.)

Frequently, husband and wife practise the same profession and contribute by their work to an almost equal extent to the family budget. On the other hand, these very working conditions lead to a way of life which is independent one from the other. But what about the care, the protection, the education and the instruction of the children whom God has given them? They are very often given over, We shall not say abandoned, to strangers to be formed and guided, and these latter have a greater hand in their education than the mother herself, whose professional duties keep her far away. Is there any reason for surprise that the sense of the domestic hierarchy is weakened, thus tending to its elimination and that paternal authority and maternal care do not harmonize in forming a loving and happy family life?

388
(36, 96)

(The family in Roman history.—Christian restoration.)

God has reserved to woman the pains of childbirth, the labor of nursing her children and giving them their first instruction. The most devoted care of outsiders will never be able to make up for the affectionate care of maternal love.

(Christian exercise of the husband's authority and the wife's obedience.—The fruits of their sacrifices.)

AUTHORITY, HIGHEST MANIFESTATION OF
PATERNAL LOVE

All. to newly-weds, September 24, 1941.

(Authority of parents: their first duty, Baptism.)

389
(40)
"What manner of child, think ye, shall this be?" (a) Children are like the "reed shaken by the wind"; they are delicate flowers whose petals fall with the slightest breeze; they are virgin soil on which God has sown the seeds of goodness but which are stifled by "the imagination and thought of man's heart" which "are prone to evil from his youth" (b) through the "concupiscence of the flesh and the concupiscence of the eyes and the pride of life." (c) Who will straighten the reed? Who is to protect these flowers? Who will cultivate this soil and make the seeds of goodness bear fruit against the snares of evil? In the first place, it will be the authority which governs the family and the children: namely, parental authority.

Children today not submissive

390
(85, 97)
Fathers and mothers today often bewail the fact that they can no longer get their children to obey them: stubborn little children listen to nobody; growing children spurn all guidance; young men and women are exasperated by any advice given, are deaf to all warnings and insist on following their own ideas because they are convinced that they alone are fully in a position to appreciate the exigencies of the modern way of life. Their only ambition is to make a name for themselves on the sports field. In short, the new generation (of course, with many wonderful exceptions!) is ordinarily not disposed to submit to the authority of father and mother. And what is the cause of this insubordi-

389a Luke 1:66.
389b Gen. 8:21.
389c Cf. 1 John 2:16.

nation? The reason generally given is that the children of today no longer possess the sense of submission and respect due to the commands of their parents. The heady fumes of youthful vanity which they breathe tend to extinguish in them all reverence for their parents. Everything they perceive around them serves the sole purpose of increasing, exciting and setting fire to their natural, untamed passion for independence, for mocking the past and thirsting avidly for the future.

If We were now speaking to children and young people, We would have analyzed and studied the reasons for these deficiencies in obedience. But since We are speaking to newly-married couples who will soon have to exercise paternal and maternal authority, We should like to call your attention to another aspect of this important question.

Effective authority

The normal exercising of authority depends not only on those who have to obey, but also, and in large measure, on those who have to command. To put it more clearly: we must distinguish between the right to possess authority and give orders, on the one hand, and, on the other, that moral excellence which is the essence and spirit of an effective, operative and efficacious authority which is able to impose itself on others and to exact obedience. The former right is conferred on you by God in the very act of your parenthood. The latter privilege must be acquired and preserved: it can be lost and it can be strengthened. Now, the right to command your children will not be worth much if it is not accompanied by that control and personal authority over them which ensures that they really obey you. But how and in what way can you acquire, preserve and strengthen this moral dominion?

391
*(7,
86)*

To some, God gives the natural gift of being able to command, of knowing how to impose their own will on

392
(85,

86)   others. This is a precious gift (though it is often hard to say whether it belongs wholly to the spirit or whether, for the most part, it reveals itself in the personality, the bearing, the speech, the gaze or the physical aspect). But at the same time it is an awesome gift. If you possess it, do not abuse it in the treatment of your children; otherwise you will run the risk of closing up and hardening their hearts in fear, of making them slaves and not loving children. This authority must be tempered by returning their affection with loving kindness and patient encouragement. Listen to the great Apostle St. Paul who exhorts you: "Fathers, provoke not your children to indignation, lest they be discouraged." (a) Remember that severity is meritorious only when it stems from a heart steeped in kindness.

Domination of self

393   To temper authority with kindness is to triumph in the
(40,   struggle which belongs to your duty as parents. For the
86)   rest, all those who would advantageously rule over others, must, as an essential element, first dominate themselves, their passions, their impressions. There is no real submission to and respect for any authority, unless those who obey feel that this authority is exercised with reason, faith and a sense of duty, because then only do they realize that a similar duty binds them to obey.

394   If the orders you give your children and the punish-
(40,   ment you inflict proceed from the impulse of the moment
86)   or from outbursts of impatience or imagination or blind, ill-considered sentiment, they will mostly be arbitrary or inconsistent, and perhaps even unjust and ill-suited. Today, you will be most unreasonably exacting and unrelentingly severe with your children. Tomorrow you will permit everything. You will begin by refusing them some small thing, and then, a moment later, worn out by their crying

392a Col. 3:21.

and sulkiness, you will grant it with a great show of tenderness, anxious only to be over and done with a situation that was getting on your nerves.

But how are you going to rule over your children, when you do not know how to conquer your moods, to control your imagination and to dominate yourselves? If on occasions you feel that you are not completely master of your feelings, then put off to a later and better time the correction you want to make or the punishment you think you must inflict. This quiet dignity with which you speak and correct will be far more effective, far more educative and authoritative, than ill-regulated bursts of passion.

Do not forget that children, no matter how small they **395** may be, have a very observant eye and will immediately *(86)* be aware of the changes in your moods. From the cradle itself, once they are able to distinguish their mother from other women, they soon become aware of the power their childish whims and fits of crying have over weak parents, and, with innocent cunning, will not hesitate to exploit it to the full.

The things that prejudice authority

Avoid everything that may lessen your authority with **396** them. Beware against ruining this authority by a non-stop *(40,* series of recommendations and criticisms, which only serve *84,* to annoy them; they will go in one ear and out the other. *85,* Avoid deceiving your children with fake reasons and ex- *86)* planations, given at random, to save embarrassment or to escape tiresome questions. If you feel you should not tell them the true reasons of some order or action of yours, it will be more helpful to appeal to their trust in and love for you. Never falsify the truth. It is far better to keep silent. You have no idea of the disturbance and crisis you may produce in those little hearts the day they find out that their natural credulity has been abused. Take care also that no sign of disagreement between you appear, in the way of treating your children: they will soon seize upon it to use the mother's authority against the father's and vice versa, and will not easily resist the urge to exploit such a situation. Do not, finally, make the mistake of waiting till your children are grown up in order to make them feel the calm weight of your authority, which must also be firm and frank, and not prone to tears or caprice. From the cradle, from the first glimmerings of their infant reasoning power, let them feel your tender care, but let them also experience your prudent guidance and firm vigilance.

Authority flows from love

397
(29,
40,
85,
86)
Your authority must be devoid of weakness, yet it must be an authority which stems from love and is seeped in and sustained by love. You should be the first instructors and first friends of your children. If you really have this parental love (a love, namely, which is Christian through and through, and not a more or less subconscious self-complacency) in the commands you give your children, these commands will find an echo in the intimate depths of the hearts of your children, without there being need to say very much. The language of love is more eloquent in the silence of labor than in much speech. A thousand little signs, an inflection of the voice, an almost imperceptible gesture, an expression of the face, a little hint of approval...all these tell them, more than any protestations, how much affection there is in the prohibition that annoys them, how much kindness is hidden in the order they find troublesome. Then only will authority appear to them, not as a heavy weight, a hateful yoke to be cast off at the earliest possible opportunity, but as the supreme manifestation of your love.

Example

398
(39,
83,
Must not example go hand in hand with love? How can children, who, after all, are naturally inclined to imitate, learn to obey, if they see the mother paying no heed

to the orders of the father or worse, quarreling with him; *86,* if the home is full of continual criticism of all form of au- *96)* thority; if they see that their parents are the first not to obey the commands of God and the Church? You must give your children the example of parents whose manner of speaking and acting serves as a model of respect for legiti- mate authority, for faithfulness to duty. From this edifying sight, they will learn the true nature of Christian obedience and how they should practise it towards their parents, in a far more convincing manner than any sermon to that effect. Be firmly convinced that good example is the most pre- cious heritage you can leave your children. This vision of a treasure of words and deeds, of encouragement and ad- vice, of the practices of religion and virtue, will always remain fixed in their minds and hearts, a moving and be- loved memory which will recall you to them in times of doubt and uncertainty between good and evil, in danger and victory. In times of darkness, when even the heavens seem obscured, your example will light up and lead the way, the way you have already travelled with that effort and labor which is the price of happiness here below.

Is this perhaps only a dream? No. The life you are about to begin with your new family is no dream. It is a road along which you walk, invested with a dignity and authority that is designed to be a school and a novitiate for those of your own blood who follow you.

May the Heavenly Father, Who, in calling you to par- **399** ticipate in the grandeur of His paternity, has communicated *(40)* to you His authority, grant you the grace to exercise this authority with His wisdom and love!

TRAINING IN THE HOME

All. to mothers of Italian families, October 26, 1941.

As We look around this splendid gathering of mothers, **400** teaching sisters, school-mistresses, representatives of the *(44)* children of Catholic Action and others who devote themselves to the work of education, Our thoughts go beyond the threshold of this hall, beyond the confines of Italy, and reach to the ends of the earth as We embrace all those dear children who are the flower of the human race and the joy of their mothers' hearts. (a) At the same time We are mindful of the immortal Pope Pius XI, who in his Encyclical *Divini Illius Magistri* of December 31, 1929 (b), dealt so profoundly with the Christian education of the young. In discussing this important subject he judiciously allocated the parts which belong respectively to the Church, the family and the State, and then went on regretfully to observe that parents are often unprepared or ill-equipped for their work as educators. Accordingly, and since the limits of that lucid and exhaustive document did not permit him to deal in detail with education in the home, he exhorted in the Name of Christ all pastors of souls "to use every means, by catechism and instruction, by word of mouth and by widely published writings, to ensure that Christian parents are well instructed both generally and particularly in their duties in the religious, moral and civic education of their children, and as to the best methods—apart from their own example—of achieving that end." (c)

401
(36,
39,
44)
In so exhorting the pastors of souls the great Pontiff was exhorting parents also, fathers and mothers alike. But We believe that We are acting in accordance with the desire of Our venerated Predecessor in reserving this special audience for mothers and other instructors of children. It is true that when We speak to the newly-wed Our words are expressed also to you. Nevertheless We are glad to have this opportunity of speaking to you in a special way, dearly beloved daughters, because We see in mothers, and in their

400a Cf. Ps. 112:9.
400b Cf. above, Nos. 240-304.
400c Cf. No. 287.

expert and pious helpers, those who exert the earliest and
the most intimate influence upon the souls of little ones and
and upon their growth in piety and virtue.

We need not remind you of how important and necessary is this work of education in the home, how grave is
a mother's obligation not to neglect it or to perform it with
indifference. Speaking as We are to Our beloved daughters
of Catholic Action, We can have no doubt that they regard
this obligation as the first of their duties as Christian mothers and as a task in which none can fully take their place.
But it is not enough to be conscious of an obligation and to
have the desire to discharge it; it is necessary also to render
oneself capable of discharging it competently.

Preparation for the role of parents

It is strange and, as Pope Pius XI remarked in his En-   **402**
cyclical (a), lamentable, that whereas no one would dream   *(36,*
of suddenly becoming a mechanic or an engineer, a doctor   *80,*
or a lawyer, without any apprenticeship or preparation,   *96)*
every day there are numbers of young men and women
who marry without having given an instant's thought to
preparing themselves for the arduous work which awaits
them of educating their children. And yet, if St. Gregory
the Great could speak of the government of souls as "the
art of arts," (b) surely the art of fashioning the souls of
children is difficult and strenuous. Those souls are among
the most fragile and the most difficult to guide. On them,
a harmful influence or culpable neglect imprints an indelible, ruinous mark. Fortunate the child whose mother stands
by his cradle like a guardian angel to inspire and lead him
along the path of goodness!

And so while We congratulate you upon what you   **403**
have already achieved, We cannot but exhort you warmly   *(58)*

402a Cf. No. 286.
402b Liber Regulae Pastoralis. lib. 1, c. 1. Migne. P.L. 77, 14.

and anew to develop those splendid organizations which are doing so much to provide for every rank and social class, educators conscious of their high mission, in mind and bearing alive to evil and zealous to promote good.

(*Works of assistance to young mothers.*)

Importance of training during infancy

404
(31,
32,
36)

To the mother, more than to anyone else, is entrusted the first education of the child in its early months and years. Of heredity, which may exercise such an influence upon the future cast of a child's character, We will not speak except to say that this hidden heritage sometimes points an accusing finger at the irregular life of the parents, who are thus gravely responsible for making it difficult for their offspring to lead a truly Christian life. Fathers and mothers, whose mutual love is sanctified by the faith of Christ, see to it that before your child is born you prepare a pure family atmosphere in which it may open its eyes to light and its soul to life so that the good influence of Christ may linger upon every step of its moral development.

405
(36,
39,
41)

Mothers, because your sensibility is greater and your love more tender, you should keep a vigilant eye upon your babies throughout their infancy, watching over their growth and over the health of their little bodies, for this is flesh of your flesh and the fruit of your womb. Remember that your children are the adopted sons of God and are especially beloved by Christ. Remember that their angels always behold the face of the heavenly Father. (a) So you too, as you rear them, must be angels in like manner, in all your care and viligance keeping your eyes fixed upon heaven. It is your task from the cradle to begin their education in soul as well as body. If you do not educate them, they will begin, for good or evil, to educate themselves.

405a Matt. 18:10.

Many of the moral characteristics which you see in the **406**
youth or the man owe their origin to the manner and cir- *(36,*
cumstances of his physical development in infancy. Purely *37)*
organic habits contracted at that time may later prove a
serious obstacle to the spiritual life of the soul. And so you
will make sure that your care of the child will be in perfect
accord with the rules of hygiene so that when he comes to
the use of reason his bodily organs and faculties will be
healthy and robust and free from distorted tendencies. This
is the reason why, except when it is quite impossible, it is
more desirable that the mother should feed her child at her
own breast. Who can say what mysterious influences are
exerted upon the growth of that little creature by the mother upon whom it depends entirely for its development?

Have you ever observed those little eyes, wide open, **407**
restlessly questioning, that dart from this thing to that, fol- *(36)*
lowing a movement or a gesture, already expressing joy or
pain, anger and obstinacy, and giving other signs of those
little passions that are to be found in the heart of man even
before the tiny lips have learned to utter a word? This is
perfectly natural. Notwithstanding what certain thinkers
maintain, we are not born endowed with knowledge or
with the memories and dreams of a life already lived. The
mind of the child as it comes forth from its mother's womb
is a page upon which nothing is written. From hour to
hour as it passes on its way from the cradle to the tomb its
eyes and other senses, internal and external, transmit the
life of the world by means of their own activity and record
the images and ideas of the things among which it lives.

Hence an irresistible instinct for truth and goodness **408**
turns "the simple soul that nothing knows" (a) towards *(76,*
sensible things. All these powers of feeling, all these child- *80)*
ish sensations, by which mind and will come gradually to

408a Dante, Purgatory, 16, 88.

their awakening, need to be educated, trained and carefully guided. Otherwise the normal awakening and proper direction of these noble faculties of the spirit will be compromised and distorted. From that early age a loving look, a warning word, must teach the child not to yield to all its impressions and, as reason dawns, it must learn to discriminate and master the vagaries of its sensations. In a word, under the guidance and admonitions of the mother it must begin to educate itself.

A threefold education

409
(1,
84)
Study the child during his tender age. If you know him well you will educate him well. You will not misconceive his character. You will come to understand him, knowing when to give way and when to be firm. A naturally good disposition is not the lot of all the sons of men.

410
(34,
50,
84,
86)
Train the mind of your children. Do not give them wrong ideas or wrong reasons for things. Whatever their questions may be, do not answer them with evasions or untrue statements which their minds rarely accept. Rather, take the opportunities they give you to train their minds lovingly and patiently. Their minds want to grasp the truth with the first ingenuous gropings of their reasoning and reflective powers. Who can say what many a genius may not owe to the lengthy and trustful questions of childhood at the home fireside!

411
(34,
76)
Train the character of your children. Correct their faults. Encourage and cultivate their good qualities, coordinating them with that stability which will make for resolution in later life. Your children, as they begin to grow up, think and exert their will, realizing that they are guided by a good paternal will, steady and strong, free from violence and anger, not subject to weakness or inconsistency, will learn in time to see therein the interpreter of another

and higher will, the Will of God. Thus they will plant in their souls the seeds of those moral habits which fashion and sustain character, train it to self-control in moments of conflict or sacrifice and imbue it with a deep sense of Christian duty.

Train their hearts. Frequently a man's destiny, the **412** ruin of his character, or the threat of grave danger, may be *(34,* traced to his childhood years when his heart was spoiled *76,* by the fond flattery, imprudent fussing and foolish indul- *80,* gence of misguided parents. They accustomed that impres- *96)* sionable little heart to see all things revolve and gravitate around it, to find all things yielding to its will and caprice, and thus they sowed in it the roots of a boundless egoism of which the parents themselves were later to become the first victims! All this is often the just penalty of the self- ishness of parents who deny their only child the joy of having little brothers and sisters, who, sharing the mother's love, would have accustomed him to think of others besides himself. What deep and rich potentialities for love, goodness and devotion lie dormant in the heart of a child! You, mothers, must awaken them, direct them, raise them up to Him Who will sanctify them, to Jesus, to Jesus and Mary, their heavenly Mother, who will open the child's heart to piety, will teach it by prayer to offer its pure sacrifices and innocent victories to the divine Lover of little ones. She will teach it to feel compassion for the poor and unhappy. How joyous is the spring-time of child- hood, unruffled by wind or storm!

The crisis of adolescence

But the day will come when the child's heart will be- **413** gin to feel new impulses stirring within it; new desires will *(37)* disturb the serenity of those early years. In that time of trial, Christian mothers, remember to train the will to resist the attacks of evil and the insidious temptations of passion. During that period of transition from the unconscious purity of infancy to the triumphant purity of adolescence you have a task of the highest importance to fulfill. You have to prepare your sons and daughters so that they may pass with unfaltering step, like those who pick their way among serpents, through that time of crisis and physical change, and that they may pass through it without losing anything of the joy of innocence, preserving intact that natural instinct of modesty with which Providence has girded them as a check to wayward passion.

414
(33,
34,
73,
77)
That sense of modesty, which in its spontaneous abhorrence of the impure is akin to the sense of religion, is held in little account these days. But you, mothers will take care that they do not lose it through indecency in dress or self-adornment, through unbecoming familiarities or immoral entertainments. On the contrary, you will seek to make it more delicate and alert, more upright and sincere. You will keep a watchful eye on their steps. You will not suffer the purity of their souls to be stained and contaminated by corrupt and corrupting company. You will inspire them with a high esteem and jealous love of purity, advising them to commend themselves to the sure and motherly protection of the Immaculate Virgin.

415
(37,
38,
78)
Finally, with the discretion of a mother and a teacher, and thanks to the open-hearted confidence with which you have been able to inspire your children, you will not fail to watch for and to discern the moment in which unspoken questions have occurred to their minds and are troubling their senses. It then will be your duty to your daughters, the father's duty to your sons, carefully and delicately to unveil the truth as far as it appears necessary, to give prudent, true and Christian answers to those questions and set their minds at rest.

If imparted by the lips of Christian parents, at the proper time, in the proper measure and with the proper

precautions, the revelation of the mysterious and marvellous laws of life will be received by them with reverence
and gratitude and will enlighten their minds with far less
danger than if they learned them haphazard, by some unpleasant shock, by secret conversations, through information received from over-sophisticated companions or from
clandestine reading. Your words, if they are wise and dis-
creet, will prove a safeguard and a warning in the midst
of the temptations and the corruption which surround
them "because foreseen, an arrow comes more slowly." (a)

The aid to home education

But in this great work of the Christian education of
your sons and daughters, you will understand that training in the home, however wise, however thorough, is not
enough. It needs to be supplemented and perfected by the
powerful aid of religion. From the moment of baptism the
priest possesses the authority of a spiritual father and a
pastor over your children. You must cooperate with him in
teaching them the first rudiments of the catechism and the
piety which are the only basis of a solid education, and of
which you, the earliest teachers of your children, ought
to have sufficient and sure knowledge. You cannot teach
what you do not know yourselves! Teach them to love God,
to love Christ, to love our Mother the Church, and the
pastors of the Church who are your guides. Love the catechism and teach your children to love it. It is the great
handbook of the love and the fear of God, of Christian
wisdom and of eternal life.

**416
(41,
44)**

In your work of education, which is many-sided, you
will feel the need and the obligation of having recourse to
others to help you. Choose helpers who are Christians like
yourselves, and choose them with all the care that is called
for by the treasure that you are entrusting to them. You are

**417
(42,
43,
46)**

415a Dante, *Paradise*, 17, 27.

committing to them the faith, the purity and the piety of your children. But when you have chosen them you must not think that you are henceforth freed from your duty and your vigilance. You must cooperate with them. However eminent school teachers may be in their professions, they will have little success in the formation of your children without your collaboration. Even less success will they have if instead of helping and lending support to their efforts you were to counteract and oppose them. What a misfortune it would be if at home your indulgence and fond weakness were to undo all that has been done at school, at catechism or in Catholic associations to form the character and foster the piety of your children!

Difficult natures

418
(81,
85,
86,
97)
"But," some mothers may say, "children are so difficult to manage nowadays! I can do nothing with that son of mine. That daughter of mine is impossible!" Admittedly, many boys and girls at the age of twelve or fifteen show themselves intractable. But why? Because when they were two or three years old they were allowed to do as they pleased. True, some temperaments are difficult and rebellious; but however unresponsive, however obstinate, the child is still your child. Would you love him any less than his brothers and sisters if he were sickly or deformed? God has given him to you. See to it that you do not treat him as an outcast of the family. No child is so unruly that he cannot be trained with care, patience and love. It will rarely happen that even the stoniest and most unpromising soil will not bear some flower of submission and virtue, provided unreasonable severity does not run the risk of exterminating the seed of good-will hidden within it.

419
(86)
The whole education of your children would be ruined were they to discover in their parents—their eyes are sharp enough to discern—any signs of favoritism, undue prefer-

ences or antipathies in regard to any of them. For your own good and for the good of the family it must be clear that, whether you use measured severity or give encouragement and caresses, you have an equal love for all, a love which makes no distinction save for the correction of evil or for the encouragement of good. Have you not received them all equally from God?

Our words have been addressed principally to you, **420** Christian mothers. But with you We see around Us today **(51)** a gathering of nuns, teachers and others engaged in the work of Christian education. They are mothers, too, not by nature or blood, but by the love which they bear for the young, who are so dear to Christ and His Spouse the Church. Yes, you, too, are mothers, you who work side by side with Christian mothers in the work of education. You have a mother's heart, burning with the charity which the Holy Spirit has poured out in you. In this charity, which is the charity of Christ that urges you on the path of well-being, you find your light, your comfort and the work that brings you so close to mothers, fathers and children. You gather together these living branches of society, these children. You are the hope of their parents and of the Church, and form them into a great family of thousands and thousands of little ones. You train their minds, characters and hearts, bring them up in a spiritual and moral atmosphere in which the joyousness of innocence appears side by side with faith in God and reverence for holy things, with a sense of duty towards parents and country. Our praise and gratitude, joined with the thanks of all mothers, go out to you in full measure. In your schools, homes, colleges and associations you emulate and continue the mother's work of training. You are truly a sisterhood of spiritual mothers whose offspring is the pure flower of youth.

We have briefly described the glories of your incom- **421** parable mission, Christian mothers and beloved daughters, **(36,** which are fraught in these days with so many difficulties **37,**

41,
46)
and obstacles—how much you tire yourselves in cultivating the growing domestic olive branches. (a) What a majestic figure is that of the mother in the home as she fulfills her destiny at the cradle side, the nurse and teacher of the little ones! Hers is truly a task full of labor, and we should be tempted to deem her unequal to it were it not for the grace of God which is ever at hand to enlighten, direct and sustain her in her daily anxieties and toil; were it not, too, for those other educators, mother-like in spirit and energy, whom she calls upon to aid her in the formation of these youthful souls.

(Blessing.)

THE PRINCIPAL END OF MATRIMONY

All. to newly-weds, March 18, 1942.

(The common burden of family life.—Cooperation towards the essential and principal end of marriage: procreation.)

422
(7,
28,
30,
80)
Besides collaborating in giving physical life and health to the child, you must also collaborate in his education and spiritual life. First impressions are all-important during those tender years. The principal end of marriage is not only to procreate children, but to educate them (a) and bring them up in the fear of God and in faith, so that in this collaboration, which fills your entire married life, you may find and taste that happiness, the seeds of which God has prepared and watered by His grace in the Christian family.

(The will and ability to effect this cooperation.—Blessed Anna Taigi.)

421a Cf. Ps. 127:4.
422a C.I.C., can. 1013, art. 1.

GOD'S RIGHTS

All. to newly-weds, March 25, 1942.

(Vocation.—The needs of the Church.)

What will you do if the Master should claim His rights, **423** namely, call one of your sons or daughters (whom He Him- **(35)** self has given you) to be His priest, His religious? What will be your response to the confidences which your children may make to you, namely, that they have heard the voice of the divine Lover murmuring in their hearts: "If you will be perfect"? In the name of God, We implore you: do not let your cruel egoism shut the door of the soul against the whispering of the divine call. You have no idea of all the varied phases of the growth and decline of God's love in these young hearts, the obstacles and the encouragement, the desires and hopes, the grandeur and the misery! The heart has depths which are hidden even from father and mother, but the Holy Spirit "Who helpeth our infirmity . . . Himself intercedes for us with groans beyond all utterance and He Who can read our hearts, knoweth what the spirit desireth." (a)

Undoubtedly, when faced with the desire for the priestly or religious life, parents have the right—and in certain cases it is also their duty—to make sure that this desire does not spring from the impulse of the moment or a fancy that conjures up a beautiful dream outside home, but is the fruit of serious deliberation, whose supernatural character is vouched for by a wise and prudent confessor or spiritual director. But if parents put obstacles in the way—obstacles that spring from unreasonable and unjustified causes—then they are fighting against God Himself. And it is far worse when they claim to try out or test or (as they say) strengthen the quality of this desire by useless, and even dangerous and

423a Rom. 8:26 f.

risky trials, which serve not only to upset and discourage the vocation, but to endanger the very salvation of the child.

(Appreciate this grace.—Pray for it in a supernatural and apostolic spirit.)

424
(72)
Make your sons and daughters grow up in the faith, which is "the victory which overcometh the world." (a) Do not suffocate in their souls that spirit which comes down from heaven. Establish firmly in their hearts that faith, which is sincere and "unfeigned", which the Apostle Paul was certain existed in his beloved disciple Timothy: "which also dwelt first in thy grandmother Lois and in thy mother Eunice." (b) Do not be miserly with God: Give Him His share of what He may ask of your family.

(Blessing.)

ATTITUDE OF THE FATHER IN THE FAMILY

All. to newly-weds, April 8, 1942.

(Duty and responsibility of the man in the family.)

425
(32,
38,
39)
Never should there be lacking in the husband's entire behavior towards his wife that note of natural and chivalrous dignity and warm attention that is proper to God-fearing men of integrity. Such men are well aware of the tremendous help this mutual love and esteem between husband and wife is to the education of the child. Powerful is the father's influence upon his children: his example is a strong incentive for them to look upon their mother, and their father himself, with respect and loving reverence.

(Dominate your troubles in order to respond to the gentleness of your wife.)

424a 1 John 5:4.
424b 2 Tim. 1:5.

DIVORCE

All. to newly-weds, April 29, 1942.

(Natural necessity for marriage to be one and indissoluble.—Divorce destroys the future of the family.)

Perhaps you will ask yourselves why We extend these consequences to include the children. The reason is that they receive three very important things from their parents: existence, nourishment and education, (a) and they require an atmosphere of happiness in order to develop in a healthy manner. Now, this serenity, this well-balanced formation and instruction is quite impossible without complete faithfulness on the part of the parents to one another. Do not children strengthen the bond of wedded love? To break this bond is, cruelly, to deny your own flesh and blood, to submit your children to humiliating ignominy, to divide their hearts and tear them away from their own flesh and blood, to embitter the carefree days of their youth, and worst of all, to cause serious damage to their souls by moral scandal. **426** *(29, 32, 96)*

(Social repercussions.)

THE CHOICE OF DOMESTIC SERVANTS

All. to newly-weds, August 19, 1942.

(Relations between employers and domestics.—Responsibilities and consequences.)

At home, these consequences are evident first of all in the children. Parents are sometimes stunned and bitterly disillusioned by sudden and quite unexpected revelations concerning their sons and daughters—young adults, adolescents, or children. They could have understood the natural **427** *(33, 37)*

426a St. Thomas Supple., q. 41, a. 1.

caprice or even disobedience of youthful ardor; but it seems impossible to explain certain bad tendencies, certain traits in their character that make them difficult to get along with, independent, critical, secretive, lacking in candor. It comes as a shock to parents to see in their children certain wicked traits that, quite suddenly, drag them down to moral ruin and are of a gravity far above the usual moral crises of adolescence.

And what do parents do? What do they think? Frightened, they torment themselves with self-examination to find the cause: has everything been done to give the children a good education? Yes; nothing seems to have been lacking: good example, good advice, well-timed admonitions, firmness, kindness, a check upon their friends, their reading, their outings, their recreations. There has been nothing, till now, that could have led to this! Thus they examine the present and immediate past in great detail. And yet, the real cause goes back to the days of childhood: to hidden memories, that, so long dormant, have now been reawakened and have begun to occupy the mind, such as words, shady jokes, behavior, improper or even only too familiar liberties on the part of an imprudent or not too modest servant!

Do not say that these children could not understand. Perhaps—who knows?—they did not understand at the moment; but later on, grown up, they remember and understand. You must not forget that nature has given children a very acute sense of observation and retentiveness, and that, from his birth, man has the tendency to imitate in word and deed. Hence what a great responsibility fathers and mothers have from the very fact that servants are in permanent and continual contact with their children!

428
(33, 39)
Note that We are not speaking of children, who, out of negligence (as so often happens) are completely left in the hands of servants who are more assiduous in looking after them and helping them than their own mothers, who may

be elsewhere occupied or just frivolous. Neither are We referring to servants—God forbid!—who are themselves corrupt or out to corrupt others.

In any case, what has happened? A rotten tree has **429** been planted in the house, which can only give fruits like *(33)* itself. With what care should servants and domestics be chosen! How they should be watched over and warned! Let fathers of families not deserve the reproof of having made an ill-considered choice, or of having had very incomplete references, or of having acted from mere whim or false impression.

It is a delicate responsibility that, for parents, grows together with growing or grown children. Innocent though it is supposed they be and really are—and the same holds good for those who are around them if they, perhaps, are also young—this innocence will not stop the natural awakening in the ardent years of adolescence. Moreover their inexperience, which accompanies this innocence, will only serve to hide and cover up the danger until the day when the mysterious thrill they experience in their hearts and in their senses will announce to them that the battle is near, but that they, alas, are unarmed! What a frightening responsibility before children and servants in the inevitable contact of daily life!

(Responsibilities in relations between parents and servants.—In the 18th century, revolutionary ideas were spread among the people, even through servants.—Influence of family life on the society of today, through servants.)

THE CONDITIONS FOR MUTUAL TRUST BETWEEN THE PUBLIC SCHOOL AND THE FAMILY

R.M. to the whole world, December 24, 1942.

(Internal order of States.—Unity and order: God, the person, the State.—Peace in tranquillity.—The working-

man's world.—*Foundations for peace: dignity of the human person, of the family.*)

Let those who desire the star of peace to appear and to hover over our society try to see that every family has a home, in which a healthy family life (material and moral) may find its fullest expression. They should see that the place of work is not so far away from the home of the worker as to render him, who is head of the family and educator of his children, almost a stranger in his own home. Above all, they should re-establish, between public schools and the family, those ties of trust and mutual help, which, in other times, were of such great benefit, and which, today, have been substituted by mistrust wherever the dominant influence of materialism poisons and destroys in the school whatever the parents had instilled into the souls of their children.

(*Dignity of work.—The Christian State.—The world war and the renewal of society.*)

THE ACQUISITION OF VIRTUE

All. to newly-weds, April 7, 1943.

(*What is virtue?—Natural moral virtues.—Supernatural virtues.*)

431
(1,
34,
36,
39,
76)
Baptism makes children sons of God and, in itself, suffices to make them angels before they attain the use of reason and the right knowledge of good and evil. However, their education must begin from their childhood, because natural good tendencies can become warped when they are not well-directed and developed by good actions. The repetition of these good acts transforms them into virtue, under the direction of the intellect and will, when they have passed the age of childhood. Is it not the training and the watchfulness of parents that moulds the character of the

children? Will not their exemplary behavior be for their children the sign-post leading the way to virtue and a protection of the treasure of grace and of all the relevant virtues received in baptism? Remember that

"The root of human virtue seldom bears
Like branches; and the Giver wills it so,
That men might know it is His gift and not
   theirs." (a)

Hence it is necessary that even those children, whom nature has endowed with a good character, should be well looked after so that they may grow up properly and be an honor to the home and to their parents.

(Ask God the grace to pass on virtue.)

THE CULTIVATION OF YOUNG PLANTS

All. to newly-weds, April 14, 1943.

(Virtues come from God but must be cultivated by man.)

First of all comes the education of the child on the part of the father and mother, and then the personal correspondence on the part of the child itself, as it gradually grows up to adolescence and manhood. **432 (30, 34, 87)**

If the cooperation of parents with the creative power of God, in order to give life to a future citizen of heaven, is one of the most wonderful plans of Providence to honor humanity, is it not a more wonderful thing that they should be called on to form a Christian? This cooperation is so real and efficacious that a Catholic author was able to write a very pleasing book on the mothers of Saints. What parents worthy of the name would not appreciate such a great honor and strive to attain it?

431a Dante, *Purgatory* VII, 121-123. Taken from the translation by Dorothy Sayers.

433
(39,
41)
But you must cultivate virtue in yourselves also, or rather, primarily in yourselves. Your mission and dignity demand it. The degree of perfection and sanctity of the parent will correspond with the excellence of the education which they give their children in every case. Children are "like a tree which is planted near running waters, which shall bring forth its fruit, in due season, and its leaf shall not fall off." (a) What influence will your behavior and tenor of life, which they will have before their eyes from their birth, have on them? Do not forget that example is of far greater effect on those little creatures, even before the age in which they will be able to understand the lessons you may give them. But even supposing that God were to supplement the defect in education by exceptional means, how can you call real family virtues those which, while they flourish in the hearts of the children, have withered away in the hearts of father or mother?

434
(32,
33,
34)
Now, the gardener has two things to do: he must first place the plant in such a manner as to benefit, and not suffer, from external conditions; and then till the earth and cultivate the plant itself in order that its growth, its flowering and its fructification may be assisted.

Therefore it is your duty to guard the child and yourselves from everything that can endanger the honest and Christian life which you and your children are supposed to lead. You must shield your own souls and theirs from everything that might darken or destroy the faith or tarnish the purity, clarity and freshness of spiritual life. How deplorable is the behavior of those who are in no way conscious of this responsibility and have no care for the evil they do to themselves and to the innocent creatures they have brought into the world! Without a thought for the danger involved, they allow themselves and their children to indulge in imprudent reading, shows, relationships, and practices, and they do not realize that a day will come

433a Ps. 1:3.

when imagination and sensuality will revive all these in the minds and hearts of the adolescent which, as a child, he saw without being able to understand! It is not enough to be on the defensive: we must seek the light, the sun, the warmth of Christ's teaching, we must look for the dew and the rain of His grace in order to receive its life, its dynamism, its energy.

But there is still more. If there had been no original **435** sin, God would have commanded fathers and mothers of **(1,** families, as He did our first parents, to till the earth and **32,** to cultivate flowers and fruits, but this would have been **34)** a pleasant task for man, and not a burden. (a) But sin, so often, alas, forgotten or openly ignored, has made work a hard thing. Nature, as well as the earth, demands the sweat of the brow: an unceasing battle must be waged to weed out, to uproot dangerous tendencies and the germs of vice, to destroy harmful influences. Even our good inclinations tend to become warped and, therefore, must be purified and adjusted. In particular cases it is necessary to stimulate apathy in the practice of some virtues and to restrain and regulate natural enthusiasm and spontaneity in the exercise of others, in order that the whole personality may develop harmoniously.

This is a task that we face at every moment of our lives. . . .

(The model: the Holy Family of Nazareth.)

MODEL FOR EDUCATION

All. to the "Frances Xavier Cabrini" Institute, April 29, 1945.

(The Patron Saint of the Institute.—Her zeal for the reign of the Sacred Heart.)

To fulfill these aspirations and to achieve her mission **436** in all its multiple undertakings, she directed her efforts **(46,**

435a St. Thomas, *Summa Theologica*, 1, q. 102, a. 3.

92,
108)
above all to the family, and made the education of youth her principal aim. In her eyes, in Italy as well as in the United States (as everywhere else), every school, from the humblest village-school to the most high-class institution, was a center of action and extended its beneficial influence not only, in the first place, to the home, but also to every stratum of society.

(Her Daughters continue the same apostolic mission.)

It might seem strange to enumerate ignorance, inertia and lack of character as some of the causes of today's evils. Do not our times exalt knowledge, action and independence almost to the point of idoltary? And yet (We have no intention of generalizing about or of ignoring many and excellent exceptions), is it not true that very often our modern culture is superficial and sacrifices clarity, depth and solidity for more far-reaching qualities? The mind is clogged by a jumble of vague notions which the intelligence is unable to grasp and thus is not in a position to acquire that particular light which gives secure guidance to the will in performing good works.

(Zeal is not capricious agitation; strength of character is not obstinacy.—Extension of the Christian education of women in the modern world.)

THE VOCATION OF THE EDUCATOR

All. to Italian Catholic teachers, November 4, 1945.

437
(80,
92)
My dear children, your oft-repeated desire and persistent wish to listen to the words and advice of your common Father and Shepherd during this your Convention in Rome is a sufficiently clear indication of the extent to which you realize the sublime importance of your mission and of the responsibility that rests on your shoulders. Not that such proof was necessary. Your actions and your entire conduct have already provided ample proof! It is beyond

doubt that the life of a whole nation feels the effects of the first education given to its youth: "Train up a child in the way he should go and, when he is old he will not depart from it." (a) It is a truth that finds an echo in one of the greatest and wisest of the poets of Rome: "Quo semel est imbuta recens, servabit odorem testa diu." (b)

This is true always and everywhere, even in the most normal times and among the soundest peoples. But how much more true is it in these days of universal agitation, when the world, nations, Italy itself depends on the children—whether they come from Christian or irreligious families; from refined surroundings or from the slums; yes, even those urchins you meet on the street and who perhaps greet you with jeers and who sometimes unfortunately carry about quite openly the cruel brand of their misery and precocious vice.

Teachers are the delegates of parents

If, granted the best of conditions and the most favorable circumstances, the education of children is the glorious mission of parents, and particularly of the mother, their task needs to be assisted and completed by the cooperation of teachers, both men and women, to whom they entrust their children. Should we say "completed," or not, rather, very often, "replaced"? There are mothers—it grieves Us to say so—who are quite incapable of realizing their sacred duty and sublime office, who have no idea of the aim of education, who, on account of their own lack of formation or of their deformation, are ignorant of the basic rules of pedagogy. All they desire is to be left in peace and to be allowed to pursue the selfish pleasures and material interests which occupy their minds. But how many others, in spite of their good will and devotedness, find themselves

438
(29,
31,
36,
46)

437a Prov. 22:6.
437b Horace Ep. 1, 2, 69f.

today, more than ever before, unable to carry out their duty adequately, on account of present-day living conditions. Innumerable household chores, often even work outside the home, allow them neither time nor possibility to perform a labor so dear to their hearts and which is the only reason of their life here on earth. Add to this the fact that the ever-growing demands of child education oblige parents to hand on (sometimes entirely) to others their precious privilege of educating the little creatures to whom they have given life.

You are, then, delegates and representatives of parents, acting in their place. What an honor this is! But, at the same time, if you did not realize that you have received it from God, how you should tremble when considering the dignity, the consequences, the responsibilities, the difficulties and the gravity of such a task!

The work of the teacher is hard and difficult

439
(53,
81,
86)
A certain type of romantic literature, very fictitious, sentimental, and now almost out of fashion, liked to portray the child as nothing else but charming and delightfully "poetic." For the Christian, the child is entitled to respect (even the pagan Juvenal warns us, that the "greatest respect is due to the child") (a) and he inspires an incomparably higher sort of poetry: he is a child of God; his angel always beholds the face of the Father Who is in heaven (b) and men are asked to make themselves like children in simplicity and humility. (c) Putting aside sentimental poetry, which is only the fruit of fantasy, and in spite of the poetry of the sublime reality, it must be admitted that the first formation of the child, or, as the case may be, of a group of children, can be a hard and

439a Satire 14, 47.
439b Matt. 18:10.
439c Matt. 18:3-4.

difficult task. Monsignor Dupanloup, the famous Bishop
of Orleans, wrote: "The long years I have devoted to their
care have been the sweetest years of my life. But they have
also been the most fatiguing, and if my hair has become
prematurely grey, it has been in the service of children." (d)

Truly, life can often be hard for one who passes long,
weary days with children: coping with their thoughtlessness,
their whims, their lightheadedness, the defects each one
has. Add to this, miseries of every kind, even when these do
not, like poisonous weeds, destroy the natural charm and
freshness of the supernatural innocence of the child. Not a
few of them have seen and heard everything, and have perhaps even gone through the grinding millstone of life.
Others have grown up without having ever heard about
God, the Blessed Virgin, the angels, the saints, their souls
or their eternal destiny, and they are quite indifferent to
whatever you try to tell them about the truths of faith.

However, We have no desire to paint too dark a picture. Many, indeed, very many children are born and bred,
or at least are re-educated in a truly Christian atmosphere.
But even the best of them, even those possessed of exceptional qualities, are a strain on one's patience, not only because of their little defects, but also on account of their
childishness, involving as it does persistent questioning,
quarrelsomeness and noisiness!

In spite of all this, the good teacher must pursue his **440**
work with zeal and, at the same time, calmly, not allow- *(53,*
ing himself to display any sign of fatigue or annoyance that *81)*
might, in a moment, compromise the results of weeks and
months of hard work or that might destroy or even diminish
the child's trust in him. Finally, even when all has gone
well, when so much care has been lavished on the initial
formation of these little children, just when one can expect
the bud to burst into flower and produce the fruit, they

439d De l'Education, lib. 2, c. 1.

must be handed over to others and the work must be begun over again, from the beginning, with new pupils.

441
(50,
82,
86)
Not only is a teacher's work fatiguing, however, but it is also difficult. It demands, even in the case of little children, specialized knowledge, experience and teaching ability. It requires study, practice, help and support, .aborious training and a complete possession of oneself. Certainly, your Association will help you to acquire these. But We recommend that an attempt be made to inspire higher sentiments, under the conviction that all purely natural means are not able to triumph over all obstacles. This conviction is certainly well-founded.

The three principal motives of the teacher's vocation

442
(53,
54)
How do you explain the fact that, in spite of the sorrows and difficulties which pertain to your profession, in spite of the arduous preparation it demands and the hardships it involves, so many candidates aspire after it? They may be influenced by three chief motives: natural inclination, material interest, an ideal.

It is not hard to understand the passion for teaching in colleges and universities, and even in high schools. The professor feels a peculiar pride in seeing young minds and hearts opening out under his influence: he communicates his own thoughts, his own convictions, his own likes and dislikes, all this to start youth off on a career that may be great or modest, but is always useful and to the credit of society. This noble pleasure greatly compensates for the annoyances, hardships and disillusionments which will surely not be lacking. But when it comes to little children, it is so easy, from afar, to feel attracted, with almost paternal or maternal affection, to them. But if some other principle or some other interior impulse is absent, this attraction soon turns into disgust. But, you will say, there are many (yourselves among them) whose desire is only made stronger with experience and in the face of hardship and sacrifice. That is, no doubt, true. But the reason is that, in this case, the inclination is not present alone, like a blind instinct, but is sustained and spurred on by one of the other two motives, material interest or an ideal.

Let us not be quick to despise or find fault with material interests. The teacher is a man; he must live and therefore has a right to a just and honorable recompense for his work, which will enable him to provide for himself and his family. This, however, is only his stipend. He does not teach for the sake of this, but for love. The ideal is the force that moves and spurs him on. Moreover, faced with the necessity of living, a young man (or woman) thinks about finding the means to provide for his future and to look after his parents. Among the various states of life, he chooses the one he esteems most and which he considers most useful to him. Even if the needs of his daily bread occupied his thoughts at the beginning, a higher sentiment prompted his choice and therefore entitles him to respect and esteem. On the other hand, he who looks upon teaching merely as a job, which he would willingly leave if he could obtain a more lucrative post, is only a poor mercenary, who leads a joyless and loveless existence, something like a prisoner dragging his heavy chains and thinking only of escape.

It is clear, therefore, that the real stimulus to the teaching vocation can only come from a real ideal. Only an ideal can lead one to master an art which excels all others, according to the well-known opinion of St. John Chrysostom. (a) This is the ideal that inspires all teachers, men as well as women, whose zeal achieves excellent results.

The ideal of the Catholic teacher

We are talking of an ideal, and here again, we are faced with so many alternatives. What ideal? There are

443
(54)

444
(79,

443a In Matt. *Homilia* 59, No. 7. Migne. P. G. 58, 584.

80,
106) men and women who profane their gifts of intelligence
and their fatherly and motherly instinct, in the service of
impiety and hatred of religion and their fellowmen. They
consecrate the years of their youth and maturity to this
fiendish task; they take upon themselves the hardships of
teaching to attain this end, sacrificing their own rest
and their own interests and even their consciences. But
there are other men and women inflamed with a holier
ideal and anxious to perform their duty in conformity with
the principles of the Gospel. These feel themselves irresistibly drawn to protect children from evil in order to
give them to God, to undergo weariness and discomfort in
order to form men who will serve Christ, the Church and
human society in a worthy manner. And this is your ideal;
this is the love that has conquered your hearts and to
which you have pledged your lives!

It is this splendid ideal, this love which participates
of the love of God Himself, which inspires you and which
sweetens the severity of your work.

The child is the future, either a dangerous future or
a future of promise. As he strolls down the street, carrying within him unknowingly the seeds of every virtue and
vice, the passers-by ask themselves: "What a one, think ye,
shall this child be?" (a) You too have anxiously asked the
same question: what will be his future for himself, for
society, for the Church? The question has worried you and
you have carried that child, those children, all children,
in your hearts; you made the firm resolution, you promised
God to make of those children the architects of the social
restoration in Christ.

Associations for the formation of teachers

445   But a feeling, not just of discouragement, but almost
(50, of fear, immediately enters your hearts. Your number,

444a Luke 1:66.

thank God, is great, but it seems inadequate to the immen- 58)
sity of the task. But then, you have realized that by uniting
yourselves, every one would double his influence for good.
It is the application of the well-known saying, which the
leaders of your Association show they have understood
well: Union is strength. Union achieves, first of all, moral
strength, and if it only did this, it would already be a great
deal! Just picture to yourselves the situation of a teacher,
man or woman, thrown on his or her own resources,
without any support or understanding from the people
around, sometimes even without any sympathy. That will
give you some idea of the great help this union for mutual
aid can be.

But We want to emphasize above all the specific end
of your Association: namely, to encourage and to obtain the
perfect formation of the teacher, to furnish him with all
the means necessary to accomplish his hard, but grand and
noble task, in the best way possible.

What is essential in this formation is not so much the
sum-total of knowledge, of methods, of clever moves, as
the spirit. Anybody who is working for the triumph of a
cause, whether good or bad, whether vital or simply superficial, is well aware that it is necessary to imbue the
hearts of his followers with this spirit. This, then, is the first
aim of your Association: the progress of your personal,
formation—intimate, but as complete and well-balanced as
possible.

Furthermore, since education cannot be really sound **446**
and beneficial if it is confined to the sphere of mere natural *(54,*
uprightness, your ideal must be, and in reality it is, super- *72)*
natural. It follows from this that both your personal life
and your professional activity must be imbued with a
supernatural spirit which, then, must flow out into those
committed to your care. How wonderful it is to see
teachers, both men and women, who, in the morning,
imbued with God through prayer and meditation, fortify
themselves with the flesh of the Immaculate Lamb, and

thus, with burning, radiant hearts, are able, with fatherly and motherly love, to communicate these spiritual riches to the minds and hearts of the little baptized children entrusted to their care. It is to this that your yearly Retreats, your bi-monthly days of recollection, and the Holy Mass you offer in common, all tend.

447
(50,
58) But, as We have already indicated, your formation must be complete. For this reason, it is not only opportune but also indispensable that your professional, pedagogical standing—precisely because you desire to tend toward perfection in the supernatural order—be eminent, superior. You should always be up to date with the uninterrupted progress of ideas and methods. The Association takes care of this aspect by courses of religious and social formation and techniques, by preparing young teachers for competitive examinations, by monthly reunions, by your journal and your libraries. It extends its interest to cover problems that relate to the kindergarten, to recreation centers and to teacher-training schools.

To obtain just legislation

448
(58) And this is not all. You must demand your rights and the means to keep them. You must defend, protect and assert your rights as Catholic teachers and the possibility to fulfill the obligations involved. Evidently, you cannot do so individually and by yourselves. Hence the need for united action through your Association. The Association proposes (and particularly in these days of universal reorganization) individual and social action to obtain educational laws that respect what is demanded by Catholic doctrine. This action is all the more legitimate in Italy, where this important matter is treated in a solemn Concordat between the Holy See and the Italian State.

449
(22, Finally you are also concerned with assuring to teachers, whether men or women, a standard of living in keep-

ing with their needs and the dignity of their work. We have 58)
already spoken more than once of the only "Sindacato"
that exists in Italy and to which Catholics also belong, and
of the requirements for membership. Well then, from the
moment that you also become members, you should refuse
to allow yourselves to be carried away passively by the
current which unites the professional or social activity of
our youth of today. You will therefore have to achieve the
necessary degree of specialization, which will enable you to
give your opinion on all matters dealth with by "the Sindacato" and to exert your influence in defence of the Religious and moral principles of the Church. You will be able
to cooperate with your colleagues (and with perfect loyalty)
in whatever is good or at least not illegal. On other points,
you will have the possibility of striving for a more Christian
understanding of the work of education and teaching as
also of the interests of your class.

(Blessing.)

PUBLIC MORALITY AND YOUTH

All. to the young men of Italian Catholic Action, April
20, 1946.

(*Hours of crisis in which important decisions are being
made for the nation.*)

The slogan you have launched, "Save the child," ex-   **450**
presses at one and the same time, the fears and hopes of   **(4,**
present times, but above all, its crying needs.   **97,**

The child is the center of all the most vital questions,   **112,**
of all the most essential values: marriage and the family,   **113,**
wife and mother, education and public morality. Wherever   **117)**
these questions are settled according to the divine law and
the Christian spirit, wherever these important values are
safeguarded and defended, then also is the child and youth
saved. But where the forces of destruction and evil have
gained the upper hand, harmful results soon make their ap-

pearance, even in small boys and adolescents. But surely you yourselves have seen them! Do you not have before your eyes the terrible spectacle of a corrupt and contaminated youth, sick with contagious germs of moral and physical infection which they pass on to future generations, in virtue of the inexorable laws of nature?

(The material want of children is a faint image of the misery of their souls.)

451
(22,
28,
66,
95,
97,
107,
110)

History always teaches us that all great catastrophes, not only economic and political, but especially spiritual and religious, are preceded by the decay of public morality and the corruption of the people's way of life, which forces its way boldly ahead and concentrates especially on the young generations. Present-day experience only confirms the lesson of history. We shall never weary of condemning, on every possible occasion, at least three of the most terrible forms of the hideous Moloch which devours so many victims: divorce, schools without God, licentious literature and entertainments. Inhuman mothers feel no twinge of remorse in taking their children to the most immoral shows and "reviews."

Undoubtedly there are always, even among a youth so depraved, miracles of grace, heroes and saints who have overcome the seductions and the attractions of the world that surround them. But these miracles are rare, and these heroes and saints are the exception. It would be a fatal illusion to think that these exceptions can become the rule without an improvement in social conditions. It would be unfair to attribute to faulty pastoral care all the responsibility for this spiritual ruin, which, in children of six, ten or fifteen years, is almost inevitably caused by the continual influence of schools that have no religion or are even antireligious, by the dangers on the streets, by the morally tainted air of factories and offices. In the natural order of things (or better, according to the dispositions of divine Providence) the child must be born and must grow in the healthy atmosphere of the family and Christian society. There he must gradually make progress until he attains that maturity which will enable him, in turn, to support, to promote and to perfect an honest and a Christian social order.

(In Italy, Christian culture is threatened.—Catholic Action must come to the aid of want, must enlighten Catholics as to their religious interests and civic duties, must defend and inculcate Christian teachings and morals.—The "Alleluia" of the Easter victory.)

THE JOY OF TEACHING

All. to French Catholic professors and students, April 24, 1946.

(Search for the light.—Various attitudes of men.—The Church, sure guide.—For the wise man who believes, the central point of the synthesis of knowledge is in God: here is situated the "joy of knowing" according to Father Termier.)

No matter how soul-satisfying be the "joy of knowing," it finds its complement in the joy of teaching. To teach! What a sublime task, by which man, in the humble measure of his created capacity, participates in the action of the Incarnate Word. St. Thomas sums up admirably this dignity of the teacher: "As it is a greater thing to give light than to shine alone, so also it is a greater thing to pass on to others things we have contemplated, than to contemplate alone." (a) The Divine Master has said of Himself: "No man hath seen God at any time: the only begotten Son Who is in the bosom of the Father, He hath declared Him." (b) Your colleagues in the University, admired for the high degree of their learning, revered for their outstanding

452
(51,
53)

452a Summa, 2a, 2ae., q. 188, a. 6.
452b John 1:18.

virtue: Ferrini, Toniolo, your own great Ozanam, are witnesses to the sublime beauty of your mission. "After the infinite consolations that a Catholic experiences at the foot of the altar, after the joys of family life, I know no greater happiness," wrote Ozanam, "I know no greater happiness than that of speaking to young men who have intelligence and a heart." (c)

(In every profession: spread the light of Christianity.— Catholic professional meetings.—Material progress cause of two wars in fifty years.—Return to the Heavenly Father.)

BASIS OF EDUCATION

All. to the Sisters of the Assumption, May 19, 1946.

(A portrait of the foundress.—Two tendencies in her social surroundings: middle-class principles and the fight for a radical reform.—The value and danger of same.)

453
(60,
63,
64,
69,
105) ... The danger was derived from a common origin: insufficiency or, much more, the lack of equilibrium, of a solid foundation in the intellectual, moral and religious education of youth, including girls, and, consequently, the almost total deficiency of a real social formation of womenfolk. The way to overcome this very soon became evident to her: complete and stabilize all that education on its indispensable foundations. She outlined her program in a summarized statement to the great educator of the time, Monsignor Dupanloup, Bishop of Orleans. She wanted her daughters to receive a broad education, which besides the study of the mother tongue and national literature, arithmetic and geography, history of peoples and natural science, would include the history of the Church, the knowledge of philosophy, the beauties of art and, most important of all,

452c Letter to M. Benoit, Feb. 28, 1853.—*Complete Works, XI, Letters, II, 470.*

religion. It was to be an education which, more than imagination and sentiment, was to bring the intellect back to truth and faith, and direct the will to the good, to renunciation and sacrifice, in order to form the character of the Christian woman, making her wise and strong, courteous and frank, honored and active.

In fact, the entire pedagogical structure of your Foundress has two main concerns. The first of these is the blending of religion and of life, a blending which reigns where thought and action, where all human life, even public life, is not discordant with the truths of faith and moral law, but is, in fact, in perfect agreement with them and is intimately permeated by their spirit. The other is faith, a conscious and alert faith, not a vague religious sense, the result of pure habit or custom. Without doubt, religious habits and pious customs are of great value, but only when from one generation to the other they awaken, stimulate, support and further the personal life of faith. What value would all the splendor of God's houses have, what would be the scope of God's own home among men, if the faithful no longer took care to build in themselves, within their very own spirit, the temple of the Lord, if they no longer believed?

454
(2,
4,
26,
59,
71,
72,
74)

With extraordinary intuition, Mary Eugenia of Jesus had foreseen how the future of the world, no less for woman than for man, would depend upon the stability of these two fundamental columns.

(Human calamities which occurred after 100 *years.— Far-reaching causes: life separated from religion.)*

To take in hand the education of young female persons and to form for the family, the people and the Church women capable of complying, by virtue of their faith, with the requirements of their time, was the ideal at which Mary Eugenia of Jesus aimed, and was the work which she accomplished.

(A work which is even more necessary today.)

THERE IS NO REAL EDUCATION
WITHOUT RELIGION

All. to the Postmaster General and other authorities of the United States, July 20, 1946.

(The Lord, an example for those who help the victims of war.—Spiritual needs are greater than corporal needs.)

455
(4,
60,
105,
107)
The most needy of all are the children who, if they are deprived of the knowledge of the faith, will be hindered in their moral development and led astray in their spiritual education. No education is really complete if it omits religion just as no training is complete if it does not develop man as a whole. The child of today will be the citizen of tomorrow.

(If a real restoration is desired, that which concerns the spirit must not be left to one side.)

PROBLEMS OF MODERN EDUCATION

Letter *Le sujet qu'ont choisi* to Rev. Father Archambault, July 27, 1946.

(Twenty-third Social Week of Canada.—The rebuilding of the world with the young generations.)

456
(109,
112)
There is a volume of truth on this question which, especially lately, has been the subject of profound teaching by the Holy See. Is it perhaps necessary to recall the code on the education of youth, constituted by the Encyclical, *Divini illius Magistri?* (a) In this, the respective positions of the family, of the Church and of the State are perfectly outlined. If it is really desired to educate youth in a way which will lead to a better future for the society, it is absolutely necessary to remember the imprescriptible and natu-

456a Cf. Nos. 240-304.

ral rights of the Church and of the family in this field. Without doubt, the State has an important part in this which, however, is certainly not that which is attributed to it by the totalitarian conception of ancient and modern paganism. Hence the necessity of making the just laws of teaching triumph everywhere, which are required by natural moral and the most elementary justice, as well as by the teachings of the Gospel and of the Christian order.

Other associated problems will make an equal claim on your attention. The youth of today, through present-day hard economic conditions, is aware of the difficulties the Government has to meet to avoid being hindered in its normal development, both on the educational, professional and family levels. Also the problems of modern pedagogy will have to be studied in the light of the pontifical teachings with regard to the evolution of systems of life and technique. We cherish, in particular, the idea of an organization for entertainments and a moderate practice of sports which, if properly understood, can and must help in the complete formation of man and of the perfect Christian who thinks and acts according to reason illuminated by faith. **457** *(5, 21, 82, 91, 102)*

(Encouragement.)

PREPARING FOR THE FUTURE

All. to the Catholic Association of School Teachers, September 8, 1946.

(Theme of the Congress: Save the child.)

The most important thing today is the permanent basis of the whole education of youth and of the people—a basis that ought to be incorporated in and decreed by the future Constitution. Without doubt, this will be one of the most serious problems that will be taken up by the Constituent Assembly; two opposite trends are brought face to **458** *(23, 92, 106, 187)* face: one which supports the Christian, Catholic school, and the other which advocates those schools commonly called lay schools; that is to say, school without religion.

But the clear results of the last decades have proved to be unfavorable to the school without religion, which is, in fact, or comes to be, anti-religious. This type of school, according to the experiences of the past and of the present century, too, has produced some bitter fruits, and has therefore failed in its true purpose; on the other hand, for almost two hundred years, Christian education has gloriously overcome all trials. Is it not significant that precisely today, even among some who do not profess our faith, the vast majority of parents who have been able to express their will freely have asked for a Christian education and Christian schools for their children?

Those responsible for education

459
(8,
14,
15,
20,
21,
117)
Your motto has, therefore, the following meaning. Let the child grow in the pure atmosphere of a Christian family and give him a school which, by mutual cooperation between the family and the Church, will work for the sound formation of youth. Parents naturally have a primary right in the education of their children, a right, as declared Our glorious Predecessor Pius XI, inviolable and superior to that of civil society and of the State. (a) But the Church has a direct and pre-eminent right in the field of education, and the right to all the necessary and useful means to procure that end, since the Church is teacher and supernatural mother of souls, to whom is committed the religious care of men and who, as a consequence, is also responsible for the spiritual and moral formation of the child. Surely We would not deny or diminish the right proper also to the State in the matter of education; this right finds its founda

459a Encyc. *Divini Illius Magistri*, December 31, 1929.-
Cf. No. 257.

tion, and at the same time its measure and its limit, in the common good of the nation. But the common good requires that the State should protect and respect the right of education which belongs to the family and the Church.

The aim to be attained is always—according to the natural law and the will of Christ, and in view of the common good—that the family, the Church and the State should cooperate together in the instruction and education of youth. This principle constitutes the essential presupposition of Art. 36 of the existing Concordat with Italy, in which "the teaching of Christian Doctrine according to the manner handed on by Catholic tradition" is proclaimed as the "foundation and culmination of public instruction." Therefore, exert yourselves to the utmost in order that these foundations, ratified and confirmed by the widest experience, be exactly maintained and observed and in order that, in every respect, this type of school should be fully assured to the parents who desire Catholic schools for their children.

460
(6,
117)

The important function of the Christian teacher

We live at a time of widespread social upheaval; it could happen, therefore, that one or another among the Catholic teachers, especially among younger teachers, might be tempted to think and to ask himself what is the meaning and what is the value, in the midst of colossal events, of his little task in a school that is perhaps very small, among children of the more simple and humble people. May no one of you, dear sons, permit himself to become agitated by thoughts or feelings such as these, which are misleading. The magnitude of these events which we are daily witnessing certainly cannot be denied. However, neither can we omit any consideration as to how often, even during the last three centuries, have these words of the Psalmist been verified: "Dominus dissipat consilium

461
(4,
52)

nationum; irritas facit cogitationes popolorum": At the Lord's bidding, a nation's purposes come to nothing, a people's designs are thwarted. (a)

The future is hidden from us as in an impenetrable mist. But you can control it because in your hands are fashioned those who shall dominate and mould future generations. These generations—that is to say, the children of today—will succeed in forming and mastering a new society for the greatest good of the human family, if those who undertake this work in soundness of mind and body are composed of honest citizens who are good Christians.

462
(45,
46,
52,
54,
83)
But all this depends essentially on your action, for nothing, with the exception of the home, has a more lasting effect on the souls of young people than the school. Here is the importance of your task, even if, perchance, it should be accomplished in a poor school lost in a mountain village —a task that, in our times, is much more important and delicate because is it not a fact that quite often you must supplement the failings of many parents who, as a result of poverty, the difficulties of life and other external circumstances are less capable of carrying out their holy and arduous educational mission?

Always consider your school, whether large and neat, or small and mean, as a temple where dignity and purity prevail, where truth and justice have their prominent places, where religion is resplendent, that religion which raises and ennobles the mind in God, in God Who is present everywhere. In the same way, may God govern the movements of your own minds and hearts; God Who is the infallible discerner of your thoughts and affections, which must all be turned toward the acquisition of goodness and the moral virtues in order that you may become yourselves the moulders of young souls.

(*The protection of the Blessed Virgin Mary.*)

461a Ps. 32:10.

CONQUERING THE SPIRIT OF EVIL

All. to a group of French students, April 7, 1947.

The apostle St. John, in his wonderful letter to the **463** faithful, reveals his predilection for youth: "I am addressing *(76,* myself to you, young men, because you are strong, because *94)* the word of God abides in you, and because you have con- quered the spirit of evil." (a) We experience a like joy in receiving you, young students, because it enables Us to express the singular affection and confidence We have in you.

The spirit of evil, which knows no disarmament, at this very moment redoubles its efforts in a battle against the Church, human society, and against God and Christ Him- self. And the blind fury which the spirit of evil puts into this fight would almost make us think that the battle was on the verge of ending in a definitive solution if we did not already know that it is going to last till the end of the world and that it will end in a final victory for God and and for His Church. Inasmuch as the spirit of evil spreads ruin, it makes innumerable victims: victims of those who, blindly, let themselves be conquered, carried away and made slaves by it; victims also—fortunate indeed but none- theless suffering—are those who persevere in the holy lib- erty of the sons of God but at the price of heroic sacrifices.

Who will be the victor? The strong! And you are the strong, you, the youth, the authentic youth, whose strength is developing healthily and vigorously, whose spirit rises without equivocation into the light of the word of God, whose heart, pure, high-spirited and generous, knows how to conquer in itself, above all, the spirit of evil. *Fortes estis? Verbum Dei manet in vobis? Vicistis malignum.*

463a 1 John 2:14.

The Church depends on the young

464
(5,
61,
93)
It is quite well-known that you, the young, are the first prizes which the forces of good and evil are striving to win over to their side. It is you, before all else, that they aim to win. If the spirit of evil intimidates you or entices you in order to conquer you, to enroll you in his army and in his shock troops, the Church, too, calls you to action; and We Ourselves proclaim that We are counting on you more earnestly. For this reason it is that you see Us so intensely interested in everything that concerns you—your well-being, your safety, your progress, and your activity, in every order, whether the physical, intellectual, moral or supernatural. Yes, We mention physical as all these are very closely connected. Healthy Christian youths, fortified by sports that are wisely understood and played, willingly bring to spiritual battles and the service of holy causes their contribution of ardor, agility and resistance. When the opportunity presents itself, with a daring answer or with a frank and resounding burst of laughter, they are always ready to disarm an enemy who is inclined to lie, to reason fallaciously or to calumniate.

465
(17,
66,
107)
Throughout her long life the Church has always been attentive to the intellectual life of youth; not only to safeguard the true doctrine for youth, but also to advance youth in the realm of lay and sacred knowledge. Ideas, basic philosophical ideas, lead the world, they say. Where do they lead it? These ideas, offspring of learning, but reflections of eternal truth, rays of uncreated light, lead it, in orderly fashion, toward its perfection for its own good and happiness. When truths are cut off, however, from their divine source they are no more than shadows: woe to the world on that day when, deceived, it takes shadow for light and light for shadow. (a) The world walks in the darkness, it runs amid disorder to its ruin, the ruin of society and the

465a Is. 5:29.

eternal souls that compose it. In order that the world may shine with truth, it is above all in the hands of youth that the torch of ideas must shine forth.

Youth, you have the enthusiasm which engenders enthusiasm. The future is in your hands. Make the word of God which dwells in you burn within you and shed forth its rays of eternal light to illuminate every man in this world. (b)

Strong in this way you will overcome the spirit of evil.

The internal victory

But above all, it is within yourselves that you must conquer this spirit of evil. You will conquer it by a battle that is at once courageous and prudent—and yet the battle will never end definitively here below. Do not be like those who become conscious of their own weakness and the imminent reality of danger only through sad personal experience; nor do We want you to be like those deaf or presumptuous children to whom the cautions and counsels of a wise mother seem always exaggerated. Do not be surprised, then, at the cautions of your Holy Mother, the Church. On her part it is wisdom and not austere severity if she puts the young on their guard against dangerous recreations which constitute a peril for the senses; against the high-sounding but erroneous teachings which in the scientific, historical, philosophical and social domains compromise right reason and health of mind; against the frivolous distractions and premature and casual love affairs in which young hearts squander away what ought to be given only once and for their entire life. Besides this prudence, and even in order to be faithful to this prudence, you now have need, as you always will, to struggle and therefore to have the necessary strength to struggle against the attractions of pleasure, against the repugnance of sacrifice, against the

**466
(76,
87)**

465b John 1:9.

seductions and suggestions of your companions, against vain curiosity and human respect, against passions and temptations—to struggle even against the momentary cessation of temptation in which, during this temporary truce which he cleverly offers, the spirit of evil seeks to lull you into lack of vigilance.

467
(72,
73)
Yes, the battle is harsh and unrelenting, but it should not frighten you, dear young people, provided that you have the secret of victory. And you have it! *Haec est victoria quae vincit mundum? Fides vestra:* This is the victory which overcomes the world, your faith. (a) Strengthen and illuminate your faith! Live your faith! Live in Christ, in His Light, in His strength, and in His grace. Nourish yourselves on His body and blood in the Sacrament of the Eucharist; then you will be strong, then you will conquer. Make your prayer ascend to Him, to the Father, through the hands and heart of Mary, His Mother and your Mother. Through her hands and motherly heart an abundance of divine help will descend upon you, in token of which, dear sons and daughters, We give you with all Our heart's affection Our Apostolic Blessing.

BLESSED BENILDO

All. to the pilgrims for the Beatification of Brother Benildo, April 5, 1948.

(*A eulogy of Blessed Benildo. His life.*)

468
(59,
81)
When justice and duty did not limit his charity, it was extended to all with a smile and thoughtful kindness. He was on the alert to discover and ease the needs of families, especially those of his pupils; but he used so much discretion and intelligence that even the most suspicious would not have been able to feel any humiliation in receiving

467a 1 John 5:4.

what, in normal circumstances, would have had the appearance of alms-giving. He gave away books and other scholastic material; he cared for the sick, especially for those whose sickness caused some repulsion; he instructed them with special lessons.

How much he loved his boys! At the same time, what a heavy cross they placed on his shoulders! The Martyriology tells us of the prayer of a school teacher who had all the more to suffer from his pupils, who had become his executioners, because their weak blows prolonged the torture. (a)

469
(53,
54,
80,
59,
81)

This is an isolated case, but how many teachers have to suffer for years, for the whole of a long religious life, almost a kind of slow martyrdom from the children who do not for a moment think that they are in any way the cause of suffering.

Brother Benildo let slip a sentence that permits us to catch a glimpse of what he had to suffer during his life as teacher and director: "If we did not have faith, our task would be an arduous one; the children are difficult, but with faith everything changes."

If children were all obedient and good, the consolation that they would offer would not hinder their tendency to be often troublesome, tiresome with their foolishness, their distractions and with their difficulty sometimes to understand even the most simple matters. Then, the moment they have gained some refinement they leave school and pass into other hands, forgetting their teacher, who patiently sets to work with the new generation; so it goes on, year after year. If it were nothing but this, it would still be the ideal; but for all those subjects who correspond to the cares showered upon them, how many are those others who give nothing but trouble and difficulty, and whose education merely causes sweat and tears!

469a St. Cassiano, martyr, *Martyrologium Romanum*, August 13.

470
(54,
57,
59)
The unfailing constancy in the fidelity to the humble duties of daily life, in the practice of all the virtues and at all times, must necessarily be an external manifestation of a deep and vigorous interior life, overflowing with divine sap. Only those who can make the motto of St. Paul their own: "It is to heaven that we look," (a) are capable of setting an example with the unchanging calm of Blessed Benildo.

Unceasingly occupied in the care of the Brothers of his community and of his boys, he was nevertheless in constant union with God. He was to be seen habitually with the Rosary in his hand and, effortlessly, by a spontaneous overflowing of his devotion, he inspired everyone with the love of Jesus, Mary and Joseph.

An admirable model, but also a model imitable by all....

(Intercession of Blessed Benildo for the Brothers of Christian Schools and for their works.)

CONTENTED STUDENTS

All. to the professors and pupils of the "Overseas School of Rome," April 10, 1948.

(Welcome.)

471
(45,
47,
80,
86)
For children whose minds and hearts are opening to their spiritual need to grow in wisdom and grace while they advance in age, as well as for mothers and fathers who enlist the precious aid of the teacher to help them meet that need, the school must indeed be a holy place for much the same reason that the home is holy.

"Maxima debitur puero reverentia—We owe the utmost reverence to the child," (a) is a perennial exhortation,

470a Phil. 3:20.
471a Juvenal, *Satire*, 14, 47.

as well as a warning, addressed to parent and teacher alike
by the classic wisdom of pagan Rome, ages before the great
Christian teacher of the East, Saint Gregory Nazianzen,
reminded you both, parents and teachers, that the direction
and formation of youth is τέχνη τεχνῶν, καὶ ἐπιστήμη ἐπι
στημῶν — "the art of arts, the science of sciences." (b)

Even the delicate irony of your poet Shakespeare **472**
alludes to this holy duty of home and classroom when he *(31,*
represents for us the "woeful pageant" of the seven ages of *45,*
man, played too often on the stage of the world: *51,*
".... the whining schoolboy, with his satchel *69,*
And shining morning face, creeping like a snail *73,*
Unwillingly to school." (a) *87,*
    Children who do not whine are those whose school has *88,*
been made a holy and wholesome place in which to live *101,*
and play, to love and know Him Who is the Way, the *102)*
Truth, and the Life; parents and teachers aware of their
sublime privilege and duty of suffering the little ones to
come unto Him (b) for light and strength during the years
when mind and character are formed—these actors on the
stage of life are playing a glorious part, not in a pageant
of woe, but in the true drama of peace, redemption and
resurrection for men and nations of good will.

    May your hearts and homes, your schools and your
countries be spared the terrible horror We have lived to
witness and lament in Christian Europe as children by the
hundred are torn at a tender age from the hands of their
parents, and the hallowed halls of their little schools are
formed or deformed by alien teachers at the bidding of
their sacrilegious masters.

471b Or. II, Apologetica.—Migne P. G. 35, 425.
472a *As You Like It.* Act II, sc. vii.
472b Cf. Matt. 19:14.

All. to the Italian Association of Catholic Schoolteachers, September 2, 1948.

(The Congress on the organization of the new State schools.)

473
(2,
36,
60)
Above all, We are happy that the scholastic reforms now in preparation, and especially the organic structure of teaching, from the kindergarten to the secondary school, correspond to the primary aim of your Association, namely that of instructing and forming the entire human person, his intellectual faculties not less than his will and instincts, the future industrious and honest citizen, as also the Christian, Son of God, "sharer of a heavenly calling." (a)

In the second place, the new school presents a great possibility of beneficial and fruitful collaboration between the family, the Church and the school.

474
(36,
46,
89)
As regards the kindergarten, We consider that the child, during those years preceeding his or her entry into the primary school, must be left as much as possible to the mother. However, when she is unable to attend personally to the education of the child, and this is not a very rare thing, given modern economic and social conditions, then the sub-primary school or kindergarten is called upon with its appropriate methods and chosen supervisors, to substitute or complete as best as possible the work of the mother. And, beloved children, would it not be an apostolate of rare quality for you to train mothers to be good educators of their children?

475
(50,
54)
Finally, keep it in mind that even the best of programs are of little avail if the master is not fitted for his task, and that, on the contrary, even with a scholastic system that is wanting and falls short in certain regards, a good teacher can always obtain notable results. The "ethical-religious"

473a Heb. 3:1.

conscience in him is the first and indispensable element; but, by itself, it is insufficient, and scholarship and capabilities are also needed. For example: the popularizing of the sciences and of technical productions—immediately ꞏthe "school films" come to mind—offer the schools of today great possibilities, though only if the teacher has a wide knowledge and knows how to employ these means correctly. Hence the necessity of "an adequate cultural and professional preparation," taking care that at the same time the future teacher, in the course of his formation, does not lose the love for the child and the will to dedicate himself with ardor to school work, work that is apparently humble, but which in reality, because of the high end that it serves, is one of the most noble.

During these weeks the youth of Italy are flocking into Rome by hundreds and thousands. Youth in such a great number cannot deceive; they show themselves as they really are. You have seen these young people—in the churches, in the streets, visiting the places of interest in the City, at large gatherings, in St. Peter's Square—sincere, happy, frank, open, enthusiastic for all things beautiful, great and good, but at the same time deeply pious and full of God. Well, these youths have passed through your schools; you have helped to be their co-educators; they are your joy, your consolation, and your encouragement. **476** *(119)*

(Protection of our Blessed Mother.—Apostolic Blessing.)

THE DEMANDS OF OUR TIMES

R.M. to the Inter-American Congress on Catholic Education, October 6, 1948.

(Importance of the Congress.)

The essence and the goal of education—to use the expression of Our immediate Predecessor—consist in collaboration with divine grace for the formation of the true and **477** *(26, 82)* perfect Christian. (a) In this perfection is included the ideal that the Christian, as such, be in a position to face ·and to overcome the difficulties and to correspond to the demands of the times in which it is his lot to live. That means that the work of education, since it must be carried on in a specific environment with a specific method, must constantly adapt itself to the circumstances of this environment, wherein perfection has to be obtained and for which it is destined.

The naturalistic approach to education

478
(69,
116)
Against the pernicious attempts of those who would completely separate religion from education and from the school, or who would at least place the school and education upon a purely naturalistic basis, put forward the ideal of a teaching vocation that is enriched by the inestimable treasure of a sincere faith, vivified by the grace of Our Lord Jesus Christ.

See that your children, your young boys and girls, as they advance in age receive religious instruction that is ever more ample and more deeply established; not forgetting that the full and profound consciousness of religious truths as well as doubts and difficulties usually manifest themselves in the last years of higher studies, especially if the student has come into contact, as hardly can be avoided today, with persons or teachings that are contrary to Christianity. For this reason, religious instruction has every right to demand a place of honor in the program of universities and centers of advanced studies.

479
(63,
69,
72,
97,
113)
See to it that with this instruction there goes, closely united, the holy fear of God, the habit of undistracted prayer, and the full and intelligent participation in the spirit of the liturgical year of Holy Mother Church, the source of countless graces. But in this work, act with caution and prudence, so that it will be the youth himself who will al-

477a Cf. 300.

ways be seeking something more and, little by little, working by himself, will be learning to live and to practise his life of faith.

As against the lack of principles in this age when all things are measured according to the criterion of success, propound a training which renders youth capable of discerning between falsehood and truth, good and bad, right and injustice, firmly establishing in his soul the pure sentiments of love, fraternity and faithfulness. If the dangerous motion pictures of today, appealing as they do only to the senses, and in an excessively one-sided way, carry with them the risk of producing in souls a state of superficiality and spiritual passiveness, the reading of good books may supplement what is here lacking, thus playing an ever more important role in the work of education.

Technical education—Physical training

To the exaggerated importance that is accorded today **480** to whatever is purely technical and material, reply with an *(61,* education which always gives first place to spiritual and *102,* moral values; both to the natural and, above all, to the su- *118)* pernatural ones. The Church, without any doubt whatever, approves of physical culture, if it be in proper proportion, that is to say when it does not lead to a worship of the body, when it is useful to strengthen the body and not to dissipate its energies, when it serves also as a recreation for the spirit and is not a cause of spiritual weakness and crudeness, when it provides new incitements for study and for professional work and does not conduce to their abandonment or neglect or to the disturbance of the peace that should reign in the sanctuary of the home.

The pursuit of pleasure

Immoderate pursuit of pleasure and lack of moral dis- **481** cipline likewise seek to invade even the ranks of Catholic *(72,* youth, trying to make them forget that they bear within *73,*

116)   themselves a fallen nature weighed down with the sad legacy of original sin. Counteract this with an education to self-control, to sacrifice and renunciation, beginning with smaller things and gradually going on to greater ones; training in fidelity in the fulfillment of one's own duties, of sincerity, serenity and purity, especially in the years of development into maturity. But never forget that it is impossible to reach this goal (of personal integrity) without the powerful help of the sacraments of confession and of the Most Holy Eucharist, whose supernatural educative value can never be duly appreciated.

The spirit of independence

482   Develop in the souls of children and youth the hier-
(75,   archic spirit—which does not deny to each age its proper
87)   development—so as to dissipate as far as possible this atmosphere of independence and excessive liberty which our youth breathes in today and which would lead it to throw off all authority and every possible check. Try to arouse and to mold a sense of responsibility and to remind them that liberty is not the only one among all human values, though it is numbered among the foremost, but that it has its limits, intrinsic in the inescapable rules of decency and extrinsic in the correlative rights of others, both as regards the rights of each one in particular and the rights of society in general.

Preparing youth for Apostolic Organizations

483   Since the education of the child and youth must be
(27,   the result of the common efforts of many coordinated ele-
42,   ments, give all the importance it merits to cooperation and
96,   agreement between parents, the school and the organiza-
117)   tions which help the school and which continue its work when the students leave school, such as Catholic Action, the Marian Congregations, study centers and other similar institutions. Not rarely the parents themselves need spe-

cial help, since often times they have not themeselves received the necessary preparation for the exercise of their educative duties; and upon a good understanding with them will ordinarily depend the success of education, however good the schools may be, and even though the teachers be the best.

We take this opportunity, beloved sons, to express Our paternal joy in the great steps you have taken towards your ideal; and with pleasure We propose as an example and stimulus for all, those countries which are leaders in this enterprise of the Christian education of youth. At the same time We express Our hope that the governments of your countries will recognize to an increasing extent the value—and more so—the almost irreplaceable character of your work of education and training, and that they will readily grant you every facility and opportunity, so that you may be able to form a reliable nucleus of teachers who are faithful Catholics as well as excellent in their profession. We likewise trust that the public authorities, in cordial cooperation with you, will bar from print and from the screen everything that might be a cause of scandal or ruin to youth. **484 (22, 82, 112)**

Thus, the Christian ideal of education is identified with the latest findings of educational psychology, and it surrounds it with a light that perfects it. This ideal also facilitates the educative process with the unified and fruitful development of the individual presonality.

(The members of the Congress of La Paz, should educate for peace.)

THE IDEAL OF COMPLETE CHRISTIAN EDUCATION

All. for the second centenary of the Beatification of Saint Joseph Calasanctius, November 22, 1948.

(A reference to the Papal Brief declaring the Saint Patron of all the Christian schools for children of the masses, August 13, 1948.)

485
(16, 50, 72)

Saint Joseph Calasanctius, who was born in Catholic Spain, founded the primary school for children, but more exactly for poor and abandoned children. Others later, and most nobly, followed the same road; he, however, preceded them all, a humble and brave apostle in the sacred work. Without doubt, Calasanctius and the Order founded by him, according to how circumstances advised or demanded, also led to the opening of high schools for youth of higher standing. However, the great love of your Founder was always for the children of the poor and simple people, and the school which he instituted, not only aimed at teaching and educating them in the Christian faith—which always remained his highest ideal—but also at imparting to them, by means of a wise and tested pedagogic method, a solid foundation to prepare and train them in life. He, therefore, really deserves the honorary title which was recently conferred upon him.

(1648, Sowing in tears; 1748, Harvesting in glory.—His children follow the ideal of his life and his thought: the complete Christian education of youth.)

The teachers' part

486
(26, 54, 60)

This ideal is very high, because its aim is supernatural formation and, consequently, the eternal destiny of the pupils entrusted to your care. It is also very vast, because it aims at making them into perfect men here below, in the intellectual, moral, scientific, social and artistic sphere of culture, according to the condition, the aptitudes and legitimate ambitions of each, so that no one may turn out to be poorly adjusted or incapable, and also so that no one may find the road to the heights closed to him. This is a magnificent and sacred duty and it requires of educators the gift of wisdom and tact, which will place them in a position to give each pupil what is suitable in the way of solid and ample knowledge. It also requires the ability to adapt one's teaching to the intelligence and capacity of the

adolescent. Above all, this duty presupposes devotion, love
and, to the extent of one's powers, a holy enthusiasm which
will awaken a spontaneous interest from pupils and stimulate their eagerness for work.

Whence, then, will you draw this treasure of superior **487**
pedagogy which you need? From your inward spiritual life, *(57,*
from prayers, from studying—in other words, in the exact *81)*
and faithful exercise of the duties of your state which the
sacred Founder has inculcated in you by his example, by
the Constitutions dictated by him, by his admirable letters
which a filial love, together with a diligent and keen erudition, has placed, or will shortly place, in your hands. From
this incomparable Master you will learn still more perfectly
what you have to know and do and how you must do it,
what you have to suffer and how you must imitate his
magnanimity in suffering, because education is, before all,
a work of love, and the great school of love is the Cross.

The pupils' part

But to you also We turn, dear pupils, to you, the object **488**
of so much care, to you who can already understand or, at *(3,*
least, get a glimpse of what a great work your education *87,*
is; great for the aim it presupposes, great for what it costs *88)*
your educators and for the collaboration it requires from
you. Thus, the Saint conceived it, the Saint whom today
you especially honor, but to whom you must be devoted
and pay constant homage, not less with acts of piety than
by doing the best you can to correspond to the intentions
of his love towards you. Therefore, you who grow in the
aura of the Calasanctian schools certainly cannot go to
school every day, diligently study the lessons, and conscientiously perform the duties assigned to you only because
you are obliged to do so, or only just to enrich your mind
with still greater knowledge, to refine your intelligence
with training and culture, to assure yourselves of a
decent livelihood. No, besides these just and upright ends,

education has the superior aim of forming and bringing to perfection in you the Christian worthy of his natural and supernatural character, useful to society, whatever be the role for which Providence has destined him.

489
(53,
84,
87)
But, to form such men, have you considered the work, the fatigue and the total and continuous renunciations to which your Masters and Professors have to subject themselves! Can you imagine what it cost them, to them who love you as they do, to oblige you to do work which is perhaps liked, but certainly austere, to observe discipline, loving but yet strong? The work of formation inevitably involves some compulsory hardship. Now, this can be borne either willingly or unwillingly. It will be done willingly if it is generously and cheerfully received by you in filial collaboration with your educators. The pedagogy of St. Joseph Calasanctius calls upon you to collaborate in the intellectual, the secular, and the religious sphere of study, as well as on the moral and supernatural plane of culture. It is a collaboration that does not merely record good results in the same passive and exact manner simply as a machine would do, but rather an active cooperation which is docile and personal at the same time.

Special duties of today's Catholic school

490
(72,
82,
116)
All this is, in general, true. But times change and Christian education must necessarily meet the times. We, therefore, believe that the Catholic school should bear in mind two special ends:

1. To the restlessness, the boundless multiplicity and pressure of modern life, which keeps man almost completely wound up as in a coil and no longer allows him to be recollected, to the frenzy of success which fortune bestows, according to which everything is judged, without minding if it is true or false, good or bad, lawful or unlawful, Catholic education is called to form the man of clear, sure, and profound convictions.

Is this not perhaps the voice of daily experience? Consider: he who does not possess sound principles is today unfailingly carried away on the tidal waves of ideological struggles. It is for this reason that so many glances now turn, full of hope, towards the Church, she who is backed by an admirable history of holiness and great works, and abounds in ancient customs, beauty and sublime forms. But that which above all else attracts the spirit towards the Church is the conviction, firm as a rock, of absolute truth, of the divine force of that faith from which all the rest receives life and value.

2. To the moral instability, to which youth is drawn in a thousand ways, by books, pictures and films, it is the duty of Catholic education to oppose the man who knows how to master himself, to preserve and defend his human and Christian dignity. **491 (72-74, 76, 97)**

Catholic moralism has a big heart; it welcomes and embraces all that is found in the ambit of that dignity. However, the boundaries which it is not lawful to overstep are clearly marked out. To maintain these limits inviolable always and in every circumstance, is the glory and merit of strong souls, but grace is necessary and humble prayer to obtain it—grace and prayer without which victory is impossible—and it is necessary that right from his first years a youth be trained to renunciation, sacrifice, and the mastery of self.

(Intercession of the saintly Founder and of the Most Holy Virgin Mary.)

CHRISTIAN AND LATIN CULTURE

All. to Roman students, January 30, 1949.

(The privilege of "Roman" youth is to grow in an atmosphere which is unique in the world.)

Indeed, among the many subjects which constitute the programs of your studies, you foster the Latin language. **492 (64)**

Latin! A language, ancient but not dead, whose superb echo, even if not heard for centuries in the ruined amphitheaters, the famous forums and the temples of the Caesars, is not silent in Christ's basilicas, where the priests of the Gospel and the heirs of the martyrs repeat and sing again the psalms and the hymns of the first centuries in the reconsecrated language of the Quirites. Now, the language of Rome is principally a sacred language, which is heard in the divine rites, in the theological halls and in the Acts of the Apostolic See, and in which you yourselves often address a sweet greeting to the Queen of Heaven, your Mother, and to your Father Who reigns above. But it is also the key which opens the sources of history to you. That which belongs to the past, Roman and Christian, has reached us in inscriptions, in writings and books, bringing, save for partial exceptions during the last centuries, practically the full authority of the Latin language.

493
(64,
113)
 Do not, however, construe Our words almost as an indication of a lesser interest for the other branches of your studies. No one more than Us is convinced that whosoever is called to hold a responsible office, whosoever wants to write or speak, must perfectly master his own native language, in all its purity, free of useless and condemned barbarisms. Therefore, always keep good Italian books close at hand, *nocturna versate manu, versate diurna.*

Precisely in these times of the cinema, in which you are living, books acquire greater importance. A film, even if irreproachable, is by its nature unilaterally visual, and therefore runs the risk of making the youth's mind superficial if it does not at the same time receive nourishment from useful and sound readings.

We know, also by experience, how profitable and often necessary it is to learn other living languages in addition to our own. Therefore, at your age We Ourselves were ardently devoted to the study of foreign languages, even those which may seem too hard to a beginner, like the German language.

We are not unaware also of the present tendency of techniques to prevail more and more on speculative sciences. The danger would be if you were to immerse yourselves so strongly in the material elements as to lose or diminish the sense of Christian culture, so rich in values of truth and wisdom and saturated with what ancient times had of eternal worth. But such a danger will be more easily avoided if you will consider it worth your every effort to master the Latin language, too. **494 (64, 102, 108, 118)**

Backed by this knowledge, you will one day be in a position to keep people from becoming increasingly more unfamiliar with the thought and spirit of that civilization by means of which their ancestors, for more than fifteen centuries, kept themselves firmly rooted in the principles of their Christian faith.

(The Roman Empire has passed, but the Church remains.)

THE DUTY OF A CATHOLIC UNIVERSITY

Letter, *La imminente celebrazione*, to Rev. Father Gemelli of March 17, 1949.

(Resumption of courses at the Catholic University of Milan after the war.)

In accordance with absolute fidelity to Christian principles, which are the whole reason for existence of the Catholic University, it must, in fact today more than ever, watch the aims for which it arose, and with persistent purpose of mind keep faith with the engagement solemnly undertaken to provide the nation's social body with leaders and lovers of science and learning who will honor both the faith and the Church, and be for Italy, which is recovering, a transforming leaven, not the least among the factors of its success. **495 (62, 68, 72, 76, 79, 118)**

The enlightened zeal with which you, beloved Son, have so far upheld the University's fate, is a good guarantee to Us of the elevated conscience with which you will continue to keep watch, and your collaborators with you, so that in this temple of truth and knowledge, the doctrine will be safe and the practice of good morals be preserved by example. May directors and teachers continue to direct every effort of theirs not only to the cult of knowledge, which, when not associated with piety, easily becomes vain and dangerous pride *(scientia inflat)* (a), but at the same time and above all to the formation of men of firm and resolute character who, having finished the courses, will stand fast before the difficulties of life and the allurements of the world.

Catholic Italy expects from its University men worthy of its faith and of its Christian civilization. And such will our graduates reveal themselves in the field of studies and in the professions if, in all their actions, beyond every human interest, they show themselves to be constant upholders of those principles with which their higher education was imbued, in order to make of them the basis of their professional life and of a glorious apostolic service for the spiritual elevation and restoration of the society that receives them.

(Appeal to the generosity of Italians.)

RULES OF CATHOLIC PEDAGOGY

Letter *Sobremaneira grata,* May 7, 1949, to the Cardinal Archbishop of Rio de Janeiro.

(Coming convocation of an inter-American Catholic Education Congress.)

496
(58, Well-organized Congresses of a like nature are very useful for promoting inter-cultural exchanges. They consoli-

495a 1 Cor. 8:1.

date the union of wills and efforts, thus realizing the great
desire of the Divine Master: "So that they may be one" (a).
They contribute, in addition, to the perfecting and constant progress of theories and methods of teaching.

*112,
118)*

Among the valuable consequences will also be record-
ed: the diffusion, among the Catholics of America, of the
principles of Catholic doctrine concerning the rights of the
family and of the Church; the solid formation of lay professors and of the very small number of religious educators;
lastly, the multiplication and finishing of the educational
centers, as powerful defences against the spreading of secular and Protestant teachings.

However, what We would like to see dealt with by the
coming Congress with particular attention is the "integral
formation of the adolescent," according to the Church's authoritative tradition, always accessible to scientific progress,
but indissolubly anchored to the progress of the Gospel.

497
*(13,
75)*

The Divine Master, Way, Truth, and Life, founded
His Church on a revealed doctrine, on a positive law and a
living magisterium. (a) In an epoch in which freedom is
exalted, Catholic pedagogy insists on remembering that
the exercise of freedom is confined in its origin by some
unchangeable duties, inherent to our human condition.

Catholic educators must not be afraid of completing
the notion of freedom with the affirmation of responsibility
which confirms the former, subordinating it, however, to
the respect due to our neighbors, our superiors and to our
Creator.

The crisis concerning authority is another great evil of
our time. It is necessary to study the manner of introducing
into Catholic educational establishments, those organiza-

498
(87)

496a John 17:22.
497a O divino Mestre, Via, Verdade, e Vida, fundou a sua
    Igreja sobre uma doutrina revelada, uma lei positiva e un
    Magisterio vivo.

tions in which the pupils, while exercising personal responsibility, learn by themselves that in order to achieve the common welfare in an orderly society, respect and obedience towards the directing authority are altogether indispensable.

499
(63,
71,
118)
Catholic educators must not allow themselves to be corrupted by the errors which certain modern theories, infected by materialism, try to introduce into the field of education. The wise precepts of Christian humanism, concerned more with formation than with the multiplicity of notions, with education more than with pure teaching, will escape the damage done by those philosophies which have developed for many into a condemnable pragmatism.

It is praiseworthy to learn the modern schools of thought, but let us first acquire a deep knowledge of the history and pedagogy of the Church. Often, one admires in others what they have copied from Christian tradition.

(Wishes for the successful result of the Congress.)

SPIRITUAL PATERNITY

All. to the Italian Catholic Union of secondary teaching, September 4, 1949.

(Welcome.—The Holy Father sees, in spirit, youth looking towards the future to ensure for mankind greater and more lasting conquests.)

500
(51,
52)
Of this unrestrainable and perennial movement toward human perfection, started and guided by Divine Providence, educators are the most directly responsible leaders; they are associated with that very Providence for the realization of Its designs. On them depends, to a great extent, whether the stream of civilization advances or retreats, whether it strengthens its impetus or languishes through inertia, whether it hurries its pace straight forward towards the goal, or on the contrary indulges at least momentarily,

in vain twistings and turnings, or worse still, in dangerous
and unsafe meanderings.

In recalling to your conscience as educators this dignity and responsibility, We Ourselves, Vicar by Divine
Providence and, therefore, invested with the same office
by Him Who on earth loved to be called "Master," We
include Ourselves in the number of those who in various
measures represent the hand of Providence in leading man
to his appointed end.

Is not perhaps this Seat of Ours mainly a Chair of
Teaching? Does not Our first duty consist in teaching? Has
not the Divine Master and Founder of the Church given
to Peter and the Apostles the fundamental precept: μα-
θητεύσατε, teach, make disciples (Matt. 28:19).

Collaborators of God and of the Church

We feel Ourselves to be, and We are, educators of
souls; the Church is a sublime school, and that not in a
secondary measure, since a great part of the sacerdotal
office consists in teaching and educating. Nor could it have
been otherwise in the new order established by Christ,
which is founded completely on the relations of the paternity of God, from which derives every other paternity in
Heaven and on earth (a), and from which, in Christ and
for Christ, Our paternity emanates towards all souls. Now,
he who is a father is, by this very fact, an educator since,
as the Angelic Doctor so clearly explains, the fundamental
pedagogical right appertains, above all, to paternity. (b)

501
(7,
14,
19,
52,
55)

That is why, while We express Our gratitude in welcoming you, We speak to you as direct collaborators in that
which is the work of God and of the Church, perhaps the
most noble enterprise according to the unanimous judgment of that very human knowledge represented by Cicero

502
(51,
52,
60,
71)

501a Eph. 3:15.
501b Cf. St. Thomas, *Summa Teologicae*, 2a, 2ae, Q. 102, 1.

who, however, looked upon the world with pagan eyes: "Quod munus rei publicae afferre maius meliusve possumus, quam si docemus atque erudimus iuventutem?" (a) Hence, immense is the responsibility which we together shoulder, though in different degrees, but not in completely separate fields: the responsibility for souls, for civilization, for the improvement and happiness of man on earth and in Heaven.

If, in this moment, when speaking to you, secondary school teachers, We have embraced a vaster field, as is that of education in general, We have done so having in mind the erroneous doctrine which separated the formation of the intellect from that of the heart and which can now be considered as superceded, at least in principle. We must moreover deplore the fact that during the last few years, reasonable limits have been exceeded in interpreting the norm which identifies teacher and educator, school and life.

Rights of the Church and of the family

503
(101,
102,
109)
Having acknowledged the school to be of powerful value in the formation of consciences, certain countries, regimes, and political movements have recognized it as one of the most efficacious means for winning over to their side those hosts of supporters of whom they have need, in order to ensure success and triumph for some specific conceptions of life that they wish to bring forward. With tactics as cunning as insincere, and for purposes in opposition even to the natural ends of education, some of the movements of the past and present century have sought to remove the school from the aegis of the institutions which, in addition to the State, hold a primordial right—the family and the Church, (a)—and have attempted or are attempting

502a *De Divinatione*, Bk. 2, chap. 2.
503a Pius XI, Encycl. *Divini Illius Magistri*, December 31, 1929. Cf. no. 263.

to obtain exclusive possession of these same schools. In other words, they are attempting to impose a monopoly, something which, apart from other respects, is seriously injurious to one of the fundamental rights of man.

But this Chair of Peter, the vigilant sentinel of the welfare of souls and of real progress, having never relinquished this essential right in the past, has in fact admirably and at all times exercised it by means of its institutions which at times were the only ones that dedicated themselves to it. Nor will it relinquish it in the future, not even in the hope of obtaining earthly advantages, nor through fear of persecution. It will never consent to let the Church, which received this right by divine mandate, or the family, which claims it through natural justice, be deprived of the effective exercise of their native right. The faithful of all the world are witnesses of the firmness of this Apostolic See in defending freedom of education in such a variety of countries, conditions and races. For the sake of the school as for the sake of divine worship and for the sanctity of matrimony, it has not hesitated to face every difficulty and danger, with the tranquil conscience of one who is serving a just and holy cause willed by God, and with the certitude of rendering an inestimable service to civil society itself. **504 (16, 110, 112, 117)**

In the countries, therefore, in which the freedom of the school is guaranteed by just laws, it is up to the teachers to know how to avail themselves effectively of it, demanding the concrete application thereof. **505 (58)**

(The teachers are awaiting directives from the Pope.)

Preserve and innovate with criterion

While, therefore, We exhort you, amid the pressing needs of the present time, to stand firmly by the rules which are the results of the age-old conquests of human wisdom, We at the same time warn you against a blind attachment to the past, which today might frustrate the **506 (82)** efficacy of your work. If, however, it is an excellent rule to treasure systems and methods corroborated by experience, it is necessary to sift most carefully the theories and practices of modern schools of education, before accepting them. In fact, good and successful results, achieved perhaps in countries different from yours as to nature of population and degree of culture, do not always give sufficient guarantee that those doctrines can be applied everywhere and without distinction.

507
(3, 82)
The school cannot be compared to a chemical laboratory in which the risk of wasting more or less costly substances is compensated by the probability of a discovery; in the school, the salvation or ruin of every individual soul is involved. Therefore, the innovations which will be deemed opportune are those which regard the choice of secondary teaching means and directives, while the end and the essential means to that end firmly remain always the same, as always the same is the final end of education, its subject, its principal author and inspirer, Who is the Lord our God.

508
(51-53, 82)
Having set forth these principles, you may safely fix your own time and hour for scrutinizing new needs and for studying adequate remedies; fix your eyes confidently on the future, which you mould by your hands in the souls of your pupils, and make it Christian, imbued by a still higher sense of justice, inspired by still greater charity, open to an ever more profound and harmonious culture. In the daily exercise of your office, you will thus be fathers of souls rather than propagators of useless knowledge—that is to say, fathers who, living life to the full, know how to raise up around them other lives similar to their own. From this follows the full devotion that the school demands of you, the school which, together with the family of which many of you are head, will constitute all your world and will take up, without fear of regret, all your energy. A world thus formed—where religion, family and culture

constitute the daily bread and water of life—is more than sufficient to fill one's life and to repay those renunciations which even lead to the total immolation of self.

Society's debt

Because of this, however, society, or more positively the State, to whose welfare you devote your life—mindful of that "maius meliusve" quoted above—is not less obliged to offer you adequate and public gratitude, as well as such compensation as is indispensable for procuring economic conditions that will enable teachers to devote themselves completely to the school. Likewise, God, the just rewarder of our works, promises a special reward to educators of souls in the well-known passage of Daniel: Qui ad iustitiam erudiunt multos, fulgebunt quasi stellae in perpetuas aeternitates. (a)

509
(22,
53)

Example

The teacher, that is, the educator who derives inspiration from paternity whose term or end is to generate other beings similar to himself, forms his pupils by the very example of his life, no less than by the rules and precepts. Otherwise, his work would be, as St. Augustine says, mere "word vending" (a) and not that of moulding souls. Even moral teaching, if not corroborated by deeds, will touch the spirit only superficially. In fact, not even the explanation of what is merely scholastic discipline will be fully assimilated by young students if it does not issue from the teacher's lips as a living personal expression: neither Latin nor Greek, neither history and still less philosophy will be received with advantage by students when they are presented without enthusiasm, as things extraneous to the life and the interests of him who teaches them.

510
(83)

509a Dan. 12:3.
510a Cf. *Confessions*, Bk. 4, chap. 2—Migne, P.L., 32, 693.

Formation of the Christian of Today

511
(26,
75,
79,
92)
Educators of today, you who draw safe rules from the past, what is the ideal of a man that you have to prepare for tomorrow? You find him fundamentally outlined in the perfect Christian. And by saying perfect Christian, We intend to refer to the Christian of today, the man of his time, a connoisseur and cultivator of all progress wrought by science and technique, a citizen who is not extraneous to the life which is today being unfolded in his country. The world will not have any regrets if a still greater number of such Christians will enter every order of public and private life. It is principally up to you, Teachers, to lay the groundwork for this beneficial entrance, directing the minds of your pupils to discover the inexhaustible power of Christianity in the work of improvement and renovation of all peoples. Therefore, do not spare hardships in promptly awakening their moral conscience so that in the years to come, the "honest man" will not come along as a surprise, almost as a stroke of good luck, as the last adventure of a life which has more than once been wrecked.

512
(102,
107,
108)
On this foundation, form men of science and technique. It will not come about that men so formed will instill fear into the world, as happens today, science having created —along with admiration—almost a terror of itself among the people and also formidable political, social and international problems—a reprisal, perhaps, for the sought-after severance of science from religion. Among the scientists themselves, at least a few are suffering, struck by the disproportion created by technique between the immensely augmented material forces available to mankind and the smallness and weakness in which their souls have remained. (a)

513
(76,
Form strong men who will be able to diffuse goodness around them and to direct others with clearness of princi-

512a Cf. H. Bergson, *Le deux sources de la morale et de la religion*, 1933, pages 334-335.

ples. Our times require that pupils' minds be turned   87)
towards a more effective sense of justice, and that they be
shaken out of the innate tendency to consider themselves
a privileged caste and to fear and shun a working life. Let
them feel themselves workers and really be such, today,
in the persevering fulfillment of scholastic duties, as they
will have to be tomorrow in positions of authority in society. It is true that among peoples troubled by the calamity
of unemployment, the difficulties arise not so much from
the want of good will, as from lack of work, but none the
less, it is still absolutely necessary that teachers instill a
spirit of industry into their pupils. Consequently, it is necessary that the latter be accustomed to severe intellectual
work, and that they learn to bear the difficulties and demands of work in order to enjoy social rights, the same as
manual laborers.

It is time to enlarge their views on a world less fettered   **514**
by reciprocally envious factions, by the extreme national-   *(66,*
istic spirit and greed for supremacy, from which the   *75)*
present generation suffered so much. May the youth of
today be receptive to the breath of Catholicism, and feel
the fascination of that universal charity which embraces
all peoples in the one Lord. Give them, yes, the consciousness of their own personality and, therefore, of the great
treasure of freedom, train their spirit, yes, to sound criticism, but instill in them at the same time the sense of
Christian humility, of just submission to law and of the
duty of brotherhood.

And encourage them. Tell them that the Church and   **515**
society are expecting a lot from them, that there is a great   *(14,*
deal of good to be accomplished and many noble enter-   *82,*
prises to be undertaken.   *87)*

Religious, honest, cultured, frank and active: thus We
would like young people to leave school, the young people
whom families and society entrust or, better, whom God
entrusts to you because before the family and society, souls

belong to God, to Christ and the Church by a pre-eminent right of origin. Have courage and confidence. Though the enterprise is great and the goal arduous, nothing is lacking for the Christian educator to obtain it. You have sufficient human means available, but above all you are rich in supernatural help furnished by grace. You and your pupils can draw abundantly from the fruitful torrents of that grace in the Sacraments and prayer.

(Blessing.)

SACRIFICE ONESELF FOR THE IDEAL

All. to the teachers and students of the University of France and of the Catholic Teaching, April 10, 1950.

(Contribution of the University of France to Europe and to mankind.—The impossibility of conflict between science and faith.—The inheritance of Christian Rome.)

516
(51, 63)
Open, expand, illuminate and progressively adorn the child's and the adolescent's minds which are awakening to life; guide the curious and ardent youth whose holy ambition is to discover the truth and who is eager to investigate every branch of learning: is there perhaps a task more lovely, more vast, and more varied in its admirable unity than this? In fact, in all ages and in all achievements of study, one thing only is sought: to find and possess an even fuller and purer light in order to love and enjoy it, to defend and propagate it; to give it to each and all, according to one's ability, and to multiply and spread the benefits of this light everywhere.

517
(54, 80, 92)
We therefore congratulate you, Catholic School Teachers; to you is entrusted such a difficult mission and your work might sometimes seem thankless if you were not sustained by your ideal. For without an ideal, without the highest ideal, who would have the courage, the right to sacrifice, as it would seem, the research and discoveries of an intellectual life, which is rewarding and exhilarating,

the luminous conquests of an apostolic life which makes the heart throb with the desire to give oneself entirely to the service of souls and of the Church, the joys of family life during the hours—often so short—of relaxation at the fireside of a home which though often modest, gives security for the future? Who would dare, who would have the right to sacrifice all this in order to devote himself without respite and without reserve to the teaching of children not his own, in such a thoughtless age in which neither profit nor progress is noted, and in which pupils allow themselves to be influenced only when they are about to pass on to another class? And of each of his pupils, one asks: "What will become of this child?" (a) Yes, disappointments are frequent and failures are numerous and bitter! But, thanks be to God, while you exhaust your lungs speaking, and ruin your eyes trying to understand their writing and correct their lessons, your heart flies to God, to Jesus Christ, to Whom you want to lead those children He entrusted to you. A good number of them, even if they will forget you, will still owe you the strength and the charity of a Christian life, while the greater part of those who would have gone astray will recall the ideas and the sentiments of their childhood, reawakened at the last hour. The pagan poet had said: "Quo semel est imbuta recens, servabit odorem testa diu." (b) But how much truer is this of the Christian youth!

(*Protection of the Virgin, Seat of Wisdom.*)

THE PATRON OF EDUCATORS

Apostolic Letter *Quod ait,* May 15, 1950.

The words of St. Bonaventure—"A real teacher is he **518** who knows how to enrich the mind with thoughts, to illu- *(52,*

517a Luke 1:66.
517b Horace, *Letters,* 1, I, 2, 69.

83,
94,
107)
minate it, and instill virtues in the disciple's heart" (a)—
should be carefully meditated on in these times, more than
ever, when we often see that the teaching given to children
is not only dissociated from moral formation, but is accompanied by contempt for God and Religion, which most
unfortunately effects the ruin of souls. For this reason,
Holy Mother Church surrounds with solicitous affection
those whose duty it is to work for the education of youth,
inasmuch as on them greatly depends the salvation and the
progress of the Christian community.

519
(16,
59)
Now, there was a man, distinguished for sanctity and
learning, St. John Baptist de la Salle, who personally and by
means of the Institute he himself founded, gave and continues to give to children a sound and complete formation,
and has even arrived at suitably preparing in schools called
"Seminaires de maitres d'ècole pour la campagne," the
teachers called upon to practise this serious duty, especially among the ordinary country-people; therefore, this kind
of school from which teachers themselves come, and which
has spread to many places, is rightfully attributed to him.

520
(55,
59)
On the other hand, the same famous pedagogue had so
much consideration for the office of educator as not to want
his Brothers, of whom he was Father, to become priests so
that they might not be drawn away from teaching, convinced as he was that it is an efficacious means to reach
religious perfection. Hence, that they who dedicate themselves to the education of youth, or who are preparing
themselves for this office, may have an example to imitate,
an ideal to copy faithfully. . .

*(At the request of the Brothers of the Christian
Schools . . .)*

> 518a Ille solus verus est doctor qui potest specimen impri-
> mere et lumen infundere et virtutem dare cordi audientis.
> *(De reductione artium ad theologiam, no. 18.)*

...We proclaim and declare St. John Baptist de La Salle, Special Patron, at the throne of God, of all teachers devoted to the education of boys and of youth.

SLOW BUT SURE ACTION

All. to the Italian Association of Catholic Teachers, September 6, 1950.

(Congratulations for the development of the Association.)

The fundamental thesis of your present Congress places the office of the teacher as educator of the people in its true light, the essential contents of which office can be summarized as follows: educate the children entrusted to your care so as to make them God-fearing Christians, living their faith intensely; thus a people will be formed, as it were by itself, of men "each of whom—in his proper place and in his own way—is a person conscious of his responsibilities." (a)   **521** *(72, 75)*

The normal young person—We should like to say the average scholar—rarely needs a particularly adapted individual education. Look at the healthy and young plant in the field or on the mountain: by virtue of its vital principle, it absorbs from the soil and from the air the elements which it needs for its development. Thus too, the child, the adolescent, with a prodigious gift of observation and receptiveness, takes from all that surrounds him—the family, the church, the school and from what he sees, hears, reads and experiences—the elements which go to form his temperament, his nature and personal inclinations.   **522** *(87)*

My beloved sons and daughters! Have you well considered what an enviable field of action and magnificent   **523** *(83)*

521a Cf. R.M. *Christmas,* 1944.

ministry has been entrusted to you? When, during those five or eight years of intimate contact with the same young people, you convey to them precious and useful knowledge? When, at the same time, almost without noticing it, you set them an example of the Christian life completely directed toward God and firmly rooted in the faith? An institution such as the school acts like a force of nature, slowly and in an almost imperceptible manner, but constantly and with sure success, for good or for evil—but in your case, for the good.

Therefore, We bless you and your holy activity; We bless your battle against the "conspiracy of bad habits."

(Blessing.)

THE CATHOLIC UNIVERSITY: ITS REASON FOR EXISTENCE

All. to the members of the Catholic Institutes of France, September 21, 1950.

(Three-quarters of a century full of self-sacrifice and abnegation, thus supporting the conviction that there is a major interest at stake.)

524
(67) What then, at present, is the explanation for the existence, for the usefulness of Catholic Institutes—a question on which some doubt seems to arise even in the best of circles? One might at first regard it as a question of dignity that the Church should seek to conserve a work of more than a thousand years which owes to her its origin, its growth, as well as its extraordinary and fruitful development. But would a mere consideration of dignity, of venerable historical tradition, be sufficient to justify, to explain such liberality with money and generosity of efforts? There is, in Our opinion, a more vital and important reason. The permanent timeliness of Catholic Institutes and Universities lies in their usefulness, in the necessity of

constituting an orderly and solid body of doctrine, and of creating a purely Catholic cultural environment.

Faultless teaching, in all branches of learning, integrated moreover with a superior religious instruction on the side, is not sufficient. Directly or indirectly, all studies have some connection with religion—not only theology, philosophy, history, and literature but the others too: the juridical, medical, physical, natural, cosmological, palaeontological and philological sciences. If it should be supposed that they do not include any positive connection with dogmatic and moral questions, they would often risk being in contradiction with themselves. It is therefore necessary that even if the teaching does not directly touch religious truth and the religious conscience, the teacher be wholly imbued with religion, the Catholic religion. **525** *(13, 50, 72)*

Yet this is not all. In certain countries, and for completely extrinsic reasons, the name of Catholic University has been replaced by another. Only the name, however, has disappeared; the nature is retained and must so remain. University does not mean simply an overlaying of curriculums which are extraneous to one another, but indicates rather a synthesis of all the subjects of learning. Not one of them is separated from the others by a water-tight compartment, but all must converge towards the unity of the integral intellectual sphere. Modern progress and the steady advance of specialization make such a synthesis more necessary today than ever; otherwise there is the great risk of the alternative of excessive independence, the isolation of specialization to the detriment of culture and general values on the one hand, and on the other the development of a general formation, more superficial than profound, to the detriment of precision, of exactness and of competency in a specific field. To actuate this synthesis as best as possible is the task of the University; to actuate this synthesis from its center up to the main key that unlocks the whole edifice is the task of a Catholic University. **526** *(67, 108, 118)*

527
(68) If the vicissitudes of time have paralyzed or slowed down the effort, it has not, however, been in vain. Your Catholic Institutes of France may be proud of their Golden Book. Without mentioning the eminent masters in all fields, professors, writers, inventors, initiators, whose names are among the most renowned, what a great number of men famed for professional worth, faith and Christian life has been given by them to the Church and to society!

528
(62, Continue, therefore, along your road, beloved sons,
70) with your gaze fixed on the ideal which, as men of learning and faith, you have set as your guiding star. Proceed in its light; it unfailingly shines in the heavens; should it become pale, you know the guide to whom Christ Our Lord entrusted you. To help you proceed with a steady step in its light, We recently wrote the Encyclical letter, *Humani Generis*. Study it; be actively docile to its teachings, and put them into effect.

And do this with that courage of which you were set the example by the most celebrated scientists, thinkers and leaders in all ages of the Church. Neither the surprises brought on by the discoveries of science nor the needs of the moment succeeded in confusing them for a single instant. Quite firm in the conviction that between science and faith, between the definite conclusions of the former and the dogmas of the latter, no contradiction, no irreducible position is verified, they lived in the serene certainty that the Catholic faith, without disguise and without reticence, remains always, today as in the times of the Apostles, the ark of salvation. Such it must be in the thought and feeling of mankind.

Let no effort discourage you, no misunderstanding make you timid and tire you; you have divine assistance on your side, in pledge of which We impart to all of you, to your Institutes, your colleges, your pupils and to all those who are dear to you, Our Apostolic Blessing.

WORK OF CATHOLIC ACTION

R.M. to the Catholic Action men of Portugal, December 10, 1950.

(The one-time Portuguese navigators: apostles of the faith.—A similar duty, at the present, for Catholic Action.—Field of work.)

This zeal has, of course, its immediate field of action within one's own family. Greatly deserving of praise from the Church and society are they who, permeated by their great responsibility, undertake to be the first educators of their own children by word and example, educating them in the Christian doctrine and its daily practice. Where this responsibility is not felt and where family life is not fully lived in the light of the Gospel, religion will always be considered as something of an accessory nature from which it is easy to prescind. Fortunately, in Portugal the family is generally sound; but, unfortunately, harmful propaganda arrives there also and there is no lack of pathogenic germs, which if allowed to act unobserved, can produce devastating epidemics. **529** *(31, 96)*

Catholic action in the family is followed by Catholic action in favor of youth. And in this respect, how many problems claim the prudent, vigilant, and persistent action of Catholic men. There is the problem of catechetical instruction for children, promoted by all the means that art and pedagogy offer, at home, in the church, and in the elementary schools. Your attention was particularly called to this problem by Our Predecessor in his letter (a) which serves as the fundamental code of Portuguese Catholic Action. **530** *(68, 69, 89, 90)*

530a Pius XI, Apostolic Letter *Ex officiosis litteris,* November 10, 1933. AAS, 26, 628-633.

There is, moreover, the very serious problem of superior moral education for the young, especially for young students, who in the future will hold in their hands the fate of the country. Without this moral education, all literary and scientific formation, no matter how perfect, remains absolutely incomplete and deficient.

(Social question.—Missions.—Increase in quality and number.)

CATHOLIC TEACHERS AND PUBLIC INSTRUCTION

All. to the Union of Catholic Public Teaching, March 26, 1951.

(The University of France: what was once its place in the history of the Church and of France.)

531
(93,
94,
102) Who would wonder if the opponents of the Church, ignoring the true welfare of France, labored to produce some small crevices that, in their designs, should little by little grow wider and wider? Lacking precise and steady doctrinal principles, the intellectual world, most of all towards the end of the 18th century, was ill-prepared to denounce detrimental infiltrations and to stop their imperceptible and progressive penetration. Even without voluntary hostility and premeditated design, the uncertainty of teachers, even of the most renowned, the fluctuating and vague thought, could not but have its effects on the superior level of instruction, as well as on the secondary and elementary education of the young—effects which grew more extensive and profound in every succeeding generation.

532
(93,
102) Then, as regards conscious impiety, it watched and exploited the evolution, or better the deviation, of the ambiguous words *neutrality* and *secularism*. Blinded by its successes, however, it failed to see the spark of Christian life which lay hidden under the mass of ashes, almost suf-

focated by restrictions—the spark of fervor and zeal which
continued to burn in the hearts of the most famed scientists and intellectuals and of the heroic teachers of the
children of the masses.

(Christian vitality that has revived.—A craving for spiritual perfection.)

The possibilities of the apostolate

In fact, the efficacy of your apostolate derives obviously from the example of your faith and of your Christian
life, and less obviously from the superabundance of your
supernatural interior life, which is poured out on all souls,
beginning from those nearest to you, those souls who are
entrusted to your care. **533** *(116)*

Thus, with good reason, seek to exercise a more direct
influence on souls through your teaching; in this is the intimate aspect of your apostolate. **534** *(96, 116)*

This apostolate is indisputably opportune; and the
evolution, though partial, which was revealed in souls during this last half century has not made it less opportune.
Notwithstanding the continual solicitude and insistence of
the Church on inculcating in Christian parents their principal duty of giving their children an education in which
the religious, doctrinal and moral element is not separated
from purely human instruction but, on the contrary, is intimately connected therewith; notwithstanding the liberal
encouragement which she gives to militant Catholics who
work with disinterested effort and sacrifice to promote and
support those schools that are avowedly Catholic; it remains nonetheless true that a great number of young people
do not attend them, owing to circumstances which are too
often inevitable, such as the impossibility of finding such
schools, the apathy or negligence of families, or other
temporal considerations. Will these souls therefore be completely deprived of the Christian formation to which they
are entitled?

535
(116) At first, it would seem that too many obstacles paralyze your good will: prohibition to invade the so-called "confessional field," a term which is often abusively extended to all that has anything to do with religion; an unlimited variety of scholars, pupils and students who come from diverse environments, having already received an initial impression, in which may be noted strangely different forms of education or its complete absence; a reserve that imposes itself with regard to young people, some of whom are already following completely different religious observances; while others, unfortunately, have no religion.

In spite of all this, you think you will be able to do good and must do it, a great good to these souls, without the slightest illegitimate or simply illegal interference. And can you perhaps do this in any way other than that of the secret influence of grace which spreads itself—of which We have already spoken—and of prayer?

Science and history reveal God

536
(64,
116) The Apostle St. Paul, in his Epistle to the Romans, opens up a very wide horizon before your eyes. The invisible perfections of God, he says, His eternal power and His divinity, have been made visible to the intelligence by means of His works, since the creation of the world. (a) By "works" is it necessary to indicate solely material creations that are perceptible to the senses? Or is it not more certain and necessary to include also the great universal laws that support the world and which, even without revelation and faith, manifest themselves to natural, loyal, and attentive reason? Well now, it is precisely the various branches of human knowledge which manifest to the intelligence both the works of God, His eternal laws and their applications to the physical, moral, and social progress of the world. In fact, it is impossible for anyone to expound amply and im-

536a Romans 1:20.

partially, the history of events and of institutions—leaving
dogmatic and apologetical insinuations aside—without seeing the light of Christ and of the Church shining brightly in
its superhuman clarity.

(Courage and confidence.)

THE FULLNESS OF EDUCATION

All. to the College of St. Joseph, Rome, May 6, 1951.

*(Centenary of the College.—Following in the footsteps
of predecessors.)*

The secret of their solid and lasting success, which is of **537**
great value, is that they have not stood still, nor have they *(82)*
deviated from the path of light traced by their fathers, by
your incomparable Founder, John Baptist de La Salle, from
whom they have gathered and in turn transmitted wise and
holy traditions.

Etre à la page: it is said today with a certain pleasure.
This may be so, but on condition that this is not made a
pretext for tearing up a precious book by destroying the
preceding pages, just as one does when removing the
leaves of a calendar.

In fact, the art of education is, in many aspects, the
art of adapting oneself, adapting oneself to the age, to the
temperament, to the character, to the capacity, to the needs
and just aspirations of the student; adapting oneself to all
the circumstances of time and place; adapting oneself to
the general rhythm of human progress.

However, in such adaptation, what characterizes the **538**
true Christian education is that it tends towards the com- *(60,*
plete formation of the child, of the adolescent in order to *63,*
make of him a man, a citizen, an integral and well-balanced *69,*
Catholic, rather than a pretentious erudite with a mind *105,*
encumbered with encyclopedic knowledge of a dispropor- *108)*

tionate and disorderly nature. To develop intellectual culture according to a wise pedagogy; to avail oneself of the soundness and strength of the body and the agility of the limbs achieved through physical education, in order that they may serve to render the spirit fit and ready; to refine all the faculties with an artistic formation which, through a successful harmonizing of the senses and the intellect, will result in amiability coupled with grace whence will flow greater efficiency, more far-reaching and acceptable—all this is indeed beautiful and good, but it would not have an eternal value nor a satisfactory fullness if religious culture, through its amplitude and magnificence, did not bestow on education its unity and true value.

539
(62,
115) An error which is very common restricts religious instruction and education to a determined period of time though with complete and wisely distributed programs. But the real Christian education exacts much more: it must be a continuous, permanent and progressive work; it must permeate all teaching, even profane, penetrating right to the depths of the soul. It, therefore, consists, in addition to the methodical exposition of doctrine, in seeing and making all things be seen in the light of the great and divine truth, just as in the contemplation of the material creation, things are not properly seen in their true colors, if not by the light, even if sometimes concealed by clouds, of the beautiful sun of God.

540
(4) But education would still be incomplete, if it did not achieve but a part of its aim; if, in other words, it limited itself to procuring the personal, physical, moral, temporal and eternal welfare of the pupils. It must in addition form and prepare them to exercise a healthy action on their time and on their generation—in fact, on future generations—so that they may pass through the world, leaving it better, sweeter and more beautiful than they found it.

(Works of charity of the pupils of the college.)

EDUCATION AND THE PRIEST

All. to the Marcantonio Colonnna Institute, May 27, 1951.

(The fiftieth anniversary of the Institute.—The family of the "Christian Brothers" has spread from Ireland overseas.—Vocations given to the Church.)

It is an indisputable fact that the frequency of the priestly vocations, although not the only norm, is still one of the safest for measuring the worth of a Catholic school and of every other educational institution, its contribution, not only to the ecclesiastical ministry but also to every branch of secular activity. **541 (79)**

On Our part, beloved children, it is a pleasure for Us cordially to thank you and your excellent secular collaborators for the assiduous work accomplished in these fifty years. Continue, then, to advance, always according to the spirit of your founder. The action of the best school and the best family would be sterile and inefficient if they left unheeded the serious warning given to their conscience by the fact that strong and dangerous influences strike and often conquer the young man, his character and his faith on the way from his father's home to the school, there where the people converge in crowds and especially at every kind of cinema show. **542 (22, 33, 97)**

An observation, however, is called for here. In some countries persons competent in questions of education and of Catholic schools have inquired in great detail into the method of modern psychology, the religious life of the pupils, mainly in their adolescent years. If their evidence is to be believed, they have come to this surprising conclusion: the danger that the cinema may weaken the faith of the pupils is less seriously threatening than that which can derive from the possible defects of the priest; and then from those of teachers and educators in general. In posi- **543 (52)** tive terms: the influence of the priest and of the educator in the home, in the church and in the school, still remains the first and strongest element for making a young man a real Christian. What a powerful call to a sense of responsibility! But for you, what a strong incentive also!

(The Pope confirms the mission already entrusted to the Institute by Leo XIII.)

SCHOOLS IN THE MISSIONS

Encycl. *Evangelii praecones*, June 2, 1951.

(The Missions.—Progress over the past twenty-five years.—Persecutions.—Work yet to be finished.—Principles of action.—Aim.—The clergy.—The laity.)

544
(47, 68, 79, 116)
Since young men, and those especially who have had the benefit of a classical and liberal education, will be responsible for the course of the future, no one can be blind to the supreme importance of devoting the best of care to elementary schools, high schools and colleges. Therefore with paternal solicitude We exhort Superiors of missions to spare neither labor nor expense in proportion to their means in vigorously promoting this phase of missionary activity.

The utility of schools for the young lies especially in the fact that they establish advantageous relationships between missionaries and pagans of every class, and, above all, they more easily influence the docile minds of the young to understand, appreciate and embrace the Catholic doctrine. As we all know, the educated youth of today will form the governments of tomorrow and the masses will follow their leadership and guidance. The Apostle of the Gentiles propounded the sublime wisdom of the Gospel before a learned audience when in the Areopagus of Athens he proclaimed the unknown God. Even though this method does not make many converts outright to the teaching of the

Divine Redeemer, still there will be many who, as they contemplate the supernatural beauty of this religion and the charity of its disciples, will feel its benign influence.

Schools and colleges are, moreover, especially helpful in refuting the errors which, now especially, are daily infecting more and more through non-Catholic and Communist activities and which are being openly and covertly instilled into the minds of youth especially.

(The press.—The social question.—Native customs and traditions.—Missionary work.—An appeal to the Catholic world.)

THE IMAGE OF GOD

R.M. to the IV Inter-American Congress of Catholic Education, August 5, 1951.

(Congratulations.)

Is there perhaps something more important in human life than education? It has been truly said that a child, an adolescent, is "a hope": a promising hope for the family, the country, and human society; and at the same time, a precious hope of the Church, of Heaven, and of his God, in Whose image and likeness he was made, and Whose child he is or must become. If this hope is not to be vain, but is rather to be fully realized, he must be fully brought up and educated well. He must receive physical education, which strengthens the energies of the body; intellectual education, which develops and enriches the capacities of the spirit; and above all, moral and religious education, which illumines and guides the intelligence, forms the will, disciplines and sanctifies moral life, and is the only education which gives to the image of God likeness to the divine Model and makes him worthy to take his place in eternal glory. **545** *(3-5, 60, 72)*

Education which does not bother about being moral and religious fails in its greater and better part, in that it neglects the noblest faculties of man, deprives itself of the **546** *(13, 60,*

72,
74,
106-
108)
most efficacious and vital energies, and ends up by "dis-educating," mixing up uncertainties and errors with truth, vice with virtue, and evil with good. Today, the best educators are aware of this, and they spare no effort to remedy the deficiences of the past, perfecting the methods, and at times working anxiously for a new education. But true morality and true religion are only one, just as Truth is but one—fundamental and substantial Truth: God; revealed Truth: Christ; Truth conserved and taught without error or deficiency: the Catholic Church. It was a non-Catholic thinker who said: "Catholicism is the greatest and holiest school of respect that the world has ever seen." (a)

Decline in family education

547
(28,
29,
46,
96)
But the subject in question, while important at all times, is all the more so in our day, first of all because it should fill a deplorable lack that today is, unfortunately, greater than ever.

Man's education starts from the cradle; and the first school that cannot be substituted is the home. "Early as one starts, it is never too early to form the character and habits of the child," as pagan wisdom had already asserted. (a) As in science, so also, analogously, in life: everything depends on the first principles.

Among Christian families of today, there are some which are models and in which is felt and lived the great responsibility of bringing children up well, a responsibility which goes with parenthood, according to natural law; but "the deplorable decadence of family education" is also true, sadly true, and is deplored in very serious terms by Our immortal Predecessor in the Encyclical, *Divini Illius Magistri:* "The employments and professions of temporal and earthly life . . . are prepared for by long and careful study, but for

546a Guizot, cited by Dupanloup in *L'Education*, I, p. 112.
547a Plutarch, *De Educatione Puerorum*, no. V.

the fundamental duty and obligation of educating their children, many parents have little or no preparation, being too engrossed in the care of temporal things." (b)

Here is the first and very serious task which is incumbent on the Catholic educator of today: to make up for the deficiencies of home training.

Youth in the whirlwind of life

The uneducated and "dis-educated" child is entrusted to the public school, where the officially neutral teaching does not form, but on many occasions deforms the spirit; where the surroundings, with frightful frequency, are not sufficiently healthy; without mentioning "the other occasions of religious shipwreck for inexperienced youth... principally impious and immoral books...cinema shows ...radio," as Our Predecessor deplores in the afore-mentioned Encyclical. (a) **548 (3, 26, 97, 107)**

It is in coping with all these difficulties that you must educate the adolescent to form the final image of the Creator, according to the model of the First-born of every creature, and give it such strength that it will not be deformed but will rather become perfect when hurled into the whirl of present-day civil and social life, that is to say, into an atmosphere that is covered in all directions by cleverly organized propaganda, by contrasting interests that do not distinguish what is just and honest from what is immoral and unjust; where on many occasions are heard the most absurd errors upheld as rules of good-living; where the very rhythm of existence keeps man bent on the material interests of the fleeting moment, without giving him time to rise up and look at the sky, to take his bearings and to think of things eternal.

If youth, once education is finished, are not soundly formed, if the image of God is traced in too superficial a

547b Cf. No. 286.
548a Cf. No. 298.

manner, it is unlikely that, subjected to such contrasting passions and battered by so many winds, they will not become in a short space of time completely deformed.

549
(3,
76)
Still worse would it be if they carried within themselves active principles of deformation in unrestrained appetites, unsubdued and dissipated passions, which would not fail to arouse disorders and vices, "similar to the myrtle that is seen in princely gardens"—and which, as the prince of your orators would say—"as soon as the gardener ceases to take care of it, and it is left to itself, it loses its shape in four days and becomes a thicket again as it was before." (a)

It is necessary that your education give a youth a character as strong as the bronze and granite of your mountains, and thus, the continuous battles and the inevitable shocks of modern life, far from deforming him, will serve to improve and perfect him, and he will appear "a still more perfect man, and sometimes a saint that can be given the honors of the altar." (b)

550
(82,
92)
This is an exceedingly hard and difficult task, that can only be successfully accomplished by a Christian and Catholic formation, which can benefit by all pedagogic progress, carefully selected however, so as to detect gold from tinsel. This formation, by acting directly on the best powers of man, indirectly influences instruction and personal hygiene, animating them with a new spirit, raising and preserving them from fatal deviations and baneful aberrations; it adds supernatural help to the natural—to the disciplined energies of the intelligence and will, it adds the light of faith and the force of grace, which alone renders possible what humanly seems impossible. (a)

(It is Catholic pedagogy which educated Brazil.)

549a Cf. A. Vieira, *Sermões,* Vol. 3 (1683), p. 404.
549b *Ibid.,* p. 420.
550a Cf. Luke 18:27.

It will still be this Catholic pedagogy, suitably rendered practicable and up-to-date, which will make your countries still more prosperous, in such a way that their hopes will flower in a wonderful spring; preserving them from many dangers that threaten faith, morals and the very social order, so that they will advance safely along the road of real progress towards the fate that Providence has laid down for them.

(Blessing.)

THE TEACHING SISTERS

All. to Teaching Sisters, September 13, 1951.

We particularly welcome the opportunity offered by your presence at the Congress of Teaching Sisters to express Our heartfelt and paternal praise of the activities of Sisters in schools and in other educational activities both in Italy and throughout the Catholic world. **551** *(16, 55)*

How could the Church have fulfilled her mission of education and charity during recent years, especially in the immediate past, without the aid given, with so much zeal, by hundreds of thousands of Sisters? How otherwise could the Church fulfill her mission today?

Without a doubt, there are many valuable and zealous efforts on the part of other women working at the side of nuns or in affiliation with them, in schools and in other educational activities, or dedicating themselves to the apostolate of the laity. We have in mind especially the good Catholic women teachers in the State schools. But even they must not wonder if, today, We turn to you, beloved daughters, gathered around Us as representatives of religious orders and congregations devoted to the apostolate of the school and education. May the dedication, love, and sacrifices that more often than not you bear in obscurity for the love of Christ and the benefit of young people bring forth fruit a hundredfold in the future as they did in the past. May Our Lord reward you and shower upon you the abundance of His Divine favors.

We hope all the more fervently that this may be so because with you We are aware of the crisis through which your schools and educational institutions are passing. It is a question distinctly shown in the comparison of the youth of today and schools taught by Religious.

(The theme studied in the Congress.)

Crisis of misunderstanding

552
(84)
1. If it be your painful experience that the teaching Sister and the modern girl no longer understand each other well, this is not a phenomenon peculiar to you. Other teachers, often parents themselves, are not in a very much better position. It is not merely an empty phrase to say that young people have changed, have become quite different perhaps. The chief reason for this difference in the young people of today may be that which forms the subject of the frequent complaint, namely that young people are irreverent toward many things that, formerly, were naturally regarded with the greatest respect from childhood up. But young people of today are not solely to be blamed for their present attitude. In childhood, they have lived through horrible things and have seen many highly esteemed ideals, formerly held in high esteem, topple before their very eyes. In this way they have become distrustful and aloof.

553
(84)
It must be remembered also that this complaint about lack of understanding is not something new. It is one which occurs in every generation and is reciprocal between maturity and youth, parents and children, teachers and pupils. Half a century ago, and even some time before that, there was a good deal of sentimentality. People were fond of believing that they were "misunderstood" and said so. Today, the complaint, not devoid of a certain amount of arrogance, is more concerned with the intellect. The result of this misunderstanding is, on the one hand, a reaction which may

sometimes exceed the limits of justice, a tendency to repudiate anything that is, or appears to be, new, an exaggerated suspicion of rebellion against any tradition. On the other hand, it is a lack of faith that shrinks from all authority and, spurning every competent judgment, seeks solutions and counsels with a sort of infatuation more ingenuous than reasoned.

Conditions for a confident understanding

To try to reform young people and convince them by making them submit and to persuade them by force would be useless and not always right. You will succeed very much better in inducing them to give you their confidence if you, on your side, strive to understand them and to make them understand themselves—except always in the case of those immutable truths and values which admit of no change in the heart and mind of man. **554 (56, 84)**

Understanding young people certainly does not mean approving and admitting everything they maintain in their ideas, their tastes, their whims, their false enthusiasm. It consists fundamentally in finding out what is sound in them and in accepting this trustfully without remorse or anger; in discovering the origin of their deviations and errors which are often nothing but an unhappy attempt to solve real and difficult problems; and, finally, in following closely the vicissitudes and conditions of the present time.

Making yourself understood does not mean employing words that are not sanctioned by good usage and construction, that are ungrammatical, leading, as they do, to inaccuracy and vagueness of thought. It means rather the clear expression of one's own thoughts in different yet always correct ways, an attempt to fathom the thoughts of others, always keeping in mind their difficulties, their ignorance, and their inexperience.

On the other hand, it is still true that even the young people of today are fully capable of appreciating true and **555 (80,**

84) genuine values. And it is precisely in this regard that you must assume your responsibility. You must treat young people with simplicity and naturalness, each of you according to her own character. But at the same time, you all must show that religious seriousness and reserve which even the world of today expects of you and through which your union with God should make itself felt. You need not speak of God all the while you are in the midst of the girls. But when you do so, it must be in such a way that they can say to themselves, "This is really a sincere feeling born of a deep conviction." In this way, you will win the confidence of your girls, who will then allow themselves to be persuaded and guided by you.

Religious life and teaching

556
(55,
57,
112)
2. And now We come to that which concerns you particularly: the religious life, your habit, the vow of chastity, your rules and constitutions. Do these render you less fit or downright incapable where the instruction and education of today's young people are concerned?

In the first place, We say that those who possess the (primary) right to education, namely the parents, are not of this opinion. Sisters' schools are still sought after and preferred even by many people who care little or nothing for religion. In many countries, vocations to the life of a teaching Sister and the number of Sisters' schools are much below demand. This is not a matter of mere chance. Therefore, We may add, and not only in regard to Italy but speaking in general: from those who have a part in drawing up school legislation, We must expect sufficient regard for justice, and sufficient democratic sense—so to speak—as to correspond to the will of the parents in such a way that the schools founded and directed by religious institutes will not be placed in a worse condition than State schools and that they will be given that freedom which is necessary for their development.

And now, let Us briefly discuss religious life in itself. **557**
The religious habit: let it be such that it is the ex- *(56)*
pression of inward naturalness, of simplicity and spiritual
modesty. Thus it will edify everyone, even modern young
people.

Chastity and virginity (which imply also the inner re- **558**
nunciation of all sensual affection) do not estrange souls *(57)*
from this world. They rather awaken and develop energies
needed for wider and higher offices beyond the limits of
individual families. Today there are many teaching and
nursing Sisters who, in the best sense of the word, are
nearer to life than the average person living in the world.

The adaptations

Followed in letter and in spirit, your constitutions, too, **559**
facilitate the Sister's task and procure for her all she needs *(56)*
and must do in our time to be a good teacher and educator.
This also applies to purely mechanical matters. In many
countries today, for example, even Sisters use bicycles when
their work demands it. At first this was something new,
though not against the Rule.

It is possible that some details of the school schedules,
certain regulations—simple applications of the Rule—certain customs which were, perhaps, in harmony with past
conditions but which today merely hinder educational
work, must be adapted to new circumstances.

Let superiors and general Chapters proceed in this matter conscientiously, with foresight, prudence, and courage
and, where demanded, let them not fail to submit the proposed changes to the competent ecclesiastical authorities.

You wish to serve the cause of Jesus Christ and of His
Church in the way that the world of today demands. Therefore, it would not be reasonable to persist in customs and
forms that hinder this service or perhaps render it impossible. Sisters who are educators and teachers must be so pre-

pared, so well versed in all with which young people are in contact, in all which influences them, that their pupils will not hesitate to say: "We can approach Sister with our problems and difficulties; she understands and helps us."

Needs of the school and education

560
(56,
60)
3. In this way, We come now to the needs of the school and education which We particularly wish to recommend to your care.

Many of your schools are being described to Us and praised as being very good. But not all. It is Our fervent wish that all endeavor to become excellent.

This presupposes that your teaching Sisters are well-versed in the subjects they expound. See to it, therefore, that they are well trained and that their education corresponds in quality and academic degrees to that demanded by the State. Be generous in giving them all they need, especially where books are concerned, so that they may continue their studies and thus offer young people a rich and solid field of knowledge. This is in keeping with the Catholic idea which gratefully welcomes all that is naturally good, beautiful and true, because it is an image of Divine goodness, beauty and truth.

561
(55,
56)
Most parents entrust their daughters to you because their consciences bid them do so. But this does not mean that their children should suffer by receiving in your schools an education of inferior value. On the contrary, you must do all that you can to assure parents that their children are getting the best education possible right from the elementary classes.

And then, do not forget that knowledge and good teaching win the respect and consideration of the pupils for the teaching Sister. Thus she can exercise a greater influence on their character and their spiritual life.

Formation of the perfect Christian

In this respect, there is no need for Us to repeat that **562** which you know well, that which has been the object of *(26,* ample discussion during your Congress. According to the *72)* Catholic concept, the object of the school and of education is the formation of the perfect Christian, that is—to apply this principle to your situation—to exercise such spiritual and moral influence and to train girls and young women in such a way that when they are left to themselves they will remain firm in their faith as Catholics and put this faith into daily practice. At least, there must be the well founded hope that the pupil will later on lead her life according to the principles and rules of her faith.

Your entire school and educational system would be useless were this object not the central point of your labor. Our Lord wants you to strive towards this aim with all your strength. He has called you to the vocation of educating girls and making them perfect Christians. In this He demands your complete dedication, and one day He will ask you to render an account.

The modern girl! You can measure better than many **563** others the still unsolved problems and the grave dangers *(56,* resulting from recent changes in the woman's world from *76)* her sudden introduction into all walks of public life.

Was there ever such a time as the present when a girl had to be won and formed interiorly, according to her convictions and will, to the cause of Christ and of virtuous conduct, so that she will remain faithful both to Him and to that cause despite all temptations and obstacles, beginning with modesty in dress and going on to the most serious and distressing problems of life?

Conclusion

Let it never happen that material advantages, per- **564** sonal authority, wealth, political power or similar consid- *(57,* erations induce you to renounce your educational ideals *58)* and betray your vocation! An examination of conscience during your Congress may have salutary effects. The reason for this paternal exhortation is Our benevolence for you, because your cares are Ours also, your happy success is Ours, too.

In obtaining favorable results, harmony and generous accord between the different religious congregations can play a major part. Reciprocal understanding and encouragement, holy emulation can only redound to your mutual advantage. The most encouraging steps have already been taken in this respect. All you have to do is to continue them.

Just as Christian education in general is not an objective easily to be achieved today, your mission is not an easy one, but insofar as the inner formation of the young girl is concerned, your religious vocation is a powerful ally. Living faith, union with God, the love of Christ with which each of you has had the chance to fill herself in the spirit of the Congregation from the first day of the novitiate; the vow, not only of chastity, but especially of obedience; a common task under one guidance in the same direction— all these things act strongly on your minds, always supposing, of course, that you live up to your vocation.

May Divine Providence direct and lead you in all that you propose and undertake. May the grace of Our Lord Jesus Christ fill your minds and hearts. May the Blessed Virgin, Mary our Mother, be your model, protectress, and advocate. Together with the expression of these wishes, We most cordially impart Our apostolic blessing to you, beloved Sisters, and to all the young people entrusted to your care.

CORRUPTIVE INITIATION

All. to the French Fathers of Families, September 18, 1951.

(The Christian rule of family rights and duties is: the family is not for society; it is society that is for the family.—

As the fundamental cell of society, the family has rights which the State, in its own interest, must safeguard.)

Let us indicate, by way of example, just a few which at present are found to be most endangered: the indissolubility of marriage; the protection of life before birth; suitable dwellings for families, not made up of only one or two children, or even without children, but of a normal, larger number; work opportunities, because the unemployment of the father is the most bitter distress for the family; the parents' right over their children before the State; their full freedom to rear them in the true faith, and consequently, the right of Catholic parents to a Catholic school; conditions of public life, particularly public morality, which are such that the families, and especially the young, will not be morally certain of suffering corruption. **565** *(22, 102, 106, 112)*

On this point, and also on others which more deeply concern family life, there exists no difference between one family and the other.

(On other questions of an economic and political nature, it may be necessary, in certain instances, to sacrifice particular interests.)

One must not give way on family rights

But insofar as the essential rights of the family are concerned, the faithful who are true to the Church will undertake to support them from the beginning to the end. It may be that here and there, it is necessary to yield on this or that detail in the face of political forces. In this case, it is a matter of being patient but not of surrendering. It is still necessary that, in similar cases, the doctrine be saved and all efficacious means be adopted in order that the matter may be gradually brought to its proper end, which must never be renounced. **566** *(111, 112)*

Among these efficacious means, even the most powerful, is the union among fathers of families having the same

convictions and the same intentions. Your presence here
bears witness that such, too, is your own standpoint.

567   Another means which, even before achieving the de-
(111) sired result is never sterile, and which, in the absence of
the pending success that one continues to work for, always
brings its benefits, is the effort—through this coalition of
fathers of families—to illuminate public opinion and convince it little by little to favor the triumph of truth and
justice. No effort whatsoever which seeks to bring this
about should be disdained or neglected.

Sex literature which is called Catholic

568   There is one field in which the work of educating pub-
(99, lic opinion and correcting it imposes itself with tragic ur-
113) gency. It finds itself, in this field, perverted by propaganda
which one would not hesitate to term fatal, even though,
in certain instances, it originates from a Catholic source
and aims at making way among Catholics, and although
they who promote it do not seem to realize that they are
unknowingly deceived by the spirit of evil.

We here wish to refer to writings, books and articles
concerning sex initiation which today very often obtain
enormous editorial successes and flood the whole world,
gaining possession of childhood, submerging the new generation, troubling engaged and newly-wed couples.

569   With all the gravity, attention and dignity that the
(78) question calls for, the Church has treated the problem of
instruction on this matter, according to the normal physical
and psychological development of the adolescent or the
particular cases advised by diverse individual conditions.
In all truth, the Church can declare that, while deeply respectful of the sanctity of marriage, she has in theory and
in practice left the married couple free in whatever the
impulse of a wholesome and upright nature allows, without
offense to the Creator.

One is appalled at the intolerable impudence of such **570** literature; and while paganism itself, in the face of the *(97,* secret of matrimonial intimacy, seemed respectfully to draw *99)* the line, We are compelled to witness this mystery violated and its vision—sensual and dramatized—offered as food to the public at large, even to youth. It is the case really to ask oneself if the dividing line is still sufficiently visible between this initiation, which is said to be Catholic, and the press which with erotic and obscene illustrations purposely and deliberately aims at corruption and shamefully exploits, for vile gain, the lowest instincts of fallen nature.

And this is not all. Such propaganda also threatens **571** Catholic people with a double punishment, not to use a *(99)* stronger expression.

First of all, it greatly exaggerates the importance and range of the sexual element of life. Let us even admit that these authors, under the purely theoretical aspect, keep themselves within the limits of Catholic morality; this does not however do away with the fact that their way of explaining sexual life is such as to attribute to it, in the mind and practical judgment of the average reader, the sense and value of an end in itself. It makes the real and primordial aim of marriage to be lost sight of, that is, the procreation and education of children and the serious duty of the married couples with regard to this end, which the writings in question leave obscure.

Secondly, this literature, if such it could be called, **572** does not seem in any way to take into account, based as it *(5,* is on nature, the general experience of all times, whether it *99)* be that of today or yesterday, which attests that neither initiation nor instruction in moral education offers any advantage of itself. Rather it becomes seriously unwholesome and prejudicial when not closely allied with constant discipline, with vigorous self-control, and above all with the use of the supernatural forces of prayer and the sacraments. All Catholic educators worthy of this name and of their

mission know very well the decisive part played by supernatural forces in the sanctification of man; whether young
or old, single or married.

But it is already much if, regarding what We have
said just now, even some slight mention is made in those
publications; often they are completely silent on the matter.
Even the principles so wisely illustrated by Our Predecessor
Pius XI, in the Encyclical *Divini Illius Magistri,* on sex-
education and questions connected thereto (a) are set
aside—a sad sign of the times!—with a smile of compassion:
Pius XI, they say, wrote twenty years ago, for his times!
Great progress has been made since then!

573   Fathers of families here present!—there are many other
(111, Christians throughout the whole world and in all countries,
fathers of families like yourselves, who share your own
sentiments. Unite with them therefore—under the direction
of your Bishops certainly; call to your aid all Catholic wom-
en and mothers with their powerful contribution, in order
to fight together, without human timidity or respect, to stop
and curtail these movements under whatever name or under whatever patronage they conceal themselves or are
patronized.

*(Patronage of St. Pius X and of the Most Holy Virgin
Mary.)*

PRUDENT INITIATION

All. to the Professors of the Discalced Carmelites,
September 23, 1951.

*(The glory of the Order.—The young religious.—The
religious home.—Obedience.—Chastity.)*

574   When the ancient Greeks and Romans wanted to indi-
(78) cate things concerning chastity, they made use of the parti-

572a Cf. No. 282.

cular term "αἰδοῖα =verenda," that is modesty, thus signifying that such things must be treated in a respectful manner. Modesty, however, must not be intended as maintaining an absolute silence on this subject so that no mention of it be made in the moral education of the young, not even with sobriety and precaution. On this subject, let adolescents be instructed with suitable advice and be allowed to open their minds, to question without hesitation, and let them receive answers which will give them sure, clear, and sufficiently full enlightenment and which will instill confidence into them.

(Poverty.)

How greatly it pleases us to hear that you desire to give your pupils a much broader education in the literature of the humanities. This literature is very suitable for training young people's minds in order that they may think and speak in a logical, clear manner, avoiding a useless excess of words and also for procuring other excellent qualities proper to the well-formed man. As regards these studies, however, We must complain of an unpleasant fact. Unfortunately, the Latin language, the glory of priests, has only a few languishing promoters. How can the praise of this regal language—called by the Greeks βασιλικὴ γλῶσσα —be worthily sung; this language which not only expresses, but depicts the truth, which in edicts and sentences stands out for its particular solemnity; this language which is the liturgical language of the Latin Church and which, lastly, is the bond of maximum value in the Catholic Church! Let there be no priest who does not know how to read and speak it fluently and with ease! Oh, if only there would arise among you many excellent individuals capable of writing it in a clear and concise manner!

575
(63,
64)

And indeed, it is the Latin and also the Greek language which, since the first Christian era, is the depository of many ecclesiastical writings and is a treasure of incomparable excellence. Consequently, the sacred minister who ignores it, is to be regarded as a man of deplorable intellectual poverty.

(*Little esteem for the Encyclical*, Humani Generis.)

THE EDUCATION OF CONSCIENCE

R.M. for the closing of "Family Day" in Italy, March 23, 1952.

576
(2,
7,
16,
26,
28,
29,
30)

The family is the cradle of birth and development of a new life which, in order that it may not perish, needs to be attended to and educated: this is a right and a fundamental duty given to and imposed immediately by God on parents. The subject and aim of education in the natural order is the development of the child into a complete man: the subject and aim of Christian education is the formation of the new human being, reborn in Baptism, that he may become a perfect Christian. This obligation, which has always been a custom and boast of Christian families, is solemnly decreed by Article no. 1113 of the Code of Canon law which reads as follows:

"Parentes gravissima obligatione tenentur prolis educationem tum religiosamet moralem, tum physicam et civilem pro viribus curandi, et etiam temporali eorum bono providendi."

"Parents are bound by a most serious obligation to provide to the best of their power for the religious and moral as well as for the physical and civil education of their children, and also to provide for their temporal welfare."

The most urgent questions of such a vast subject have been clarified on various occasions by Our Predecessors and by Us Ourselves. We therefore now propose not to repeat what has already been amply explained, but rather to draw attention to one element which, although the basis and the fulcrum of education, especially Christian education, seems instead to some, at first sight to be extraneous to it. We would like, that is, to speak of that which is deeper and more intrinsic in man: his conscience. We are induced to do so by the fact that some currents of modern thought are beginning to alter the concept of it and impugn its value. We shall therefore treat of conscience inasmuch as it is the object of education.

Conscience

Conscience may be called the most personal and secret nucleus of man. There he takes refuge in absolute solitude **577** with his spiritual faculties: alone with himself, or better, **(75)** alone with God—Whose voice conscience echoes—and with himself. There he makes up his mind, for good or for evil; there he makes his choice between the road to victory and the road to defeat. Even if he wanted to, man would never succeed in ridding himself of his conscience; with it—either as approving or condemning—he will proceed along the whole road of life, and likewise with it—a truthful and incorruptible witness—he will present himself before God's judgment. Therefore, conscience is, to use an image as old as it is apt, a ἄδυτον, a sanctuary on the threshold of which everyone must stop; whether child, father, or mother. Only the priest, as guardian of souls and as Minister of the Sacrament of Penance, has access to it; yet not for this does conscience cease to be a jealous sanctuary whose secret God Himself wishes to be kept with the seal of the most sacred silence.

In what way then can one speak of the education of conscience?

The Christian conscience

It is necessary to refer to some fundamental concepts **578** of Catholic doctrine to realize fully that conscience can **(75)** and must be educated.

The Divine Savior has brought His truth and grace to man, ignorant and feeble: truth to show him the way that leads to his goal, and grace to give him the strength to reach it.

To travel along that road means, in practice, to accept the will and commandments of Christ and to adapt one's life to them, that is, every individual action, both internal and external, that the human will chooses and determines. Now, what spiritual faculty is it that dictates the will, in particular cases, so that it may choose and determine those acts that conform to the divine Will, if not the conscience? It is therefore the faithful echo and the clear reflection of the divine rule of human actions. Such expressions as "the judgment of the Christian conscience," or "judge according to Christian conscience," have therefore this meaning: the rule for the final and personal decision of a moral act is to be taken from the word and will of Christ. He is in fact the Way, the Truth and the Life (a) not only for all mankind as a whole, but for each individual person: as much for the adult, as for the child and youth.

579
(75) From this it follows that the forming of the Christian conscience of children or youth consists, first and foremost, in illuminating their minds concerning Christ's desires, His law and His way, and in addition, in influencing their souls insofar as this can be done from the outside, in order that they may execute the divine Will freely and constantly. This is the highest duty of education.

580
(12, But where will the educator and the one educated find
74) the Christian moral law in the concrete easily and surely? He will find it in the law of the Creator imprinted on each one's heart (a), and in Revelation, that is, in the complex of truths and precepts taught by the divine Master. Both of these, the law written in the heart, that is, the natural law,

578a Cf. John 14:6.
580a Cf. R.M. 2, 14-16.

and the truths and precepts of supernatural Revelation have been placed by Christ our Redeemer, as a moral treasure for humanity, in the hands of His Church so that she may preach them to all nations, illustrate and transmit them, intact and defended from all contamination and error, from one generation to another.

A "new moral"

Though it was undisputed throughout the centuries, difficulties and objections now arise against this doctrine so that it is necessary to shed light on it. **581** *(97, 100)*

As in dogmatic doctrine, so in the Catholic moral order, there are some who would like to institute an almost radical revision so as to arrive at a new valuation.

The first step, or better the first blow, to the Christian moral order would be that of unchaining it—as is claimed— from the narrow and oppressing supervision of the Church authorities, so that, freed from the sophistical subtleties of the casuistic method, morals may be led back to their original form and simply referred to the intelligence and decision of the individual conscience.

Everyone sees to what fatal consequences such an upsetting of the fundamental basis of education would lead.

Without commenting on the manifest ignorance and immaturity of judgment of those who hold such opinions, it will do good on the other hand to point out the central shortcoming of this "new morality." In referring every ethical criterion to the individual conscience, closed jealously in upon itself and made absolute arbiter of its own decisions, far from facilitating its progress, it rather deviates it from the main Way, which is Christ. **582** *(12, 100)*

The divine Savior has delivered His Revelation, of which moral obligations are an essential part, not just to mere individual men but to His Church, to which He has entrusted the mission of leading souls to embrace faithfully that sacred duty.

(The individualistic autonomy of conscience is irreconcilable with the dispositions given by Christ.—The Church does not want to humiliate man, but to introduce him into supernatural riches.—This presupposes precise moral obligations.)

Permanent value of the precept of purity

583
(12,
77)
Conscious, therefore, of the right and duty of the Apostolic See to intervene authoritatively, when necessary, in moral questions, in Our address of October 29 last year, We proposed to illuminate consciences on the problems of married life. With the same authority, We today declare to educators and to the youth themselves: the divine Commandment of purity of soul and body in its full force is binding on the youth of today, too. They too have the moral obligation and, with the help of grace, the possibility of keeping themselves pure. We therefore reject as erroneous the affirmation of those who consider falls in the years of puberty inevitable and for this reason deserving of little heed, almost as if they were not serious faults for the reason that ordinarily, according to this opinion, passion removes the liberty necessary for an act to be morally imputable.

584
(76,
77)
On the contrary, it is a duty and a wise rule for the educator, while not neglecting to convey to the young the noble values of purity, so as to win them over to loving and desiring it for itself, clearly to inculcate the commandment as such, nevertheless, in all the gravity and seriousness of its divine ordination. He will thus encourage the young to avoid all future occasions, encourage them in the fight the harshness of which he will not hide from them. He will induce them to embrace courageously those sacrifices which virtue exacts, and he will exhort them to persevere and not to fall into the danger of laying down their weapons right from the beginning and of yielding to perverse habits without offering resistance.

(More than from the field of private conduct, it is from the field of public life that the attempt is being made to exclude the moral law.—The sciences, politics, art, etc., have their own laws but, in substance, their practice through the activity of man cannot escape a moral valuation.)

Therefore, Our Predecessors and We Ourselves, in the confusion of the war and in the troubled vicissitudes of the post-war period, have not ceased to insist on the principle that the order willed by God embraces life in its entirety, not excluding public life in all its manifestations, convinced as We are that no restriction of real human freedom is involved, nor any intrusion in the State's sphere of activity, but rather an assurance against errors and abuses from which Christian morality, if justly applied, is capable of giving protection. These truths must be taught to young people and inculcated in their conscience by those who, in the family or school, have the obligation to attend to their education, thus sowing the seeds of a better future. **585** *(66)*

This is what We intended to tell you today, beloved sons and daughters who are listening to Us, and in telling it to you, We have not hidden the anxiety which weighs on Our heart over this formidable problem which concerns the present and future of the world and the eternal destiny of many souls. How much comfort would We receive were We certain that you share with Us this anxiety of Ours for the Christian education of youth! Educate the consciences of your children with constant and persevering care. Educate them to fear as well as to love God. Educate them in truthfulness, but be truthful with yourselves first and banish from educational work what is not frank and true. Imprint on the consciences of the young a genuine conception of freedom, the only true freedom worthy of a creature created like unto the image of God. Such freedom is quite different from dissolution and unrestraint; it is rather a proven capacity for goodness, it is the self determination to **586** *(63, 75, 95)* will and to accomplish what is good (a); it is the mastery over one's faculties, over instincts, and the events of life.

587
(72,
73,
75)
Educate them to pray and to draw from the well-springs of Penance and of the most Holy Eucharist that which nature cannot give them: the strength not to fall, the strength to rise again. Let them realize while still young that without the help of these supernatural forces, they cannot be good Christians, nor even upright men whose reward is a serene life. Prepared in such a way, they will be in a position to aspire to what is best, they will be enabled to dedicate themselves to that great employment of their being, the fulfillment of which will redound to their glory: the living of Christ in their own lives.

(To be united in the spreading of the kingdom of Christ.—Blessing.)

A NEW MORALITY

All. to the World Federation of Young Catholic Women, April 18, 1952.

(Theme of the Congress: The Faith of the Young.)

588
(74,
75,
100)
Today, We should like to take the opportunity of this meeting with you, in order to tell you what We think of a certain phenomenon which is manifesting itself in some degree everywhere in the life of Catholics and which to some extent affects everyone, but most especially youth and the educators of youth, and which is referred to in several passages of your memorandum, particularly where it says: "Confusing Christianity with a code of precepts and prohibitions, young people have the feeling that they are being suffocated in a climate of "demanding morality"; nor is it a negligible minority which seeks to cast off this 'wearisome burden'."

586a Cf. Gal. 5:13.

We could call this phenomenon a "new conception of moral life," since it involves a tendency which manifests itself in the domain of morality. But it is on the truths of faith that the principles of morality are based, and you know how fundamentally important it is for the preservation and development of faith that the conscience of the young man and the young woman be formed at a very early age and developed according to correct and sound moral standards. Thus the "new conception of Christian morality" affects very directly the problem of the faith in youth.

We have already spoken of the "new morality" in Our Radio Message of last March 23, to Christian Educators. (a) What We say today is not merely a continuation of what We then expounded, for We wish today to uncover the hidden sources of this conception. We might term it "ethical existentialism," "ethical individualism"—all understood in the restrictive sense of which We shall speak, and which has also been called "Situation-ethics," or "morality according to the situation."

"Morality according to the situation"

The distinctive mark of this morality is that it is not **589** based in effect on universal moral laws, such as, for exam- *(100)* ple, the Ten Commandments, but on the real and concrete conditions or circumstances in which men must act, and according to which the conscience of the individual must judge and choose. Such a state of affairs is unique and is applicable only once for every human action. That is why the decision of conscience, as the proposers of this ethic affirm, cannot be commanded by ideas, principles, and universal laws.

(According to those who favor the new morality, conscience may make decisions contrary to the divine law, and

588a See No. 581 ff.

even as regards God Himself, to violate this law.—For con-
science, nothing exists other than God, the Father, and the
ego of man, the child of God.—In this way, some Catholics
think that they can soften the requirements of Christian
living.)

590   This is especially true of the negative obligations of the
(74) moral law, those which oblige us not to do something.
The fundamental obligations of the Christian law, inasmuch as they supercede those of the natural law, and
are based on the essence of the supernatural order established by the Divine Redeemer, do not apply only to the
essence, the nature of man and his essential relationships,
but to every sphere of his activity.

(Some applications.)

591   For the rest, against the "situation-ethics" We pro-
(74, pose three considerations or maxims. The first: We grant
100) that God wants, first and always, a right intention. But this
. is not enough; He also wants good work. A second principle
is that it is not permitted to do evil in order that good may
result. (a) But this new ethic, perhaps without being aware
of it, acts according to the principle that the end justifies
the means. A third maxim is that there may be situations
in which a man, and especially a Christian, must remember
that it is necessary to sacrifice everything, even his life, in
order to save his soul. We are reminded of this by all the
martyrs, and they are very numerous, even in our time. The
mother of the Machabees along with her sons; Saints Perpetua and Felicitas, notwithstanding their children; Maria
Goretti, and thousands of others, men and women, whom
the Church venerates—did they, in the face of the "situation" in which they found themselves, uselessly or even
wrongly incur a bloody death? No, certainly not, and, by
their blood they are the most explicit witnesses to the truth
against the "new morality."

591a Cf. Rom. 3:8.

(According to Saint Thomas, Catholic morality guides conscience when there are no absolutely obligatory rules independent of all circumstances.)

The faith of youth and morality

The Christian education of the conscience definitely **592** does not neglect personality, even that of the young girl *(26,* and the child, nor does it check its initiative. All sound *75)* education aims at rendering the educator unnecessary, little by little, and making the one educated independent within proper limits. This is also true of the education of the conscience by God and the Church. Its aim is, as the Apostle says, (a) "the perfect man, according to the measure of the fullness of the age of Christ," hence, a man who is of age, and who also has the courage which goes with responsibility.

But it is necessary that this maturity be on the right **593** plane. By means of His Church, through which He contin- *(26,* ues to act, Jesus Christ remains the Lord, the Head, and *75)* the Master of every individual man, whatever be his age and state. The Christian, for his part, must assume the grave and sublime task of putting into practice in his personal life, his professional, social and public life, insofar as it may depend on him, the truth, the spirit, and the law of Christ. This is what We call Catholic morality, and it leaves a vast field of action for initiative and the personal responsibility of the Christian.

This is what We wanted to say to you. The dangers **594** besetting the faith of our young people are today extraor- *100)* dinarily numerous. Everyone knew this and knows it, but your memorandum is particularly instructive on this subject. Nevertheless, We feel that few of these dangers are as great or as laden with consequences as those which the "new morality" creates for the faith. The bewilderment oc-

592a Eph. 4:13; Cf. 4:14.

casioned by such deformations or such softening of moral
duties, which duties flow naturally from faith, would in
time lead to the corruption of its very source. Thus the
faith would die.

595
(73,
76)
From all that We have said on faith, We shall draw
two conclusions, two directives, which We wish to leave
with you in conclusion, in order that they may orientate
and animate the whole of your activity and life as valiant
Christians.

The first: The faith of young people must be a praying faith. Youth must learn how to pray. Let this prayer be
always in the measure and in the form suitable to the age
of youth, but it must ever be realized that, without prayer,
it is impossible to remain firm in the faith.

The second: Youth must be proud of their faith, and
ready to accept the fact that it will cost them something.
From earliest childhood, the young must accustom themselves to make sacrifices for their faith, to walk before God
with an upright conscience, and to reverence whatever He
orders. Then youth will grow naturally, as it were, in the
love of God.

(Blessing.)

THE FIRST TRANSMISSION
OF THE GOSPEL MESSAGE

All. to the World Union of Catholic Women's Organizations, April 24, 1952.

*(Peace, a condition for a healthy female life.—The
establishment of peace is the task of the woman.—The psychological and moralizing effect on men.)*

596
(34,
36,
39,
66)
. . . above all, it is a synthesis and a crowning of spiritual labor to educate the young according to the Christian
aspect of the world as revealed to us by the Divine Savior.
To whom, in practice, does the initial teaching of the gospel message belong if not to mothers?

What wisdom and benevolence has Divine Providence displayed! It has ordained that every generation at its birth should pass through the sweet care of the mother—at whose side stands the Mother of all, the Church—so that it may receive that goodness, gentleness, and devotion that are natural to the woman. Without this periodic return to the beneficial source, humanity, surrendering itself to the hard-heartedness and bitter battles of daily life, would in a short time decline into the most abject savagery. You, who through natural duty and divine calling form the souls of children, ought then to guide the coming generations into a sense of universal fraternity, and into an abhorrence of violence.

(Exterior action in public life.—Woman in Christian life.—The Christian woman is necessary for civilization and progress.)

THE BLESSED ROSE VENERINI

All. to the Religious Venerini Sisters on the Beatification of their Foundress, May 5, 1952.

While St. John Baptist de La Salle, the glorious Patron **597** of Catholic educators, was founding his first schools in *(59)* France to fight religious and secular ignorance, Divine Providence was mysteriously preparing your Foundress, beloved daughters of Blessed Rose Venerini, to render the same service to little girls in the Papal States.

The origin of her Institute was modest like the source of great rivers, because God always takes pleasure in exalting the humble. Invited by her spiritual father to gather women, maidens and young girls, around her to recite the Holy Rosary, she began to explain the meaning of the prayers to them, and afterwards the principal mysteries of the faith and the rest of Christian doctrine, which she would conclude with wise spiritual counsels. In this modest apostolic activity, the program of the Religious Venerini Sisters was gradually outlined.

598
(54,
72)
Right from the outset, Blessed Rose taught in order to sanctify. This was her aim, and it is still yours after more than two centuries and a half of fruitful devotion. Your Mother deeply felt the spiritual requirements of a Christian education. Illuminated by her first experiences and guided by the supernatural instinct of divine grace, she desired that not only the text of prayer be taught in the schools, but also their meaning and the manner to meditate on them. Now, prayer is not taught like a secular science. One who teaches prayer must himself be solid in prayer, prayer that is fervent, simple, and habitual. But this calls for deep devotion, that real devotion which the Angelic Doctor rightly defines as "the will to give oneself promptly to those things that concern the service of God." (a)

(Her habitual exclamation was: "Provided it gives pleasure to God, everything is dear to me.")

599
(51,
54,
55)
You have certainly not forgotten the lessons of your Mother. Imitate her, sanctify yourselves in order to sanctify, as she did, the many girls entrusted to you, not only in Rome and Italy, but also overseas, in the great America. You will thus deserve the praise that Blessed Rose heard from the lips of Our Predecessor Clement XI of happy memory, the day when the venerable Pontiff personally visited her first school in Rome. Having requested that the usual lessons be held as if he were not present, he was so satisfied that to Blessed Rose, who was kneeling at his feet, he uttered those memorable words: "Lady Rose, you help Us to perform Our office; you do what We cannot do, and with these schools you will sanctify Rome. We are deeply grateful to you."

600
(14,
26,
"You help Us to perform Our office." Yes, the Church is essentially an educator. To give her children more abundant life is something which belongs to her maternal of-

---

598a St. Thomas, *Summa Theologicae*, 2a, 2ae; Q. 82, A. 1, in corp.

fice, and as the period of childhood is the most delicate
and susceptible to progress, she tenderly stoops down to
nourish the spirit and soul of her children. As, in fact, Our
glorious Predecessor Pius XI taught, "The proper and immediate aim of Christian education is to cooperate with
divine grace in forming real and perfect Christians: i.e.,
Christ Himself in those who are regenerated with Baptism,
according to the vivid expression of the Apostle: 'Little
children of mine, that I again carry in my heart until Christ
is formed in you.'... Therefore, Christian education includes the whole sphere of human life, sensitive and spiritual, intellectual and moral, individual, domestic and social; not to lower it in any way whatsoever, but to elevate,
regulate and perfect it according to the example and doctrine of Christ." (a)

60,
80)

Who would marvel then that to this program alone,
so noble and so vast, you have always wanted to restrict
your activity? Faithful to the wish of your Foundress, you
have never accepted any other activity but that of teaching,
so that in this manner you have been able to improve your
methods and adapt them to the conditions of modern life,
though maintaining intact the spirit that at all times animated your activity. The respect and admiration which you
so thoroughly deserve thus rises, almost through you, to
Blessed Rose, your Mother, who today, from the glory of
the elect, delights in seeing the work, which she so humbly
began, prosper in your hands.

601
(82)

(*Blessing.*)

600a Cf. 300 above.

BOY SCOUTS—AN EDUCATIONAL MOVEMENT

All. to the VII International conference of Catholic Boy Scouts, June 6, 1952.

(Theme of the Conference: the apostolate in Boy Scouts and with Boy Scouts.—The aim conforms to the spirit of the Boy Scouts.)

602
(26,
60)
Everyone knows that right from the beginning, religion has always occupied first place; but you are equally aware of the strength and aim which Catholicism contributes to the educational activities that you pursue. It is not sufficient for you to train the best citizens, the most active and the most devoted to the common good of the terrestrial city; it is more essential to train them as the best sons of the Church.

(All the faithful are called to collaborate in the apostolate.—Scouting ought to prepare them for this and experience affirms that it actually does.—The Scout does not seek to escape the services and the obligations of civil life.)

603
(26,
60,
90)
He has taken to heart a complete and harmonious culture well in keeping with his faculties and present necessities. To attain this ideal, the promise to keep the Scout Law, with the grace of God, is a potent lever which raises youth above weaknesses and temptations. Based on the principles of the natural law, the Scout Law, together with an education designed to stimulate endeavor, and the daily practice of voluntary good deeds, makes an appeal to uprightness and loyalty. Youth have such a great desire for loyalty and are happy when they find the means of preserving it steadfastly. It makes them detest lies, fraud and false pretenses. The young, feeling their strength grow, tend to be generous; they want to fight and to test themselves in difficulties; they feel the need to give and offer themselves, to excel, discovering in open-air life and in the trying out of their physical capacities means well adapt-

ed to their age. Purity, so favored by such a moral climate, is clearly defined and gives their energies a Christian reserve and refinement.

Who could deny the advisability of such an education in a society where egoism, mistrust, cowardice and an untamed love for pleasure reign supreme?

(The first apostolate: Example in the Group.—Preparation for entry into society and the responsibilities it entails.)

In conclusion, the formation of character, which is the main aim of Scouting, ought to tend in a social and apostolic direction. It ought to prepare the young for the service of their neighbor, whether it be in personal contact or in civil and religious institutions.

604
(66, 88, 90)

(Apostolic Blessing.)

THE IDEAL OF UNIVERSITY STUDENTS

All. to the University Students of Rome, June 15, 1952.

(Welcome.)

You, on the other hand, are not unaware of the assiduous care with which We follow university life, its progress, its problems and its battles; likewise, you are not unaware of the tokens of Our predilection, particularly that which We would like you to consider as a gift that has sprung from the bottom of Our heart: the University Chapel, ardently desired by you and received with joy, to serve as a spiritual center and the crowning edifice in the City of Studies.

605
(21, 45, 119)

And what better gift could We offer to the youth of the University of Rome than a Temple which, while continuing to be a perennial token of Our affection, might also, with its Hall destined for worship, with its Crypt dedicated to the pious memory of those who fell while still young, with its dedication to Eternal Wisdom, be the sanctuary where youth can find the means of nourishing the triple flame which must inspire and light up their journey through life: their country, an extension of the family, as it were—learning, and religion, which are the three pillars of a modern and well-ordered society?

Responsibility towards the fatherland

606
(68)
1. Now, you are those who determine the future of your native land, although not exclusively, but more so than any other group of young people, because among civic activities, the liberal arts or professions are those which in a greater degree give tone to the life of a nation and mark out its course. The direction of future society depends mainly on the mind and heart of the university students of today. And as you have come to Us for some healthy inspiration, it seems to Us that We can say: deepen the understanding and penetrating awareness of the nation's future leaders, and the sense of special responsibility toward the country in the individual professions to which you will devote yourselves when you have successfully completed your studies.

The future of a nation, among modern and civilized peoples, therefore, depends fundamentally on its University youth.

(The nation relies on University youth in the hours of danger, and also in the normal course of national life.)

607
(87)
Your love for your country, your learned and professional ideals, must therefore be realized now in assiduous and methodic study, which exacts a sense of discipline that is desired rather than imposed, a life of austerity, constant concentration, and purity of life, which is the most valid support of real gains in learning.

Love of knowledge

608
(69,
2. The other torch which will illuminate your path is knowledge itself and its many branches, which you your-

selves will feel the need to cultivate unceasingly. As you   70,
grow older you will realize how grateful you must be to   88)
God for having directed you along the path of knowledge
which, in return for the many hardships it calls for, gives
its followers such inestimable satisfactions as, art excepted,
no other work can give. What splendid dignity profound
knowledge confers on persons who have command of it,
and therefore utilize it for the benefit of others! What
great satisfaction it brings—We do not mean to self-love,
but to the natural human yearning for knowledge and the
broader visions it affords. Very few other earthly goods
can be compared with it for perfecting man.

However, while you appreciate its charm to the full,
do not think that it can fully satisfy you. Such an expectation, aside from being an error of overestimation concerning
its power to perfect, would also cause bitter disappointment on the day when, with full maturity of spirit, the realization of the deepest and fullest human values will arise
in you—since man acquires the consciousness of his full
being only by degrees. On that day, not even philosophy,
which is the interpreter of nature and of natural knowledge, and thus in some way, the rule of life, will be able
to deal with all the problems and difficulties to be overcome. It will be necessary to ascend to higher sources, to
which a sincere love of truth and its sure possession will
lead; We mean to say, to supernatural religious sources.

Genuine Christian faith

3. Our discussion has led Us to the third point which   **609**
We intended to deal with, that is, the Christian Faith—this   *(70,*
third torch illuminating the road of life, this certainty that   *87)*
comforts and encourages on every occasion, this "sweet
joy on which every virtue is based." (a) Infused in Baptism,
it has been nourished and cultivated in you since your first

609a Dante, *"Paradise"*, 24, 89-90.

years through prayer and the Sacraments, through the teaching of the Catechism, through the example—We hope— of those who surrounded you. Now that you are adults and have reached the age in which you must yourselves choose and decide, it is necessary that you make it your conscious possession, as it were, that you understand still more deeply and live more intensely the treasure of the Catholic Faith and the wealth of truth and grace that Jesus Christ gave you through His redeeming grace and through His Church, and Whose seed He placed in your souls since your cradle days.

This is the highest duty in your life, the fulfillment of which exacts the concurrence of the whole person: mind, heart, inward conviction and will.

610
(69)   An early experience should cause you to reflect: how is it that this or that companion of yours who was at first a believer and pious, having entered the University, suffers a crisis which gradually turns into religious indifference or into other more or less clear forms of atheism? You cannot, beloved children, expect Us to deal with such a delicate problem in a few words. On the other hand, however, your future and you yourselves are so close to Our heart that We cannot fail to express some brief thought on this subject.

611
(73,   We shall leave to one side the question as to how
76)   intellectual difficulties and other circumstances concur in causing these crises; rather than in the seat of pure reason, however, the causes should be sought in the jungle of un- restrained passions and moral deviations, or perhaps in the untrustworthy ground of concessions which it is considered must be made to the requirements of a coveted career. In any case, one thing is certain: there is no religion and con- sequently no personal religious life without the worship of God. But the worship of God is not a simple, cold intel- lectual act; it is praise of God, service of God, the confident abandonment to God of one's whole heart and soul. (a)

Similarly, "to believe" certainly means in the first place, to admit and penetrate—as far as possible—the truths revealed by Jesus Christ; but it also implies accepting the consequences that they involve in moral life. Therefore, if some should consider the brief half hour of Sunday Mass dedicated to the worship of God sufficient for their religious life, how can they hope to prevent it from withering away and becoming arid?

Consider also the fact that the religious truths presented to you in your childhood and school days were done so in a manner in keeping with a child's and adolescent's intelligence. The intellectual maturity which enables deeper problems and relations to be understood has come only in the course of years, and only now have you fully realized this. Therefore, though you may progress by degrees in secular sciences, you do not make similar progress in religious knowledge and in the life of the spirit, so why wonder at being subject to such crises? Be therefore conscious of your responsibility, try to improve the intellectual understanding of your faith, and try to live in accordance with the rules of great Christian virtues.   **612** *(69)*

(Supposed contrast between faith and natural sciences. —Although these are competent in the domain of perceptible things, they must not cause metaphysical realities to be forgotten.)

We will add only one more word on the religious crisis. Difficulties concerning faith must not be considered by themselves, but must necessarily form part of the complete and complex problem of religion and the world. Particular questions have already been, or will be solved some day, you may be sure; but among the facts which come to our mind when considering the ancient and modern history of humanity in the face of sociological data, especially con-   **613** *(54, 92)*

611a Cf. Matt. 22:37.

temporary, is the law that presents itself to us with pressing evidence, namely that a life in keeping with the dignity of man is possible only if individuals as well as communities and public authorities are grounded in religion, if they recognize a personal God, His order and His commandments. The "masses" without God do not allow themselves to be kept in order for long except by means of terror. This law has always been valid, but no generation has had to experiment its value so tragically as the present generation. Is not all this, for every calm soul, powerful evidence of the existence of God?

With God in your mind, in your heart and in your profession, conforming yourselves without hesitation to His wise law and to His amiable, sometimes mysterious dispositions, you will be able to face with an easy mind the difficult course that awaits you with an easy mind. Without Him, even your professional fields and especially those which are more closely connected with the human spirit, like philosophy, teaching, jurisprudence, medicine, and politics, would lose some of their vitality.

614
(87)   You can be sure that the best way to avoid useless shipwreck and to preserve the torch of faith is to practice the precepts with the same frankness with which you learned the divine commandments at your mother's knees, and almost under her eyes; particularly you who are far away from your homes, who sometimes feel yourselves engulfed and almost made anonymous in the big city, and consequently, much more exposed to the enticements of evil.

That is how, beloved children, We would like Our dear university youth to be: conscious of their serious social responsibilities, assiduous in preparing to meet them, generous in aspiring to perfection, masters of knowledge, strong in the faith, devoted to the nations, continuators of the noble traditions of the Roman Athenaeum which gave so many famous men to the Church and to Italy. May the kingdom of God, which is the harmony of heaven and earth, of human work and moral virtues, of serenity during time and eternal beatitude, establish itself in your souls!

With these good wishes We heartily impart Our Paternal Apostolic Blessing to you, to your distinguished fellow colleagues, to the families of which you are and will become the precious treasure, for your present life, for the success of your studies and the coming tests, and for your future.

CONCRETE RELIGIOUS EDUCATION . OF CHILDREN

All. to the children and women of Italian Catholic Action, July 15, 1952.

(Twenty-five years of Catholic Action for children.— Be ready to make sacrifices, be pure and strong.—Become like glowing flames.—Congratulations to the Women of Catholic Action.)

During these latter times youth have passed and still are passing through difficult moments. More than ever, it may be said that the enemy, "like a roaring lion, is prowling around seeking whom it may devour and whom you, strong in the faith, resist." (a) Therefore the Church relies upon your watchfulness and your motherly care to ward off the dangers and preserve children from corruption. Too often the family and the school do not give that solid religious education which is needed. You, happily, make up for this deficiency. And what method is more efficacious and more fruitful than that which not only imparts to children a theoretical and abstract teaching, but above all endeavors to make the events in the life of the divine Model come alive in their minds, to emphasize the great happenings which the liturgy commemorates, and thus to impregnate

615
(52,
69,
79,
89,
111)

615a 1 Peter 5:8-9.

with divine examples, not only their minds but also their hearts and sentiments, which are so delicate and so receptive at that age?

It is more than natural that souls placed in intimate contact with the Divine Master should endeavor to imitate Him, to consecrate all their lives to Him and to dedicate themselves also to the salvation of others. From this comes that blossoming of vocations who constitute the most radiant crown of your labor and its best claim to glory. And they whom Our Lord does not call to the priestly or religious state will one day be, no matter what their social function, faithful servants of the Church and citizens conscientious of their duties towards the nation.

Beloved daughters! The work which you represent calls for a profound dedication and many sacrifices, but for the Church it is of inestimable value.

(*Apostolic Blessing.*)

THE MISSION OF THE UNIVERSITY

Letter *Quel motif de joie*, August 12, 1952, to the presidents of "Pax Romana."

(*The XXII International Congress will be held in Canada.*)

616
(16,
67)
For this reason We wish, first of all, to confirm that the directives We addressed to you lately on the role of intellectuals in the Church, for they are always timely. Furthermore, the theme of the present Congress, "The mission of the University," prompts Us to define today those directives regarding a point that is particularly dear to Us. For We remember the decisive action of the Roman Pontiffs in the creation of the first Universities and in the course of their brilliant history. If the changing circumstances have sometimes relaxed the age-old links between the Church and the Universities, the present-day bewilderment of man-

kind, eager for unity and concord, and the spiritual anguish
of so many persons of good will, invite you to re-establish
those links once again. It is with that thought in mind, that
you, Catholic students and intellectuals, will apply yourselves to the study of the mission (traditional, yet ever new)
of the University. Your duty is to know it well in order to
serve it well.

In the first place, anyone who considers the Univer-   **617**
sity as a community of teachers and students dedicated to   *(66,*
works of the spirit cannot deny that its mission is to be a   *68)*
center radiating intellectual life for the benefit of the national community, in the atmosphere of healthy freedom
proper to all culture. This is a permanent task in which
Our children have never ceased to take part. However, if
the University wishes to render the age-old treasures entrusted to its keeping fruitful to the new generations, it
must bear in mind particular contemporary conditions. For
is not this a time when, in many countries, large sectors of
the population aspire to authentic learning, when the
economic and social difficulties of student and professional
life give rise to grave problems for those in authority, and
when, finally, modern means of information are ever increasing their influence, sometimes to the detriment of the
real education of personal thought?

If we broaden the perspective, We find that an anal-   **618**
ogous task confronts the great family of Universities, heir   *(66)*
to mankind's cultural patrimony. In order to avoid harmful
narrow-mindedness, it is necessary to multiply contacts
between teachers and students of the various countries, to
develop, by the study of languages and by useful collaboration, an appreciation of the intellectual riches proper to
each. It is thus that people, far from becoming involved in
competition and opposition to one another, will rather
delight in complementing each other. Here We cannot but
express Our good wishes to the *Pax Romana Movement* for
its patient efforts directed toward this end, and We are

likewise appreciative of the development of planned activity on an international plane, in the service of learning and culture.

619
(63,
67,
68,
108)
Now this mission of the University, which brings together men and nations in peaceful intellectual collaboration, would be deceptive if it were not achieved in a progressive coordination of the knowledge which they possess. Could the communion of minds be usefully achieved outside the unity of truth?

"A University," as We observed a short time ago, "does not mean merely the juxtaposition of abilities which are foreign to one another, but the synthesis of all the objects of knowledge .... And modern progress, with the steady development of specialization, makes this synthesis more necessary than ever before." (a)

In truth, modern progress also makes such a synthesis more difficult and insecure, and the University must protect it from two opposing dangers. The first would be the undue interference of the State, which, going beyond its powers, would presume to impose on education, for political or ideological ends, the specious unity of an arbitrary philosophy. On the other hand, the University would fulfill its mission badly were it to abandon itself to pluralism or to a superficial eclecticism. On the mere plane of natural knowledge, its task is to master a diversity of subjects, to promote wisdom, and to form the intellectual personality of the student. It should be on its guard, therefore, lest it fail in its highest mission, namely, that of giving young minds a respect for truth, and of guiding them to independent lines of thought, indispensable to their intellectual maturity.

620
(67,
A delicate mission, requiring both firmness and discretion, to which We especially invite Our Catholic Universi-

619a All. to the Catholic Institute of France, September 21, 1950. Cf. 526.

ties, enlightened in their task by the splendor of the faith.   *68)*
They alone can pursue the effort for synthesis in providing
the keystone of the edifice itself, for "this unity will tend
towards its perfection only in the measure in which it seeks
itself in God, in charity enlightened by knowledge according to the single truth of the Gospel, under the guidance
of the Church, one and holy." (a) Such Universities at
the service of the young student, crowned by the teaching
of Christian philosophy and theology, will be schools of
truth; they will also be teachers of life, Christian, moral,
civic and social.

(Best wishes for the success of the Congress.)

MODERN AND COMPLETE EDUCATION

Letter of the Secretary of State to the IV Portuguese
Social Week, October 16, 1952.

*(Appropriateness of the chosen theme: Problems of
Education.)*

The rights and duties of the family, of the Church and   **621**
of the State as regards education, can never be stressed too   *(21,*
much, nor can the mission of each of these three societies   *22,*
with their attributions and proper field of activity, be   *25,*
brought out too clearly.   *43,*

The school ought to assist the family but never sub-   *46,*
stitute it. Not only ought the State not obstruct the work of   *109)*
the Church and of the family, but it should assist them and
facilitate their activities and the exercise of their divine,
natural and positive rights.

Now, the Portuguese concordat sufficiently applies
these principles, recognizing the rights of the Church to
teach and to have her own schools and reminding the

620a All. to the International Committee for the unity and
universality of culture, November 14, 1951.

State of its duty to direct its entire teaching according to Christian doctrine and morals.

622
(60) From another aspect, modern education must be complete. It must not limit itself to simple instruction, or to religious training only. Today, a good education demands, among other things, suitable physical education, too, making use of various sporting activities, whatever form they may take, as a means and not as an end in themselves; it demands social education which forms in the minds of young people a sincere love of justice and charity, pillars of a true new order; it demands civic and political education, which renders youth aware of their duties towards the nation and which at the same time guides them in the exercise of their rights which, as a consequence, will make them participants in the public life of the State.

(Best wishes of the Holy Father.)

ADULT EDUCATION

All. to the Teachers and Students from the schools of Adult Education, March 19, 1953.

(The numerous present-day activities for the general or professional education of adults.—The contribution of the Association of Italian Catholic Teachers.)

623
(14,
16,
17,
18) It is for you to occupy an outstanding place in this field of the apostolate because the Church has always considered education not only as very important, but as one of her essential duties. She has been the great educator of peoples, both by exercising this mission through her priests and religious and by being the guide and inspiration of institutions controlled by the laity. She preserved ancient culture during centuries of barbarism. In the Middle Ages she exercised the ministry of teaching in all its stages. In the modern era she founded the first public schools and to the mission lands she brings, along with the Gospel, general culture.

Has she not the function of bringing man to the perfect development of his being, to the fulfillment of his earthly and heavenly destiny?

If, then, the Church, as in duty bound, devotes herself in a special way to education, it can well be understood with what care she attends to the needs made manifest in our own days by the multitudes who, in their infancy and adolescence, were not able to receive the education they needed and to which they rightly aspired. **624 (91)**

(The evolution of modern society renders these needs more demanding.—The importance of political and economic questions ought not to overshadow the preparation for family life.)

If the worker is aware of the dignity of his office as a father, and if the mother devotes herself to her mission as educator, giving suitable instruction and guidance, the life-cell of society will be healthy and strong. Mothers must acquire the elementary knowledge necessary for the government of a family, the art of keeping a house in order and of dealing with the family budget, useful ideas about bringing up children and, above all, enough understanding of the rules of pedagogy to profit by the experience of others without placing too much confidence in their maternal instinct which, of itself, will not always and without fail keep them from harmful mistakes. **625 (44, 91)**

As for the father of the family, one of his principal functions undoubtedly is to procure for his wife and children the financial means indispensable for living. Is he not, however, above all, the enlightened and wise guide, strong in his own personal experience, a prudent counsellor in matters regarding the important laws of life and the intimate aspirations and difficulties of those dear to him, to whom he gives spiritual support more valuable and more necessary than material protection? If the schools of adult education should achieve so much so as to initiate their stu- **626 (38, 91)** dents properly in the art of educating, what inestimable service would they not render to the family, society and the Church!

(The ignorance of the masses in political and economic matters leaves them defenceless and at the mercy of astute agitators and unscrupulous politicians.—The Christian point of view.—The professional formation aiming at a genuine, human and spiritual culture.—Sense of Christian destiny.—Industrial materialization.)

627
(69,
91)
　If adult education does not wish to fail in its purpose, it must endeavor to put these wayward ones back into contact with a living tradition—especially that of the Church—through the simple and at the same time profound lessons of the Catechism, Holy Scripture and the Christian feast-days. In adult education the teacher will not overlook national and local advantages, oftentimes so picturesque and entertaining and so much adorned with the wisdom of the centuries. Thus, reunited to his human and religious past, man will be given the surety he needs to guide himself and enlighten others. He will the more easily carry the weight of his responsibilities, once he realizes that his activity reaches out beyond the limits of his individual life and prepares for the future a world enlightened by Christian hope.

Possibilities of adults

628
(82,
86)
　To carry out such a mission, which is worthy of your efforts, you understand the need of a long and carefully planned preparation. Consequently, We would call your attention to some conditions of adult education and the qualities which it calls for in teachers.

The term "adult education," as you well know, indicates various degrees of teaching and formation. If we consider the human race as a whole, we find that a notable part of it is still illiterate. Hence the first duty is to teach millions of men to read and write. The second degree of adult education is the completion of elementary studies which were either never finished or were badly made. The majority of persons now benefiting by adult education in Italy belong to this second category. We are happy to know, however, that a third grade has already numerous students who wish to gain further useful knowledge in order to perfect themselves in their trade and so become a greater asset to human society.

Besides, it should be noted that adult students come **629** forward of their own accord. It is often necessary to begin *(86,* by persuading them that further education is useful. Then *87)* their attention must be held and their interest kindled in order to make them diligent. Without this the work would not be worthwhile.

The first objection to be overcome is the belief that an **630** adult is no longer able to better himself by schooling. On *(86,* the contrary, however, many experiments have clearly *91)* shown that the adult between the ages of twenty-five and forty-five is in full possession of his capacity to learn; he is capable of greater voluntary application, has a better appreciation of what he learns, organizes his knowledge to better effect, and knows how to use it more wisely. The desire for knowledge exists at all ages and one who has felt the drawback of ignorance is always happy to have someone offer to help him make good. It is quite true that in many adults the desire for knowledge is smothered by occupations or lulled to sleep by idleness. In this case, the intellectual faculties are dulled and there arises the false idea that they are no longer capable of learning and retaining. On the other hand, facts demonstrate that numerous adult schools are succeeding in attracting a remarkable number of students. It is the task of the teacher to seek out the reasons why each one wishes to complete his education and to see how this desire can serve as a basis for the development of personality and a deeper understanding of things.

The duty of the adult educator

631
(54,
83,
86,
87)

Rare indeed are the adults who have the courage to complete their education by themselves. Such a method leads often to a dangerous and defective training. The presence of, and contact with a teacher are, generally speaking, irreplaceable for the adult as well as for the child, because the adult adapts himself more slowly and needs to discuss and reason about his knowledge. The teacher must make his teaching live, make his students think, and uncover for each of them the talents he has at his disposal. The teacher will put the student into more intimate contact with himself, nature, the family, his fellow-citizens, the Church, which is the city of the children of God, with God, Who is the origin and goal of all life. To this end the teacher does not need to be a person of superior intelligence or a great scholar, but he should have a worthy character, generous and disinterested. His manner of speaking and behaving with his students, answering their questions, putting questions to them, praising and admonishing them—all this is a lesson they will never forget. In order to succeed well the educator must not count solely on himself. There are methods and techniques of adult education which have already proved their value. Among these, audio-visual methods have played a great part. Beginners' texts have been written, adapted to the degree of culture of those who frequent adult schools. They aid the teacher who, however, must always continue to be a guide to his students in their reading.

632
(86,
91)

Still he must aim higher and give the adult a share in the conquest of knowledge through the practice of reflection and expression, carried out with small groups on concrete topics, in order to train them to transform into vital learning the endless wealth of daily experience. As far as possible, the adult must be made capable of preserving his freedom; this, however, does not mean that he should segregate himself and refuse his cooperation in those activities which solicit it. He must be made aware of the influences by which he is daily surrounded—advertisements, the press, the radio, motion pictures—and placed on his guard against all those factors which, knowingly or unknowingly, try to lead him to act in spite of himself, try to take advantage of his good faith, or to extort his approval or his money—in a word, against those responsible for the "de-personalizing" which We have already denounced.

Public life as educator

From what We have said it is easy to conclude that the effective and generalized education of adults cannot be the work of one institution only but must be the result of an interplay of effort made by all those who have any authority over the people. Whoever addresses himself to the public, under any title whatsoever, shares in the responsibility for adult education: those in charge of newspapers, the radio, motion pictures, the theater, advertising firms, publishers and booksellers; also, the employees, the representatives of the State, the public officials, for there is an educative manner of organizing work and popular celebrations and in establishing and ensuring the observance of regulations and service to the community. In a sense it can be said that the popular culture of a country is a sign of its character. Centuries have contributed to it; the institutions, the language and customs are at one and the same time both the result of it and the instruments whereby it is produced, because they reflect the spirit of the age in which they began and they also contributed towards maintaining it. It suffices to pass from one country to another to perceive the sometimes noteworthy differences which mark even neighboring peoples. Beneath the differences of individuals we find a common background of culture and a heritage of art, literature and folklore, in which all share in greater or lesser degree. In speaking to you We do not need to tell you of the riches of this treasure in your beautiful fatherland nor of how grateful one ought to be to those who have handed it on.

633
(86, 91, 111)

634
(52,
86)
Beloved sons and daughters, you, who are dedicating yourselves to adult education, have understood how important is your activity, how involved it is, and how many qualifications it needs. Persevere courageously so that many may follow your lead. It is not so much a question of a gainful occupation. Rather it is a question of a genuine apostolate which is at the same time both human and Christian. It is also a source of intimate joy to realize that you are giving service of high value. The admiration and affection of your students will not be wanting, because they are happy to have received from you the gift, not only of your knowledge but especially of your mind and your heart.

We congratulate you, who are enrolled as students in the courses of adult education, on your desire for intellectual progress and on your aim to fit yourselves even more perfectly for the duties and responsibilities which fall on you today. Your perseverance will find its reward, not only in your own personal perfection but also in the advantages accruing from it to your family and to all your social circle.

(Apostolic Blessing.)

SCIENCE AND FAITH

All. to the students of the Sorbonne, April 9, 1953.

(The growing Church and the old Roman Empire.— The false modern divinities seem young and the Church old. The Church is continually young and outlives all errors.—Be conscious of your own Baptism.)

635
(73,
79)
Be men of prayer, daily prayer, personal and fervent prayer; drink of the streams of grace that flow from the sacraments, above all from the Holy Eucharist. This you have often heard repeated. Still We cannot refrain from stressing it once more, because it is fundamental.

Be careful to observe moral law; do not be satisfied with the minimum. The Church can and must insist that you do so; for the important tasks within and without—to-day more than ever as We insistently repeat—have need of Christians of solid faith and blameless life. The weak do not conquer the earth nor can they reach heaven.

In your studies and scientific research, be strong in the conviction that between the indisputable truths of faith and admitted scientific facts, there can be no contradiction. Both nature and revelation come from the same God, and God cannot contradict Himself. Be not disturbed even if you hear the contrary repeatedly stated, even if research must wait for centuries for the solution of apparent conflicts between science and faith. **636**
(70)

Love your neighbor, and sharpen your sense of social justice; We mean that social justice which concerns all conditions and all classes of men. **637**
(66)

(The Church wants to reunite all men in one family.)

Broaden your outlook and open your heart to take in all countries and all peoples. The Catholic Church is unsurpassed in having at its disposal powers of reconciliation, of understanding, of unity, which can act on the ultimate and most profound convictions, those which rule lives. It is for all the children of the Church to translate these powers into action, but it more especially behooves you, who belong to the class of leaders, to perform this mission.

You have your directors who speak to you in the name of the Church; follow them as young people should, and prepare yourselves thus for the tasks of the morrow. The Church counts on you. The talents which you have received are not to be buried. Diffuse the light, be the salt of the earth, and you will have an abundance of the purest joy that is given to man on this earth; namely, to imitate his God.

(Blessing.)

EDUCATION BY RADIO

R. M. to Colombia on the occasion of the inauguration of a Catholic Radio Station for the education of rural peoples, April 11, 1953.

638
(91,
97)
Beloved sons, farmers of Colombia, who are wont to listen to the Catholic Radio Station of Sutatenza, zealous students of the radio schools, so commendably organized by the Movement for Popular Culture:

We have been asked to say a few words which may serve for the inauguration of the new station. How can We decline such an invitation, since it has to do with a Radio Station, and a Colombian Radio Station, which specializes in promoting the welfare of Our dearly beloved farmers?

The radio—like so many of the other wonders of modern science—is a precious gift of God. Yet it is the kind of gift that would seem to Us to be badly misused if it should serve only to satisfy curiosity, to give pleasure, or to distract. On the other hand, We think it is properly used when, in the service of truth, of morality, of justice and of love—as We have repeatedly said—it is made a means of promoting Christian formation and of helping towards the intellectual and moral uplifting of nations.

Colombia, Catholic Colombia, the country of the Sacred Heart of Jesus and of the Virgin of Carmel, has clearly understood the problem. Scattered throughout their extensive territory, so broken up by mountain ranges—where even today communications are difficult—thousands and thousands of Our sons, stout of heart, wise and generous, like the ground they cultivate with their daily toil, are not able as a rule to enjoy the benefits that derive from the abiding presence of ministers of the Gospel and of teachers.

It was a priestly mind and heart which found a solution of this problem, thus giving new proof of the care for the humble by which the Church of Christ sets such great store.

The history of it is well known to you. The credit for the initial efforts to set up the first small center goes to you.

(Initial difficulties, and then the interest taken by the Government and international organizations.)

Our desire in this moment is only to congratulate, to exhort, and to bless you.   **639**
                                                                    (91)

We congratulate you, indeed, because We know with what love you have welcomed this education, which shows your interest in your Christian formation and also your understanding and your good intentions; We congratulate you because you are receiving a great benefit, still another means given you by God to complete your Christian training, the basis of all genuine progress.

Moreover, We exhort you, because perseverance during one scholastic term after another will undoubtedly require an effort which you must not shirk, for the love of God and of the Church, for the love of your country and of yourselves. There may be less busy seasons when work is not urgent and when studies may even provide a pleasing change; but there may be other seasons, when, for one reason or another, every added task becomes a burden: in that case it will be necessary to display good will in order not to leave off what has been begun.

(Blessing.)

THE VALUE OF SEX EDUCATION

All. to the Fifth International Congress of Psychotherapy and Clinical Psychology, April 13, 1953.

(Scientific Christian Psychology.—Man as a psychic whole,—as a structural unity,—as a social unity.)

A word also on the method sometimes employed by the psychologist to set the "ego" free from its inhibition, in the case of aberration in the sexual domain. We refer to complete sexual initiation, which would not pass over anything in silence, leave nothing obscure. Is there not therein a harmful exaggeration of the value of knowledge in these   **640**
                                                                    (78, 99)

matters? There is, however, an effective sex education which, quite safely, teaches calmly and objectively what the young person should know, for his own personal conduct and his relationship with those with whom he is brought into contact. For the rest, special stress will be laid, in sex education, as indeed, in all education, upon self-mastery and religious training. The Holy See published certain rules in this connection shortly after the Encyclical of Pius XI on Christian Marriage. (a) These rules have not been rescinded, either expressly or *via facti.*

(*Man as a transcending unity looks to God.—Best wishes and Blessing.*)

THE WORK OF THE "DON BOSCO VILLAGE"

All. to the children of the "Don Bosco Village," April 19, 1953.

(*Let little children come unto Me.—The workers in the vineyard.*)

641
(96)   The scene thus described by the Evangelist reminds Us of something that happened comparatively recently, one of those numerous incidents which, like brilliant stars, illuminate the long history of the Church. In some of the very poor districts of Rome, the streets used to be crowded with children playing, quarrelling, cursing, blaspheming—offending God in many ways. One day a certain priest, desirous of saving these young people, made his way into their midst, and asked them: "Why do you stand about all day doing nothing?" Some replied: "My father is at work all day and my mother can't look after all her children, there are so many of us!" Another murmured: "My father is out of work, and from morning till night he and my mother are out trying to find something for us to eat." Another explained tearfully: "My mother is dead, and I do not know where my father is." All alike said: "No one gives us a wel-

640a Decree of the Holy Office, March 21, 1931. Cf. No. 306.

come; no one wants us. That's why we stand about in the streets all day long doing nothing."

At that, the priest exclaimed, "Come! We will give you a home, and we will try to take the place of your mother and father. Come! We have a little church where Jesus, the Friend of children, will show you how to become better. Come, and alongside that little church we will build schools and workshops. You will have kind, solicitous teachers who will help you to learn many things. Come! You will have food enough and medicine when you need it. There'll be fields for you to play in. In this way, you'll become strong. Come! We'll build a village all for you, and we'll be your friends. We'll work with you, study with you, play with you, and, when things go wrong, we will even cry with you! We will be one great family, entrusting ourselves to the almighty power and wisdom of Our Father Who is in Heaven." **642** *(96, 113)*

And hand in hand with the priest, the boys went—first a few, then others, then still more. Today, We are told, "Borgo Don Bosco" has more than 1,000 boys; three hundred boarders, seven hundred day pupils. There they pass the whole day working, studying and playing. The tireless Salesians, who, with admirable self-sacrifice, take care that nothing essential is wanting, devote themselves with remarkable zeal and fervor to your civil, religious and moral education, so that you may become good citizens, competent and Christian workers.

Follow generously and joyfully, my dear children, the instructions they give you. Play as much as you can, and thus grow strong in body. Set to work in school and learn as much as you can, but, above all, allow Jesus to form your young souls through the work of the priests and their helpers. Minds and bodies must necessarily develop, but what good would it be to have a healthy and strong body, and a sharp and quick mind, if the will were bad and the soul dead through lack of divine grace? **643** *(76, 87, 91)*

644   Now, a few words to you, parents and relatives of
(42) these children. We are well aware of the difficulties and
worries you often meet with, which prevent you from doing as much as you would like to do for your children. But
try, at least, to help the priest in his educational work as
much as you can. Sad to say, it has sometimes happened
that certain families have only succeeded in destroying all
that has been built up in the souls of their children in the
beautiful atmosphere of the chapel or the classroom. In the
name of God, We implore you to look after these children,
so dear to Us, and, what is more important still, so dear
to God.

(Congratulations and encouragement to the Salesians.)

THE SPIRIT OF EMULATION

All. to the graduates of the "Rencontres de la jeunes-
se," April 21, 1953.

(Welcome and congratulations.)

645   One and the other, We willingly give you, displaying
(72, at the same time Our great pleasure with your noble con-
107, tests, in which you employ genius and love, and which
119) are well worthy of the civil traditions of your country.
They are such as truly to contribute to the promotion of
the intellectual, spiritual and moral elevation of the new
generations. Where, in fact, the competitive spirit of youth
is also disposed to allow itself free play in the calm fields
of the arts, letters and sciences, under the sun of religion,
there is a well-founded hope that the future will not be an
easy prey to hedonistic materialism, nor made sterile by
fatal inertia. If the youth of a nation were not to thrill to
high ideals, or be inspired by a spirit of wholesome emulation, it would condemn itself to ruin.

In receiving Our affectionate praise, beloved children,
treasure in your hearts, also, Our exhortation: number

yourselves always among the conquerors, especially in the hard fight that every man and every Christian is called upon to fight here below against the enemies of his eternal salvation. Fix your eyes constantly on the incorruptible crown of glory which God reserves for those who, taking Jesus the Divine Master as a model, will in the end be able to assert like Him: "I have conquered the world."(a)

THE NATIONAL CONSTITUTION
AND EDUCATION

All. to the Pilgrims of Fribourg in Brisgovia, April 22, 1953.

(Memories of past times.—Upsets caused by war.)

Your visit to Rome coincides with the feast of Blessed Bernard of the noble family of Margraves of Baden, which has wished expressly to be represented by your group in pilgrimage. **646** *(24, 76, 116)*

Bernard, the second protector of your diocese, left you the example of a life of prayer and penance, the example of a simple and orderly Christian life. You honor him, above all, as the protector of your youth, when to him you pray: "Look down upon and bless our youth entrusted to you, seriously threatened by the spirit of incredulity and by the corruption of habits: with your supplications, obtain for them firmness in the faith, and strength and perseverance in the battle against temptation." It seems as though this prayer was expressly composed for our times.

In the first place, entrust to Blessed Bernard of Baden the serious problems that are troubling you at the present, namely, that the decisions due to be taken, now, by your country may pave the way for a genuine Christian culture, may ensure for your children schools and an education in

645a John 16:33.

accordance with the wishes of their Catholic parents and may respect and preserve intact the indefeasible rights of the Church.

THE CHILDREN OF THE PEOPLE

All. to some Religious and lay teachers, June 4, 1953.

(Their 36,000 pupils constitute a complete city of the future.)

647
(46,
52,
91)
But what will this future be? It will be that which the teachers and educators desire and are able to form.

We are aware of your passionate devotion to this most noble office, which We would like to define as both religious and social at the same time. As a complement to normal Christian education in the home and, as far as possible, in close union with the parents of your pupils, it strives to prepare for the Rome of tomorrow a population that is healthy and prosperous in every respect. Therefore, especially to you, beloved daughters, almost as if you were Our faithful collaborators, We express Our paternal gratitude.

We congratulate equally those in charge of Municipal administration, who endeavor to promote the moral and material welfare of Our most beloved people, threatened in more than one way due to various causes, particularly in the outskirts and the suburban districts of the city, which occupy so great a place in Our pastoral care. The institution, therefore, of post-graduate and specialization courses for both men and women is both good and expedient, as these aim at educating, helping and professionally training young people, especially those most in need. And now, after five years of activity, these courses can point to abundant good results.

648
(4,
20,
Solicitude for the children of the people is a strict duty of the community; nor would it be right for one attracted by the ideals of future reforms of the whole social struc-

ture to define such provisions as so many useless and, in *113)*
fact, actually dangerous palliatives—dangerous because
they would delay the advent of complete reform. The great
reforms, which every honest mind must hope for and wisely
favor, avoiding irreparable damage to the whole edifice,
call for sufficient time to ripen into secure and stable realities. But in the meantime, when it is a question, as it so
frequently is, of boys and girls who are left to themselves
and are, therefore, to be found loitering in places which are
hygienically or even morally unhealthy, it is necessary to
act promptly in order to save them in the best possible
manner, doing what can be done and with the utmost
urgency. Moreover, the reforms themselves would never be
put into effect if they were proposed to, or even imposed
on, a spiritually decayed people which the community had
not prepared, by means of a solid education, to welcome
such reforms.

Your office, therefore, beloved daughters, ranks high; **649**
it is a mission that is necessary but at the same time, a deli- *(52,*
cate and difficult one. Have confidence, however, in your *53,*
work, rejecting that feeling of pessimism which sometimes *92)*
overtakes those who educate, as if it were inevitable that
the years and troubled waters should destroy every sound
formation received during early years. Notwithstanding
adverse events, an education based on Christian principles
will never fail to bring beneficial results.

Have, besides, a high conception of your work, which
exerts a direct influence on souls. Does there exist a task
which is more noble, more fruitful and more acceptable to
God? They who teach others what is good will, as the
Holy Ghost says, shine like stars in the firmament. (a)

Lastly, be firmly convinced that there is no other way, **650**
no surer method to make children become honest and in- *(5,*
dustrious citizens, whose lives will not be an unbearable *92)*

649a Cf. Dan. 12:3.

weight to themselves nor constitute a danger to society, than by making of them, before all else, faithful worshippers of God. Instill into their hearts Christian faith, the observance of the Commandments and the value of virtue above every other material and perishable good. And love them, especially you, beloved daughters, with a motherly heart, every day more, as if they were your own children, remembering that children are the apple of God's eye.

In exalting what you have done and will do for the children and the youth of Rome, and as a remembrance of this hour so much appreciated by Us because it was spent with you, We wish to say to you: the children of Rome and especially those who are poorest and most destitute are the most precious treasures of the Pope! Take care of them, defend them and dedicate yourselves to seeing that their spiritual splendor will never be darkened by error and corruption, but that they will reflect honor to the Church and to the glorious Catholic traditions of Rome during their whole lives.

(Blessing.)

FORMATION IN CATHOLIC ACTION

All. to the Assistants of Italian Youth of Catholic Action, September 9, 1953.

(National week for studying principles and methods of religious education.—The present world is inhuman, because it is anti-Christian.—The Youth of Catholic Action, object of the Pope's love and hopes.)

651
(93
97)
Yet this very love that We have for the young, and the hope We place in them, sometimes gives Us cause for great anxiety, because of the dangers that beset them almost everywhere. They are, as it is plain to see, the object of so many snares, of so many attacks, in this world which deafens them with its noise and wearies them with its everlasting unrest. It misdirects them with its relativism in the

matter of truth and error, of good and evil; it fascinates them with its whirlwind changes of color, debases them with its vulgarity and enslaves them with its evil living.

Those anxious for the fate of the world live in fear for the young. It is quite evident that thieves and evil-doers lie in wait for them, ready to attack and rob them, to wound them and then vanish, leaving them half-dead by the wayside. No category of youth is spared in this spiritual slaughter, carried on as it is, day after day, and hour after hour, regardless of cost. No method of attack is left untried by this wicked and complex industry of sin. **652 (80, 93)**

(Undertake a vast action of Catholic reconquest.)

Form the intelligence and the will

However, lest We jeopardize the success of this great work through any misunderstanding or hesitation, which would be dangerous, We want the youth of Catholic Action in the first place to understand clearly what it is they are about. **653 (63, 69, 72, 87, 88)**

Definite ideas and deep convictions are needed to arouse enthusiasm, to give strength to resist, and to call forth a generous response. Little or nothing can be done with boys who are heedless, or lazy and not serious. Beware of being satisfied—as We gave warning at the outset—with questions learned by heart without any understanding of their meaning. We turn now to point out the urgent need of a method of teaching catechism which is accurate and complete, and which, whilst not neglecting the help of memory and imagination, lays stress on reason and explains, for example, that the sincere and conscious act of faith is the most rational and reasonable human act. Give the young as organic a view as possible of Catholic teaching. Make them see in Christ One Who will satisfy their vital need of knowledge that is full, orderly and enlightening.

654
(87)

Yet no amount of study, no application however earnest, can make anyone infallible, much less the young, who are more exposed than adults to the danger of error, because of their lack of experience. The young Catholic, therefore, besides having a mind rich in clear ideas, must have a docile will. This does not mean—as some would think—that he must become lifeless and lazy, unable to think for himself, and so almost useless, in practice, to the Church. Rather does the Church desire him to be full of initiative, always active and industrious. On the other hand, he must have a will strong enough to accept willingly the commands of those in authority over him, by making their will his own will.

(The Assistant, the guide of the Directors themselves.)

655
(77
79,
87)

If the young have clear ideas and deep convictions, together with a determined and docile will, you will the more effectively be in a position to show them the noble work that awaits them in life.

Some will, perhaps, one day be priests like yourselves, God's ministers, mediators between God and men. Speak to them persuasively and warmly of the greatness of the priestly state. Tell them that perhaps never more so than today has the harvest been so great. But the workers are few in number, and consequently unable to be wherever their presence is so eagerly called for.

Others, and they are the vast majority, are called by God to co-operate with Him in the procreation of new life. Explain to them the beauty of Christian love, and, in order to prepare them to raise an upright and happy family, let them taste the happiness of purity unstained.

656
(72)

Lastly, there is a goal at which all young people should aim, whatever their particular calling in life. Today is indeed the day of the Gospel; systems and doctrines which attempted to do without God have failed or are failing. Young people, then, are needed who are wholehearted in

their faith, ready to spurn mediocrity and renounce hypocrisy, if ever they have fallen into it; young people who
desire to possess the divine life, and to possess it plenti-
fully; young people who, while studying or working, speaking, praying and suffering, have in their hearts, like a
burning flame, the ardent love of Christ, and the love
of souls.

THREE DANGERS FOR THE FAITH

All. to the Winners of the "Veritas" Contest, September 30, 1953.

(Development of the "Veritas" contest of religious
education.—Preserve the faith that this religious education
has fortified.)

During the early part of this month, addressing Our-   **657**
selves to the Diocesan Ecclesiastic Assistants of Catholic   **(72)**
Action, We urged them to prepare for the Church an army
of young heroes, ready for every bold enterprise. Do you
also want to be the brave vanguard of this peaceful army?
Do you want to respond fully to what the Church expects
from her student youth?

After your success in the "Veritas" Contest, another
victory is awaiting you: victory over a world without Christ,
without God. But such a spiritual battle cannot be fought
and won without a lively, integral and coherent sense of
faith. "Haec est victoria, quae vincit mundum, fides nostra."
(a) This faith, however, could be shaky due to the weakness of its foundations, it could be dashed to pieces against
the rocks of doubt, it could even be submerged in the
mud of passion. Therefore, if you want to respond to what
the Church expects from you, you must prepare yourselves
to keep your faith and defend it by every means.

657a 1 John 5:4.

Superficial religious education

658
(69)

1. Nobody will expect from you the broad and deep learning proper to one who frequents a regular course in Theology; on the other hand, you must shun certain small manuals which are absolutely insufficient for educated men, and you will guard yourselves from a superficiality which creates easy illusions, and then brings unfailing disappointment to those who are satisfied, for example, with purely mnemonic formulas.

659
(69,
72,
116)

There is no doubt—and We gladly take advantage of the occasion to stress it—that young Catholic students must excel in every branch of learning. Duty exacts this much and the Church calls for it, since today as always, it must defend both Christian and human civilization from the attacks of a materialism that is often well-disguised. But it is equally certain that an ever-increasing development of your historical, literary and scientific acquirements without an adequate and corresponding deepening of religion, which is truly necessary, could be highly dangerous to your souls. That is why, my dear young people, We entreat you to continue in your studies with the same diligence and consistency which brought you success this year in the "Veritas" Contest. Do not let yourselves be satisfied until you have penetrated, as far as possible, into the intimate meaning of religious truth, and until the truth itself has not penetrated you—your intelligence, your imagination, your heart and your whole being.

Doubt and uncertainty

2. This assiduous, attentive and deep study, in addition to ensuring the solidity of the foundations of your faith, will make you avoid or overcome the stumbling-blocks of uncertainty—another danger which the souls of young people must encounter.

We are not speaking here of the kind of doubt which might be called "dynamic" and which is fruitful and constructive,—doubt, that is, which "is born at the feet of truth" and is a stimulus to fresh studies and fresh conquests. We refer, instead, to the "static" doubt which is nearly always rooted in ignorance, or at least in knowledge that is inadequate and imperfect. It will, therefore, be necessary to solve each difficulty as it arises and to do so in a decisive manner in order to save from danger the many certitudes which may have cost you much fatigue to acquire. To achieve this, you must avail yourselves of your teachers, of books that contain deep and objective doctrine, of your very companions who may be more prepared and ready than you, without forgetting that lively and well-directed discussions could also be an excellent means for clarifying ideas, both for yourselves and for others.

Do not fear that this desire for clarification on your **661** part and this spirit of research may come up against some *(70)* solid scientific truths, as some erroneously think. Real science can never be contrary to faith, because a truth can never be in real conflict with another truth, there being but one Truth, the true God, the Author of every truth.

The vice of impurity

3. We will add another word, beloved sons and **662** daughters, and We wish to say it to you more from Our *(76)* heart than from Our lips. Too often, it is not an insufficiency of sound religious learning that causes young people to abandon the Faith, nor is it the rocks of rational doubt. Rather, it is the mire of passion which today—even more than yesterday, perhaps—causes such havoc, because the devil and the devil's disciples have multiplied beyond measure the snares which attack your virtue.

It is the chains of the impure vice which thrust so many young people into the darkness of a mysterious prison of gilded walls and prevent them from seeing the light; it is the mire of bad habits which troubles the hearts of the young and drops over the eyes of their spirit the cataracts of vice. And when souls have become almost blind, a strong flow of the light of grace is necessary in order to dispel the darkness and awaken them from their torpor.

Listen to the grieved voice of your Father, beloved sons and daughters. Look upwards, as it befits human beings. Rather, look even higher, beyond the stars, as is fitting for children of God. Up there in Heaven is your home; there God your Father is awaiting you with His crown, with His glory and with His joy.

663
(72, 73, 77) Tell Us, dearest children, that to keep yourselves pure, you will not hesitate before any martyrdom, whatever it may be, a martyrdom of blood or an unbloody, silent one, to which God and the angels bear witness. Ask Mary, our Mother most pure, the strength to preserve yourselves immaculate in the midst of such filth and slime.

Be comforted by the certainty that you are not alone in the fight or in the victory. In a deplorable spectacle of darkness and of death, a glimpse of light and of life is already discernible. In fact, if you look well about you, you will discover a multitude of young people engaged in the same battle and aiming towards the same victory—perfumed flowers, full of charm in their hidden beauty.

They may either remain flowers forever, through divine predilection, by the consecration of their whole lives, or, after an immaculate youth, become fruitful in a home blessed by the Lord.

This flowering of purity, certainly, is not readily found outside the garden of the Church, and thus you, dearest children, in addition to procuring a protection for your faith, will be another proof that if mankind today wishes to save itself from disaster, it must look to the Church as to its only true guide.

THE DUTY OF WOMEN TEACHERS

All. to the Delagates of the Young Girls of Italian Catholic Action, December 30, 1953.

(Prayers, deeds, sacrifices for the work of Catholic Action.)

But perhaps you would not be satisfied if We allowed you to leave without taking advantage of your presence here to express to you Our paternal gratitude and to say to you a simple word of exhortation and comfort. It is, first of all, addressed to you, beloved daughters, who belong to the various religious Congregations; you are truly heroic souls who spend your lives in Institutes, in Orphanages and in Kindergartens, in the renunciation of every human satisfaction, working tirelessly and silently, often unknown and at times even disregarded by others; real spiritual mothers, in whose care the Church anxiously but confidently places the most delicate flowers of her garden. And then, Our grateful greeting and exhortation go to the Delegates of the *Minor Sections,* to whom are entrusted the littlest recruits of the women's army of Italian Catholic Action. With a holy pride in your work, trusting in the grace of God, devote yourselves to the Christian formation of girls, urged on by an enlightened and generous love.

664
(4, 28, 46, 51, 52)

1. Above all, We are eager that you greatly esteem your sacred and delicate mission.

In educating the little ones—naturally in collaboration with the family, whose function is indispensable—you must be persuaded that you are accomplishing a work which is one of the choicest. Your work is perhaps not too visible, but it exacts great effort and self-denial, while at the same time it is one of the most efficacious forms of apostolate for the fate of the Church and of the nation.

Balanced authority

665
(80,
84-
86)
Consider, in fact, those whom with a charming word you call your "little angels"; your three groups known as "little tots," "favorites," and "aspirants" are young girls entrusted to you by God so that you may lead them to the threshold of adolescence. Therefore, you must be their guides during that time of greater receptiveness, so to speak, that is, when they more easily receive the impressions of good and evil. Conscious of this, though wisely making your authority respected, you see to it that it does not weigh too heavily on their spirit. They would suffer it with fear and perhaps anguish, and instead of opening their hearts with confidence and joy, would close up within themselves. And the memory of the treatment received might weigh on their psychological consciousness for many years. It is not rare that cases of serious psychological disturbances among adults are explained by the misunderstanding on the part of their teachers of which they were victims in their childhood. But you, beloved daughters, are well aware of the consequences of your work, which helps to form and mold those attitudes and tendencies which in their future lives will play a considerable part. Thus, your educational activity will be carried out in its every phase with calm, balance, and coherence.

Detachment of the heart

666
(4,
5,
81)
2. The esteem for your work will make you love your little girls. They represent the hope of families, of the nation, and of the Church because for the greater part, they will be the mothers of the future. And in the meantime, they are favorites of Jesus, as they were during the times in which the Divine Master was journeying over the roads of Palestine. Powerful in their pleading for graces, living models for those who want to enter the kingdom of

Heaven, they avert the divine chastisements from our families and our cities and therefore deserve your most tender love and affectionate kindness.

You will, however, avoid excessive external demonstrations of affection which would easily lead to detrimental weaknesses and would make the girls domineering and arrogant. Nor must love be confused with the joy they can give you by their presence, candor and innocent freshness. Such joy will certainly help to give you incentive and fervor in accomplishing your duty, but you will always remember that love is a gift that entails sacrifice and renunciations. Therefore, in your total devotion to the children, you will not seek your own selves, nor will you aim at winning the exclusive affection of the girls, but truly and sincerely loving them, you will arrive at that detachment of heart which often proves to be arduous but is indispensable. **667**
(51, 53, 81)

The supernatural and apostolic aims you pursue make this detachment even more necessary, because you desire to make the love of Jesus Christ blossom in those souls which belong to Him and which He redeemed with His precious Blood. This generous self-restraint will permit you to know better every deficiency of yours and to endure the difficulties and also the possible unsuccessful results with a smile. You will, thus, be worthy collaborators in the work of redemption, living symbols of Christ and of His love for children.

Psychological knowledge

3. But in addition, beloved daughters, you must seek the integral formation of your little girls; and as it is not sufficient to love in order to be good educators, you will endeavor to learn what is necessary and useful so as to maintain the educational obligations you have assumed. **668**
(50, 84)

This is why We exhort you to serious and assiduous study: study the girls and the best way to instruct and educate them. The physicist, the chemist, the biologist, the doctor, study over a period of years; they interest themselves in the analysis of a ray of light, in the contemplation of a flower, and they aspire to the profound knowledge of phenomena and physiological laws. How much more wonderful is the study of a free spirit, springing up and containing the mystery of a life!

669
(36,
80)
You must not ignore the characteristics of girlhood, its anxieties and desires, its aversions and preferences. There is the love of motion in it, a quivering of the senses and the restlessness of a growing intelligence. Children love to play, crave affection, are inclined to fancy, live on illusions and dreams, are spontaneous and have the instinct of imitation.

But they also develop precious religious and moral energies. We will here limit Ourselves to quoting two examples derived from the results of experimental psychology: "The second period of childhood from six to nine years," the author observes, "is characterized by love of parents, God and the truth"; and in addition: "The years from seven to ten number among the more important for the prevention of juvenile delinquency." This is a comforting encouragement and at the same time a serious warning to those who shoulder the responsibility of young people up to their years of puberty.

670
(2,
50,
82)
You will without doubt acquire this knowledge through the gift of psychological penetration, which is necessary for every educator, but also by utilizing the results of research and recent experiences in the field of education. We do not certainly expect that you become scientists in human psychology in general, or in that special sphere of child psychology, but you cannot ignore—and still less despise—the new conquests in the field of pedagogy. Not that all attempts are to be unconditionally praised, but without foregoing the solid principles and the tested Christian traditions, you can usefully bring your methods up-to-date

and improve them. The Catholic educator—here still more than elsewhere—must not remain behind. The rapid evolution of the present conditions of life makes your role more delicate and complex. It would be too easy to rest on comfortable customs and neglect necessary progress. Therefore, make the effort required for adaptation and you will, in this manner, be able to achieve the goal of every education: the integral formation of the person, in full accord with the absolute exigencies of his supernatural destiny and with the characteristics of contemporary society.

The natural and supernatural transformation of children

4. You will, therefore, see to the normal human development of your girls, without forgetting that they are souls redeemed by the Blood of Jesus, made participants of the divine life. **671 (26, 60, 76)**

If it is true that you will not be able to give them physical beauty, which is God's gift, you will, however, apply every care to help them achieve that grace and above all that smile which illuminates and transforms even less attractive features. Therefore, make them your little serene and carefree girls, strong and loyal, and do not let them neglect anything that will make the truth they possess and the virtues with which they are adorned be attractively visible in them.

5. Now, a final word, beloved daughters, a final recommendation. **672 (72, 82, 90)**

The case is not rare of girls who abandon the Association when they become irresolute and impatient, daring and timid, happy and anxious about facing the new roads which unfold before them; when the heart begins to become excited and swells with an unknown tenderness; when the intelligence re-awakens and the will is born to a new life, more personal and independent. This, sometimes, is due to the insufficient structure of the Association itself, which does not offer enough attraction to make group life desirable to the adolescent and the youth; but in most cases, it could be that no effort was made to penetrate deeply the mind, heart and will of the girls.

Theirs were scattered notions, learned distractedly, without method or order, as they should have been; a spiritual life formed of praiseworthy habits, but not rooted in firm convictions, nor nourished by a living and vivifying faith; defects that were unknown or not corrected in time; small vanities, unrepressed or at least not guided by an understanding patience. Certain defections, which often make the "graduation celebration" held in Catholic Action a sad event, must be attributed quite correctly to the insufficient solidity of the edifice which was perhaps built with great fatigue but with insufficient method during the preceding years.

673
(60,
76,
80)
We exhort you, therefore, beloved daughters, not to be content with yourselves until you have seen your girls receive a profound formation that will result in their complete transformation. You have often received them in a restless and disorderly state, dominated almost entirely by their instinctive impulses: you must bring them to a state of balance and order, and instill into them obedience to a superior law. You must establish a logical order in their perception, teach them to discipline their affections, and see that their actions be consistent with the principles of morality; you must, above all, teach them to place themselves in real contact with God, at first trying to make it more and more frequent, then later on continuous.

You must not imagine that early age is an obstacle in the path towards consummate perfection, towards sanctity. "There will be saints among the children," Our saintly Predecessor Pius X exclaimed when he admitted them to the Eucharistic Banquet. He knew—as We know—that "the age of the body does not prejudice the soul, so that man, even in his childhood, can achieve the perfection which belongs to the age of the spirit." (a)

When Jesus laid down a childlike spirit as a condition for admittance to Paradise and then implored, "Let little children come to Me," can it be denied that even the child is in a position to reach evangelical perfection?

Aim high, beloved daughters! Propose to your girls, **674** with simplicity but with clarity and vigor, high goals; *(73)* then accompany them with patience, support them with sweetness and lovingly raise them up again when they fall along the way. See to it that they nourish themselves frequently, even daily, with the Immaculate Flesh of Christ: "As natural motion, the more it nears the end, the faster it becomes . . . , so the soul in the state of grace, the more it approaches the end, the more it should grow." (a)

See to it, therefore, that the young souls entrusted to your care do not place any barrier to the action of God in them; teach them to abandon themselves in the arms of Mary and you will witness with amazement miracles of grace transforming your little girls into living tabernacles of Christ, into docile instruments of life for Him.

TELEVISION

Letter *I rapidi progressi,* January 1, 1954–to the Bishops of Italy.

(Progress of television in Italy.—It is a gift from God to be employed only for the good of men and of the family.)

Neither may We be indifferent to the beneficial conse- **675** quences which television can have in social matters, in re- *(91)* lation to culture, to mass education, to teaching in schools

---

673a St. Thomas, *Summa Theologica,* p. 3, q. 72, a. 8.
674a St. Thomas, *Letter to the Hebrews,* c. 10, lect. 2 in fine.

and to the very lives of nations which, through this means will certainly be helped toward greater mutual knowledge and understanding, and the achieving of cordial union and better reciprocal cooperation.

Serious dangers of television

676
(91,
97)
    Such considerations, however, should not make one forget another aspect of this delicate and important question. If, indeed, television, when well-regulated, can be an effective means of a sound, Christian education, it is also true that it is not free from dangers, because of the abuses and evils to which it can be perverted by human weakness and malice. These dangers are all the more grave in view of the greater suggestive power of this invention, and its larger and more indiscriminate audience.

    Unlike the theater and the cinema, which limit their plays to those who attend of their own free choice, television is directed especially to family groups, made up of persons of every age, of both sexes, of differing education and moral training. Into that circle it brings the newspaper, the chronicle of events, the drama. Like the radio it can enter at any time, any home and any place, bringing not only sounds and words but the detailed vividness and action of pictures, which make it more capable of moving the emotions, especially of youth. In addition, television programs are made up in great part of motion picture films and stage productions, too few of which, as is known from experience, can fully satisfy the standards of Christian and natural moral law. Finally, it should be noted that television finds its most avid and rapt devotees among children and adolescents who, because of their very youth, are more apt to feel its fascination and, consciously or unconsciously, to translate into real life the phantasms they have absorbed from the lifelike pictures of the screen.

It is easy, therefore, to realize how television is very **677** intimately bound up with the education of youth and even **(22,** the holiness of life in the home. **33,**

Now, when We think of the incalculable value of the **96,** family, which is the very cell of society, and reflect that **112)** within the home not only the physical but also the spiritual development of the child, the precious hope of the Church and of the nation, must be begun and carried out, We cannot fail to proclaim to all who have any position of responsibility in television that their duties and responsibilities are most grave before God and society.

Public authorities, especially, have the duty of taking every precaution that the atmosphere of purity and reserve which should pervade the home may be in no way offended or disturbed. In this regard even the wisdom of antiquity, moved by religious respect, declared: "Let no improper word or sight cross the threshold of this home . . . for the child one must have the utmost reverence." (a)

We have constantly before Our mind the painful **678** spectacle of the power of evil and moral ruin of motion **(33,** picture films. How, then, can We not be horrified at the **97)** thought that this poisoned atmosphere of materialism, of frivolity, of hedonism, which too often is found in so many theaters, can by means of television be brought into the very sanctuary of the home? Really, one cannot imagine anything more fatal to the spiritual health of a country than to rehearse before so many innocent souls, even within the family circle, those lurid scenes of forbidden pleasure, of passion and evil, which can undermine and bring to lasting ruin the whole structure of purity, goodness and wholesome personal and social upbringing.

For these reasons We think it opportune to stress that **679** the normal vigilance which must be exercised by the **(22,** authorities responsible for public entertainment is not suf- **33,**

677a Juvenal, *Satires*, XIV, 44, 47.

96,
112,
113)

ficient in regard to television, for securing broadcasts un-
objectionable from the moral point of view. In television,
where it is a matter of programs that will invade the
sanctuary of the family, a different criterion of judgment
is necessary. So one sees the groundlessness, especially in
this field, of the pretended rights of the absolute freedom
of art, or of the recourse to the pretext of freedom of
information and of thought, since here higher values are
at stake which must be safeguarded; and those who offend
against them cannot escape the severe sanctions threatened
by the Divine Savior, "Woe to the world because of of-
fences . . . woe to that man by whom offence cometh." (a)

We cherish the heartfelt hope that the noble sense of
responsibility of those who have authority in public life
will serve to forestall the deplorable occurrences which We
have deprecated above. In fact, We should like to hope
that as far as programs are concerned, judicious measures
will be forthcoming, aimed at making television serve as a
healthy recreation for people and at contributing as well
in every way to their education and moral improvement.

The duty of Catholics

680
(91,
97,
111,
112,
113)

But, if these desired measures are to achieve their full
effect, all must be alert and on the watch.

To you, Venerable Brothers, We turn first of all, and
to all the clergy, in this matter, making Our own the words
of St. Paul to Timothy: "I charge thee, in the sight of God
and Jesus Christ, Who shall judge the living and the dead,
by His coming and His kingdom: preach the word, be instant in season and out of season: reprove, entreat, rebuke
in all patience and doctrine." (a)

But no less urgently do We turn to the laity also,
whom We wish to see in ever greater numbers, and in

679a Matt. 18:7.
680a 2 Tim. 4:1-2.

closed ranks around their pastors, also in this holy crusade. In particular let those whom the Church, through Catholic Action, calls to work alongside of the hierarchy, understand the need for timely action, before it is too late, to make their presence felt in this field. No one has the right to look on idly at the rapid development in television, when he realizes the extremely powerful influence it undoubtedly can exercise on national life, either in furthering good or in spreading evil.

And when there are abuses and evils, it is not enough for Catholics to confine themselves to deploring them; these abuses must be brought to the attention of the public authorities in quite precise and documented particulars. Indeed, it must be admitted that one of the reasons, less noticed perhaps but nonetheless real, for the spread of so much immorality is not the lack of regulations, but the lack of reaction or the weakness of reaction of good people, who have not known how to make timely denunciations of violations against the law of good morals.

However, your efforts would still be far from fully **681** satisfying Our desires and Our hopes if they should be re- *(91,* stricted simply to setting up safeguards against evil and *113)* did not result instead in a vigorous accomplishment of good. The goal We wish to point out to you is this, that television should be not only morally irreproachable but that it should also become an instrument of Christian education.

In this regard, the wise considerations which Our Predecessor of happy memory, Pius XI, addressed to the motion picture industry are to the point: "Just as the advances in art, science, even in technical perfection and industrial production are true gifts of God, so also they must be directed to the glory of God and the salvation of souls and must contribute in a practical way to the spreading of the Kingdom of God on earth, so that, as the Church bids us pray, we may profit by them in such manner as not to lose the eternal good: 'Let us so pass through the good things of the present as not to lose those of eternity.' " (a)

In order to attain this aim, it is easy to understand how important is the preparation of the programs to be televised. Certainly, in a country of such age-old and profound Catholic traditions as the Italian nation, We have every right to hope that Catholicism will have a place in television in proportion to the importance which it occupies in the national life.

(Catholic Central Office for Television.—Union of Catholics.—Form the conscience of Christians.)

THE CONDITION OF THE CHRISTIAN TEACHER

All. to the Executives of the Italian Catholic Union of Secondary Education, January 4, 1954.

(Tenth anniversary of the Association.)

682 Teachers who adhere to your ideals form the major-
(58) ity in various national organizations which, on the occasion of elections in this field, manifested their trend of thought. This happy result would not have been achieved without the great organizing efforts carried out by the executives of your Union nor without the generous cooperation of many subordinate leaders. It will permit you—at least We hope so—to carry the demands of your economic program through to a happy conclusion.

The material condition of teachers

683 We are aware of the fact that the salary of the greater
(22) number of teachers, far from assuring them the free time and money necessary to complete their personal training and

681a Encyclical *Vigilante cura,* June 29, 1936. Cf. *Oremus* of the 3rd Sunday after Pentecost.

perfect their teaching methods, is instead barely enough for the daily needs of life, especially for those who have had the courage to take on the responsibilities of a family.

Besides, that salary cannot be considered to be on a par with your serious social responsibility. A society that is really interested in intellectual and moral values, a society that does not want to slip and slide towards that materialism to which it is being drawn by the weight of the ever more mechanical life of technical civilization, must show the esteem that it has for the profession of the teacher, assuring him a return which corresponds to his social position. Let us not forget that the labor which produces spiritual values is real labor and even, in its kind, more lofty than manual labor. This should be taken into consideration in calculating a just wage.

There are still too many precarious conditions in your career, problems arising all over again each year, denying you security for the future, with consequent serious harm to continuity in instruction and to personal formation. When one thinks of the small place that the salaries of teachers hold in the national budget, there arises the desire to see set aside under this heading, insofar as is possible, the relatively modest sums which would be enough to improve the material conditions of teachers, and thus to improve instruction throughout the country and raise the the cultural level of the whole nation.

(References to the speech of September 4, 1949, on the importance of the educational mission [a].*—The ten years of activity of the Association.)*

It would be a temptation to laziness to dwell with satisfaction on statistics and testimonies, while there still remains so much work to be done to check and push back the materialistic current of which We spoke recently in our   **684** *(58, 111)*

683a Cf. above, Nos. 500-515.

Christmas Message. Everyone must constantly and energetically struggle within himself and in his professional social life against indifference and lack of supernatural faith. The tendency, so enkindled in our days, of looking for what is practical and immediately useful could transform your Union into just another of the many unions whose only real purpose is economic improvement. Instead, you must seek in it a good that is deeper, more lasting, more radiant both for yourselves and for all its members.

685
(54,
83)
Membership in your Union is first of all a sign of your firm intention of "pursuing your own moral and spiritual perfection." That means acquiring through prayer, personal application to the teachings of the Church, and the efforts of the interior life, that union with God and that dignity which give your conduct and your judgments the value of a testimony in favor of your faith. This will also make your authority more respected and more effective, not merely in school during the time when your pupils are subject to you, but in public life as well, in your dealings with families and with young people who, once they have been instructed by you, will boast all their lives of having had you as teachers.

Christian educational methods

686
(54,
84)
The first consequence for you of the deepening of your Christian life will naturally be a more elevated notion of your educational mission and a greater professional consciousness. We mean a more ardent will to achieve the greatest possible competency in your own field in anything pertaining to either theory or practice.

To carry out his job fully, the teacher worthy of the name must first know his pupils. That means the youngsters of a certain age in general, as they are described by sound Christian pedagogy, and those of his own class or Institute in particular, as their families form them.

Certainly, great progress has been made in experimental psychology and in pedagogical remedies. Men have sought, and not without happy results, to measure the importance of the different elements conducive to the assimilation of scholastic material by the memory and the intelligence of the pupil. They consider material factors, such as furniture, lighting, types of books, composition of pictures and of sounds. And they consider intellectual conditions properly so-called, such as centering of varied interests according to local circumstances and age, and associations of memory which a well-adapted education fosters. It would be inexcusable for a modern teacher not to keep himself sufficiently informed of the work that is being done in this field, and We know that your teaching associations are taking an active interest in these matters particularly. **687 (50)**

But a Christian instructor cannot be satisfied with teaching techniques. By faith, he knows something which, unfortunately, is confirmed by experience—the importance of sin in the life of the youngster—and he knows the influence of grace as well. The capital sins do not in themselves depend on remedies. Certainly there are often reasons of temperament and of health in laziness and in other defects; but there is always original sin, too. Hence, the Christian educator cannot be satisfied with letting nature do its work, or simply favoring it, as if he were a farmer dealing with the fruits of the earth. He, like the grace of God, of which he wants to be nothing more than the helper, corrects and elevates at one and the same time. He fights against the lower inclinations and works to see that the higher ones develop. He struggles patiently and firmly with the defects of his pupils and trains them in virtue. He lifts them up and improves them. In this way, Christian education participates in the mystery of the Redemption and effectively works with it. From this comes the greatness of your work, which is in a way analogous to that of the priest. **688 (32, 51, 80, 85)**

Necessary collaboration between
the family and the school

689
(42,
46,
85,
106)
The youngsters, in whom you must interest yourselves, are not abstract beings, but children of definite families. Why is it that such great efforts on the part of teachers, so many hours and years of constant dedication, sometimes show almost no results, if not because the family, with its failure to educate, its errors in teaching, and its bad example, day by day destroys whatever the teacher strives so hard to build? Has he nothing to say to the family in such a case? Should he do nothing to enlighten them, help them, make them aware of the complexity and the wide range of their mission, to implant in them proper educational principles, correct their errors and stir up their zeal? Families should not be allowed to believe, as many do, that they have satisfied their duties towards the children when they have sent them off to school, giving no thought to working hand in hand with the teachers, on whom they wrongly think they can completely unload a part of their own responsibilities. This is true especially as regards the elementary grades, but also for the secondary schools. For at this period growing adolescents begin to free themselves from subjection to their parents and it often happens that they oppose the teacher to the father, the school to the home. Many parents find themselves at such a time almost deprived of all authority before the queer moods of their children, and some errors that are committed in these years can turn out to be injurious to the equilibrium of the adolescent.

690
(42,
43,
46,
49)
This is only one point among a host of others to show that the collaboration of parents and of teachers must be constant and profound. For this reason, one of your "Conventions" (November, 1951) studied "the school as an educational community." We encourage with all Our hearts whatever will help to bring about closer cooperation between the school and the family. The family chooses the

teacher to prepare the adolescent to live his adult life in the State and in the Church. It must not and cannot abdicate its directive office. Cooperation is natural and necessary, and in order to be fruitful, it presupposes acquaintance with each other, constant relations, unity of outlook, and successive adaptations. Only the teachers can make their ideal effective. The family must be the most solid support of the teacher on all levels: local, union, national. He is first of all a delegate of the family, and only after that, if the case presents itself, a public official or employee of the State or of the teaching body.

In every association which is important and covers a wide field, the responsibility of the leaders is particularly great. They are truly the soul of the movement. It is up to them to make the Statutes live, so to speak, and to make the spirit of the Association penetrate each of its members. The "National Sessions," that have brought you together in Rome, ought to represent a definite step forward in the life of the Union. There are thousands of adolescents entrusted to you during the delicate years of their development; you have a serious responsibility for the formation of Italian youth and you are making an important contribution to the preparation of a better future for your country. As Christians, you cannot remain indifferent; as teachers, you have the joy of being able to cooperate effectively in the religious renewal of your generation. This is why We wanted to encourage you and to show you the trust that We put in your generous Union. All of you should realize and tell your colleagues that the Pope attaches great importance to the work of the Italian Catholic Union of Secondary-School Teachers.

691
(52,
58)

(Blessing.)

GOOD TEACHERS

R.M. to the Fifth Inter-American Congress on Catholic Education, January 12, 1954.

(The progress of these five Congresses.—The theme of the fifth: The formation of teachers.)

692
(50)
It is a theme of primary importance. To repeat the words of Our immortal Predecessor, "good schools are the fruit not only of good regulations but principally of good teachers, excellently trained in the respective subjects which they are to teach, and possessing the intellectual and moral qualities which their important office requires—men who burn with a pure and divine love for the youngsters entrusted to them, precisely because they love Jesus Christ and His Church." (a)

Good teachers, then, should have perfect human formation, intellectual and moral. For the teaching office is a lofty one which calls for intellectual discernment and goodness of heart, for a capacity for intuition and sensitivity of spirit, for adaptability and renunciation as well as human depth, capable of bearing everything for the love of neighbor.

693
(3,
5,
50,
52,
54,
71,
83)
Good teachers need a professional competency which should be at least above average, and better yet, outstanding on all levels of instruction and in each of the specialized fields, if it is not to be unworthy of a mission which serves not merely the people and the State, but also God, the Church and souls.

Good teachers are those with a pure professional Catholic conscience, a soul burning with apostolic zeal, a clear idea of doctrine, which must penetrate all their teaching, and a profound conviction of serving the highest spiritual and cultural interests, and that in a field of special privilege and responsibility.

692a Pius XI, Encycl., *Divini illius Magistri;* cf. No. 297.

Good teachers, finally, are careful to educate rather than merely to instruct; they are capable, above all, of forming and of molding souls chiefly through contact with their own. A great teacher, who is no stranger to your Spanish-speaking world, although inspired only by the light of paganism, has said, "*Eum elige adjutorem, quem magis admireris, cum videris quam cum audieris:* Choose that teacher whom you have to admire more when you see him than when you hear him." (a)

In not a few regions of the New World, the social and political movements which followed their independence have brought about the penetration into the field of teaching of ideas and principles which, starting out from a liberalism and a laicism which daringly claimed to dominate everything, flowed over into a monopoly on education, with manifest damage to integral Christian formation and with evident injury to the Catholic minority, and often to the immense Catholic majority. **694 (95)**

(The great Iberian-American Educators.—Amalgamation of the natives and Europeans through the work of Christian culture.)

We cannot doubt that in the future you will insist ever more on the programs so wisely outlined in your earlier meetings and in the directives which the Church has constantly offered you with maternal generosity. You will interest yourselves more in education than in mere instruction, perfect your methods, afford an ever greater opportunity for the teaching of religion, become more demanding in the choice of textbooks. You will encourage the cooperation of the families of your pupils, stop at no sacrifice for the formation of your professors, follow up your pupils after their departure from your classrooms with timely post-graduate assistance and dedicate all the attention it deserves to teaching as a part of various social works. In **695 71, 91, 92)**

693a Senecae ad Lucilium, lib. V, Epist. XI (52) n. 8.

this way, your educational activities will merit, at the very least, the respect of all, especially of the good, along with the support and the protection of the public authorities. The latter will see in your work an effective and generous assistance, contributing to the common good of society and constituting the strongest barrier against those pernicious doctrines which, like a black flood, threaten everywhere. To achieve this—We repeat—"be fathers of souls more than propagators of sterile information," form your pupils above all "by the example of your life." (a)

(Geographical environment of the present congress: Havana.—A symbolic picture: the typhoons pass through but "they will not prevail.")

EXHORTATION TO PERFECT VIRGINITY

Encycl. *Sacra Virginitas,* March 25, 1954.

(The traditional doctrine of the Church regarding virginity.—Virginity and matrimony.—The excellence of virginity.—Contrary errors.)

696   As Our duty demands, We cannot but censure all
(79)   those who strive to turn young people away from the Seminary or Religious Orders and Institutes, and from the taking of sacred vows, persuading them that they can, if joined in marriage, as fathers and mothers of families, pursue greater spiritual good by an open and public profession of their Christian life. Certainly their conduct would be more proper and correct, if, instead of trying to distract from a life of virginity those young men and women who desire to give themselves to the service of God, too few alas today, they were to exhort with all the zeal at their command the vast numbers of those who live in wedlock to promote apostolic works in the ranks of the laity. On this point, St. Ambrose fittingly writes: "To sow the seeds of

695a Cf. Nos. 508 and 510.

perfect purity and to arouse a desire for virginity has always been a function of the priesthood." (a)

(Free choice of perfect chastity.—Its difficulties.)

Flight and alert vigilance, by which we carefully avoid the occasions of sin, have always been considered by holy men and women as the most effective means of combat in this matter; today, however, it does not seem that everybody holds the same opinion. Some indeed claim that all Christians, and the clergy in particular, should not be "segregated from the world" as in the past, but should be "close to the world"; therefore they should "take the risk" and put their chastity to the test in order to show whether or not they have the strength to resist. **697 (77, 99)**

(The Church has promulgated wise laws to protect and guarantee the sanctity of the sacerdotal life and the formation of the young clergy.)

The educators of the young clergy would render a more valuable and useful service, if they would inculcate in youthful minds the precepts of Christian modesty, which is so important for the preservation of perfect chastity and which is truly called the prudence of chastity. For modesty foresees threatening danger, forbids us to expose ourselves to risks, demands the avoidance of those occasions which the imprudent do not shun. It does not like impure or loose talk, it shrinks from the slightest immodesty, it carefully avoids suspect familiarity with persons of the other sex, since it brings the soul to show due reverence to the body, as being a member of Christ (a) and the temple of the Holy Spirit. (b) He who possesses the treasure of Christian modesty abominates every sin of impurity and instantly flees whenever he is tempted by its seductions. **698 (77)**

696a "Semper spectavit ad gratiam sacerdotum iacere semina
integritatis, et virginitatis studia provocare." (St. Ambrose,
De Virginitate, Ch. 5, n. 26; Migne P.G., 16, 272.)
698a Cf. 1 Cor. 6:15.
698b Cf. 1 Cor. 6:19.

699   Modesty will, moreover, suggest and provide suitable
(78,   words for parents and educators by which the youthful
99)   conscience will be formed in matters of chastity. "Wherefore," as We said in a recent address, "this modesty is not
to be so understood as to be equivalent to a perpetual silence on this subject, nor as allowing no place for sober
and cautious discussion about these matters in imparting
moral instruction." (a) In modern times, however, there are
some teachers and educators who too frequently think it
their duty to initiate innocent boys and girls into the se-
crets of human generation in such a way as to offend their
sense of shame. In this matter, in fact, a just temperance
and moderation must be used, as Christian modesty demands.

(Fear of God, humility.)

700   Moreover, there is another argument worthy of atten-
(72,   tive consideration: to preserve chastity unstained neither
73,   vigilance nor modesty suffice. Those helps must also be
77)   used which entirely surpass the powers of nature; namely,
prayer to God, the Sacraments of Penance and Holy Eucharist, a fervent devotion to the most Holy Mother of God.

*(Testimony of the Saints as to the utility of these
means.)*

701   Nevertheless We do not deny that this Our joy is over-
(79)   shadowed by a certain sorrow since We learn that in a
number of countries the number of vocations to the priesthood and to the religious life is constantly decreasing. We
have already given the principal reasons which account for
this fact and there is no reason why We should return to
them now. Rather do We trust that those educators of
youth who have succumbed to errors in this matter, will
repudiate them as soon as they are detected, and will consequently seriously resolve both to correct them and to do

699a All. *Magis quam mentis,* September 23, 1951. Cf. No.
574.

what they can to provide every help for the youth entrusted to their care who feel themselves called by divine grace to aspire to the priesthood or to embrace the religious life, in order that they may be able to reach so noble a goal. May God grant that new and larger ranks of priests, religious men and women, equal in number and virtue to the current necessities of the Church, may soon go forth to cultivate the vineyard of the Lord.

Moreover, as the obligation of Our Apostolic Office **702** demands, We urge fathers and mothers willingly to offer to *(35)* the service of God those of their children who are called to it. But if this be a source of trouble, sorrow or regret, let them seriously meditate upon the admonition which Ambrose gave to the mothers of Milan: "The majority of the young women whom I knew who wanted to be virgins were forbidden to leave by their mothers.... If your daughters want to love a man, the law allows them to choose whom they will. But those who have a right to choose a man, have no right to choose God?" (a)

Let parents consider what a great honor it is to see **703** their son elevated to the priesthood, or their daughter con- *(35)* secrate her virginity to her Divine Spouse. In regard to consecrated virgins, the Bishop of Milan writes, "You have heard, parents, that a virgin is a gift of God, the oblation of parents, the priesthood of chastity. The virgin is a mother's victim, by whose daily sacrifice divine anger is appeased." (a)

702a *"Plerasque virgines cognovi velle et prohiberi etiam prodire a matribus.... Si hominem velent amare filiae vestrae, per leges possent eligere quem vellent. Quibus igitur hominem eligere licet, Deum non licet?"* (St. Ambrose, *De Virginibus,* lib. I, c. 10, n. 58; P.L., 16, 205.)

703a *"Audistis, parentes ... Virgo Dei donum est, munus parentis, sacerdotium castitatis. Virgo matris hostia est, cujus cotidiano sacrificio vis divina placatur."* (St. Ambrose, *De Virginibus,* lib. 1, c. 7, n. 32; Migne, P.L., 16, 198.)

RELIGIOUS TEACHING BROTHERS

Letter *Procuratores Generales,* March 31, 1954—to Cardinal Valeri, Prefect of the Sacred Congregation for Religious.

704
(55,
68,
119)
The Procurators General of eight Religious Institutes of Brothers, whose special mission is the instruction and education of youth, have presented Us with an official report of the annual meeting of the French Provinces of their Institutes, held last year at Paris, in order to inform Us of what had been accomplished there, and what they hope to accomplish in the future. At the same time, they besought Us, in a spirit of devoted respect, to point out what seems to be the best means to obtain greater and more promising developments.

This is what We gladly do in succinct form by means of this Letter. And in the first place, We rejoice because We know with what zealous and untiring will these Brothers are fulfilling the mission confided to them, a mission that can be of the greatest assistance to the Church, to the family, and to civil society itself.

Indeed, their work is of great importance. Boys and young men are the blossoming hope of the future. And the course of events in the years ahead will depend especially upon those young men who are instructed in the liberal arts and every type of discipline, so that they may assume the direction not only of their private affairs but also of public matters. If their minds are illumined by the light of the Gospel, if their wills are formed by Christian principles and fortified by divine grace, then we may hope that a new generation of youth will emerge, which can happily triumph over the difficulties, bewilderments and fears that presently assail us, and which by its knowledge, virtue and example can establish a better and healthier social order.

705
(56,
It is Our great consolation to know that these Religious Institutes are laboring to that end, guided by those

wise rules which their Founders have bequeathed to their 57)
respective Institutes as a sacred inheritance. We desire
that they perform this task not only with the greatest
alacrity, diligence and devotion, but also animated by that
supernatural spirit, by which human institutions can flourish and achieve good results. And specifically We desire
them to strive to imbue the youths confided to them with a
doctrine that is not only sound and free from all error, but
which also takes account of those special arts and processes
which the present age has introduced into each of the
sciences.

But what is most important is this, that they draw su- **706**
pernatural strength from their religious life, which they *(57,*
ought to live intensely, so that they may form to Christian *72,*
virtue the students committed to their care, as the mission *84,*
confided to them by the Church demands. For, if this *107)*
strength were relegated to a subordinate position, or
neglected entirely, neither literary nor any other type of
human knowledge would enable them to live an upright
life. In fact, these merely human attainments can become
effective instruments of evil and unhappiness, especially at
the age "which is as wax, so easily can it be fashioned to
evil." (a)

Therefore, let them watch over the minds and souls
of youth; let them have a profound understanding of
young people's indifference, of their hidden motives, of
their deep-seated drives, of their inner unrest and distress,
and let them wisely guide them. Let them act vigorously to
drive away at once and with the utmost determination
those false principles which are a threat to virtue, to avert
every danger that can tarnish the brightness of their souls,
and so to order all things about them that while the mind is
being illuminated by truth, the will may be rightly and
courageously controlled and moved to embrace all that
is good.

706a *"Cereas in vitium flecti,"* Horace, *Ars Poetica,* 163.

707
(53,
55,
80,
57,
82)

While these Religious Brothers know that the education of youth is the art of arts and the science of sciences, (a) they know, too, that they can do all things with divine aid, for which they pray, mindful of the word of the Apostle of the Gentiles, "I can do all things in Him Who strengtheneth me." (b) Therefore, let them cultivate their own piety as much as they can, as is only right, for, although they do not belong to a Congregation of priests, they are, nevertheless, legitimate members of a lay Congregation. (c) Such a Religious Institute, although composed almost entirely of those who by a particular divine vocation have renounced the dignity of the priesthood and the consolations that flow therefrom, is all the same held in high honor by the Church, and is of the greatest assistance to the sacred ministry by the Christian formation of youth. On a previous occasion We turned our attention to this subject, saying: "The Religious State is in no sense reserved to either the one or the other of the two types which by divine right exist in the Church, since not only the clergy but likewise the laity can be Religious." (d) And by the very fact that the Church has endowed laymen with this dignity and status, it is quite plainly apparent to all that each part of this holy militia can labor, and very effectively, both for its own salvation and that of others, according to the special canonical rules and regulations by which each is regulated.

708
(55,
79)

Wherefore, let no one give less consideration to the members of these Institutes because they do not embrace the priesthood, or deem their apostolate less fruitful. Moreover, it is a fact well known to Us that they gladly encour-

707a Cf. St. Gregory Nazianzenus, Orat. II; Migne, P.G., 35, 426: τέχνη τεχνῶν καὶ ἐπιστήμη ἐπιστημῶν.
707b Phil. 4:13.
707c Cf. C.I.C., can. 488, 4.
707d All. to the General Congress of Religious Orders, held in Rome; A.A.S., 1951, p. 28.

age the youths committed to their care for instruction and education to embrace the priesthood, when it seems that divine grace is calling them. Nor is there any lack of instances of their former pupils who now adorn the ranks of the episcopate and even the Sacred College of Cardinals. These Religious Institutes merit and deserve Our praise and that of the whole Church; they deserve, also, the good will of the Bishops and the Clergy, since they give them precious help, not only in providing a fitting education for youth, but also in cultivating the vocations of those students whom divine grace attracts to the sacred priesthood.

Therefore, let them continue along the way upon which they have embarked, with ever more joyful dedication, and together with the other religious Orders and Congregations to whom this work has been entrusted, let them devote themselves, united and zealous, to the instruction and education of youth.

As a pledge of the divine help, which We implore for them with earnest prayer, and as a testimony of Our personal benevolence, We lovingly impart the Apostolic Blessing to you, Our Beloved Son, and to each of the Superiors of these Institutes, to their subjects, and to their pupils.

CHILDHOOD AND THE DEVIL

All. to the schoolchildren of Italy, May 2, 1954.
(*Welcome.*)

1. We wish above all to express to you the paternal concern that fills Our heart when We see reflected in your eyes the innocence that charms men, enraptures angels, and moves even the Heart of God. Who can tell, indeed, what may some day become of this easy, blithe gladness of yours? It might be possible—and Our soul is saddened merely to think of it—that the sun of your childhood will be darkened by menacing clouds.

709
(3)

Do you remember how, when Jesus walked the streets of Judea, the little children ran to honor Him and their mothers presented them to Him, overcoming the opposition of those who feared that they would bother Jesus. Today, alas, there is great danger that this will not continue to be the case, and that some children will no longer be, as before, the little friends of Jesus.

Once upon a time there was a little boy, fine and good, who was the consolation and joy of his parents. One day they sent him on a small errand outside the village, and he walked happily along a country road towards his goal. He looked at the trees in flower, heard the song of the birds; everything summoned him to peace, to well-being. From time to time, he stopped to pick the small flowers of the field because he wanted to carry some back as a gift for his mother. All of a sudden he saw a hidden snake come out of the grass, and before he could defend himself, he felt its fangs sink in, leaving him stricken with all the symptoms of poisoning. A short while afterwards, the boy died in the arms of his mother, who kept calling him in vain in the midst of her tears.

710
(33,
87,
88,
93,
97)

2. How many little ones today are in peril of being poisoned by a snake even more insidious, the serpent of hell? Who would be able, then, to recognize them? For these, Holy Church would weep, and it would not be easy in this case to comfort the sorrowing mother and dry her anguished tears. This venomous serpent encircles the world, disguised in many ways, and now he seems to be trying to attack children in particular, to snatch them from Jesus and estrange them from the priesthood and the Church. Today there is cause for great fear that children will be struck, wounded, and their souls killed.

Watch out, dear children. While you walk in the streets or play the games of childhood; when you take up certain newspapers and books; when you happen to attend shows that progress has brought even into the walls of your own homes: watch out! Often the serpent may be hidden there to strike you, to snatch you from Jesus. Never stop watching out for him: he may bewitch you, and then you would be lost. At the first sign that you are threatened, cry out, run to your mother right away, and above all to your celestial Mother, to Mary, who has at her command the power of God and is always near you. Call on your Guardian Angel to enlighten and sustain you.

In order not to fall victim to the serpent, in order to remain good, you must do all that Jesus tells you through your parents, teachers, and priests.

(Say "yes" to Our Lady.—The children of the Gospel: the Holy Innocents; at the multiplication of the bread; on Palm Sunday.—Pray for the Church.)

PERMANENT VALUE OF THE ENCYCLICAL "DIVINI ILLIUS MAGISTRI"

Letter from the Secretariat of State, December 31, 1954—to His Eminence Cardinal Roques, Archbishop of Rennes.

(Homage addressed to the Holy Father on the occasion of the Silver Jubilee of the Encyclical "Divini Illius Magistri.")

The Holy Father is not unaware, certainly, of the great **711** sacrifices that many parents and Catholic teachers make to *(5)* remain faithful to the cause of Christian education. It is a matter that is very dear to his heart and he is glad of this opportunity to congratulate them and encourage them to continue in their efforts.

The difficulties of life today, the rapid succession of events and opinions, will not be able, in practice, to restrict in some way or dim the permanent value of the principles contained in the papal encyclical.

712 Today, as yesterday, it is of the highest importance to
(117) assure children of Christian families of an education and
an instruction that conforms fully with the demands of
their supernatural destiny and with what will be required
of them in civil life. And, precisely to recall the just conditions for such a formation, Pius XI, in 1929, laid down, in
masterly fashion, the rights and duties respectively of
Church, family and State regarding children. (a) His
Holiness appreciates the resoluteness with which Your
Eminence and his colleagues in the hierarchy instruct the
faithful on this point of Christian doctrine and take care
that it may be applied in practice according as circumstances and times allow.

713 Moreover, the bishops of France, who have so vivid a
(115) sense of their pastoral responsibilities to the flock committed to their charge, will not fail, and rightly so, to favor
equally whatever can contribute to the Christian formation
of thousands of young people, who, for one reason or another, have to grow up in institutions which are less favorable to their religious formation than Catholic institutions.
Some years ago, the Holy Father himself willed to pay
homage to the spirit of sacrifice of the Christian University teachers and to the nobility of the sentiments which
guided them in their work as educators. Their presence and the witness they have given, joined to that of
chaplains (who, unfortunately, are too few and sometimes
impeded in the exercise of their ministry), have, no doubt,
been greatly instrumental in obtaining the religious renewal of France. However, this legitimate and laudable action
obviously cannot evidently make us forget nor can it nullify
the desire of the Church, namely, that all Catholic parents
may at last be granted their rightful opportunity—in actual
practice—to give their children an education that is fully
and openly Christian.

712a: Cf. Nos. 240-304.

That is why there is cause for satisfaction over the **714** efforts that have already been made to give better recog- *(118)* nition to the religious and professional worth of Catholic institutions, to their development and to their fair distribution in the nation. To further this end, the national Committee for free education has, under the chairmanship of Your Eminence, achieved results which merit the congratulations of His Holiness, who further hopes that the good reception already given in various fields, may permit the work to develop still more.

(Blessing.)

THE FORMATION OF TEACHERS

Letter *Die Gluck-und Segenswunche,* February 12, 1955—to the bishops of Germany.

(Marian Year.—Difficulties of the Church in Germany: crisis of religious vocations; violation of the Concordat in the matter of education.)

Dear sons and Venerable Brethren, that We may not **715** compromise Our conscience, We have to state most solemn- *(50)* ly, in this matter, that, according to article 24, par. 1 of the Concordat mentioned above, it is absolutely necessary that Catholic schools be in the hands of teachers, who not only profess the Catholic faith, but have all the qualities demanded by their office. It is therefore equally necessary that these teachers be formed in special centers of formation, which are clearly mentioned in the Concordats with Germany (art. 24, par. 2) and with Bavaria (art. 5, par. 3.), where guarantees have been given that Catholic teachers will have an education of mind and heart which responds to the special needs of Catholic schools.

In the absence of these centers of formation, it is only with great difficulty that we can form teachers suitable for our needs. If, further, there is a complete lack of these teachers, it is difficult to imagine how Catholic schools can continue to exist and respond adequately to the high standard that is expected of them.

EDUCATION OF INTERNATIONAL FEELING

Letter from the Secretariat of State on the occasion of the Fifth Congress of the International Catholic Bureau for Childhood, April 28, 1955.

716
(66)
In selecting as the theme of the forthcoming Congress of the Internaltional Catholic Bureau for Childhood at Venice, "Education of the international sense in children," rest assured that you are corresponding with what the Head of the Church himself thinks. Did not His Holiness, in his last Christmas message, urge Christians and all men of good will "to work united in order to renew the foundation of unity of the human family"? And is there any better way of collaborating in this work of peace than by developing in young people the vivid realization of this fraternal union?

(Good wishes for the success of the Congress.)

717
(66)
As with all forms of education, that which you propose to study requires first of all the right spirit. At the same time, you must not neglect to have recourse to different methods of formation in order gradually to open the child's mind to the world, which his everyday surroundings are insufficient to provide.

You will find the spirit of this education, its deepest and most lasting inspiration, as also the credentials of its authority, in the faith in Christ the Savior Who makes "peace through the blood of His cross" and brings "reconciliation" to a humanity that is divided in itself because it is God's enemy. (a)

717a Col. 1:18-21.

Such an education, further, will normally lead to active participation in the life and the spirit of the Church. "Supra-national by its very essence," declared the Holy Father in his Christmas Broadcast of 1945, "the Church is placed in the midst of the history of the human race . . . she continually radiates and diffuses new healing and unifying forces." Hence it is that religious instruction to children quite legitimately takes its stand on these doctrinal foundations in order to develop in the child a truly "Catholic" conscience which is the authentic expression of a Christian vision of the world. Educators therefore must not neglect to open to the young this vast and beneficial vision: a true son of the Church has the heart of a "brother to all men."

In this light of faith, the speakers of the Congress and the special Committees would do well to consider the special problems involved in this education and the most suitable means of solving them. The field to examine is vast, and contains many as yet unexplored regions. **718** *(66)*

The spirit of the child must be awakened by study, but his sensibility must also be aroused and he must be taught to discover for himself the dimensions of the world around him. In his young heart, love for his own country must develop side by side with a realization of his duties to the human family. Attachment to the legitimate values of his own national community must be harmonized with respect and even esteem for the civilizations of the other peoples and races whom he learns about. Family and school, reading, shows and travel, all can contribute to give the adolescent this eminently Christian sense of the basic solidarity that unites him to all men, even the most distant and the poorest, over and above the frontiers and the differences of culture and mentality.

(Blessing.)

EXAMPLE OF THE EDUCATOR

Letter *Das Gelobnis univerbruchlicher,* May 13, 1955—
to Miss Mleinek.

(Congratulations for 70 years of activity of the Association of German Teachers.)

719
(4,
50)
Your maxim will be the following: "We, Catholic teachers, will not allow any other group of teachers to be better than us in the matter of cultural perfection." Thank God for the activity of your Association for the benefit of the young, and above all, for young women, which consequently redounds to the advantage of wives, mothers and families.

720
(42,
72,
74,
83)
We have a very high regard for the work of teaching and education which is performed by Catholic teachers, who contribute—today, as you are well aware, in a most substantial manner (often even to a much greater degree than the home can),—to the formation of youth from early childhood through the years of growth up to maturity in order to render them fit for life and strong in their religious and moral convictions. But you must always remember that a healthy atmosphere for this formation can be created only by the personal example of the teacher, who is completely and sincerely devoted to her mission and to the children entrusted to her care.

721
(5,
15,
19,
45)
Your Association takes its inspiration from the principles which Our Predecessor Pius XI set forth in his Encyclical, *Divini Illius Magistri.* (a) Remain faithful to your ideal, and, We may add, increase your fidelity as opposition to this ideal is increased. At all events, the Church will never voluntarily surrender her own schools and the formation of teachers according to her vision of the world and of the Catholic faith. (b)

(Blessing.)

721a Cf. Nos. 240-304.
721b Auf die Schule des eigenen Bekenntnisses und die Aus-

CHARTER FOR A CHRISTIAN EDUCATION

Letter *Pour commémorer*, to the Cardinal Archbishop of Malines, August 24, 1955.

(National Congress of Belgium on the occasion of the twenty-fifth anniversay of the Encyclical "Divini Illius Magistri.")

The inviolable principles which this document lays down regarding the Church, family and State in the matter of education, are based on the very nature of things and on revealed truth. They cannot be shaken by the ebb and flow of events. As for the fundamental rules which it prescribes, these too are not subject to the wear and tear of time, since they are only the faithful echo of the Divine Master, Whose words shall never pass away. (a) The Encyclical is a real Magna Carta of Christian education, "outside which no education is complete and perfect." (b) It lends itself to study, today as it did in the past, by all those who, in a spirit of loyalty, desire to know, in this matter, the genuine and firm thought of the Church, "to whom belongs, in a very special manner, the mission of education." (c) In times of difficulty, it provides, with its clarity of doctrine, a certain guide for the courageous efforts of Catholic parents and teachers who are desirous of assuring youth of a formation fully in conformity with the requirements of the faith.

Likewise We take pleasure in the thought that this commemoration will give all an opportunity to make a deeper study of this masterly teaching in order to appreciate its force and strength and to revive in their hearts

722
(5-
7,
10,
26,
28,
62)

bildung seiner Lehrkraffe eindeutig im Sinne des katholischen Glaubens und Weltbildes wird die katholische Kirche jedenfalls friewillig nie verzichten.

722a Cf. Matt. 24:35.
722b Encycl. *Divini Illius Magistri;* cf. No. 243.
722c Ibid., cf. No. 246.

those sentiments that a true son of God should have for the sacred cause of Christian education.

(Congratulations for the consecration of Belgian Catholic education to the Sacred Heart.)

723
*(4,
5,
26,
60,
88)*
If it is true that "Christian education embraces human life in all its forms ... in order to elevate, regulate and perfect it according to the example and teachings of Jesus Christ," (a) what wonderful graces will be obtained through this consecration to the Sacred Heart! In It are "all the treasures of wisdom and knowledge," ready to enrich all who thirst after the truth that saves. Is it not "the meeting-point of all the virtues" of which Jesus Christ is the Model, "the fount of life and sanctity" capable of satisfying ardent youth thirsting for high ideals? May the divine Heart reign over families and preserve them faithful to their serious obligations in the matter of education. May It reign over Christian schools and their teachers who perform a work of such great benefit to Church and country. May It reign also in Movements and works of the young, over all those places where, with the passing of the days and years, the long and tiresome task is performed of preparing the child to be a true Christian and a man of character.

(Blessing.)

REDEMPTION AND EDUCATION

All. to Catholic Guide leaders, August 26, 1955.

(Welcome.)

724
*(1,
2,
51,
54,
69)*
Conscious of the responsibility which you have in the Christian formation of Catholic Guides, you have made the resolute decision to take up together, under the direction of your chaplains, the serious theme of the Redemption in its relations with education. No teacher will be unaware of the importance of this study, since every Christian teacher

723a Encycl. *Divini Illius Magistri.* Cf. No. 300.

has the task of directing those under her charge not to one end in preference to another, but to the only last end of man, Christian sanctity. Now, a guide who takes up this work, must know the starting-point, the finish, the road to follow and the strength of the travelers. The starting-point is a nature created in the image of God and destined for happiness by the Creator, but deprived of grace because of original sin. The efforts of man alone would never have sufficed to obtain supernatural grace permitting him to save himself and reach the heights of sanctity to which God calls him. So God sent His Son to redeem humanity. The Christian educator is called upon to collaborate with this sole Savior, to make Him known and loved by the children entrusted to him. It is a sublime honor, but it carries the obligation of great humility and great loyalty to the precepts of Christ.

Renunciation

Because Christis defined as the Way, the Truth and the Life, "without the Way there is no going; without the Truth there is no knowing; without the Life there is no living." (a) The Redeemer presents Himself to everybody, but He does not have two truths to present, nor two ways to follow, nor two lives to offer. Have not the Evangelists given us the words of the Redeemer regarding the essential condition for attaining this new life, which must be preferred above any sacrifice, above all earthly goods or personal convenience or human affections, no matter how legitimate? (b) The educator who would forget this fundamental principle of Christian life and neglect to draw the practical conclusions first for herself and then for those in her charge, would certainly not be a good guide.

Your movement accustoms you to do without the comforts of modern life, this artificial "padding" which, elim-

725
(54,
76,
90)

725a Imitation of Christ, Bk. 3, Ch. 56, n. 1.
725b Cf. Matt. 10:37; Lk. 14:25-27.

inating physical effort, enfeebles the will. It invites you to
the practice of a more severe life and calls you to generosity in giving yourselves to your younger sisters. How could
she who at every moment is able to satisfy her every whim
feel the needs and sufferings of others? How could she
feel for herself the need of an interior life of recollection
and prayer, which alone can give the strength to mortify
selfish tendencies and practice disinterested charity?

Christian optimism

726   That is why you are capable, better than others, of
(26,   understanding the meaning of the words of Jesus and
75,   drawing the necessary conclusions. The aim of the Guide
90)   Movement is the development of your personality and the
cultivation of your natural aptitudes so that you may one
day be able to accept all the responsibility awaiting you,
shouldering it with courage and decision. But over and
above human virtues there is the Christian ideal to which
you aspire, and which is impossible to attain without a
constant battle against self. But is there not a contradiction
here? Without a doubt, if it were a question of self-denial
and sacrifice without any compensation.

But just when a difficult renunciation has to be made,
Christ transforms the soul of the Christian, (as you are
well aware) assisting him to penetrate the mystery of His
work, inviting him to collaborate, and granting him to that
end greater and greater ardor. And thus, though it is so
exacting and severe, the Christian doctrine on education is
the most optimistic of all. It relies not on mere human
strength but on the capacity every man has to become a
son of God! "Behold what manner of charity the Father
hath bestowed upon us, that we should be called and
should be the sons of God." (a)

727   Pedagogical methods differ even among Catholics and
(1,   that is a good thing. According to the character and the

726a 1 John 3:1.

condition of the educators and the pupils, one method will 54, be more successful than another. All, however, must be 72, based on what has been revealed, in the center of which 82, is the mystery of the Redemption. All the children of 84) Adam bear the consequences of original sin, and baptism, which makes them sons of God and of the Church, does not take away a certain tendency to evil, against which they must battle with the invincible help of grace. This International Congress will enlighten you certainly about this basic condition of Christian education and will suggest means to attain the desired end. You are always working under the direction of the Divine Guide and Redeemer. Hence you must, above all, follow His example: the Gospel describes His wonderful patience, His astonishing humility, His immense love for men, especially children and the poor. And (in the Eucharist) you come into intimate contact with this lovable Christ of the Scriptures. He is the vital center of your activity: "If you do not eat My flesh, you will not have life in you." (a) Indeed, in the formation of Christian men and women, Jesus Christ must always be given first place. He is the gate by which the sheep enter, He is their light, their way, their food, their life. The more you keep united to Him, the better will you be able to accomplish the beautiful mission entrusted to you.

(Blessing.)

SOCIETY AND SCHOOL

Letter from the Secretariat of State on the occasion of the twenty-eighth Social Week of Italy, September, 1955.

(Theme of the Week: Society and School.)

There is no doubt that today, more than ever, (for vari- **728** ous and even contrasting reasons) public interest is cen- *(10)*

727a Cf. John 6:53.

tered on the problems of the school. The desire, therefore, to tackle these problems in order to determine the functions of the school in the light of modern developments, is something that does credit to the sense of responsibility of Italian Catholics. At the same time, this is a solemn assertion of the right of the Church to have in her hands a mission which she has always considered one of her most important duties. This mission of teaching and educating souls is hers not by any human concession, but by Divine mandate, since the Savior commanded His Apostles to "Go and teach all nations." (a)

729
(2,
6,
24,
46,
52)
Even though the school does not constitute the only, or even the most important, factor in education, it still remains the common ground on which the family, the Church and the State meet in the field of education. From the perfect functioning of the school depends, in great part, the complete formation of the man, and therefore, the progress or retrogression of civilization itself.

You will then understand how justified is the interest of the Holy Father in the work of the coming Week, and this interest is all the greater when we consider the tremendous responsibility that Italian schools have today. They do not only have to form man for himself and prepare him for life in society, but they have to perform a task of reconstruction. They must restore many moral values which have become warped in the minds of youth today, the sorrowful aftermath of these last years of inhuman wars.

Adaptation to actual conditions

730
(26,
82)
On the other hand, if the school is to be effective and make any contribution to the preparation of the citizen and of the perfect Christian, it cannot cling to outdated points of view, and even less can it ignore the recent develop-

728a Matt. 28:19.

ments of society, which frequently find scholastic institutions incapable of meeting the problems involved. "When we talk about the perfect Christian," said the Holy Father in his speech to the Union of Catholic Secondary School Teachers of Italy on September 4, 1949, "We mean the Christian of today; a man of his times, with a knowledge of whatever progress has been made by science or industry, a citizen who does not feel that he is not in keeping with life as it is today." (a)

A heritage to preserve

In this attempt to bring the school up-to-date in its programs and methods, the Catholic must, in the first place, be careful to avoid the danger that his function as a transmitter of a heritage already acquired might be less appreciated, when comparison is made with the proportions and elaborateness of a new heritage. "And therefore, while he accepts whatever is new, he will take care not to be hasty in casting off the old which has been proved by the experience of many centuries." (a) **731** *(52, 82, 118)*

The school, in fact, as His Holiness has pointed out, "cannot be compared to a laboratory, in which the risk of wasting more or less costly material is compensated for by the probability of a discovery; in the school, every individual soul faces salvation or damnation. The novelties, which may be considered worth bringing in, will relate to the choice of secondary means and pedagogical directives, but the end and the essential means will always remain the same, as will the ultimate end of education, its subject, its chief author and prime Mover, namely, God Himself." (b)

With this in mind, nobody will fail to see that the wonderful technical progress, the appreciation of the value **732** *(82)*

730a Cf. No. 511.
731a Encycl. *Divini Illius Magistri.* Cf. No. 295.
731b Cf. No. 507.

of labor, the increasing participation of all classes of people in deciding the fate of nations, the recent achievements in pedagogy (to recall only some of the aspects of civilization today), are all really positive elements, knowledge of which, once it is duly accepted into the scheme of scholastic education, will without doubt contribute toward a more complete formation of the man of our day, and, therefore, a greater increase of the common good of society.

Supernatural values

733
(26,
69,
82)
But this assimilation of the positive values of our times is necessary, also, in order to achieve a greater affirmation of the spiritual and supernatural values in the school and in society. As the Holy Father has already noted, the intellectual life of today "is so dominated by scientific, technical and economic considerations that the sense of truths of a superior order (science calls them metaphysical truths) and the capacity to perceive them are fast disappearing.... But these metaphysical truths are fundamental to the whole of one's being, whether material or spiritual, natural or supernatural." (a)

A school that limits itself only to problems relating to the passing conditions of the times can only be insufficient. It is worthy of man only when it prepares him for the transcendent and eternal realities of faith and morals, and makes him feel the need of a more complete formation based on the most noble values, which are those that Christianity offers.

Duty of the State

734
(8,
10,
11,
14,
In order that the school may respond to the requirements of society, it is necessary for society to do its duty in regard to the school. And this will happen when the family, Church and State, each in its own field, work together to educate the young. We must, however, note in

733a Discourse to graduates of I. A. C. May 24, 1953.

this regard, that the family, which has as its end the pro- *21,*
creation and education of children, possesses a priority of *24,*
nature and therefore a priority of right over the State in *25,*
the matter of education. On the other hand, the Church *109)*
(who regenerates in the family of the spirit the men who
are generated in the family of the flesh) has the right and
duty to teach the highest truths and laws of the religious
and moral life to those who have entered her society. In
this, since it relates to the supernatural order, she has a
claim that is absolutely superior "to any claim in the natural order." (a)

The State has therefore the duty to respect the prior
rights of the family and of the Church in the matter of education, and she must protect whatever these two institutions undertake regarding schools. Were the State to substitute itself unduly for these, or worse still, were it to
monopolize education, it would not only violate the rights
of individuals, of the family and of the Church, but would
lower the cultural standards of the schools themselves.

It is sad that, in this matter, the Catholics of Italy **735**
show themselves ignorant and hesitant. Being accustomed *(112,*
for so long to the domination of the schools by the State, *115,*
many have very hazy notions about their right to freedom *117)*
of education. In saying this, We have no intention of
denying the existence of authentic and essential Christian
values in Italian State schools.

During these last few years, regular religious instruction and large groups of Catholic teachers have already
made their good influence felt. However, this does not
always and everywhere suffice to respond to the hopes of
many Catholic parents, who are desirous of guaranteeing
their children a Christian education in the best way possible. These, therefore, are perfectly within their rights, a
fact that is admitted by the Italian Constitution itself, when

734a Encycl. *Divini Illius Magistri;* cf. 246.

they make a firm demand for more comprehensive legislation in the matter of schools, in order that they may have
the possibility of choosing, without excessive expense, the
school that best corresponds to the moral and religious
aspirations they have for their children.

School and family

736
(42,
43,
46)
We must also consider the relations between the school
itself and the family. The problem is particularly urgent
today and the Holy Father has often called the attention
of educators to it. Unfortunately, the cooperation of the
parents is not always asked for and the problem of relations between these two institutions tends to be considered
from a pragmatic or a purely cultural point of view and not
from the point of view of education. This was the reason
why His Holiness only recently warned: "We willingly
encourage whatever helps to improve relations and promote collaboration between school and family. It is the
family that chooses the teacher to prepare the adolescent
to live his life as an adult in society and in the Church.
The family must not and cannot renounce this role of direction. Cooperation is natural and necessary, but, to be
fruitful, it calls for mutual acquaintance, continual contact,
the same point of view, subsequent adjustments." (a)

When this exchange of vital forces takes place on a
Christian basis, important results follow and often it can
offset the bad influences of the environment. In this case,
solidarity on the level of grace will have truly favored the
common welfare by forming the man, the citizen and the
Christian.

The Christian teacher

737
(26,
The fundamental problem for a real reform in the
schools will always be that of the teacher, because "good

736a Discourse to the Union of Italian Catholic Secondary-
School Teachers, January 5, 1954. Cf. No. 690.

schools are not so much the result of good organization as of good teachers." (a) Hence the importance of a sound formation for teachers. It is, however, evident that teachers will never be worthy of their profession, if, although possessing adequate cultural preparation, they should limit their work to instruction in the strict sense of the word, and feel themselves under no obligation to provide the deeper and more comprehensive instruction that is education. Everything in the school must be educative. If it is not to fall short of its purpose, it must be made educative in its every aspect. And who can accomplish this noble task better than the Catholic teacher? In the light of faith, he alone is able to understand fully the individual dignity of his pupil, whose supernatural life demands recognition, support and development.

50, 71)

Every care must, therefore, be taken to form Christian teachers worthy of the name. The school has no more urgent need than for educators of this sort.

738 (50, 52, 111)

"You," said His Holiness during the audience given to teachers on January 5, 1954, "have a serious responsibility in the formation of youth and you have a great part to play for the future of your country. As Christians you cannot remain indifferent. As teachers, you have the joy of being able to cooperate very greatly in the renewal of your generation." (a)

The theme you have very aptly chosen for the coming Social Week, coinciding as it does with the twenty-fifth anniversary of the Encyclical *Divini Illius Magistri* of Pius XI, of revered memory, will not fail to instill new ideas in your minds. Animated by these high ideals, Italian Catholics should, today more than ever, feel the need to unite their efforts for the triumph of Christian principles in the schools of Italy. His Holiness asks this of all. Working

737a Encycl. *Divini Illius Magistri.* Cf. No. 297.
738a Cf. No. 691.

towards this end, they will one day be the architects of the renewal of the family and of society which We hope will soon come.

(Blessing.)

TEACHERS OF EARLY CHILDHOOD

All. to the Association of Italian Women Teachers, October 24, 1955.

(The activities of the Association.—Three fundamental principles.)

739
(36,
75)
1. In order to ensure a brighter future for both the Church and human society there is no more efficacious solution than to bend down to the tender buds of the new generations from their infancy in order to direct their development towards what is true and good. During the years when their psychological and moral consciousness begins to dawn, when external ideas of good and evil begin to be added to the sensations of the sweet and the bitter, of the beautiful and the ugly, it is necessary to begin to instill in their minds the true concept of things and the right rules of conduct. Good education consists primarily in prevention—prevention in its literal sense of "arriving ahead of others," namely, ahead of error and sin—and prevention is certainly easier than a great deal of correction and repair later on.

740
(26,
118)
2. No educational method, be it based on some particular tradition or developed by modern educational science, can give perfect and lasting results if it disagrees with Christian principles, or scorns their values, or fails to use true Christian means, including supernatural ones. Christianity is not only able to complete any other pedagogical method, but it possesses its own safe method for leading souls to the highest perfection, as abundantly demonstrated by its saints.

Form within yourselves the heart of a mother

3. Anyone who either by religious vocation or free **741** professional choice wants to become an educator should *(36,* know that he or she cannot become one offhand, but must *44,* prepare for the difficult task with adequate training. In *46,* the case of early childhood it is proper that their educa- *50,* tion be left principally in the hands of women, who should *51,* strive to enrich their inborn gifts of intuition and tender *53,* feelings with the proper amount of knowledge and experi- *82)* ence to be obtained from pedagogical sciences. Here, therefore, is the reason for your Teachers' Institutes.

To form a teacher for very young children is like spiritually forming a mother, with this difference, that while a mother becomes an educator through a natural disposition—which, however, does not exclude, wherever possible, planned preparation—a professional educator must develop within herself a maternal spirit through her own efforts and her own good will.

Is there a higher and more beneficial goal for a woman than to develop within herself this maternal spirit? Perhaps never so much as today has the world needed mothers and the maternal spirit that draws men away from the turbulent currents of violence, oppression, and coarseness into which they have fallen.

Nature's providential law has decreed that each generation should pass through the gentle school of mothers so that every new life may be surrounded by brightness and goodness, thus checking the rule of evil. However, it is not always possible, nor is every mother able to carry out her salutary mission.

Examples of classical and Christian history

Your Association has the purpose of giving our educa- **742** tors a formation that, as far as possible, is both complete *(50,* and up-to-date, without depriving them of those broader *64)* visions of life and of the sciences.

We have noted with satisfaction the sujects chosen for your convention this year, such as ancient history, archeology, the art of drawing—the presentation of which has been entrusted to eminent scholars. Very appropriate indeed is the historical knowledge of our classical and Christian civilization, eloquent vestiges of which you have an opportunity to see and admire in the Eternal City.

From the contemplation of them, the mind of the educator is inspired to esteem his own work even more and to direct it along an unbroken line of ideal perfection. Patterns of this perfection, worthy of imperishable glory, are found scattered through the centuries, both in the lives of individuals and in their works, and in themselves they represent an incentive to future generations to imitate them.

But if it is not given to every nation to find examples of such exalted perfection in its own history, it is always possible to take its inspiration from the common heritage of all peoples, from the history and the glory of the Universal Church, along whose long road the Christian educator will find at each turn light and strength to enable him to equal or even to surpass the past.

THE CATHOLIC TEACHER

All. to the Italian Catholic Elementary School Teachers' Association, November 4, 1955.

(Tenth anniversary of the Association.)

743   Ten years of diligent effort, of struggles won and con-
(4,   quests achieved in the arduous and exacting field of edu-
5,   cation—such is the priceless gift you want to offer today to
31, the Vicar of Christ who, as you well know, holds children
47, close to his heart and, through them, the destiny of both
52) the Church and your country.

After parents, who is more responsible for the religious and secular destiny of the country than its elementary school teachers, through whose hands, according to law, all children must pass?

(*The work already achieved is the foundation of all future hopes.*)

The Catholic Teachers' Association is now established in all dioceses and provinces. It has 1,310 sections and its members include about eighty per cent of Italy's teachers. This has been achieved, no doubt, because there is to be found in very few groups, as there is in yours, such complete moral soundness and such a conscious seriousness of aims. It has also been achieved because your association has worked tirelessly to bring together and to preserve these precious qualities under the banner of Jesus Christ, sole Master of adults and the young. We praise the careful work you have done in preparing national and provincial lecturers, in providing teachers with both religious and professional training. We cannot fail to express Our pleasure over the dignified and intelligent way in which you have tried to obtain just economic and legal improvements without letting yourselves be influenced by a facile demagogy, which is always harmful and especially so in school matters. We must also point out that your numbers and unity have enabled Catholics to win an absolute majority at all meetings of an electoral nature. Thus We express Our satisfaction with your very valuable work and urge you to continue it with the same dedication and at the same pace as in the past, so that the grace of Jesus, friend of children, may always shine where the young people of Italy spend their most beautiful years.

But you must also hear a word of exhortation from Us, along with some simple, though necessarily incomplete, thoughts as to what a teacher should be and what he must know, desire and do in order to be worthy of the high calling entrusted to him.

744
(22, 58, 111, 112)

What should a teacher be?

745
(26,
51,
60,
63,
71)

1. First of all, *what should a teacher be?*

Some people seem to think that the word "instructor" means more than the simple word "teacher" and are inclined to replace the latter by the former. It does not seem proper to Us to do this, beloved sons and daughters, and you are right in continuing to call yourselves Catholic *teachers.* "Teacher" is the highest title that can be given to an instructor. The teacher's function demands something higher and more profound than the function of the person who merely communicates a knowledge of things. The "teacher" is a person who knows how to create a close relationship between his own soul and the soul of a child. It is he who personally devotes himself to guiding the inexperienced pupil towards truth and virtue. It is he, in a word, who molds the pupil's intellect and will so as to fashion as best he can a being of human and Christian perfection. Thus it must not be thought that, because he teaches in an *elementary* school, a teacher worthy of of the name has but little right to the unconditional and complete respect of his country. In the elementary school, children learn the basic *elements* which are for everyone the foundation of future intellectual development and which are in most cases the only scholastic heritage they will have at their disposal throughout their entire lives.

746
(50,
51,
101,
103,
107)

What, then, should you be?

True teachers must be complete persons and Christians. That is, they must be imitators of the only Divine Master, Jesus Christ.

Let Us tell you of Our grief, beloved children, at seeing here in Italy more and more schools where, in a seemingly harmless way under specious pretexts, Jesus is in reality ignored or, worse still, where pupils are taught to fight Him and to exclude Him wherever He is found—in minds, in hearts, in families and in society. What will they be able to learn inside those desecrated walls, poor little boys and girls, from teachers who do not teach the truth, who do not point out the path, who do not know—and who therefore cannot indicate—the road that leads to true life?

Fortunately, the large majority of elementary school teachers have often reaffirmed their intention not to mislead in any way the children entrusted to their care. Other groups may have gone back on such an intention. But you have been courageous and have withstood all threats and urgings. It is not enough, beloved sons and daughters, that you have declared yourselves Catholic. It is also necessary to live up to your faith. It is not enough, therefore, merely to expound the truths to be believed and point out the path to be followed. Above all it is necessary that your children see you practise what you teach. If they do not, the effectiveness of your teaching will be quite limited. We urge you, therefore, to pledge yourselves to live a completely Christian life. In order that the goal that We are setting for you may not seem too arduous, We shall point it out in words which the Divine Master used in addressing the multitudes of His listeners: To enter the kingdom of heaven, become as these children—efficiamini sicut parvuli (a): pure, simple, humble and generous.

747
(54, 83)

What should a teacher know?

2. What should you know?

You must not think that because children—the object of your educational work—are young, you can be content to be humanly, spiritually and morally mediocre. It is well known, in fact, that the more one works with "little ones" the more necessary it is to have ability. Does not the Creator of the vast universe of stars, whose movements He directs with admirable harmony, show equal power and

748
(50, 82)

747a Matt. 18:3.

wisdom and arouse an even greater sense of amazement when He regulates the imperceptible motions of the atom in its parts? Those who have called children "men in miniature" have indirectly claimed for teachers a not inconsiderable greatness of soul. We shall not speak, of course, of the knowledge you must have so that you can impart it to a child. But, although the case of a teacher who does not know what he should teach his students is inconceivable, a certain lack of preparation as to the manner in which such teaching should be imparted or as to the purpose it should have is noted in some teachers.

749
(84)
You must know a child by observing him and you will achieve this if you observe him directly and make diligent use of the help pedagogy offers you. A child is a small fragile thing, completely helpless in the face of life, who grows and blooms like a spring flower. He is a small being in search of motion and play, loving everything that helps him to feel grown up, already independent and increasingly responsible for his own actions. Exceptionally varied in their appearance and needs, some children are marked by a retarded physical development. Others give concern because of their precocity, intellectual as well as moral. There are those who are altogether backward, while others give promise of great and beautiful things because of their extraordinary intelligence or uncommon diligence. Some are restless and turbulent, others calm and contemplative.

750
(84)
It is not enough to know children. You must know how to talk to them. It may be said that few persons are capable of listening as children are, since no one else has such a thirst to learn. In fact, everything they see elicits questions, which are asked with insistence and sometimes with an indiscretion which is well known to you all. But even though children want to learn and know how to listen patiently, it is still important for teachers to learn as much as possible about the art of speech, about how to express

themselves and how to impress things on the little minds of their pupils. Without distorting things in any way, teachers must nevertheless transform them by using simple and suitable terms, refraining, meanwhile, from using words and forms of speech which are exaggeratedly childish. Futhermore, children more than adults have a great need to see. We must, therefore, neglect nothing that can aid their imagination. It is also necessary to avoid monotony, excessive lengthiness and too many explanations.

Thus wisdom more than knowledge, and depth rather than breadth of learning, are required of a teacher. Above all he should have an eager solicitude for the future of children regardless of their unsettled present and should guide their every move towards the future. A teacher is a good sower who throws a handful of seed into the ground. He chooses with foresight the time, place and manner so that no seed will be lost and so that each will be abundantly fruitful. **751** *(51, 63)*

What should the teacher want?

2. *What should you want?* **752**

As teachers you must see to it that the children acquire all the knowledge which is absolutely indispensable to life. You should, therefore, be faithful to well-established programs, gently and firmly seeing to it that the children in your care carry them out diligently according to their ability. As Catholic teachers you should be particularly careful that children learn religion in a clear, organic and therefore lively manner. "Lively" it should be made above all, not only in the sense of interesting, but also in the sense that religion is life. For religion is an indispensable factor in living. It is not only a solution to doubts and uncertainties, but also an aid in winning life's battles, small today but great tomorrow. It is a refuge in early temptations to sin and a light and guide for children's actions, duties, renunciations and relations with the outside world. Remem- *(52, 63, 69, 72, 85)* ber that quite a few children do not attend parochial catechism classes because of negligence or aversion on the part of ill-advised parents. Others may never again, even as adults, have an opportunity to learn the catechism or study it more profoundly.

In order, therefore, that these little ones may not lack the benefits of Christian doctrine, you must make firm use of your right to teach it. You must not forget that this is also your imperative duty before God and your country.

753
(60,
66)
As educators you should be eager to mold your children and urge them to exercise the human virtues: loyalty, courage, and devotion to duty, family, and country. It should be noted here that the sentiment of patriotism is perhaps too much neglected by people today, (a) although

753a In September, 1955, the Holy Father had the Secretariat of State address the following letter to the Third National Congress of the French Union of Parochial School Sisters:

"*It must be admitted that matters belonging to the civic order—which, however, ultimately refer to the Fourth Commandment—have not always in past times occupied the rightful place that is theirs in Christian education. How many Catholic women, to cite but one notable example, even today, take no interest in their duty to vote, and this because of the fact that the serious consequences which their absence from the polls might inflict on the good of society was never impressed on them. How much more desirable it would be should the children of light realize the need to set an example in this field as well as in others! They must be first n their solicitude for the common good of their homeland and possess as much zeal in the performance of their civic duties as in the observance of the domestic or professional virtues. All this, however, presupposes a diligent formation begun in early childhood. . .*" (October 16, 1955, col. 1296 ff.)

Similarly, among the directives given by the Holy Father on the occasion of the Canadian Social Weeks, by means of the Secretariat of State, there occurs the following: "*If the State has the right to claim the civic education*

it has been and may still be a priceless factor in the complete training of the child. It should not be feared that love for all mankind—which you must develop in a Christian manner in your little charges—is necessarily contradictory to special love of one's country. Does love for the families of others contradict the special love which everyone must have for his own family?

Lastly, *as Catholic Educators,* you must do all you can to make every person a good Christian and to make many of them attempt a direct ascent of the holy mount of God, encouraged and sustained by you as well as by the priest. Jesus wants saints among the children of today. So you must see to it that children look upon Him not only as a beloved friend, but also as a model of every virtue. If it is true, as We firmly believe, that God is preparing a new springtime for His Church, We should like to think that among the little ones—as among adults—He will find an army of souls ready for any call and any heroism. **754**
(26, 45, 88)

Individual formation of children

4. You will achieve this end if you try as hard as possible to deal with your children *individually.* There is a certain amount of education and training which must be given to them in common. This must be done not only for practical reasons, but also and especially because child psycholo- **755**
(46, 84)

not only of youth but of all ages and of all conditions" Pius XI, no. 270, *"it is clear that this task can have no other foundation but those rules of right over which the Church is the divinely appointed Guardian and guide. It is necessary, besides, to recall the very grave obligation which falls on parents to give their children that civic education which it is their right to receive"* (cf. C.I.C., can. 1113, cf. also can. 258); *"this surely forms an integral part of the educative mission of the family and of the Christian school which extends its action." (La Documentation catholique,* October 16, 1955, col. 1292 ff.)

gy finds unquestionably useful the acceptance by all the children together of certain rules and principles of life. There are also times, however, when each child must be regarded individually and when it would be harmful to deal with him as a part of a group. Some children, for example, need encouragement. Others must be restrained. One may need comfort and another reproach or punishment. Remember, God creates souls individually, not in a series in which one soul is the same as another. Created as God's flowers in order to reflect His glory, souls bloom in different ways. This produces the wide variety provided by the sight of the field in which the Divine Gardener labors diligently and lovingly.

756
(84) Be mindful, lastly, to ask *gradually* for what you want to obtain from your children. Except in very unusual cases Jesus wants—and you too must want—the plants entrusted to your care to grow gradually and not hurriedly. Therefore, if you want to raise them to a certain height, if you want to see them flourish and flower to the utmost, you must know how to tend them. If children are allowed to run too much they will stumble and fall. Likewise, placing burdens on their shoulders too heavy for them to carry may slow down their steps, if it does not stop them altogether.

757
(51) We have outlined for you, beloved sons and daughters, some practical suggestions for yourselves in your noble task as educators, which is close to Ours as pastor of all souls. Accept them as you have in the past with filial docility and trust.

758
(16,
54) May the memory of our meeting remain always with you as a vivid proof of the earnestness—We might say jealous earnestness—with which the Holy Church, the common and loving mother of the generations of humanity, regards the education of children. Is it necessary to put into words what is so eloquently expressed and proven by the arduous struggle which the Church carries on almost constantly to

assure you of a sound Christian education? You, too, might be given the honor of meeting such a test, as many valiant Catholic teachers have already met it elsewhere. In such a case the Church will not abandon you, as, We are sure, you would not abandon the Church in the throes of a long struggle—a struggle which, by God's promise, would end in peaceful victory.

Do not be deceived by the claims often made by the enemies of Christian education that they are guardians of culture, freedom or merely of public economy. How unfounded these claims are is shown by the fact that never have culture, true freedom and economy been better protected than when private and public schools are given a chance to develop in conformity with the principles, natural aims and desires of families. **759** *(45, 92, 101, 103)*

It is by divine plan that the activities of the Church are always in happy accord with the right interests of families. This means that the measures taken by the Church in the various fields of public life prove themselves in time to be right, that is to say, in accordance with God's wishes.

Beloved sons and daughters, make yourselves worthy achievers of these divine plans along with the families of the Church.

(Blessing.)

THE WORK OF EDUCATION IN BOARDING SCHOOLS

All. to the Students and Staff of the National Boys' Boarding School of Rome, April 20, 1956.

(Welcome.—The Boarding School, heir to the traditions of the Noble Pontifical Clementine College.—Present prosperity.)

Notwithstanding the fact that it has given good results in the past and is giving them at present, boarding school **760** *(46)* education has been the object of severe criticism, mainly from some of the promulgators of the pedagogical systems who would like to see it all abolished as though it were totally useless. But criticism even if substantiated by this or that defect, does not constitute a sufficient motive for the general condemnation of boarding school in itself.

761
(28,
41,
43,
46)
Undoubtedly, family environment, almost like a nest provided by nature, when assisted by the Church and supplemented by the school, is the most adapted for assuring a good and perfect education; but often the family is hindered from carrying out the task single-handedly, whether by circumstances of locality, work or persons. In these cases the boarding school becomes a providential institution, in the absence of which many young people would be deprived of great benefits.

However, these boarding schools do not exempt the parents from the duties they have towards their children; in fact, it is necessary that the parents exert their influence in the school also, even though they themselves remain out of sight, in order that their children's formation may be completed. Between the education in the family circle, often impeded, and the education offered in the boarding school, necessarily of an imperfect nature, a middle way is found in the semi-boarding school where the boy reaps the advantages of both family and boarding school life.

Advantages of boarding school life

762
(46,
76)
The principal advantages of this are the formation of the spirit to a more austere realization of duty, to the idea of discipline and carefulness, to the habit of coordinating personal occupations and to the sense of responsibility for one's own actions. In the boarding school the young person is taught how to act in society; this is due mainly to the different dealings which he has with his superiors, with his fellow-students and even with his juniors. Healthy competition urges him on to a correct sense of honor and the ac-

ceptance of necessary sacrifice. The attainment of these talents from his earliest years will undoubtedly assist the young man to set out in life. It will sustain him in times of vicissitude and in carrying out the obligations proper to his state.

Drawbacks of boarding school life

The attaining of these results, however, are exposed to risks either by excesses or by defects of method; these, in turn, can lead to an opposite result, and, as a consequence, supply ample motive for judging boarding school education as negative and harmful. Undoubtedly community life, being outside its natural environment and under the surveillance of a rigid rule which makes no distinction between one individual and another, presents its dangers. If the slightest mistake is made, there will be students with anything but a sense of personal responsibility; rather they will be led almost unknowingly by the mechanical nature of activities and actions to a pure formalism in their studies, their discipline and their prayers. **763 (48, 84)**

Strict uniformity tends to suffocate all personal initiative; the secluded life tends to restrict a wide vision of the world; the strict imposition of the rules at times encourages hypocrisy, or it imposes a spiritual level which for one is too low, and for another, unattainable; extreme severity ends in converting the strong characters into rebels and the timid into dejected and closed characters.

Remedies to these drawbacks
Better judgment

These dangers can and must be averted by better judgment, by moderation and by kindness. In the first place it must be known how to identify every single case among the students. So-called mass education, as also class education, is certainly far less tiring but runs the risk of assisting only a few, whereas all have the right to benefit **764 (84)** by it. The students are never alike, whether in intelligence, in character or in other spiritual qualities: this is a law of life. They must, therefore, be considered as single persons, whether it be in assigning them a tenor of life or in correcting and judging them. It is necessary to avoid the stamp of uniformity which calls a few hundred boarders to study, sleep, eat and play in one single building, with one single time schedule and under one single set of rules.

765
(46,
75,
84)
Certainly, with an eye to avoiding this drawback, they can be divided into homogeneous groups in such numbers as not to render things impracticable, so that they may be assisted and followed with paternal attention in their single subjects. But even when they are thus divided into groups—to which it would be helpful to give a schedule, regulations and proportionately varied exercises—and when the normal youth is taking in for himself what he needs for a right formation from the complex of moral and spiritual values offered by the training and the school in the form of good example and good books, it is essential, nevertheless, that each and every pupil feel himself the object of the teacher's special attention, and never must he have the feeling of being lost in the mass, his particular needs, demands and weaknesses overlooked and only his physical presence counting. From such particular concern, the student will derive an incentive for affirming and developing his personal temperament, the spirit of enterprise, the sense of responsibility towards his superiors and his fellow-students, just as he would have had he been living in the bosom of a numerous and well-ordered family.

Discretion and moderation

766
(84)
Moderation is the second characteristic on which boarding school education should be based. The ancient saying, "ne quid nimis," similar to this other one, "in medio stat virtus," ought to inspire the teacher's every act, whether it be in laying down a rule or in demanding its

observance. A profound sense of discretion is needed in determining the length of the periods for study and recreation, the distribution of rewards and punishments, the granting of freedom and the observance of discipline.

Even religious practices ought to be within just measure, so that they do not become an almost insupportable burden and do not fatigue the soul. The deplorable effects of excessive zeal on this point are frequently noticed. Students of boarding schools, even Catholic boarding schools, where moderation is held in little regard, where the tenor of religious practices and duties imposed is perhaps not even suitable for young clerics, on their return home, have been known to neglect the most rudimentary elements of the Catholic faith, such as attendance at Sunday Mass. Undoubtedly youth must be helped and exhorted to pray; but always in such a manner that prayer remains a sweet need of the soul. **767** *(73, 84)*

Gentleness

Thirdly, an air of serene gentleness ought to permeate every boarding school, though not such as to compromise the formation of strong characters. The sense of duty is communicated by means of personal persuasion and by arguments of reason and affection, especially to the younger students who come from wholesome families. A pupil who is certain of the love of his parents and his superiors will not hesitate to respond to their care. To be avoided, therefore, are orders for which no reasonable justification can be given or presumed, corrections that are the result of a personal grudge, punishments that are exclusively vindictive. Gentleness is to be given up only as a last resort, and then only for a short time and in individual cases. It must be present in every decision and must overcome strict and water-tight justice, as the soul of youth is never mature enough to comprehend all the evil, nor is it so tenaciously attached to it as not to know how to take up the good path again when it is pointed out. **768** *(85)*

769
(50)
These requirements of a more general and practical character, and those known to you as formulated by pedagogical methods, provided that they are diligently applied, will not fail to ensure excellent results from your educational labors.

The boarder's duties: a high ideal

770
(46)
Now We would like to direct Our words to the young people who are being educated in schools such as yours, so that they may be better aware of what their families, the Church and society expect of them, and of how they ought to correspond to the many cares showered upon them.

Families do not always resort to the boarding school as a result of the above-mentioned abnormal exigencies; rather some select this kind of education for their children in the deep conviction that they are placing them in more favorable conditions for the reception of a more perfect formation and, if possible, a more complete one. Schools such as yours have as their main end, though not exclusively, the preparation of learned men in all respects, men a cut above mediocrity, in whom religious and civil society can place trust for the future.

771
*(50,
88)*
But how will a school, even if perfect in every aspect, be able to form eminent men if you young people are not the first to yearn to become such? The first step to an excellent education, then, is to keep before your eyes the highest possible level. The intelligent and healthy boy is spontaneously borne along by his youthfulness to propose for himself great and attractive ideals. However it often happens that apathy and laziness develop or external influences conspire to smother these impulses and to reduce to ordinary proportions the urge to excel. It is impossible to imagine a worse beginning on the path of life than the failure even before the trial, the surrender before the battle, the resignation in the face of the adversary.

Unfortunately in our times, there are many youths who are insensible to the attraction of the greatness of wholesome and high ideals, sluggish youths who are content to attend to their little world of personal comforts, and whose ideals, when they have any, are short-lived, of mere surface value and immediate advantage. Admittedly they can grow into good citizens, even useful to society; but what would become of a nation in which not enough youths were ardently aspiring to great and distinguished things? Its future, which demands progress, advancement and development, would remain seriously compromised. So it is that We want you all to open your souls to great aims, and, while justly estimating your own capacities, make bold plans, so that in the immense field of life, you can make valuable contributions to knowledge and art, or to action in a society which eagerly awaits your valuable direction in the future.

Active Collaboration

Undoubtedly one of the special values of boarding school education is that it stimulates souls to know and seek great things, by the existence of noble traditions through spontaneous emulation and the influence of distinguished teachers. However, finding yourselves assembled in such praiseworthy institutions, which do their utmost to impart a complete and excellent education, might lead you to believe that merely the act of living in them passively for a number of years suffices to achieve the ends aimed at—just as it is sufficient to remain on a ship, and worry about nothing else, in order to arrive at a far-distant port. Well, to resolve to attain certain goals in life is only the first of many difficult steps that must be taken. There is no such thing as a magic virtue which mysteriously brings ideals into reality; rather it takes a strong will and the utilization of the entire forces at your disposal. The initial desire must be followed by dedicated labor, which in its turn must be constant, undeterred by difficulties, prepared

772
(46,
50,
76,
87)

for trials and renunciations, for as the ancient saying goes, what costs nothing is worth nothing. Moral benefits cannot be received as presents from others as, for instance, an inheritance; they are to be won by your own personal efforts. Nonetheless, the school can be of real help, according to the extent you collaborate with your teachers. But in what manner will you put your collaboration into action? Above all, by placing your trust in them.

Trust in teachers

773
(51,
87)
    Trust, the result of esteem, consists in the conviction that all that is counselled and taught to you is the result of affection and is meant for your good, even if, at first glance, the motives are not clear. Many lives have been shipwrecked because of the initial refusal to place any trust in parents and teachers; many bitter experiences could have been avoided had more trust been placed in those with greater experience. Place full trust in those over you, those who have taken upon themselves from the hands of Providence the responsibility of your future and who have the necessary talents of mind and heart. Among these the foremost are your parents, whose advice ought never to be placed under discussion, at least until you are sufficiently mature to face everything.

Docility and Obedience

774
(50,
87)
    Trust ought to be accompanied by a certain docility, which consists in putting into practice all advice, in accepting corrections, in complying with the directives given to you with affection. The growing critical spirit of your times will often induce you to doubt this or that rule, while the suggestions of those who are not in the slightest interested in your future will often incite you to brush aside the guiding hand. Then you must bear in mind that maturity of judgment comes with years and in no other way, if you are not to suffer the consequences of thoughtless steps.

Constant Generosity

Let unchanging generosity in dedication to duty be **775** the third virtue of those who desire to become eminent. *(50,* The boy who hesitates to begin, who alternates weeks of *87)* study with weeks of laziness or frivolous occupations will never reach the heights. You now possess a precious treasure: your youth. Its wonderful qualities are a natural aptitude for truth and goodness, an adaptability of spirit, abundant physical energy, complete spiritual faculties and vigorous impulses. Such riches, just as the evangelical talents, will not be always at your disposition. Well, the school, through the fatherly vigilance of the teachers, the wise division of the time schedule, the training in method and precision and the other rules to which the teachers will conform, will help you to obtain the best results from your talents; but the fact will always remain that it is up to you to further this work and to be on the lookout so that they will not be lost.

Boarding school friendships

Further, it is necessary that the young collaborate **776** among themselves in building up their splendid future. *(46,* Although they themselves are often unaware of it, they are *50)* dependent upon each other due to greater natural comprehension. Notwithstanding the work of well-informed teachers, a bad fellow-student can destroy all that they form, while on the other hand, a good companion will strengthen the directives of the master more than he himself can ever hope to do. Just as it is up to each and every one of you to guard against the destructive influence of this or that companion, easily recognizable by the discord between his suggestions and the advice of the teachers, so it is also your duty to exert your influence on the others to their advantage. In this manner, among the fellow-students of the same school, wholesome and deep friendships are formed that neither years nor distances will ever weaken. They will be the dearest and most valued results of those long past school years.

Collaboration between the family and the school

777
(41-
43,
46)
Finally there is a third collaboration which cannot be overstressed and which brings together the school, the students and the families. Above all a perfect concordance of principles and directives is needed between the school and the family, so that the action of one does not destroy that of the other. In particular, the family, as We have already pointed out, does not renounce its own rights nor does it relieve itself of its responsibilities in entrusting a son to the boarding school. It is up to the family to complete, uphold and continue the work of the teachers. Sometimes it will call for greater trust in the student, while at other times, it will entail greater severity or a more diligent interest, or even the sacrifice of sentiment. But above all, it is essential that the young should realize the existence of a perfect understanding between the school and the family.

With this threefold collaboration, to which will be added that higher, more efficacious and intimate one which religion exercises by means of its ministers, it can be reasonably hoped that the high ideals proposed by the young, encouraged by the family and pursued by the school, will one day become a joyful reality.

The need to grow in age, wisdom and grace

778
(72,
80,
87,
88)
As regards your practical conduct, beloved sons of the National Boarding School of Rome, We would like to remind you of the first rules of the "Pontifical Noble Clementine College" which specially recommend three things: piety, obedience and study. After the passage of three centuries, We could not give better rules for carrying out your collaboration with the teachers. Be devout in the joy and

in the purity of your heart, convinced that the faith is the solid foundation of life. Be obedient, not merely compelled by fear but rather convinced of the good intentions of your superiors, those who love you. Be attentive to your study; study with method and assiduousness, not merely to enrich your minds, but also to fulfill the common obligation of work.

To this We would like to add a special duty, peculiar to your age, whose character lies essentially in growing. As each new day finds the young better equipped physically, so ought it also to find the young more advanced in study and virtue. The highest praise which the Holy Gospel bestows on the Child Jesus, lies in the statement that, "And so Jesus advanced in wisdom with the years, and in favor both with God and with men." (a) Make the divine Companion your model, not only for unceasing growth in wisdom and grace, but also for the comfort your conduct will give to those who look on you as their most valuable treasures in this world: your parents and your teachers.

(Greetings and Apostolic Blessing.)

INTERIOR LIFE AND EDUCATION

All. to the members of the General Chapter of the Brothers of the Christian Schools, May 23, 1956.

(Words of welcome to the members of the Chapter.)

You know, O Beloved Sons, how much We admire your religious family, not only in view of the incomparable successes it has achieved in the field of education throughout the world and in the training of future workmen, but especially for the fruits of sanctity it has produced over three centuries and will continue to produce if, in the future, you remain faithful to the spirit of your holy founder. **779** *(54, 57*

778a Lk. 2:52.

The total dedication of yourselves in loving abnegation, in profound fidelity to the Rule, in a conscientious and intelligent application to the duties of your state ought to be the axis of your religious life, because it is from your interior life that the spiritual fruit of your work depends.

Never get the impression that you fall short in charity in reserving for God and for your soul's good the entire period set aside by the Rule for private and community prayer. Such a sign of humility and confidence will ensure yourselves and your pupils the grace of light and strength from the Divine Master of your soul, which is more necessary today than ever in the task of Christian education. In this manner you will continue to maintain that position which the Church has assigned to you, namely to form without interruption new generations of Christians proud of their faith and well prepared to carry out all their family and social duties in society.

(*Apostolic Blessing.*)

THE FIRST LESSON IS ONE OF EXAMPLE

All. to the Primary School Supervisors of Spain, July 3, 1956.

(*Welcome.—Teachers and pupils.*)

780
(4,
5,
69,
71)
Give them a degree of learning that is in proportion to their young age; prepare them for the later phases of their education; inspire them with a holy love for the family and the nation. But, above all else, form them with a religious and moral training that is healthy, solid, clear and well founded, a formation that will produce good sons of the family, good citizens of the nation and good members of the Church. Give them this formation, as our hopes depend on them.

781
(4,
51,
You are obliged to be honest men, exemplary Catholics and perfect members of your profession. Without doubt, you consider your entire lives as a response to the

special calling by the Lord; but if you are to realize your
ideal, "To God through the profession," We say that these
three characteristics ought to be summed up in one, since
the man, the Catholic and the member of the profession are
not three separate entities: they form only one person, a
person able to teach first and most of all by example rather
than by words. And when We look to the future of the
beloved Spanish Nation, We must sincerely confess that
We visualize it as placed in your hands, and that We experience a singular satisfaction in knowing that today almost
the entire body of Supervisors belong to your Association.

(Album.—Review.—The Spanish College.)

54,
83)

Beloved Sons, continue along the path you have
chosen, well assured that Our affection and Our constant
interest accompanies you. As your prayer says, ask for firm
faith, burning charity, Christian fortitude, unshakeable
constancy and unalterable patience. May the truth always
be on your lips, love in your actions, and your whole lives
a shining example. It is only thus that you will be worthy
of the position you occupy and of the graces that Our Lord
is continually showering upon you.

(Apostolic Blessing.)

782
(54,
83)

TIMELY EDUCATION

All. to the members of the General Chapter of the Congregation of the Holy Cross, July 19, 1956.

(Greetings.)

Your schools will do more than set an example of
scholarship. Youth has need not only of a sane and sound
culture, but it must develop a calm and well-balanced
judgment, capable of discerning between truth and error,
good and evil, justice and the opposite. Firmly grounded

783
(60,
63,
72,
88)

in convictions planted by faith and reason, they must be strong enough not to be carried away by false illusions of violent passion or a fickle public opinion that measures everything by the rule of immediate, apparent success. Such youth the Church reasonably expects to see leaving with sure step the portals of your schools. The supernatural truths of Christ's teaching and example have become the background of their thoughts and conduct, and you may confidently look forward to their being a joy to His Spouse, the Church, and an asset to society.

784
(69,
75,
76)
Now the task of molding youth must begin early; rather, it cannot begin early enough. Consequently one understands the immense importance of the work done in the Secondary Schools, where the adolescent, entering on a period of transition and powerful emotions, senses perhaps for the first time the smoke of battle, glimpses the glory of victory, and has no intention of stooping to compromises. He is in dire need, however, of a conscience that reflects the truth steadily and clearly, and a will of steel.

(Missionary work of the Congregation.—Blessing.)

THE TEACHER CANNOT BE NEUTRAL

All. to the Catholic School Teachers of Bavaria, December 31, 1956.

(Welcome.)

785
(21,
22)
It is an obvious principle, not only in all truly democratic States, but also in all lawfully constituted States, that the more the school is dependent upon the State, the more the State must carefully consider the wishes of those who are concerned with education. In your country, regarding the education given all children, that is, elementary education, not only is the law of obligatory attendance in force, ruled by the State, but also an obligatory school law— the system of maximum dependence of schools on the State.

Consequently, it is indeed the duty of the State in regard to its school system to respect conscientiously the expectations and the will of those who have rights in education, as to the educational system itself and in particular the training of teachers.

In applying this principle to Catholic students, the State must fulfill its duty in such a way that between the Catholic home and the school, between Catholic parents and the teachers of their children, there is a warm atmosphere of understanding, mutual confidence and cooperation. The State must be conscientious about the most important and profound question, the question of religion, so that parents and teachers have the same thoughts, the same convictions and the same faith. **786 (22, 42, 46)**

The fundamental importance of the training of teachers for this basic problem is clear and We have no reason to press it further. The teacher is the soul of the school. It is he who gives it spirit. **787 (48, 50, 62, 80,**

The school, giving instruction day after day throughout the year, acts like a force of nature, slowly but constantly, almost imperceptibly, and therefore most profoundly. It should not be said that teachers must set aside their personal convictions while they teach. That would be asking the impossible even for teachers said to be neutral, and even more so for teachers with strong convictions. It would offend the elementary rights of man to compel parents by law to send their children to schools where the teachers are indifferent, negative or even hostile to the religious and moral convictions of the parents. **102, 106, 116)**

Catholic education is the most complete

Probably no other institution has as broad an experience as the Catholic Church with ideological influence upon young people in schools. She has gathered experiences from all parts of the world, and the conclusion reached **788 (15, 19, 50,**

69,
92,
101)   may be stated in these terms: prescinding from lay schools, in all other mixed religion or "neutral" schools, the Catholic Church suffers the most. This is so for the simple reason that its religious faith is by far the richest and most complete. Therefore it is understandable that the Church will fight to the end for Catholic schools and the Catholic training of teachers in such a way as to assure the existence and well-being of Catholic families and their children.

789
(92)   The objection cannot be raised that the school should also give solid training in citizenship to young people—as if the Church has not done this and will not continue to do so! The Church fully recognizes this necessity. As far as this is concerned, We believe that the Catholic schools can proudly hold their heads high before whatever State authority there may be. Look at your own country! Since 1914 it has had to face the worst trials and catastrophies. Did Catholics fail to do their duty? On the contrary, did they not, precisely in the most crucial moments, produce men of great worth who rendered precious services to their country, their fellow countrymen and the common good?

(*Blessing.*)

THE PROTECTION OF CHILDREN

R.M. for the "Mothers' and Children's Day," promoted in Italy by the National Council for the Protection of Maternity and Infancy, January 6, 1957.

(*Mary Most Holy, model for all mothers.—Congratulations in that the National Council for the Protection of Maternity and Infancy aims at recalling adults to their duties towards children.*)

790
(96)   While recognizing the great number of Christian families in which the child is the object of the most tender and constant care, Our heart is moved with sincere compassion and profound affection when Our thoughts turn

towards the numerous children whom poverty, sickness, the war or other sorrowful events have deprived of the normal means of formation: children who are orphans, morally or totally abandoned, whom life has snatched very early into its violent whirl and has plunged into the most bitter sufferings. There are already too many whom unknown events wound in body and soul, but how many others are the innocent victims of sins not their own, of material and moral miseries resulting from the very social environment in which they live!

The family environment

In what way can such sad conditions be bettered? Who should be the first to prevent a renewal of the bitter weeping of mothers which, in the very mystery of the Epiphany, cast a shadow over the serenity of Christ's infancy? First of all, beyond any doubt, the parents. Yet, how many couples, on the day of their marriage, have at the most a very vague idea of the duties which they will later have to perform as educators, and of the demands this task imposes! The child who enters this world ought to have a family circle to welcome him which is capable of providing him with all that he will need to keep healthy, to develop and gain control of his mind, will and heart, so that he may be able in time to take his place in society.

791
(28,
30,
96)

Modern psychology and pedagogy show quite clearly the importance of the education received in infancy; that which then forms the child is not a more or less systematic teaching by words, but, above all, the homey atmosphere, the presence and behavior of the parents, the brothers and sisters, as well as that of the neighbors, the course of daily life with all that the child sees, understands and experiences. Each of these elements, perhaps minor in itself and apparently unnoticed, nonetheless leaves its mark on him, and bit by bit determines the fundamental attitudes that he will adopt in life: trust in the persons he has about him,

792
(32,
80,
96)

frankness, docility, the spirit of enterprise and of discipline, respect for authority or, on the contrary, selfish individualism, insubordination and rebellion. The gentle but constant action of the wholesome family, united and well-founded, regulates the natural instincts, directs them in a definite manner, coordinates them and thus shapes well-integrated personalities, fully developed both individually and socially. Lack of balance in the family, on the other hand, has its repercussions on the children leaving them unstable, victims of dissensions and shocks, incapable of forming any real accord between innate tendencies and the moral ideal.

Homes incapable of carrying out their educational function

793
(29,
96,
97)
    If some homes present more or less notable imperfections, inherent in every human work, others, unfortunately, have such upheavals as to render them really unfit to fulfill their educational function. Without speaking of those children born out of wedlock, who give rise to particular problems, it must be pointed out that present social conditions face parents with serious handicaps, and, at times, with the practical impossibility of assuring the essential material and social needs of their young. We are thinking of the families of emigrants and refugees; of those in which fathers are unemployed or receive insufficient wages; of those wherein mothers are forced to leave the home regularly to go to work; of those whose dwellings are inadequate in size, unhealthy or lacking in privacy; of those increasingly invaded by means for spreading ideas, useful perhaps to mature and prudent people, but disastrous to the simple minds of children, and tending, because of the wickedness of interested parties, to uproot the influence of the father and mother. Even in the most favorable cases an evil that too often today must be lamented is the thoughtless conduct

of parents, who, without a reasonable motive, refuse to exercise personally their mission as educators.

The duties of parents

We would like to exhort fathers and mothers to realize the importance of their calling and to use their authority effectively, to teach the child with wisdom and moderation, to dominate his instinctive tendencies, to stimulate his good will, to awaken his intellect and affection and to transmit to him the precious inheritance of the most beautiful and elevated traditions of human and Christian culture. How many special joys can be enjoyed by parents in their attention to education, parents who do not consider the child as a burden or an amusement and are deeply moved by their task! The worries and sufferings which education exacts are largely compensated for by the stupendous wonders offered by the physical and spiritual progress of the child.

794
*(31,
40,
53,
63,
71,
76)*

The responsibility of all the members of the community

But the duty of protecting infants does not belong exclusively to the parents, but rather in due proportion, to the entire community. Ought not every adult—man or woman—contemplating the shining faces of children who are advancing trustingly along the path of life, examine himself and ask himself whether by word, or by action, by thought or by desire of the soul, he is not a cause of disturbance or of deviation for the young entrusted to his responsibility or for those whom he meets daily in the streets? Even though he has not the slightest intention of causing evil, his example has far-reaching effects; wide-open, iniquisitive eyes follow and observe him. Does he sometimes consider what scenes, what impressions hold the attention of those highly receptive little beings, who are sensitive to whatever is about them, and suffer, almost

795
*(39,
111)*

defencelessly, the influence of everything which presents itself to them, good or bad? How much better the world would become if the thought of not wounding young souls occupied men's minds more often!

Means to be adopted

796
(89,
96,
97,
113)
The absolute protection of the child demands further that the specialized aids—medical consultations, orhanages, boys' towns, settlement houses, reformatories—look more specifically to the treatment and care of cases in which the family has gravely failed in its natural function as regards physical, intellectual and moral training. Those children, deprived of material support, and even more, of all affection of which this age is gravely in need, and abandoned to their fate, would become too easily not only useless elements but often even dangerous ones, thus adding to the number of delinquents. Therefore, with great satisfaction, We see developing generous enterprises, both public and private, aimed at promoting and assisting institutions established for the protection of children and youth. In particular, We are well acquainted with the work done by the "National Organization for Maternity and Infancy," which is connected with the "International Union," and by means of the "Medical Consultors for Child and Maternal Care" and "Infant Homes" has offered outstanding assistance and service to more than 770,000 children. The progressive action which is its distinguishing mark is aimed epsecially at combatting the causes of mortality among mothers and children and at contributing in many ways to the consolidation of the family as a society wherever the family does not conform fully to its mission. Those who dedicate themselves to these or similar works well deserve the encouragement and support ᵒf all, as the responsibility and duty of coming to the assi⸱   ce of those children who have been left helpless in unfortunate circumstances rests on human society as a whole.

As modern technical progress in every field calls for more suitable and better adapted persons and as social and political evolution renders more essential the active participation of citizens in order that institutions may be better run, child education demands a more prolonged and strenuous effort and more burdensome means. But this is not a reason for withdrawing from such a vast undertaking. Social unrest is the cause of disturbances; by means of far-reaching and well-organized collaboration, it must be kept from dissipating the nation's greatest treasure, the strength of its youth. Youth must not, through the negligence or indifference of the responsible bodies, swell the ranks of those who are unskilled in any qualified trade and lack the power to perfect themselves, morally or culturally.

797 (4, 31, 111)

Beloved sons and daughters! These Our thoughts We desired to express to you on this day of Christian solemnity, with the intention of enabling you to participate in the anxieties of Our heart for the future of the Church and civil society. Each one of you, but especially parents, must consider it a personal duty to ensure that the nation has more vigorous energy, and is healthier and more aware of the true sense of human brotherhood and of the superior ends it pursues.

(Glance at the Child of Bethlehem.—Prayer to the Divine Infant.)

EDUCATIONAL TRADITIONS OF THE "COLLEGIO ROMANO"

All. to present and past students of the Ennio Quirino Visconti High School and College, of Rome, February 28, 1957.

(The E. Q. Visconti High School and College has, in part, inherited the glories of the "Collegio Romano.")

798
(82)
It has been rightly said that one of the chief characteristics of Romans—almost the secret of the perennial greatness of the Eternal City—is respect for traditions. Such
respect does not mean fossilization in forms that are now
outmoded, but keeping alive that which centuries have
proved to be good and fruitful. Tradition understood in
that sense is not in the least an obstacle to sound progress.
It is rather a powerful stimulus to keep us on the right path
and at the same time to restrain the adventurous spirit that
wants to embrace every new thing rashly and without dis-
crimination. Tradition is, furthermore, as has often been
said, a safeguard against decay. How then can the tradition
of the "Collegio Romano" still guide you in your present
course, and strengthen modern methods which, with new
ideas, have as their goal the thorough intellectual and moral training of youth? As a kind of partial payment of the
debt We owe the beloved Visconti School, We wish to set
forth three features of the ancient "Collegio Romano"
which, if preserved with honor, will ensure the new plant
the benefits of the original tree.

An ardent love of study

799
(63,
87)
1.—First of all, an ardent love of study common to
both teachers and pupils was the constant tradition of the
"Collegio Romano." Regard for culture as an incomparable
human value reached such a high degree in the "Collegio
Romano" that it became known throughout Europe. Less
than ten years after the foundation of the College, Our Predecessor, Pope Pius IV, referred to it in a note to the King
of Spain, calling his attention to it and asking his protection
for it as the "nursery of other colleges which are spreading
both in Italy and elsewhere, even in Germany and France."
For three centuries, each sovereign, prince or eminent person who came to Rome wished to visit the College and
spend some time with its famous teachers and its select
students. Students at the College learned to appreciate

knowledge above other human values, and as a primary factor of spiritual perfection. What a wise precept for young people who, although studying much, might mistrust the usefulness of studies and apply themselves in a superficial way, without making any of the sacrifices or renunciations which the conquest of knowledge demands in exchange! One certainly could not reproach a young man for desiring an education also in order to follow a profession or obtain a position sufficient to provide the necessities of life. But it would be unfitting to aim at this without serious and adequate preparation. Such preparation can be achieved only through application to study almost for the sake of study alone, apart from any immediate interest. Therefore, encourage in and around yourselves an ever increasing love of study, mindful that a society in which there is a decline in appreciation of culture is doomed to lose its other blessings.

Harmony between culture and life

2.—A second feature of the "Collegio Romano" and its educational system was the fostering of a perfect harmony between culture and life. First of all, religion, which was not separated from education, guided and upheld the training of minds, from the sovereign position rightly attributed to it. Upright behavior and civic virtues were cultivated with the greatest care, since they were believed to be of absolute value to learning. There was no doubt then, as there should be no doubt today, that religion, uprightness and learning are the fundamentals of a perfect education. In fact, they are the very basis of the harmony of life itself. To achieve this harmony, the educators of the Roman College made use of classical subjects, especially of philosophy. In addition to the immediate aim of educating minds to appreciate beauty and to search for truth, the Roman College aimed at educating minds to orderliness and stead-

800
(62, 64-66, 69, 70, 72, 74)

fastness. All its graduates were distinguished by their mental balance and by their devotion to the service of truth.

801
(67,
69)
How wonderful it would be if modern methods of teaching were to keep to the same lines! Then much happy inspiration could be had from young people—energetic, talented, rich in many kinds of learning, yet capable of making a clear synthesis of such knowledge; youths neither hesitant and doubtful nor tottering on the shifting sands of uncertainty; youths with sound ideas, clear vision, without confusion or suspicion, who do not permit their love of research to die, or the innermost foundations of certainty, the most elementary truths, to be undermined.

"Good understanding" between teacher and student

802
(84,
85,
87)
3.—The third characteristic of the "Collegio Romano" worthy of attention was the mutual understanding between teachers and students. In the classrooms of the College, the faculty was not considered as a practically inaccessible stronghold of authority, the cold source of lessons. The classroom was, rather, a proper meeting-point for a loving teacher and a youth eager to share in his knowledge. In Our youth, We Ourselves witnessed this unity between teachers and students. Even today We feel that the affection that linked us with distinguished teachers whom We particularly admired is still strong and unchanged. There is no doubt that mutual esteem and faith strengthen education more than any other method. They convert the school into another family, where respectful love successfully replaces severity, removes the need for corrective discipline, and eases the task of both teachers and students.

(Good wishes for the realization of this ideal.)

STUDY IS A DUTY

All. to Students of State Secondary Schools in Rome, March 24, 1957.

(Welcome.—Spiritual preparation for the Papal audience.—The presence of Catholics in Roman scholastic circles.)

Since We follow your affairs with paternal anxiety, We are not, on the other hand, unaware of some of the bewilderment and mistrust that you feel. These feelings have their origin in the consideration of the great scientific progress and consequent technical development as compared with the grief that afflicts many over what is happening today and what may yet happen tomorrow. Your mistrust touches upon a little of everything, and does not even spare the school. Either the teachers sometimes may not fulfill your expectations, or the curricula may seem out of date to you, while often everything appears to be no longer adapted to the new requirements and new trends.

Those, such as your teachers and especially your priests, who can penetrate beneath your outward appearances, easily discover the reason for this impatience and uneasiness. You are discontented with the way the world is going and you want a reconstruction. If it is true that many young people are still vague and uncertain and groan about the uselessness of every attempt at rebirth and recovery it is equally true that others—many others—are full of confident hope.

You are among the latter, dear children. Indeed, one cannot say that you represent "wasted" youth. It would be better to say that you are burning, flaming youth, ready to light and keep aflame the fire that Jesus came to bring upon earth. But, in order that your intentions may be more than mere words, it is necessary that from now on you do not neglect anything that your state of life demands of you. And herein lies your duty to study, to study seriously in an organized and complete manner. Here we come to the search for truth, the effort to possess it, and, finally, the will to put it into practice with deeds.

1. *Study the truth*

804
(2,
87,
92)

Your young intellects are open to life, eager to know, and nature is spread before you with her marvels and her mysteries. The problems of existence, human events, your aspirations, the goal to aim for, the roads to follow, the means to use,—everything is a query. Everything demands clear light and a definite answer. Study, therefore. Apply yourselves to your studies, expend every effort and do not pass over anything that your teachers and your curricula offer you. Being indifferent and lazy would mean betraying yourselves and renouncing a complete and harmonious development of yourselves. You would also be betraying your parents, who have probably made great sacrifices and have gone without many things in order to keep you at school. You would deprive your native land and the world of a necessary number of capable men, men of science and of the arts, experts in politics, economics and law.

2. *Study seriously*

805
(63,
64)

a) To this end take care before everything else not to assess the importance of studies by the criterion of immediate usefulness. You do not yet know what life has in store for you, nor do you yet know how your career will develop.

It is a well-known fact that future Masters of ships and Naval Officers are first taught how to handle sails. No one would imagine, at first, that this could be necessary for the solution of complicated problems about the course of an ocean liner and the gunfire of a battleship. But if you ask experts why future navigators must learn how to sail a boat and perfect themselves in that art, they will answer that it is in that way that sailors more easily acquire that sixth sense which is appropriately called "sea sense."

The application of this to your case seems natural and easy to Us. Every time you open a book, every time a lesson begins or an examination takes place, you should not ask yourselves: What use is this to me? Do not say: I shall be an engineer, what use is philosophy to me? I shall be a lawyer, of what use is physics? I shall be a doctor, why study art? The truth of the matter is that certain ideas and certain information, certain habits of thought, a certain mental discipline, the sense of measure and intellectual harmony—in short, a wide and deep training in fundamentals—help in life and are often useful in an unanticipated and unhoped-for way. This is also generally true of Latin and history.

b) In order to study seriously, you must guard against the belief that the amount of knowledge acquired is the fundamental element on which to build the edifice of your future culture. There is no need to know too many things, but only to learn what is necessary and suitable, and to learn it well, to understand it properly and study it thoroughly and intensely. It is therefore necessary to avoid compelling yourselves to make an almost superhuman effort and to run breathlessly after everything that learning has enshrined and tries to bring to the student's desk. This is all the more true if one is thinking of methods of learning which are pure memory aids. These methods are a far cry from serious and pleasure-giving study, from a real and profound cultural formation, and because of them, some schools are running the risk of involving themselves in a drama which saddens parents and irritates the students. **806** *(63)*

807 *(63)*

c) But there is a third error which students must avoid falling into, with the help of conscientious teachers and those who are in charge of arranging their curricula.

Those who are aware of the problems of the schools know that there is nothing more harmful than a mass of ideas accumulated in a confused and disorderly way— ideas which neither meet nor integrate, and which, rather, often clash and cancel one another out. Frequently the teaching and study of scientific matters is completely divorced from the total training of the intellect. The intellect should constantly increase its capacity for synthesis and profound research through serious philosophical studies. Science and philosophy must therefore complement one another, coming together in those places where the study deals with the most profound and hidden structures of matter and where the greatest harmony must be achieved or discovered.

808
(69)   The teaching and study of religion is sometimes passed over by some students, or looked upon with distrust and suspicion by the teachers of other subjects, who might not refrain from witticisms and insinuations. And, just as they once resorted to the certainties and lights of science to deride the doubts and shadows of philosophy, so do they today compare the "reasonableness" of certain philosophical ideas with the "indefensibility" of mysteries. Anyone can imagine the chaos that derives from such a method of teaching and studying. Unfortunately, your delicate and unprepared young minds know it.

809
(64,   Much better results would be obtained if the teach-
67)   ing of all subjects were conducted in a perfectly systematic and organic manner. As a matter of fact, the "corpus doctrinae" obeys, in much the same way, the laws of every living body. A living body develops as the result of the interior development of its members, which in turn find nourishment for their own life from the whole body. The interior impoverishment of some members or their inordinate growth creates in the rest of the "corpus" a loss of vitality, weakness, and thus ineffectiveness of action. The

same thing happens in the various branches of human knowledge. An inordinate growth would be of no use to the cultural whole, just as a lack of distinction between that which is fundamental and essential and that which is only accessory would be harmful.

The much-hoped-for organic unity of culture will be achieved when the "corpus doctrinae" has Christ as its head. "I am...the truth," He one day exclaimed. (a) When you study nature remember that "All things were made by Him and without Him was made nothing that was made." (b) When you learn history remember that it is not a simple enumeration of more or less bloody or edifying facts, for one can easily see in it a structure which should be studied in the light of universal Divine Providence and the undeniable freedom of man's actions. You will particularly note how you would see the events of the past two thousand years with different eyes if you were to consider them as the development of Christian civilization, starting with those events which marked the dawn of the Church, dwelling upon the great and unsurpassed syntheses made in ancient and medieval times, giving some thought to the painful apostasies but also to the great conquests of modern times, and looking with confidence at the many signs of rebirth and recovery.

3. The need for complete studies

But in order that this organic culture may be possible, **810** it is necessary that your studies be complete. **(65)**

(a) First in the order of precedence comes the natural world which presents itself to you, impresses itself on your senses and arouses your curiosity. It is necessary that nature should have a powerful attraction for the youth of the modern generation. Lift your gaze to the mysterious depths of the nebulae and the clusters of stars scattered

809a John 14:6.
809b John 1:3.

throughout the immense universe. Stop and contemplate the marvels of your man-ruled planet. Penetrate into the deepest structures of the atom and its nucleus. In order to read the stupendous book of nature, you must take science as an interpreter, interesting yourselves in its problems, its solutions, its hypotheses and its mysteries themselves. While small, presumptuous minds are satisfied with the few notions they have learned, you will notice that the disproportion between what you know and what you would like to know is always growing. If your teachers—to whom We turn Our affectionate and grateful thoughts—know how to guide you in reading this book, in this study, you will be greatly astonished at the ease with which one can discover in every creature the Creator Who is glorified by this knowledge and fills your heart with happiness in recompense.

811
(66,
75)
(b) From the experimental sciences, move on to the truths of philosophy, which is the basis of all knowledge. We know well that often such a noble and necessary study is confined, unfortunately, to an enumeration of errors coming from agitated minds and disordered hearts. Such a study is certainly harmful to students, as is clearly shown by the ever stronger and more distressed complaints of parents who are justly concerned about the things that their children are taught. We do not understand why one who sows the seeds of scepticism in the unprepared minds of the young should be called a "teacher." Freedom of the intellect consists in the possibility of penetrating always more deeply into this or that truth, of considering one aspect of it rather than another, and of making deductions and syntheses of major or minor importance. It is, therefore, an entirely positive freedom, and the more it is enlightened and protected against error, the greater it is.

812
(66)
It is, therefore, necessary to have a knowledge of the history of philosophical thought, but it is even more neces-

sary to insist on the study of reality in all its aspects and its elements. Each one of you will have to be able to answer with precision and clarity the questions which you will inevitably ask yourselves or will be asked by others: What is reality in general? What specifically is the world? What validity does human knowledge have? Does God exist? What is His nature and what are His attributes? What are the relations between Him and the world? Between Him and men? What is the meaning of life? And of death? What is the nature of joy, and what is the function of pleasure? With what criteria must human society, the family and civil society be ruled?

In order that these questions may be given adequate answers, it is necessary to appeal to the everlasting philosophy which was elaborated by the great intellects throughout the past centuries. It has lost none of its objective value and its didactic effectiveness, all the more so since the development of scientific knowledge is not in contrast with the definite theses of that philosophy.

(c) From philosophy, move on to the science which derives its knowledge from the doctrines of the faith, learned through Divine Revelation.   813 (69)

All Christians, but especially those dedicated to study, should have a religious education as profound and as organic as possible. As a matter of fact, it would be dangerous to develop all other forms of knowledge and leave the religious heritage unchanged from the first days of childhood. Incomplete and superficial, it would necessarily be suffocated and probably destroyed by non-religious culture and the experience of adult life, as is proved by the fact that the faith of many was shipwrecked by doubts left unclarified and by problems left unsolved. Inasmuch as it is necessary for the foundation of your faith to be rational, a sufficient study of apologetics is indispensable. Afterwards you should sample the beauties of dogmatic theology and the harmonies of moral theology. Finally, try to include Christian ascetics in your studies and press on, on, beyond to the high planes of mystical theology. Oh, if you could see Christianity in all its greatness and splendor!

814
(72,
88)
One last word, beloved children. Let truth, known and possessed, become your rule of life and action. Free yourselves thereby from passions and prejudices. Grow in Christ through truth. "Rather are we to practice the truth in love, and so grow up in all things in Him Who is the head, Christ." (a)

A call to rebirth and a cry for recovery sounds throughout the world: it will be a Christian recovery. As We said in the beginning, you want a new structure to arise from the ruins heaped up by those who preferred error to truth. The world will have to be rebuilt in Jesus.

Let those who dream of non-existent decay, and foresee impossible downfalls of the Church, look back into history, reflect on the present, and foresee—for it is not impossible to do so—the future. Let them remember what happened to those who tried to destroy the Handmaid of Christ and see what is happening to those who are obstinate in their insane designs. Those who go against the Church will smash themselves against the rock on which Christ, her Divine Founder, wished her built.

Young people! do you want to cooperate in the gigantic enterprise of reconstruction? The victory will be Christ's. Do you want to fight with Him? To suffer with Him?

Do not, then, be weak and lazy. Rather, be inflamed and ardent youths. Enkindle the fire which Jesus came to bring into the world and make it blaze up!

814a Eph. 4:15.

INFLUENCE OF PRIMARY EDUCATION

All. to a Pilgrimage of Catholic Teachers from Spain, July 18, 1957.

(Welcome.)

1) First of all, in a society in the process of a complete change, such as the present one, keep intact the high ideal of your divine mission because: **815** *(31, 80)*

a) your mission is and always will be a vital necessity since the formation and primary education of children is the foundation for all future social changes;

b) your mission is the natural basis of all that is to follow, since it provides early impressions and guidance the influence of which can never be overlooked, but must rather be regarded as something definitive;

c) although the field of culture is always expanding, it is certain that in some of its forms and to some degree it will never be available to all, whereas the primary elements of learning necessarily reach the whole of society, and can thus make an ever more definite impression on it.

Duty to mold souls

2) However, for your mission to attain full efficiency, you must have a clear concept of it, always remembering that: **816** *(2, 46, 47, 71, 92)*

a) your mission as teachers cannot be reduced simply to a means of imparting knowledge which is more or less profound and broad; you should be, above all, educators of the spirit, and, in due proportion, molders of the souls of your pupils;

b) your work cannot be regarded as simply an individual responsibility, but as a social function, in full accord with the family and with other legitimate authorities, sharing views and teaching aids with them, and required mutual respect—all with a common purpose: the good of society;

c) your vocation can be said to transcend the merely human and earthly; it makes you cooperators with the priest and with Christ's Church in that training of souls to which you can contribute so substantially but which you could also, unfortunately, impede.

Necessity of a profound spiritual life

817
(*81,*
83)
3) Finally, the satisfactory fulfillment of such important duties will require on your part:

a) assiduous dedication to your work, shunning no sacrifice and putting aside personal gain;

b) exemplary conduct, so that your little ones, who will watch you closely, will learn more from your deeds than from your fine words—especially from your upright living, your self-abnegation, your patience, and your sincere piety;

c) continual contact with the Lord, especially through prayer and frequent reception of the Sacraments, because in such a sublime and delicate work as the primary education of children, the principal part is reserved to the grace which descends from above.

(Blessing.)

THE CHALLENGE TO CHRISTIAN EDUCATION

Letter to the Third International Congress of the World Union of Catholic Teachers, August 5, 1957.

818
(*111)*
Beloved sons and daughters of the World Union of Catholic Teachers! At the invitation of the Catholic teachers of Austria, you are about to hold your third world congress in Vienna. Indeed the idea of a world organization of Catholic teachers rose among Catholic educators of

Austria, and the World Union of Catholic Teachers was founded in Vienna during the Eucharistic Congress of 1912 The time of troubles and storms which Austria underwent thereafter also affected the Union. But after 1945 the idea animating that World Union revived all the stronger. The Holy Year of 1950 brought the founding of your Union, which took up its seat at the center of the Church, very close to Us. We are pleased with the youthful vigor and growth of the Union. It began with ten unions of teachers; today it already numbers forty unions all over the world. It has 320,000 members, all united in an outlook and a program which Our immediate Predecessor of happy memory, Pius XI, established as the ideal of Catholic education in his encyclical *Divini illius Magistri*. It is with some satisfaction that We infer the prestige of your Union also from the fact that it has been included by UNESCO among its advisory bodies. The Catholic teachers of Austria, charged with the preparation of this year's world Congress, have asked Us to give it Our blessing. We are happy to comply with this request; but We think We owe it to the importance of your profession and of your Union to speak first a few words of counsel.

Education in the era of technology

During the last hundred years and more the Church has striven to give her youth a Catholic upbringing and schooling. Wherever constitutions and laws allowed Catholics to form their own schools by their spiritual and financial strength, they made truly heroic sacrifices to attain this goal. **819** *(16, 117)*

But, in the meantime, mankind has entered the age of technology. Technology is beginning to change the psychic structure of man, but it must not be permitted to change the Catholic ideal of education. Teachers have pointed out correctly that moral and religious education is now of even **820** *(60, 67, 70)*

greater importance than professional education and com-
munication of knowledge; for modern advances make for
excessive activism, for a tendency to adapt oneself without
responsibility or resistance, and for an undue receptiveness
to sense-impressions that is accompanied by a crippling of
reflective thought. It is man in the age of technology who
stands most in need of that consistent and uniform education based on absolute truth and on God as the center of
existence, an education which only Christian faith and the
Catholic Church can provide. We must, therefore, continue
our traditional ideal of education in these new times.

The Catholic teacher

821
(50,
52,
83)
The Church likewise adheres in these new times to the
ideal of the Catholic teacher. The teacher is the soul of a
school. For this reason the Church is as interested in the
character of the teacher and in his formation as it is in the
Catholic school itself. A genuinely Catholic teacher is the
essential requirement for a Catholic school. It does not
matter whether the professional work of Catholic teachers,
men or women, belongs to the lay apostolate in the strict
sense of the word. For you may rest assured, beloved sons
and daughters, that a Catholic teacher who stands at the
peak of his profession in expertness, training, and devotion,
who is deeply convinced of his Catholic faith and practices
it as his second nature before the youth entrusted to him,
serves Christ and His Church as well as he would in the
highest form of the lay apostolate. This is true of the
Catholic teacher at a Catholic school and almost more so
at a non-Catholic school.

822
(4,
21,
56,
66,
"The work of the Catholic teacher in international
life" is the theme of your congress. Surely you will have
much to discuss. We would like to touch only briefly on a
few great questions and tasks confronting Catholic education today. In view of the deadly dangers which the

Catholic Church sees threatening her in Latin America, it   79)
is necessary that the number of teachers there be greatly
increased and a thorough professional education be given
them; that the Catholic spirit and the quality of those higher Catholic schools from which priestly vocations are
expected, and which are charged with the formation of
devout young Catholics for the other professions, be im-
proved and perfected. As for Catholic upbringing and
schooling in Asia, the First Asian Congress in the Lay
Apostolate at Manila (and similarly the first meeting of
leaders in the lay apostolate at Kisubi [Uganda] for Africa)
developed valuable policies and programs: the professional
formation of Catholic teachers who can serve as examples;
schools for girls and the education of women; the relation
of the Catholic teacher to ecclesiastical authority, and—in
the case of Africa—relations with native governmental
authorities; the attitude of the Catholic teacher toward
neutral, governmentally created unions where they are the
only unions permitted. At Kisubi the following healthy
principle was laid down, which is in entire harmony with
the principle of subsidiarity: the state should leave the
family and the Catholic mission-school alone as long as
they do not need its protection and assistance; the school,
in its turn, should develop good citizens.

International Christian sentiment

In Our Christmas message of December 24, 1955, We   823
considered the relation of Europe to the younger, non-   (60)
European states while discussing ways of securing world
peace. These states, We said, should not forget how much
they owe Europe; and Europe should continue to be
generous in putting at their disposal those genuine values
in which it is rich. What We said then you may apply,
mutatis mutandis, to the problem of schooling and education. But We hold it self-evident that those young and,
perhaps, still under-developed peoples must adopt cultural

values organically, that is, just as a living organism absorbs and incorporates what is given to it. They must grow in a way and to a measure that corresponds to the condition of a young nation, and always in such a manner that psychic and moral growth keep pace with technical, economic, and intellectual advances. The genuine building of culture aims at whole persons oriented to God. This is the task of all those who can influence intellectual development, particularly Catholic teachers.

824
(66,
91,
97)
In connection with the subject of your congress We would like to direct your attention to a simple but related subject. Radio, motion pictures, and television—however injurious their effects frequently are—surely have the advantage that they bring people all over the world closer to one another, not only by increasing their knowledge of one another, but also by promoting common sentiment and temperament.

A Catholic teacher knows how to elevate these feelings to the height of their moral purpose. He will point out that those far-away people feel as we do, that they too have achievements to point to and can serve as our models in many things. Above all, he will stress the fact that they too have God for their Creator and Father, that they too are included in the love and salvation of Christ and called to His Church. Thus young people will, with all due pride in the history and attainments of their own people and with all love of their country, also have respect and good will for all other nations. What power there lies in such education against excessive nationalism which lacks that respect and good will, and which is incompatible with Christian thinking! Here too the effect of your school reflects in a precious way the world-wide unity of the Catholic Church.

You are going to end your international congress with a pilgrimage to the Mother of Grace at Mariazell. In fervent prayer commend to her, the pure and powerful

Virgin, your tasks, sorrows, and hopes. May Jesus Christ,
the Son of God and Mary, fructify all your work, with His
grace and bring it to completion.

As a pledge thereof We give the Apostolic Blessing
from the fullness of Our heart to you, beloved sons and
daughters, who have met in Vienna, and to your entire
association.

CLASSICAL STUDIES

All. to the Minor Seminaries of France, Sept. 5, 1957.

*(Rome and the priesthood.—The priesthood, glory of
the Church, who has care for the formation of her priests.)*

You must rejoice first of all at pursuing classical **825**
studies, for they remain unequalled for the exercise and *(64)*
development of the most valuable qualities of the mind:
penetration of judgment, broadmindedness, finesse of analysis and gifts of expression. Nothing helps to understand
man today as much as a profound study of history. Nothing
can teach one how to weigh the value of words, to grasp
the nuances of an expression, the logic of an essay and the
strength of an argument as well as the exercise of versions
and themes in classical languages. For you Frenchmen,
Latin and Greek are the origin of your national tongue and
literature. But every clergyman owes it to himself to be
able to read the most important and venerable documents
of the Scriptures and of tradition in their original texts.
During your brief sojourn in Rome you have seen a great
many Greek and Latin inscriptions that remain in ancient
cemeteries and in museums, on pagan and Christian monuments. You know that ancient Christian literature constitutes an immense treasure of knowledge and of piety,
which is examined with great admiration by a great many
scientists throughout the world. It will not be possible for
each one of you to engage upon special and more profound
studies. But what joy for a Christian to be able to come

into immediate contact with these texts and to hear ring out today the powerful voices of the Fathers of the Church, of St. Chrysostom or of St. Augustine!

(Conditions for the formation of minor seminarians.— Usefulness of minor seminaries.—Cooperation of the young men in their own formation.)

THE PRIVATE SCHOOL

All. to the Congress of European Private Schools, November 10, 1957.

826
(66) We are pleased to greet you, gentlemen, who have come to Rome to discuss the common problems of European private schools. This is a fortunate initiative, the idea of which was born during an excursion to Vienna made by some Italian students. The warm welcome they received in that city made it evident that similar intentions and preoccupations exist which are entirely natural to those who give to the private school, or receive from it, the best of their human, spiritual and intellectual resources. The present meeting aims at emphasizing various characteristic aspects of the private school, and the mission that it intends to carry out in a society at grips with the rapid and profound transformations that prompt it to overflow national boundaries to establish a cultural, economic, social and even political European community.

The Attitude of Modern States

827
(22,
23,
95,
109,
117) One can state without fear that the legislation which a country reserves for private schools—We use this term in the sense which you yourselves give it, namely, a school which is not managed by the state—reflects rather exactly the level of spiritual and cultural life of that country. A state which relegates to itself exclusively the task of educa-

tion, and prohibits private organizations or independent groups from assuming their responsibility in this field, makes a claim which is incompatible with the fundamental requirements of the human person. The ideal of the freedom of the school is admitted by all political regimes that recognize the rights of the individual and the family.

In practice, however, all degrees of freedom are possible. At times the state more or less disassociates itself from the efforts of private initiative, does not support them financially and reserves for itself the right of awarding all academic titles. At other times, however, the state recognizes, under certain conditions, the value of private teaching and grants it subsidies. But even more than concessions of material assistance or the legal recognition of degrees, the fundamental attitude of governments toward private instruction is important. Often, in fact, a liberty that is admitted in theory, remains limited and even opposed in effect; it is at most tolerated, when the state considers itself to have a true monopoly in matters of teaching.

Now, a serious analysis of the historical and philosophical foundations of education clearly proves that the mission of the school does not belong to the state only, but first of all belongs to the family, and then to the social community to which the family belongs. The formation of the human personality, in fact, springs primarily from the family; and because, to a large extent, the school aims at the same goal, it is only an extension of the family's action; and receives from the family the necessary authority for that purpose. The supremacy of the family in education shows itself, furthermore, in the frequent incapacity of the school to effect by itself a remedy to grave family deficiencies. **828** *(7ff, 21, 24, 46, 49)*

On the other hand, to the extent that the school communicates the knowledge of an entire body of matters geared to the exterior activities of individuals, it depends also on the community—on its traditions, its demands, its cultural level, the direction of its tendencies. The needs of the community will be interpreted on the school level by individuals, organized groups, religious and cultural institutions which propose the formation of young people for their future tasks as their own proper aim. The state, the political power as such, will intervene only to exercise a supplementary function; to insure to the action of private organizations the required extension and intensity. Far from considering the private school as a complement subordinated to the political power, it is necessary to grant it a real independence in its own function, and the right to inspire family principles which govern the growth and development of human persons, without forgetting the necessities imposed by the social domain.

829
(20-
22,
49,
66,
117,
119)
The administrative organization of modern states has in fact grown beyond bounds; and has absorbed all those greater sectors of public life, particularly the school. While intervention is at times legitimate when the action of individuals is incapable of satisfying the needs of the whole community, still it is harmful when it deliberately supplants competent private initiative. You are therefore right to stress the preeminence of the private school over those schools whose administration depends on public powers. And you are correct in emphasizing the eminent services that it has rendered wherever it has been given sufficient freedom of action. You intend to propose during this congress a European center for the defense of the spiritual benefits of the private school. Today this objective requires careful attention and a strong participation on the part of all those who believe in its irreplaceable function. In the majority of modern nations the private school must still, unfortunately, bear up under a hard struggle to preserve the rights it has gained; and, in short, its economic subsistence. But, because it is not subject to the servitude which weighs heavily on all State entities, it possesses a greater adaptability to the new conditions of

international life. You are therefore right in hoping that an agreement among private schools will facilitate the formation of young generations, who are anxious to free themselves from the constraint of an often exaggerated and actually outdated nationalism, and to face the increased responsibilities they will have to assume in a structurally broader Europe.

The spirit of the private school

It is normal that the problems of organization and method should occupy a large part of the discussions in which the persons who are responsible for private schools exchange views, if they wish to remain perfectly up-to-date with the present progress of pedagogy. But it is important, above all else, that the spirit of the private school, its concept of men and of education, and the disinterested ideal of those who dedicate themselves to it, should be respected. Sometimes, giving in to misguided zeal, private school leaders have followed, in their methods and the structure of their curricula, the example of a teaching system that concerns itself with other interests and is less concerned with safeguarding the true values of the person. We do not doubt that you will have a part in avoiding this reef, which is more dangerous for you than attacks from outside your ranks. **830** *(54, 82, 108)*

Those who will play a primary role in public life tomorrow will have graduated, We are convinced, from schools which honor more the ideal of freedom and personal initiative, and do not hesitate in placing, at the heart of their teachings, sound moral and religious convictions; especially those of the Christian faith which, throughout the centuries, has not ceased to shape the mind of the Western peoples. European society, now in the course of formation, will be able to find its interior equilibrium and hold its place among other world powers, only if it pos- **831** *(4, 18, 49, 68, 92)* sesses an elite imbued with the best human and Christian traditions; and above all convinced of the supremacy of the spiritual realm over the more elaborate forms of technical organization. It depends on you, gentlemen, to work toward the preparation and flowering of this elite, and to give in this manner to the Western peoples the living forces which will help them achieve a common destiny in peace and fraternal collaboration. As a token of divine favors and of success for the efforts which you have already made and will continue to make for such a noble cause, We impart to you and all those who employ themselves in truth and justice to the service of private education, Our Apostolic Blessing.

PRAYER FOR TEACHERS

December 28, 1957.

832
(51ff,
60,
62)
O Word Incarnate, Teacher of teachers, our beloved Jesus, who didst deign to come into the world in order to point out to mankind, in Thine infinite wisdom and inexhaustible goodness, the way to heaven, graciously hear the humble supplications of those who, following in Thy footsteps, desire to be Catholic teachers worthy of that name, and to guide souls in the sure paths that lead to Thee and through Thee to eternal happiness.

Grant us Thy light, that we may be able not only to avoid the snares and pitfalls of error, but also to penetrate into the nature of truth so as to attain to that clarity of insight which causes what is most essential to become most simple, and therefore best adapted to the minds even of little ones, in whom Thy divine simplicity is most clearly reflected. Visit us with the assistance of Thy Creator Spirit, so that when we are commanded to teach the doctrines of faith we will be able to teach them as they should be taught.

833
(51,
Give us the power to adapt ourselves to the still immature minds of our pupils; to encourage their splendid,

youthful energies; to understand their defects; to endure   *54,*
their restlessness; to make ourselves as little children, with-   *81ff)*
out giving up due authority, thus imitating Thee, dear
Lord, who didst make Thyself as one of us without abandoning the lofty throne of Thy divine nature.

Above all, fill us with Thy Spirit of love: love for Thee,
our kind and only Teacher, that we may sacrifice ourselves
in Thy holy service; love for our profession, that we may
see in it a high vocation and not merely an ordinary occupation; love of our own sanctification, as the chief source
of our labors and our apostolate; love of the truth, that we
may never deliberately betray it; love of souls, whom we
are to mold and fashion to truth and goodness; love of our
pupils, that we may train them to be exemplary citizens
and faithful children of the Church; love for our beloved
youths and children, that we may feel toward them a true,
paternal affection that is more sublime, more deliberate,
and more unselfish than that of their natural parents.

And do thou, O Mary, our holy mother, under whose
loving eyes the youthful Jesus grew in wisdom and in
grace, be our intercessor with thy divine Son and obtain
for us an abundance of heavenly graces, that our labors
may redound to the glory of Him who with the Father and
the Holy Spirit liveth and reigneth forever and ever. Amen.

EDUCATION, A SOCIAL PROBLEM

Letter of the Substitute Secretary of State to the Forty-
fifth French Social Week, June 28, 1958.

(*Theme of the Congress: "Education, a social problem."—Versailles is a symbol: it looks to the future without
ceasing to be firmly rooted in the past.*)

A nation that is conscious of its future should give con-   **834**
siderable attention to the kind of instruction given its youth   *(4,*
and to the education which they receive. Will today's chil-   *63,*

66,   dren become, tomorrow, adults capable through their moral
92)   courage and their training of working together to face the
great tasks of their fatherland? Will they have benefited
from a formation consistent with proper attitudes, and will
they be at the same time working in a sufficiently judicious
way toward careers most useful to the nation in fields
which are not overcrowded? Will the best among them be
able to resolve, with the mastery of judgment and the capacity for adaptation which characterizes true culture, the
new problems which in ten or twenty years will be posed
for the elite?

(*Reference to the Encyclical,* Divini illius Magistri,
magistral instruction on Christian Education. [a])

The origin of the mission of the school

835   With regard to the particular aspect of the problem of
(7ff, education treated by your gathering, it is known that "the
21,   mission of the school itself is derived, not from the State
24,   alone, but first from the family, then from the social com-
46,   munity to which it belongs" (Discourse of November
49)   10, 1957). (a) And His Holiness set forth his thinking precisely in these terms: "To the extent that the school
communicates the knowledge of an entire body of matters
geared to the exterior activities of individuals, it depends
also on the community, on its traditions, its demands, its
cultural level, the direction of its tendencies. The needs of
the community will be interpreted on the school level by
individuals, organized groups, religious and cultural institutions which propose the formation of young people for
their future tasks as their proper aim." (b) These pontifical
words put the school precisely in its true setting. They
show why education is fundamentally a social problem.
The reason is that the scholastic institution derives its

834a See above Nos. 240 and 722.
835a See above No. 828.
835b See above No. 828.

rights from families and from the various groups making up society, which give it their mandate, and to which it is responsible for the formation of future generations. The Catholic may rely upon this doctrine with surety to make necessary distinctions and to explore proper ways to serve youth. But, at the same time, the analysis of present circumstances brings the confirmation of experience on more than one point to these superior principles. It brings to light the size of the educative task actually at hand, the reasons for the present complexity of this task in the context of contemporary social life, and finally the great necessity, if what is generally expected is to be accomplished, to appeal in a spirit of true liberty for the collaboration of all those responsible for the formation of the child. A rapid scanning of the situation is sufficient to convince of this.

School and family

When one turns to the family, he sees the often formulated wish to be more closely associated with the educative activity of the school. And the Church makes this desire its own: "We willingly encourage," His Holiness declares, "that which will facilitate and make always closer the collaboration between the school and the family. The latter must not, and indeed cannot, abdicate its directive function; collaboration is natural and necessary" (Discourse of January 5, 1954). (a)

836
(42,
43,
46)

The numerous voluntary efforts that have already been made in this regard can also be put forward. For how can fathers and mothers be disinterested in so many questions relative to the religious, moral, intellectual and hygienic activities of the schools to which they confide their children? How can they avoid being concerned about the principles which are inculcated in their children in order to prepare them for life, to give them a just idea of

836a See above No. 690.

true values and to discipline their wills in the pursuit of the good?

Why should fathers and mothers set aside their inalienable responsibility when it is a question of the professional orientation of their children which has such serious consequences for the future?

Undoubtedly no one can deny the advantages to be derived from mutual good relations between parents and teachers, or the benefits to be drawn from the exchange of information between them. But it is likewise of prime importance that, in the name of this same principle of collaboration—and in the names of the institutions that it supports—full recognition be given to the family's primordial mission of education which makes the family, by virtue of this mission, far more than a mere occasional collaborator of the school. Because it is first of all a family problem, education is a social problem, overflowing the limits of purely intellectual and scholastic questions.

The school and industrial, agricultural and commercial life

837
(63-
67)
A consideration of the economic future of the country leads to a similar enlargement of perspectives. For in the measure in which it is possible to forecast the future and its major orientations, it is important to prepare youth carefully. Here most assuredly one must be on guard against excessive emphasis on the technical, avoid all premature specialization and uphold the rights of culture. Apart from its permanent value, culture is in a period as uncertain and constantly shifting as ours, the most valuable capital of a people, which will give them in due time the greatest potentials with which to face new situations.

838
(65,
82)
Nevertheless, it is normal to envisage regular relations between those responsible for education and the various sectors of industrial, agricultural and commercial life. In these fields, in fact, private initiative gets appreciable

results in the formation of young people. The art of teaching has made real progress. And it can readily be seen that at different levels of education some exchanges would be fruitful as much for the perfecting of teaching methods as for the improvement of curricula and the progressive introduction of students to the great problems of economic life. In rural areas in particular, the close ties frequently existing between the family and agricultural enterprise offer the school an additional reason to collaborate with the environment in which the child grows up, for he must learn to improve his ·understanding and his service as his general knowledge gradually increases. The experiences of those involved have shown that, in this regard such collaboration should be encouraged. Youth can truly benefit from this opening of the mind and from a common will to cooperate freely.

The school and civic life

Some analogous observations can be made with even more reason with regard to the civic and social life of the nation. The education received should enable young people to approach the different fields of labor later with an informed social sense and to enter into the life and activities of the national and international community without trouble. This should always be the case nowadays. And you should recall the exhortations of the Holy Father on this subject to a previous French Social Week on civism: "If it is true that in a democratic state, civic life imposes great demands on the moral maturity of each citizen, one should not be afraid to realize that many among them, even among those who call themselves Christians, have a degree of responsibility for the present social confusion. These facts require a definite redress." (a) It is primarily with regard to youth that this redress should be made. The members of the teaching body, which is most legitimately

839
(66)

839a Letter of July 14, 1954.

involved in this matter, voluntarily realize the advantages to be derived from the collaboration of various institutions belonging to the life of the city, to the world of labor and to the relations between peoples. Some efforts made with discernment in support of scholastic instruction will initiate the child to the collective structures he too often ignores and to moral duties of great importance. By its participation in the human community and through the ramifications of its training, the school offers to the nation real possibilities for civic health and social peace.

The school and youth movements

840
(90) Considerations of this kind could be multiplied; but there is a final consideration of capital importance the point at which teachers and educators should recognize at once the limits of their professional competence and learn how to collaborate. This is with regard to the movements and activities of organized youth.

It is false to think of them as the prerogative of the schools, as a normal complement of their educative task, but on the other hand, it is to be hoped that the education realized in the home, completed in the school and pursued simultaneously in various youth movements, where it is like an apprenticeship to life, should be a continuous work motivated by a common spirit, founded on the same moral principles and leading to the same perspectives of the future.

Why must a child be exposed to the lamentable arguments, even to the dull struggles going on in different educational circles? Yet there mutual services, in respect to just liberties, appear to be of great value for the healthy formation of youth and for its unity in the heart of the nation.

Liberty of private initiative

841
(24, The leaders of the Social Week at Versailles will make further analyses in other directions. But already the lesson

of deeds has been joined to the instructions of doctrine, and some conclusions must be drawn, which in the name of the Holy Father, I should like to point out in order to enlighten your work. They may be summed up in this affirmation which only a spirit of true liberty and collaboration can bring to face, with respect to legitimate rights, the complexity and breadth of the problems of training and education which have just been evoked. Actually, it should not be a question of denying originality in the function of teaching, nor of contesting its greatness or its merits. But experience tends more and more to prove that, in order to offer everything to youth, for the benefit of all nations—a formation as rich, diversified and adaptable as the epoch needs—an appeal to private initiative would be desirable in order to promote a sound freedom of exchange and research—in a word, to enrich all the living forces of the nation by means of free concourse.

45, 49, 117)

In this case, it is up to the public powers to harmonize these multiple efforts and to organize them for the common good. But they should know how to respect and encourage them in a thousand ways.

842 *(20- 22, 109)*

The Holy Father observes, "A state which takes to itself exclusively the task of education and prohibits private organizations and independent groups from assuming their responsibilities in this field, makes a claim which is incompatible with the fundamental requirements of the human person" (Discourse of November 10, 1957). (a)

And everyone knows that beside the monopolies of law there exist today, as a consequence of economic conditions, certain monopolies of action which are no less rigorous.

But, for the welfare of the national community, advances must be made along the path of just freedom if the institutional plans for education are to be renovated for the

842a See above No. 827.

purpose of better adapting them to achieve their proper ends. This path is that of concord among all those who truly desire educational progress.

And with regard to this, much is hoped from the present Social Week, which offers the example of a brotherly meeting between Catholics of two divisions—public and private—with a common concern about resolving the questions which trouble their hearts according to Christian principles.

The good done by the Catholic school

843
(4,
5,
18,
68,
72,
92)

May we, by means of this letter, also render special homage—among all the private scholastic institutions—to the schools, colleges, and Catholic universities which in France hold so honorable a place and render such important service to the Church and to the country.

From the viewpoint of liberty which we have been contemplating, their task is considerable. And many of the voluntary efforts already made in various fields, many of the results obtained, make it seem hopeful that, in years to come, the development of so beneficial a mission can be assured, thanks to the intelligent understanding of the men who are responsible for the welfare of the country and its future.

"Those who will play a primary role in public life tomorrow," the Holy Father declares, "will have been graduated, We are convinced, from schools which give more honor to the ideal of freedom and personal initiative, and do not hesitate to place at the heart of their teachings, sound moral and religious convictions, especially those of the Christian faith which, throughout the centuries, has not ceased to shape the mind of the Western peoples" (Discourse of November 10, 1957). (a)

(Blessing.)

843a See above No. 827.

THE CATHOLIC SCHOOL IN THE FACE
OF THE REALITIES OF THE MODERN WORLD

All. to the International Office of Catholic Teaching,
September 14, 1958.

The Third General Assembly of the International **844** Office of Catholic Teaching brings you together, dear *(16,* children, and affords Us the opportunity to grant this *26,* audience which you have earnestly requested. We respond *111,* to your desire with all Our heart and thus support with *117)* Our encouragement the efforts you have exerted to found and develop your Office. Catholics of today, even more than those of yesterday, attach great importance to education. Wherever the faith takes root, schools of all types soon arise—kindergardens, grade schools, secondary schools, and universities embracing all branches of learning.

Ecclesiastical authorities are anxious to form an elite as soon as possible and to facilitate the spread of Christian culture. Aided by the admirable devotion of lay teachers and by the financial support of Christian people, they make every effort that all young baptized persons might receive in Christian institutions the religious and intellectual formation which they need. But their efforts are often carried out in a disorganized way, according to the needs of the moment and the impulses of generous enthusiasm, without that rational examination of the situation which is needed to determine with precision the conditions under which these efforts will bear the best fruit. Thus there is an evident loss of energy and a lessening of the effectiveness of the apostolate.

Catholic teaching on the international plane

Nowadays there is a great increase in international ex- **845** changes. Public and private organizations are interested *(112)* in international cultural and educational activities. The

Catholic school must, therefore, demonstrate its value, adapt itself for the formation of Christians in the modern world, and defend itself against the attacks made upon it in many areas. This was the reason for the creation of your organization which proposes, as its statutes declare (Article 3), "to affirm on an international plane the role of teaching that is conducted under the protection of the Church." It had been possible previously for Catholic universities, students, intellectuals, and teachers to discuss questions which interested them in their respective fields. But it was still necessary for some group to represent Catholic teaching in its entirety and to present its point of view to international governmental and non-governmental organizations. For this reason representatives from six nations met at The Hague for the first time in November, 1950. After the ecclesiastical hierarchy of the interested countries had approved of the project, the organizing assembly of the Office met at Lucerne in September, 1952, and drafted statutes. Since then its membership has constantly increased. Although hampered in its actions by a lack of funds, the Office has accomplished a notable amount of work since its foundation. In particular it has been represented at several meetings of international organizations, has edited a number of reports, studies, and articles, has established an extensive collection of documents on the schools of various countries, and has answered many requests for information. At present you are concentrating your attention on the UNESCO projects relating to primary education in Latin America and to the mutual appreciation of cultural values in the Far East and the West. You are also cooperating in the organization of Catholic schools in Africa.

846
(26,
50,
60ff)
Your present congress deals with a rather complex subject, "The Nature and Role of the Catholic School in the Face of the Realities of the Modern World." In doing this, you fulfill one of the important points of your statutes,

which calls for "study of the principles that are the basis of Christian instruction of youth and the study of problems that the application of these principles entails" (Article 4a). Problems of pedagogy and of the school in general have in recent years become very prominent—problems arising from the increased number of regular students, the question of lengthening of the period of education to meet the demands of modern science and industry for specialized personnel, and also the more delicate problems resulting from the rapid extension of the media and content of culture. Thus it is opportune to examine the situation of the Catholic school in the modern world and the way this school adapts itself to an accelerated rate of growth. The political and social climate of international life cannot fail to have an influence on various movements which the Catholic schools take into account, such as the conflict of political ideas and systems, the alignment of nations into opposing factions, the needs of underdeveloped regions, and the common utilization of new sources of energy. The proper solution of these formidable questions can only come from an elite with sound ideas and generous hearts who will be able to consider such problems with full technical competence and with an understanding of the essential requirements of the human conscience. The Catholic school aims at confronting its pupils with all their responsibilities, and thus it helps develop the fundamental principles of a harmonious balance between individuals and nations.

Conditions required for a school to be Christian

So that the Catholic school will not fail in its mission, all those in positions of responsibility must keep in mind the advice given by Our venerable predecessor Pius XI in the encyclical "Divini illius Magistri." For a school to be Christian it is not sufficient that there be a course of religion every week or that certain practices of piety be

847
(48, 108)

required; above all, Christian teachers must form spirit and character and communicate to their pupils the wealth of their own profound spiritual lives. To do this, the exterior organization of the school, its discipline and its curriculum, must constitute a framework adapted to its essential function, and the school must be penetrated, even in its apparently most humble and material details, with an authentic spirituality: Is it a matter of indifference what daily schedule is adopted, or what choice of subjects, teaching methods, or disciplinary systems is made? Legal requirements or other circumstances have led many times to regrettable surrenders and have greatly diminished the efficacy of religious education itself. We also believe that you will be accomplishing a very useful work in making available to Christian teachers a comparison of methods and results obtained in other countries. This project will save educators the expense of useless or harmful experimentation and will more surely eliminate from their own methods all elements that are alien to true Christian inspiration.

848
(2, 26, 60ff, 88)
In any case, the efficiency of an educational system depends, in the final analysis, on its complete faithfulness to the main goal it has set for itself. The Christian school will justify its existence in so far as its teachers—clerics or laymen, religious or secular—succeed in forming staunch Christians. Therefore, their zeal should apply itself unfailingly to bring their pupils more and more into the life of the Church, to have them take part in its liturgy and its sacraments, and then to initiate them—according to the capacities of their age—into apostolic work among their companions, in their own families, and in their walk of life. They should also be brought to look toward the missionary field, which really begins at the gates of the school or college. The school should show them the apostolic opportunities offered to their generosity in the vocation of a priest or a religious or among the varied forms of lay

action. The pupils of a Catholic school should not regard their future career as a simple social function which is undoubtedly necessary for all of them and their age group, but with no immediate relation to their condition as baptized persons; on the contrary, they must always think of it as the exercise of a personal responsibility in the work of saving the world. If they take their careers seriously as Christians on the temporal plane, they will realize through them their highest spiritual destiny.

The merits of the Catholic school

It would be a mistake to think that because of this the Christian school holds specifically scholarly tasks in less esteem or has relegated them to a secondary place. On the contrary, the intellectual objectives, which are the aims of teaching, receive from the school's spiritual orientation a firmness, a security, and an increased strength. And so it is that when pagan pupils or those belonging to another religion attend Catholic schools, they obtain a cultural training equal to that they would have received elsewhere. As a matter of fact, Catholic schools often enjoy renown in non-Catholic circles for the quality of their courses and for the eminent services which they render to the national community. Unfortunately, in spite of its obvious merits, the Catholic school does not always receive from public authorities the support that it deserves. We have already spoken of this problem in Our discourse of November 10, 1957, to the International Congress of Private European Schools. (a) It may be hoped that the movement which encourages nations to unite into larger groups will encourage governments to surmount such opposition to those who found Catholic schools. It remains for Us to urge you, dear children, to pursue with courage and perseverance the tasks which you have set for yourselves. To stimulate

849
(51,
63ff.
70,
92,
112)

849a See above Nos. 827 ff.

your zeal, you can well repeat the exclamation of St. Paul, proud in the trust that God had confided to him to proclaim the mystery of Christ. "Him we preach, admonishing every man and teaching every man in all wisdom, that we may present every man perfect in Christ Jesus." (b) Such is the magnificent scope of your work and the work of all Christian teachers: to preach the Lord to those who do not know Him, to make perfect those who do know Him.

(*Blessing.*)

849b Col. 1:28.

JOHN XXIII

elected in 1958

CHRIST, THE APEX OF UNIFIED KNOWLEDGE

All. to the Federation of Catholic Universities, April 1, 1959.

(*Welcome.—Development of the Federation.*)

May your collective labors, which have a strong salu- **850** tary effect not only within your own domestic walls, so to *(94,* speak, but also in the supreme councils and assemblies of *107,* State, become more closely knit! And may more and more *111)* effort be made that, by your common endeavors, truth may be sought and made known so that a protective wall, or bulwark, may be erected against the ever-present material- ism! Alas! many take a perverted pride in the progress of those arts by which the secret powers rooted in physical nature are controlled and turned to human use, and think they can live sufficient unto themselves, neglecting the law of God and setting aside all fear of Him. Nothing more sin- ful or more shameful than this could happen to the human race and to civilization, and in some regions of the world, it can be seen how bitter are the fruits produced and gathered from a bitter root. God is "the cause by which the universe was made, the light by which all truth is seen, the fountain from which true happiness flows." (a) Hence, what else is it to withdraw from God, except to rush into the darkness of perversity and unhappiness, and, by overturning right and justice, to destroy the very foundations of human fel- lowship? Today, humane and technical studies are increas- ingly being cultivated separately from one another.

You, therefore, rightly and with merit, are taking heed **851** that this danger is met. For when studies are examined *(66,* most minutely and separately, the truth by which all studies *67,*

850a Cf. St. Augustine, *De Civitate Dei*, S, 10; Migne, P.L. 41, 235.

70)   are consolidated and obtain their proper order and position
       can escape the eyes of the investigating intelligence with
       great consequent loss. Hence, it is especially necessary that
       deeper sources of truth be sought for, so that they may
       shine out as radiant stars for the scholar. These principles
       of higher unity must be sought in the mutual bond of all
       the arts of learning, in the perennial philosophy, and in sa-
       cred theology. We say more: the very apex of knowing and
       doing is Christ, the Word of God; He is Truth itself, from
       Whom and by Whom and in Whom are all things.

       "By faith we understand that the world was fashioned
       by the Word of God; and thus things visible were made out
       of things invisible." (a) All things are made manifest in
       their highest significance by Him from Whom they take
       their existence; wherefore, "Nor are you to be called teach-
       ers; you have one teacher, Christ." (b)

       Therefore, be bearers of God, bearers of Christ, bearers
       of the flame.

       (*Work and prayer for the Ecumenical Council.*)

THE STUDY OF CICERO

       All. to the First International Congress of Ciceronian
       Studies, April 7, 1959.

       (*Welcome.*)

852   We heartily congratulate you on the excellent studies
(63,   in which you are zealously and diligently engaged; for you
64)   are searching more deeply into the works of the greatest
       author of Latin eloquence, ready to pass on to as many
       others as possible the light you draw therefrom. To knowl-
       edge and research of this sort can deservedly be referred
       the praises which flowed from the mouth of Cicero himself

       851a Heb. 11:3.
       851b Matt. 23:10.

in the speech for Archias: "These studies are the food of youth, the charm of age, an ornament in prosperity, in adversity a refuge and solace; a delight at home, no hindrance in public life; they are our companions at night, in foreign travel, and in the country." (a) Alas, there are too many who are abnormally captivated by the progress of technical studies and take it upon themselves to disdain and limit the study of the Latin tongue and similar disciplines. They wish to be "citizens of the new age," immersed as much as possible in computations, in calculations, in the making of machines. With necessity itself urging, We think a contrary course should be pursued. For truly there is deeply rooted in our minds something more worthy of the nature and dignity of man; and that which nourishes and adorns the mind should be more urgently sought after, lest wretched mortals exist like manufactured machines, cold, hard, and devoid of love.

In the wise Providence of God, the wisdom of the ancient Greeks and Latins was often the instructor of men, the dawn of the Gospel of Christ, which is the sun, "the Orient from on high." (a) Among those ancients, Cicero holds a place of special rank: he himself, among other things, recognized God as the Creator and Ruler of all things. He set the nature of law in a clear light, and in brilliant language praised the foundation of justice: faith, constancy, truth, integrity. What more need be said? In explaining the duties of individuals, his teaching—it is pleasant to recall—truly foreshadows with prophetic inspiration the Christian law: "We wish brave and courageous men to be also good and sincere men, friends of truth, and not at all deceivers.... Therefore, it is not those who do an injury who are to be considered brave and courageous, but those who protect others from wrong doing." (b) St. Au-

853
(64)

852a Cap. VII.
853a Luke 1:78.
853b *Off.* 1, 19.

gustine, in the third book of the Confessions, shows the wonderful effect which the work of Cicero entitled *Hortensius* gave to the disposition of his thoughts and to his character: "That book truly changed the direction of my mind and turned my prayers to You, O Lord, and gave me a new purpose and ambition. Suddenly, all the vanity I had hoped in became as worthless; and, with an incredible yearning of my heart, I longed after immortal wisdom." (c) We desire with paternal prayers, beloved friends, that what St. Augustine then felt, you may experience in reading, meditating, and loving the documents of ancient wisdom; and, because you are of noble mind, may you always prefer, to fleeting and harmful things, the everlasting stable good, for the sake of which we were created and without which we cannot live rightly and happily.

(Blessing.)

THE EDUCATIONAL VALUE OF SPORTS

All. to the Sixth Congress of the Italian Athletic Union, April 26, 1959.

(Welcome.—Theme of the Congress: "Sound Athletics for a better youth.")

854
(61, 91)
The great value of athletics lies in its particular efficacy for interior perfection, consequent upon the exterior discipline with which you continually and seriously train your body. We are pleased to bring this spiritual value of athletics to your attention at this pleasant meeting today, the first which We have had with you since Our elevation to the Supreme Pontificate. We trust that you will never forget, beloved sons, that your athletic efforts are not an end in themselves; remember that the body which you train, whose agility and grace reflect a ray of the beauty

853c *Cap.* III, 7.

and omnipotence of the Creator, is only an instrument which should become docile and accessible to the strong influence of the soul. Your exercises, your competitions, which are like happy parentheses between the monotony of study and daily work, ought to develop the spiritual and immortal side of your being. If they were to have a harmful influence, if your athletic life should prove to be not a safeguard but a danger to your souls or an obstacle to the fulfillment of your religious duties, then you would find yourselves off course, like runners who, because the true course is not well marked, do not arrive at the tape in good time.

Athletics also possesses a value of the first order for the practice of virtue in your life. You train continually to preserve the elasticity and vigor of your muscles, lest their reflexes be diminished. Such continual preparation, although it aims primarily at attaining physical and technical prestige, should nevertheless bear fruitful and enduring results in the soul, which is thus enriched by the good habits acquired. Moreover, sports can also develop those true and strong Christian virtues which the grace of God later renders stable and fruitful: in the spirit of discipline one learns and practices obedience, humility, and renunciation; in team-work and competition, charity, the love of fraternity, mutual respect, generosity, and sometimes even pardon; in the strict laws of physical efficiency, chastity, modesty, temperance, and prudence. Oh, how fortunate you are to be able to practice with youthful enthusiasm these ancient virtues; without them, one can certainly be a courageous athlete, but never a truly Christian athlete. **855 (61, 75-77, 87, 91)**

The spiritual value of athletics is deduced again from that sense of temporariness which, always searching for better results, characterizes every competition. In every athletic season new records are, as your sportswriters say, "broken," conquered by the courage and tenacity of champions. The realization of this, since it makes you constantly **856 (60, 61, 91)** dissatisfied with the results which you have attained, has a very great pedagogical and spiritual value.

It teaches you, in effect, that just as in the physical world, so also, and in a special way, in the spiritual, one may never be satisfied with the level reached, but with the help of God and with good will one must seek always to reach new goals, to strive for continual improvement, which finally leads "to perfect manhood, to the mature measure of the fullness of Christ." (a)

(*Preparation for the Olympics of 1960 in Rome.— St. Paul to the Corinthians: Run to obtain an imperishable crown.—Apostolate for athletes.*)

SCOUTING: PREPARATION FOR LIFE

Letter, *Lieti di assicurare*, May 2, 1959, to the Chaplains of the Italian Catholic Boy Scouts.

857
(26,
60,
66,
69,
72,
90)

We are happy to assure you that We are present in spirit at the proceedings of the General Council of the Association of Catholic Boy Scouts in Italy and We send Our cordial greeting and good wishes to the participants. It gives Us fatherly satisfaction to draw attention to this deserving association's noble aspirations, its energetic activity, and its growth. It is a school of wholesome and competent preparation for life, with the purpose of forming young men, from childhood on, into adults of character who will be loyal citizens, well trained in discipline, hardened to sacrifice, and above all, good Christians aspiring to virtuous lives, active in charity, devoted to the Church, eager to bear witness to their faith. For so generous an undertaking We wish increasingly effective progress to the benefit of those cherished young souls, so that they may be educated to a sense of responsibility and faithfulness in their religious, family, and social duties. We are confident that the

856a Eph. 4:13.

zeal of the ecclesiastical assistants and the self-sacrifice of the directors will be crowned with new and consoling fruits. (*Blessing.*)

LOOKING TOWARD THE FUTURE
AND ETERNITY

All. to the Sixth Congress of the Italian Association of Catholic Teachers, September 5, 1959.

A widespread and paternal greeting springs from Our heart in welcoming you to Castelgandolfo, beloved sons and daughters of the Italian Association of Catholic Teachers who have come to Rome from all regions of Italy to take part in your sixth national Congress. We welcome you and are happy to express Our warm satisfaction on this occasion, particularly during these September days that already herald for you the start of a new year of hard work and rewards in the exercise of the educational mission that you chose as a vocation and which you perform in an exemplary manner for the good of the Church and of civil society. **858** *(4, 5, 51)*

By following the provident development of your meritorious association, We know the wealth of spirit and the dignity of cultural and pedagogical training you have brought to it, making possible its spread throughout Italy inside of a few years, and thus achieving its aim of training, aiding and enlightening an ever wider legion of members. You are particularly pleasing to Us because of your title of Catholic teachers, which gives you high honor and generous inspiration: two words that clearly express your convictions, your aims and ideals. **859** *(58)*

A noble mission

You are pleasing to Us above all because you are fulfilling a lofty and noble mission that makes of you **860** *(51-*

53) priceless instruments in the intellectual, civic, moral and
religious education of those who are the hope of the
Church and of the fatherland; and because you often carry
out such a function in silence, in sacrifice, in hardworking
simplicity that does not seek recognition, but is satisfied
solely by the good testimony of one's own conscience.

861
(80,
85)
At this moment Our mind is filled with the pleasant
picture of teachers (both men and women) who have
spent their entire life for the school and whom both We
and you have known: serene and smiling, modest, but firm,
bending with infinite patience over the desks of children
who at times were restless but eager to learn—to know
nature, God's work and its beauty, to drink deeply of the
fountain of truth and wisdom.

862
(51,
54)
Beloved sons and daughters! We wish on this occasion
to leave with you some thoughts of encouragement and
support for you in your daily toils, so that you may continue with renewed energy and firm and constant purpose
on the path which you have chosen.

We recommend to you "in visceribus Jesu Christi" (in
the heart of Jesus Christ), (a) always to hold your mission
in profound esteem, so that you may accomplish with holy
fervor that which is required of your good will.

The professional value of the teacher

863
(50,
56,
60,
65,
82)
1) Above all, you train the minds of your young pupils,
whose process of development is stimulated and accelerated by modern pedagogical methods, as well as by the
widespread effectiveness of the press and of audio-visual
techniques. Meanwhile, continued effort is required on
your part to add more and more to your specific training
for the work you do, which requires, and will require even

862a Phil. 1:8.

more so in the future, mastery of a secure and profound doctrine. This particular need has already been called to your attention by the subject of the congress: "Elementary Education at the School Level." We know—and We encourage all plans and efforts made in this field—that there is being studied the delicate and important problem of adding to elementary education a formative training adapted to the ability and needs of youths from ten to fourteen years, a training that will give them a more mature consciousness of their own duty, make possible the acquisition of knowledge necessary to present-day work and prepare them to attend professional institutes or to engage in their future activity—without precluding access to higher studies. Such a prospective plan opens new horizons for your beneficent educational influence, which requires of you a complete and satisfactory technical preparation. For this reason We paternally exhort you continuously to elevate and perfect yourselves in culture, so that your sphere of action may extend in depth to such new and difficult fields, respected because of your seriousness and possession of the necessary requisites.

The teacher, an educator of souls

2) Your mission, however, is something that is even higher: you form and mold the *souls* of your students. The figure of the teacher—a memory that everyone locks away in his heart as one of the dearest memories of childhood—rests entirely in the lofty function which makes him an educator of souls by words, example and the patient work he performs with difficulty and sacrifices. St. John Chrysostom outlines such an incomparable mission with the profound words so well known to you: "What is there greater than to direct the soul and mold the habits of adolescents? I deem, without a doubt, more excellent than

864
(52-
54,
82,
83)

painters, than all sculptors and artists, he who understands well the art of shaping the soul of the youth." (a)

This ability does not come from book learning or practice, but from the grace of God, from prayer and from a long apprenticeship of profound Christian living, beginning with the fruitful years of study and school.

Responsibility for the future

865
(46,
52,
80,
83)

The greatness of this educational mission is judged also by the responsibility which it entails: As we pointed out at the start, the destinies of human society are entrusted to the work of teachers because they train the men of tomorrow, instilling in their hearts—still tender and pliable—teachings and impressions that will remain dominant throughout life.

Teachers, in addition, establish fruitful contacts with the families of students; these contacts can go further than a simple scholastic relationship. They can become a beneficent influence through convinced Christian testimony.

Meanwhile, it is necessary that your efforts strengthen more and more your own Faith, in order to insure firm mastery of Catholic doctrine; that your efforts may serve to make clear your duty, professionally as well, to attain a strong Christian personality; furthermore, that these efforts may remain always an example in the conscientious fulfillment of duty and be generous in the social apostolate and in relation to civic matters.

Eternal recompense

866
(53,
54)

3) We wish to convey to you a final thought that may sustain you in the accomplishment of the duties mentioned. It is this: In educating the minds and molding the souls of your students, you are preparing for yourselves in

864a Hom. 59 to 60 on chap. 18, St. Matt., Migne 58, 584.

heaven one of the brightest crowns. Unfortunately, sometimes projects and claims, methods and problems are given first place. Although these may be useful and urgent they must not make you lose sight of the goal toward which everything must be directed if it is to have meaning. All things, as able teachers of all times teach, must be viewed "sub specie aeternitatis," in their eternal and unchangeable value, of which they shall never be divested. This is why We encourage you to discharge your duty with the most staunch faith, the most steadfast hope and the most fervent charity: in the expectation of heaven, to which your souls aspire with yearning and ardor. May there always shine before you the Biblical words: "But they that are learned shall shine as the brightness of the firmament: and they that instruct many to justice, as stars for all eternity." (a) May this be your secret longing, the desire that shall find fulfillment in the blessed possession of God. And may it give you always strength and renewed courage when life's difficulties, the harshness of duties, burdens, misunderstandings or crises disturb your serenity. May the thought of the glory that God prepares in heaven for His good and faithful servants always give you strength and renewed courage. These are the wishes that, at this eve of the National Eucharistic Congress, We entrust in your behalf with the Divine Savior, with the prayer that His grace and virtue may always accompany you in the fulfillment of your delicate and most noble work. So that your joy may be greater in this amiable meeting of children with their mutual father, We impart from Our heart to you, your dear ones, your students—together with the well deserving central president—and to leaders and assistants of the Italian Association of Catholic Teachers, Our propitiatory Apostolic Blessing.

866a Dan. 12:3.

SCHOOLS OF THE APOSTOLATE

Encycl., *Princeps Pastorum,* on the Missions, November 28, 1959.

(Fortieth anniversary of the Encyclical, Maximum illud, *issued by Benedict XV.—Local hierarchy and clergy. —The formation of the local clergy.—The apostolate of the laity.)*

867
(16, 26, 79)
It can rightly be said that the natural seat and, as it were, the training ground, where these lay executives of Catholic Action are prepared for their functions, is the Christian school; and this school will achieve it purposes, and fulfill its task, only insofar as its teachers, whether priests, religious, or laymen, educate and turn out true Christians. Everyone is aware of the great importance, present and future, of the mission country schools, and of how much effort and work the Church has devoted to establishing schools of every description and level and to defending their existence and well-being.

868
(15, 79)
It is obviously difficult to add to school curricula a program of formation for Catholic Action executives, and therefore it will often be necessary to resort to extracurricular methods to bring together the most promising youths, and train them in the theory and practice of the apostolate. The local ordinaries must, therefore, use their prudent judgment in assessing the best ways and means for opening schools of the apostolate, in which, obviously, the type of instruction will be different from that in ordinary schools.

869
(15, 26, 63, 105, 114,
Sometimes the task will be to preserve from false doctrine children and adolescents who must attend non-Catholic schools; in any event, it will always be necessary to balance the humanistic and technological education offered by the public schools with a formation based on spiritual values, so that the schools may not turn out

falsely educated men, swollen with arrogance, who can 116)
hurt the Church and their own people instead of helping
them. Their spiritual education must always be commensu-
rate with their intellectual development, and must be
planned to make them lead a life inspired by Catholic
principles in their particular social and professional environments; in time, they must be able to take their places
in Catholic organizations. To this end, if Catholic youths
should be forced to leave their communities and attend
public schools in other towns and cities, it will be expedient
to open social centers and boarding houses, in which
Christian life and morals are safely preserved, and the
talents and energies of the young people are directed
toward lofty apostolic ideals.

By thus entrusting to the schools the special and highly **870**
useful tasks of preparing Catholic Action executives, We *(9,*
do not, however, intend to exempt families from their *28,*
responsibilities, or to minimize in any way their influence, *43,*
which at times equips them even better for nurturing apos- *69)*
tolic fervor in the souls of their children, for instructing
them in Christian precepts, and for preparing them for
action. The home is, in fact, an excellent and irreplaceable
school.

(The field of Catholic Action.—Assistance by Catholics
to foreign students.—Conclusion.)

SCIENCE AND EDUCATION

Letter to the International Office of Catholic Education, December 30, 1959.

(Thirtieth anniversary of Pope Pius XI's encyclical,
Divini illius Magistri.—*Organizations created for the bene-*
fit of schools.)

. . . let Us . . . tell you of Our concern in the face of the **871**
present development of the technical world and its con-

sequences for education. The Christian faith certainly has nothing to fear from science, nor from the method which has grown out of it; on the contrary, it teaches us that these new possibilities are a glorification of the creative goodness of God, who has said: "Fill the ·earth and subdue it." (a) But it teaches us equally that they are simply means put at the disposal of men, who can use them for the best as also, alas, for the worst. That is why it seems to Us urgently necessary today that sincere Catholics be present in great numbers in this sphere, in the full vigor of human activity, in order to guide it in the sense wished by the Creator. That is why it is also expedient that it be made possible for numerous children to acquire in good Catholic technical schools a specialized training and a truly Christian education which will enable them tomorrow to constitute the professional and moral elite of whom the world and the Church have such great need. . . .

(Conclusion and Blessing.)

871a Gen. 1:28.

INDEXES

ABBREVIATIONS

References

AAS   *Acta Apostolicae Sedis*, Rome, Vatican Press, 1909-1956.

AD   *Atti e discorsi di Sua Santitá Pio XII*, Rome, Edizione Paoline, 1939-1955.

AG   *Acta Gregorii Papae XVI*, Rome, S. Congregation of the Propagation of Faith, 1900-1904.

AL   *Leonis XIII Pontificis Maximi Acta*, Rome, Vatican Press, 1881-1905.

AP IX   *Pio IX Pontificis Maximi Acta*, Vatican Press.

AP X   *S. Pio X Pontificis Maximi Acta*, Vatican Press, 1905-1914.

ASS   *Acta Sanctae Sedis*, Rome, 1865-1908.

BL   *Bullarii Romani, Continuatio. Summorum Pontificum Benedicti XIV . . . , Pio VIII, Prate*, 1845-1854.

CC   *La Civilta Cattolica*, Fortnightly Review.

CIC   *Codex iuris canonici*

CD   *Catholic Documents.*

CTS   *Catholic Truth Society*, India.
           Catholic Truth Society, London.

DC   *Documentation catholique*, Maison de la "Bonne Presse," 5, Rue Bayard, Paris.

DR   *Discorsi e Radiomessaggi di Sua Santita Pio XII*, Milan, "Vita e Pensiero," 1939-1946, Rome.

Ft.   *Iuris canonici Fontes*, Rome, 1923-1939.

NCWC   *National Catholic Welfare Conference*, Washington,

OR   *L'Osservatore Romano.* Daily newspaper.

TPS   *The Pope Speaks*, Quarterly

Nature of Documents

All. = Allocutions.
Apost. Const. = Apostolic Constitution.
Apost. Letter = Apostolic Letter.
Encycl. = Encyclical.
RM = Radio message.
Transl. = Translation.

Numbering of the text

In the margin of the text or in footnotes:

The numbers in bold type indicate the division of the Pontifical text, or refer to it.

The numbers in brackets and in italics refer to the division of the Analytical Index, and facilitates the finding of texts on the same subjects.

In the indices:

Read explanations before each index.

ALPHABETICAL INDEX

The numbers in brackets refer to the divisions of the Analytical Index; the numbers in heavy black print refer to the paragraphs of the Papal pronouncements.

ANALYTICAL INDEX

PLAN OF THE ANALYTICAL INDEX

— 609 —

ANALYTICAL INDEX

The numbers in italics between parentheses indicate the division of the present Index or refer to the division of the same;

the numbers in bold type refer to the divisions of the Papal document;

the underlined numbers refer to passages of particular importance of the Papal document;

the big numbers in bold type, for example **62,** refer to an entire document which begins at the number indicated;

the titles in bold capitals indicate a subject matter treated in several Papal documents already published or still to be published, in a separate volume of the present collection.

Introduction

NATURE AND AIM OF EDUCATION

(1) — Education is the formation of man; it helps him tend towards the end for which he was created: **243.**
— It has fallen man as its *subject:* **278, <u>288</u>, 435,**
and redeemed man: **278, 724,**
but it has not recovered the balance of its inclinations: **278, 409, 431, 727.**

(2) — It has the *aim* of forming him:
in view of his individual perfection: **245, 454, 473, 576, 670, 729, 804, 848.**
as son of God: **473,**
and for his ultimate end: **242-243, 258, 260,**
which is of the supernatural order: **<u>248</u>, 454, 670, 724,**
and is placed only in God: **242, 338,**
and of his social life: **129, 244-245, 454, 473, 670, 729, 816, 848.**

ITS IMPORTANCE

and of Her mission to save souls: **231, 515**.
which are Hers, more than of the family and society: **515**,
and which She alone can lead to the fullness of their terrestial and heavenly destiny: **623**, cf. *(2)*.
This mission, by virtue of its aim, is superior to every purely natural mission: **246, 318**,
is extended to all men: **94, 189, 215, 252, 304**,
faithful and non-believers: **253, 255**.

(15) — The right of the Church in education carries with it:
that of selecting the means suitable for carrying it out: **245, 247, 288, 319, 459**,
in particular that of opening schools and other educational institutions: **250, 721, 788, 868, 869**.

The exercise of the right of the Church in history: 231, 308

(16) — The right was always claimed by the Church as one of its essential attributes: **29, 79, 190, 215, 236, 324, 623, 758, 819**.
— She has always exercised it: **123, 201, 231, 288, 504**,
especially by founding schools: **29, 85, 253, 309, 311**,
of all kinds and grades: **86, 167, 232, 333, 519, 523, 844, 867**.
particularly Universities: **105, 207, 253, 311, 576, 616**,
and by exercising Her authority: **85, 485**.

(17) — So the Church has favored the sciences and the arts: **105, 124, 129, 132, 197, 206, 232, 276, 308, 312, 465**,
preserved ancient culture: **124, 149, 193, 232, 254, 310, 312, 623**,

(18) — and exercised her fruitful work of civilization: **123, 132, 135, 147, 237, 253-255, 303, 309, 337, 623, 831**,
for families: **237, 251-252, 256, 263, 436**,
and nations: **251-252, 843**.

(19) — The right of the Church in education lies with the Pope and the Bishops: **11, 14, 132, 176, 204, 320**,
bound to one of their most important missions: **1, 6, 84, 501**.

assure teachers conditions that are in keeping with their functions: **449, 484, 509, 683.**

(23) – It can even still, by the same right, demand from all a certain degree of culture: **163, 267, 272, 459, 729, 827,**

claim to carry out the task of civil education: **267, 270, 729,**

and the foundation of schools preparatory to certain public services: **269,**

cf. abuse of military training: *(109).*

Cf. **THE INTERNAL PEACE OF NATIONS.**

(24) – The organization of the State for the temporal common good, basis of its rights in the matter of education: cf. *(21),*

though at the same time it delineates its limits: **318.**

– The rights of the State are limited:

by the prior rights of the family: **259, 268, 351, 828, 835,** cf. *(7)-(8),*

by the superior rights of the Church, **266, 268,** cf. *(10) ff.*

– to whom the full responsibility of educating belongs: **237,**

– the rights of the supernatural order, superior to those of the State: **142, 256, 318,**

with which they are not in opposition: **237, 252, 256, 264,**

but which must be co-ordinated in perfect harmony: **256, 271-272, 274, 646, 729, 734, 841.**

(25) – The State must never hinder religious teaching: **203,** over which it has no right: **110,** cf. *(12),*

nor ought it to favor a training which is contrary to the religious one: **144, 346, 347, 370,** cf. *(94) ff.*

– But ought to help positively the work of the Church: **144, 234, 267, 307, 621, 734,**

which in Her turn renders it the greatest service: **135, 144, 252,** cf. *(92).*

Cf. **THE CHURCH AND THE STATE.**

Chapter II
THE PRACTISING OF CHRISTIAN EDUCATION

A. *The duty of education*

(29) – The very grave duty of education: **258**, <u>**288**</u>, **397, 438, 576,**
bound up with paternity: **305, 426, 432,** <u>**547**</u>, **793,**
from which no authority can dispense parents: **351, 793,**
imposes on them the duty of training their children, as a sacred duty entrusted to them by God: **371**
for the aim desired by the Creator: **130, 260,**

(30) – and as a consequence to offer them not only existence and support: **112, 370, 791**
but education: **791,**
physical and civic: **258-260, 422, 576, 730,**
especially moral: **258-260, 576, 791,** cf. *(71)* ff.,
and religious: **67,** <u>**112, 176, 229, 258-260, 367, 370, 422, 432, 576,**</u> cf. *(34)* and *(71).*

(31) – For parents the education of their children is:
a very pure joy: **404, 438, 794,**
the beginning of their true greatness: **472,**
their first apostolic field: **529,**
and at the same time a social service of fundamental importance: **130, 341, 529, 743, 797, 815.**

B. *The duty of parents in education:* **400**

(32) – Education, made more difficult by original sin: **435, 688,** cf. *(1),*
seeks from the parents:
even before the birth of the children:
a healthy inheritance: **404,**
the atmosphere of a united family: **305, 425-426, 792,**
and Christian: **377, 404, 434, 792;**

(33) – during education:
a) the protection of the family from unhealthy influences: **434,**
reading: **385,**
amusements, (cinema, radio and television): **298, 677-679, 710,** cf. *(113)*
and **PRESS, CINEMA, RADIO,**

She has an outstanding position in the education of sentiments and during the crisis of adolescence: **413, 415, 427,** cf. *(78)*.

THE TASK OF THE FATHER

(38) — It is the duty of the father, together with that of maintaining the family: **626**
to guide his sons: **626,**
above all by setting an example: **425,** cf. *(39)*
and by forming them during the crises of adolescence: **283, 415.**

C. *Conditions and aids demanded by family education*

(39) — For the effective exercise of the task of parents as educators what is needed is:
their presence at home: <u>317</u>, **401, 405, 428, 430,** cf. absence from home: *(96),*
the example of their virtues: **378, 385, 387,** <u>398</u>, **425, 431, 433, 596, 795,**
a most effective method of education: **141, 285, 364, 387,** <u>398</u>, **795,** cf. *(83),*

(40) — their authority: **389, 794,**
a participation in that of God: **257, 399,**
necessary to defend and form their sons: **287, 389,**
and which demands:
their union: **396,**
a true love for their children: **397**
self-control: **378, 383,** <u>393-394</u>, **794,** cf. *(85)* and *(86)*.

(41) — The indispensable helps to their work are: **405, 433,**
the help of the Church and its ministers: **288, 386, 416, 761, 777,**

(42) — that of the school and of its teachers: **112,** <u>417</u> **690, 720,** cf. *(46),*
that it is their right and their duty to make a good choice: **173, 327, 417, 689, 736,** cf. *(48),*
to watch over: **160,**
and to help: **387, 417, 644,** <u>690</u>, **736, 786.**
instead of opposing them: **417, 644, 689, 777.**

correct judgment: **410, 445, 692,**
a sound philosophy: **180, 209, 525, 693, 863,**
profound scientific competence: **150, 297, 475, 668, 670, 693, 742,**
and pedagogic competence: **295, 441, 447, 485, 687, 741, <u>748</u>, 769, 846, 862.**

It is the normal Catholic school that is most able to ensure this formation: **80, 167, 519, <u>715</u>, 788.**

(51) — The teaching vocation is one of the noblest: **502, 516, 724, 745, 781, 858, 862,**
it is a genuine spiritual paternity: **420, 508, 664, 741, 745, 751, 773, 833,**
and a genuine collaboration in God's work: **500, 502, 849,** cf. *(26),*
and that of Christ the Redeemer: **331, 452, 472, 667-668, 688, 724, 746,**
and the Church's hierarchy: **<u>331</u>, 335, 502, 599, 757, 832, 860.**

(52) — So it is a sacred ministry: **84**
and an excellent form of Catholic Action: **<u>294</u>, <u>297</u>, 331, 865,**
that ought to hold first place: **325, 331, <u>335</u>, 501, 615,**
as the most efficacious apostolate: **166, 335, 543, 634, 649, 664, 821,**
but which is responsible to God for souls: **461-462, <u>502</u>, 508, 518, 543, 647, 691, 731, 752, 832, 864,** cf. *(4),*
and for the future of society: **461, 500, 502, 647, 691, 729, 738, 743, 752, 860, 865.**

(53) — It carries with it great joys: **442, 452, 508, 667, 794,**
and its heavenly reward: **509, 794, 866,**
but it is a tiresome and difficult task: **130, 439-440, <u>469</u>, 489, 649, 707, 741, 794, 860, 864.**

(54) — So, although it can be aroused by inclination or interest: **235, <u>442-443</u>,**
it ought above all to proceed from a high ideal: **475, 486, 517, 631, 781, 830,**

and a supernatural ideal: **445, 462, 517, 693, 723, 833**;
it demands a fervent spiritual life: **446, 469-470, 598-599, 613, 685-686, 724, 727, 747, 779, 781, 782, 862, 864,**
and courage in bitter struggles: **758, 866.**

THE RELIGIOUS TEACHERS: **551, 704**

(55) — The teaching vocation finds its highest expression in the humble but glorious religious teachers: **145, 520, 551,**
whose value is recognized even by the unbelieving themselves: **327, 556, 561,**
They participate in the teaching mission of the Church: **109, 501, 551, 599, 707,**
who would like them to be more numerous: **556,**
and to whom they are of great assistance: **704,**
and procure vocations: **708.**

(56) — Their vocation demands from them, no less than from other teachers:
a secure doctrine: **705,**
a solid professional formation: **297, 560-561, 822, 863,**
a sufficient adaptation to new techniques: **368, 554, 559, 705, 863**
and to daily needs: **557, 559, 563.**

(57) — It demands above all a fidelity to the spirit and the obligations of their religious life: **175, 470, 558, 705, 779,**
which, far from being a hindrance to them: **327, 556, 558,**
is, on the contrary, an aid to their superior pedagogic value: **175, 487, 564, 706-707, 779.**
Cf. **THE STATES OF PERFECTION.**

CONGRESSES AND TEACHERS ASSOCIATIONS

(58) — Congresses and teachers' associations, religious or lay:
are useful for their formation: **297, 403, 445, 447, 496, 859,**

theology: **154, 374, 809,** cf. *(70),*
  can provide the key: **10, 154, 524, 526, 620, 851.**

(68) — The Catholic University ought to set a high standard
  for its scientific authority: <u>**206**</u>**, 209, 313,**
  to fulfill its proper mission which is to preserve Christian principles: **495,** <u>**619-620**</u>**,**
    amongst the students: **205,** <u>**619-629**</u>**,**
    in society: **140, 205, 527, 606, 617,**
    which they will have to direct one day: **359, 381, 530, 544, 606, 620, 704, 831, 843.**

Religious Instruction: **609, 627**

(69) — Those who have care for children ought to ensure
  their religious instruction: **7, 178,** <u>**187**</u>**, 752,** cf. *(34),*
  in the absence of which all other education would be
  incomplete: **68, 70-72, 95, 101, 159, 194, 197, 204, 252, 334, 453,** <u>**530**</u>**, 538, 608, 733, 788, 800, 808,**
  This education ought to have its beginning in the
  elementary schools: **28-29, 84,** <u>**94**</u>**, 145,** <u>**472**</u>**, 752, 784, 857,**
  by the principal points of doctrine: **95,**
  it ought to be adapted,
    under the penalty of crises to the faith: **610-611, 659-660, 801,**
    to intellectual development: **23, 45, 72, 124, 142, 306, 353,** <u>**478**</u>**, 611, 653, 658-659, 780, 784, 869,**
      for a vision of doctrine that is organic and
      profound: **192, 478, 653, 752, 788, 813,**
      and for the development of the sentiment with
      a study of the Gospel and the liturgy: **479, 615, 627, 724;**
    of its own right, it demands a place in the university programs: **478,**
    and presented in a pleasing manner: **148, 170.**

(70) — Christian doctrine is the climax of learning: **4, 64,**
  <u>**147**</u>**, 153-154, 296, 608-609, 800, 820,**
  any contradiction between science and faith being
  impossible: **4-5, 124, 132,** <u>**147**</u>**, 163, 206, 308, 528, 636, 661, 871,**

but rather a positive agreement: **5, 106, 132, 147, 276, 851,**

because both reason and science lead to God: **4-5, 206, 276, 871,**

and are directed towards faith: **64, 206, 276,**

and faith preserves reason from error and enriches it with fresh knowledge: **27, 124, 276, 528, 849.** Cf. **THE RELIGIOUS INSTRUCTION OF THE FAITHFUL.**

THE TRAINING OF THE WILL

(71) — Still more than the formation of the intelligence, the teacher must do his best to educate the will of young: **69, 156, 197, 499, 737, 745, 780 794, 816,**

on the twofold basis: **454, 502, 693-695, 780,**

of a conscientious and living faith: *(72),*

and of an intimate union between religion and life: *(74).*

a. Conscientious and live faith: **609, 647**

(72) — Religious instruction, cf. *(69),* ought to tend to the development of a conscientious and lively faith: **219, 424, 454, 485, 521, 562, 656, 720, 783, 843, 857,**

which permeates life as a whole: **219, 224, 291, 353, 659, 752, 778, 800, 814, 831,**

which is the principle for victory over the world: **71-72, 467, 490, 546, 645, 657, 706, 725,**

and of an authentic spiritual life: **152-154, 387, 479, 525, 598, 653, 672,**

very useful for studies: **153, 495,**

and indispensible for moral life: **31, 221, 278, 306, 446, 481, 491, 545, 587, 663, 700, 831, 843,** cf. *(77).*

(73) — Faith shall be nourished by prayer: **221, 491, 595, 611, 635, 700, 767,**

by frequenting the holy sacraments: **306, 481, 587, 635, 700, 767,**

especially the Eucharist: **187, 221, 364, 377, 472, 674,**

to which the child must be directed at the very
initial awakening of reason: **181-184,**
Cf. **THE LITURGY.**
and by a filial devotion to the Blessed Virgin: **208,
221, 306, 377, 414, 467, 663, 674, 700,**
Cf. **MARY**

b. Union between religion and life: **576, 588, 696**

(74) — The pupil ought to find a moral formation in the
school: **84, 159, 720, 800,**
in harmony with Christian morality: **159, 329,**
founded on the natural universal law: **159, 491, 546,
580, 590-591,**
and on revelation: **72, 580, 590-591,**
and entrusted to the Church, who alone can teach
morality in its entirety, cf. *(12).*

(75) — The training of conscience: **497, 577-579, 586, 739,**
ought to begin at a very early age: **511, 588, 784,**
and ought to develop a sense of responsibility: **301,
482, 497, 521, 592-593, 726, 765,**
and of genuine freedom: **223, 514, 811,**
which is not licentiousness: **482, 497, 586,**
but dominion of oneself and of events: **72, 587,
855.**

(76) — The will of the child must be fortified: **282, 301, 411,
463, 491, 495, 513, 653, 643, 646, 784,**
with the habit of sacrifice: **491, 584, 595, 725, 762,
772,**
and with the practice of virtue: **278, 855.**
teaching him to dominate his sensitivity: **221, 408,
673, 794,**
and his passions: **129, 220, 466, 549, 611, 662,**
and not to give away his heart: **412, 466,**

(77) — to defend his purity at all costs: **220-221, 663, 855,**
for the love of the beauty of virtue: **306, <u>584</u>, 665,**
but also to obey the precept: **583-584,**
whose observance is possible: **583,**
with the help of grace: **122, 583, 700,** cf. *(72)-*
(73),

and regard for modesty: **222, 306, 367, 414, 697-699.**

(78) — This traditional formation to chastity is the true foundation for sexual education: **283,**
as it is approved by the Church: **569,**
and which, at the necessary moment, demands a clear and prudent explanation of the laws of life: **283, 415, 574, 640, 699.**
— The errors of the new "sexual initiation": *(99),*
and of the *géminée* school: *(98).*

(79) — The formation received in school: **218, 374, 635,**
ought to prepare young people for the apostolate: **360, 867, 868,**
not solely during the years of study: **226, 360-361,**
but during their whole life: **44, 374, 444, 495, 511, 544,**
and to encourage religious and sacerdotal vocations: **145, 229-230, 615, 655, 696, 701, 708, 822,**
the discouragement of which is a blameworthy action: **696, 701,**
and whose number is an indication of the value of the education given in the school: **541.**

D. *The Art of Education*

(80) — Education is the "art of arts", it is a delicate work: **<u>297</u>, 402, 469, 471, 707, 715,**
because it leaves indelible marks: **1, 212, 244, 298, 385, 422, 437, 517, 665, 669, 787, 792, 815, 865,**
in the child that is wounded by original sin: **688,** cf. *(1),*
and particularly exposed: **152, 166, 168, 215, 252, 444, 600, 652,**
but susceptible to progress: **600, 778,**
and readily accessible to true values: **408, 412, 555, 669, 673, 861.**

(81) — It demands from the educator:
a true love for youth: **<u>297</u>, 379, 487, 666, 833,**
together with a detachment of the heart: **468, <u>667</u>, 817,**

but which ought to be preserved unalterable: **45**, **287**, **375**, <u>**389-397**</u>, **688**, **689**, **860**.

(86) — Authority is at times a natural gift: **392**,
but you can also procure it: **391-398**,
meditating that it is of divine origin: **287**,
with the dominion of one's self. **391-396**, **441**, **665**,
impartiality: **418-419**,
loyalty: **396**, **410**,
respect for the child: **439**, **471**,
the example of obedience: **223**, **378**.
N.B.—The method of education for adults: **628-634**.

The Collaboration of Pupils in their Education: **214**

(87) — Education demands the collaboration of the pupils:
279, **432**, **488-489**, **522**, **609**, **631**, **643**, **771-776**,
which is not a limitless autonomy: **279**,
but demands the opposite:
a respectful and trusting docility: **223**, **378**, **482**,
489, **498**, **654-655**, **710**, **773**, **774**, **778**, **802**, **856**,
a strong will: **655**, **856**,
a constant and generous effort: **772-775**, **779**,
a pure life: **466**, **607**, **614**, **856**,
assiduous work: **472**, **513**, **607**, **629**, **653**, **778**, **799**,
803, **804**,
awakened by interest: **629**, **799**.
(Students' Strikes): **177**.

(88) — Pupils ought to be animated by a high ideal: **208**,
488, **604**, **608**, **653**, **771**, **814**, **848**,
and sustained by prayer: **472**, **710**, cf. *(73)*,
by frequenting the sacraments: cf. *(73)*,
by spiritual retreats: **219**, **362**,
to follow their models: **214**,
Christ: **300**, **304**, **723**, **754**, **778**, **783**,
and the saints: **303**,
especially their protector, St. Louis Gonzaga:
133, <u>**216-227**</u>, **365-366**, **380**,
St. John Berchmans: **380**,
St. Stanislaus Kostka: **228**.

§IV. **The auxiliaries of the family and the school: 357**

(89) — Auxiliary educators: **796,**
voluntary catechists: **358, 530, 615,**
aided by the mothers of families: **474,**
ought to be reckoned amongst the first members of
Catholic Action: **358, 615.**

(90) — There must be ranked amongst the valued auxiliaries
of education:
the Marian Congregations: **315, 382,**
and other youth movements of Catholic Action: **353-
354, 356, 359-361, 530, 672, 840,**
the Boy Scouts: **603-604, 725, 726, 857,**

(91) — the educational utilization of games and sports: **333,
363, 457, 643, 854-856,**
and that of the film, of radio transmissions and television: **298, 633, 638-639, 675-676, 680-681, 824,**
where Catholicism ought to have its place: **681,**
the evening school institutes and adult education: **624,
630, 647, 695,**
which ought to aim at their complete formation in
view of their family and social life: **625-627,** cf. *(86).*
Cf. **THE LAY APOSTOLATE—THE HUMAN BODY
—PRESS, FILMS, RADIO.**

Fruits of Christian education: **336**

(92) — As history testifies: **68, 336-337, 458,**
and also the pagans: **458, 849,**
Christian education assures great benefits, both temporal and eternal, for those who have received it: **68,
88, 101, 156, 301, 334, 336-337, 339, 517, 550, 649,
804,**
and so also the families and civil and religious society:
**3, 8, 12, 18, 21, 24, 27, 60, 90, 106, 109, 114, 116,
117, 139, 156, 159, 172, 190, 191, 244, 264, 273-274,
287, 294, 330, 336-337, 340, 342, 372, 431, 436, 437,
511, 550, 613, 650, 695, 759, 788, 789, 816, 831,
834, 843,** cf. *(4)-(5).*

PART TWO

NATURALISM IN EDUCATION

CHAPTER I

THE SCOURGE OF NATURALISM

it drives the young to reject all authority: **223, 279, 390, 418,**
urges them to immorality: **46, 450, 651,**
multiplying the causes of corruption for them: literature, amusements, radio programs: **298, 355, 363, 451, 479, 491, 542, 548, 570, 638, 651, 676, 678, 680, 710, 793, 796, 824.**
Cf. **PRESS, FILMS, RADIO.**

Co-education of the sexes

(98) — Co-education of the sexes, based on the negation of original sin: **284,**
is a misconception of the true nature of man and woman: **284**
and constitutes a grave danger to youth: **57, 284.**

Sexual education: **565**

(99) — Sexual education, as is understood from Naturalism: **282,**
is praised to the skies by some Catholics: **306, 568, 570,**
offends the modesty of the young: **699,**
exaggerates the importance of the sexual element, to the detriment of the primary end of marriage: **571,**
and the efficacy of conscience, to the detriment of the necessity of grace: **572, 640, 697,**

Morality according to situations: **588**

(100) — "Morality according to situations", which aims at the freeing of morality from its universal basis, to the advantage of solitary concrete circumstances: **581, 588-589,**
is contrary to the natural truth and the teaching of the Church: **121, 159, 248, 591,**
carries with it numerous perversions: **594,**
and places faith itself in danger: **582, 594.**

§III. **The School without God: 26.**

(101) — Under philanthropic pretexts: **66, 78, 759,**
scientific: **129, 142, 280, 314, 359,**
or political: **5, 286, 307, 503,**

but with the real aim of ruining religion and souls: **25, 29, 33, 37, 43, 66, 98, 131, 280, 328, 746, 788,** and of imposing itself on children: **47, 269, 286, 307, 315-317, 472, 503,**

(102) — naturalism, thanks to State intervention: **35, 73, 138, 201, 290, 315-317, 472.**

and contrary to the rights of the family: **262, 286, 265, 272, 503, 787,** cf. *(25),*

deprives the Church of education: **13, 25, 27, 29, 31, 33, 35, 43, 50, 77, 79, 80, 103, 136, 138, 200, 315-317, 531,** cf. *(103),*

prohibiting the religious: **33, 98, 172, 328,** cf. *(104),* in order to introduce under the equivocal label of neutrality laity: **103, 532,** cf. *(106),*

non-believing teachers: **50, 73, 138, 321,** cf. *(106),* an atheistic education: **77, 131, 136, 195, 200, 307, 457, 787,** cf. *(105)* ff.,

and distorted programs: **91-92, 348, 480, 494, 512,** cf. *(108).*

Judgment on the Naturalist school

(103) — To reject the Church's right in teaching is: cf. *(10)* ff.,
an ingratitude: **132,**
and an impiety: **37,**
contrary to reason: **79, 225, 273,**
and to right: **237, 273, 323,**
fatal for the young: **29, 31, 273,**
and for the common good: **28, 32, 144, 273, 759,**
which leads to error: **79, 114, 132, 746,**
and to a hatred for religion: **210, 322.**

(104) — The prohibition for the religious to teach:
is based on a false pretext: **172, 327,**
is ungrateful and an injustice: **172, 327-328,**
and is detrimental to society: **172.**

(105) — The prohibition of religious instruction in schools: **66,**
deprives education of its essential part: **55, 79, 455, 538,**
is a danger to the faith and habits of the young: **66, 79, 80, 89, 129, 210, 869,**

constitutes a deep loss to culture but benefits that which gains in extension: 239, 436, 494, 512, 526, 546, 619,
and deprives it of its principle of unity and synthesis: 538, 619, 830, 847, cf. (67).

(109) — The encroachment of the State, which imposes itself physically and morally: 179, 191, 268, 371, cf. (102), is based on a false conception of the State: 5, 259, 456,
it is a misconception of the natural and primary rights of the family: 33, 201, 234, 258, 261, 317, 323, 344, 369-370, 503, 621, 827, 842, cf. (7) and (24),
and that of the Church and conscience: 268, 317, 503, cf. (10) ff.,
therefore it is an abuse of power: 261, 268,
contradictory to common sense: 259,
and to the doctrine of the Church: 19, 34, 290, 323, injurious to the cultural level of the school: 734.
Abuse of military training: 235, 269, 348, 369.
Cf. INTERNATIONAL PEACE.

Chapter II

REMEDIES FOR NATURALISM

§I. General Necessity for Action

(110) — To safeguard youth against the evils of naturalism, it is not necessary to count on a miracle of grace: 451. nor on the sole power of the State: 115.
— To back the action of the Church,
only one capable of remedying this evil of a spiritual origin: 37, 352,
and which, condescending to concessions that are reconcilable with her mission: 15, 83, 127, 162, 174, 251,
She remains intransigent in her right: 29, 79, 127, 190, 236, 504,

(111) — demands the efforts of all: 99, 103, 298, 566, 633, 680, 684, 795, 797,

in strict union: **11, 16, 53-54, 155, 161, 164, 355, 738, 744, 797, 818, 844, 850,** especially that of the bishops: **79,**

without which nothing ought to be undertaken: **164, 199,**

but they ought to operate with firmness: **2, 7, 17-18, 79, 80, 90, 140, 160, <u>221</u>, 680,**

and remind the faithful of their duties: <u>**17-18, 59**</u>;

those of the clergy: **6, 16, <u>111</u>, 329, 680,**

those of parents: **130, 212, <u>260</u>, 573,**

and of their associations: **112, 355, <u>566-567</u>,**

those of Catholic Action: **203, <u>294</u>, 307, 355-356, 358, 615, 680,**

and of the press: **164, 567.**

§II. Action on Legislation

(112) — This action ought before all else to be exercised on the public authorities: **17, 53, 59, 79, 456, 566, <u>680</u>, 849,**

and on international organizations: **818, 845,**

with all legal means: **138, 199, 329, <u>355</u>, 566, 744,**

and with resistance to unjust violence: **130, 260, 350,**

with the aim of obtaining from the State:

the defence of public morality: **53, 450, <u>484</u>, 565, 677, 679,** cf. *(22),*

the respect for the rights of Catholic parents: **115, 151, 161, 212, 455, 504, 646, 735;**

with the recognition of the freedom of Catholic teaching: **54, 138, 161, 198, <u>293</u>, 329, 484, 496, 556,**

and with a just distribution of the subsidies in its favor: cf. *(22),*

and with respect, in public teaching itself, for the principles in harmony with man's natural morality and his supernatural destiny: **79, 115, 151, 161, 212, 430, 456,**

conditions of every true education, cf. *(26),*

and of a complete and mutual understanding between the school and the family: **430**

1. *Education*

§III. **Direct Action**

A. *In favor of the Christian restoration of matrimony*

(113) — The salvation of youth depends on the Christian
restoration of matrimony: **6, 287, 329, 450;**
Cf. **MARRIAGE**
it demands the care of abandoned youth: **41, 642,
648, 796.**

B. *In favor of a return to morality:* **675**
— Vigilance over the press and immoral amusements:
179, <u>355</u>, 568, 573, <u>679-681</u>, cf. *(33),*
to which it opposes others, sane and formative: **298,
363, 479, 493, 681,** cf. **PRESS, RADIO, FILMS.**

C. *Action on the Neutral School:* **53**

(114) — Frequenting these schools is forbidden to Catholic
children: **30, 36, 58, 61, 94, 101, 104, 130, 134, 138,
141, 158, 260, 290, 355,**
only if there exists a twofold condition
of which only the bishop can be the judge: **61, 290,**
and which must be watched closely by parents: **62,
94, 212, 229,**
that is that there is a genuine necessity, and that all
harm for the soul of the pupil be avoided: **61-63, 82,
158, 869.**

(115) — The preservation and readmission of religious teaching into public schools,
for which there is a duty to demand: **74, <u>111</u>, 321,**
and which is desired even by the non-Catholics: **102,**
is insufficient for the construction of a Catholic school
or for the calming of the parents' consciences: **73,
153, <u>291</u>, 321, <u>350</u>, 539, 713, 735.**

(116) — Its deficiencies ought be supplemented:
by a religious instruction given outside the school: **30,
58, <u>62</u>, 68, 75-76, 107, 111, 143, 178-179, 355,** cf.
(89),
by a formation fortifying the young to resist error:
**38-39, 44, <u>51</u>, 64, 146, 299, 312, 345, 478, 481, 490,
646, 659,**
indispensable above all in the higher classes: **478,**
and assured above all in the free school: **544,** cf.
(117).

The delicate apostolic task of the Christian teachers in public neutral teaching: **533-536, 787.**

D. *The free school:* **100**

(*117*) — The best remedy to the Godless school is the Catholic school: **18, 59-60, 79, 104, 113, 118, 138, 152, 165, 382, 459-460, 712,**
— from which depends the salvation of the infant: **450.**
— It is established by virtue of its vindicated freedom of teaching:
not as a universal principle: **52, 128,** cf. (*95*),
but as the free exercise of a right: **53, 101, 128, 229, 504, 735, 827, 841,** cf. (*10*),
and is not a discriminating work, but a duty of conscience: **294, 302, 347.**
— It is a duty for all
to demand it: **293,** cf. (*112*),
to support it: **59, 81, 100, 113, 130, 162, 194, 293, 483, 819,**
and to collaborate in its development: **59, 163, 165, 496, 714, 844.**

(*118*) — As a reply to the deformed methods of today, particularly those of history: **93,** cf. (*108*);
it must remain faithful to the traditional methods of Christian education: **193, 222, 306, 494, 499, 731, 740,** cf. (*64*) ff.,
which have already undergone their tests: **167, 519,**
and insist on its spiritual values: **480, 499,** cf. (*63*) and (*69*) ff.
— The task of the Catholic Universities: **331, 499, 526,** cf. (*67*)-(*68*),
of the normal Catholic schools: cf. (*50*).

(*119*) — In virtue of the heroic dedication of Christian teachers: **33, 100,**
the free schools, opposing the crimes of the lay school: **196, 330,**
have greatly contributed to the maintenance of Christian life: **88, 101, 330,**
and rest as the best hopes of revival: **205, 208, 374, 476, 605, 645, 704, 829.**

INDEX OF QUOTATIONS

The numbers in heavy black print refer to the paragraphs of the papal pronouncements.

SACRED SCRIPTURE

LAY AUTHORS

INDEX OF DOCUMENTS AND SOURCES

The numbers in bold type refer to the division of the Papal document; numbers in bold followed by a letter of the alphabet refer to a footnote corresponding to the division of the text indicated by the same number.

CHRONOLOGICAL INDEX OF DOCUMENTS

PIUS VII (1800-1823)

May 15, 1800	Encycl. *Diu satis*	**1-2**	BL. 1, 5 Transl.

LEO XII (1823-1829)

August 28, 1824	Ap. Cost. *Quod divina sapientia*	**3-5**	BL. 1, 54 Transl.
December 25, 1825	Encycl. *Caritate Christi*	**6-7**	BL. 1, 114, Transl.

GREGORY XVI (1831-1846)

June 21, 1836	Letter *Cum christianae*	**8**	A.G. 2, 101 Transl.

PIUS IX (1846-1878)

October 9, 1847	(S. Congreg. of Propagation)	**9-11**	Ft. 7, 4820 Transl.
December 8, 1849	Encycl. *Nostis et Nobiscum*	**12-13**	A.P. IX, 1, 198 Transl.
May 15, 1850	(Nunciature of Paris)	**14-18**	Annal. de Phil. crét. 40, 398 Transl.
November 1, 1850	Consistorial address	**19**	A.P. IX, 1, 251 Transl.

ALPHABETICAL INDEX
OF WRITTEN DOCUMENTS